# Willa Cather's Pittsburgh

CATHER STUDIES

CATHER STUDIES 13

# Willa Cather's Pittsburgh

Edited by
Timothy W. Bintrim,
James A. Jaap,
and Kimberly Vanderlaan

UNIVERSITY OF NEBRASKA PRESS | LINCOLN

Portions of chapter 1 previously appeared in *Becoming Willa Cather: Creation and Career*, by Daryl W. Palmer. Copyright © 2019 by the University of Nevada Press. All rights reserved. Used by permission of the University of Nevada Press.
An earlier version of chapter 2 by Michael Gorman was previously published as "Willa Cather's Imperial Apprenticeship: Rudyard Kipling, the Celestial Empire, and San Francisco" in *Studies in English Language and Literature*, vol. 20, March 2012, pp. 41–67.

The series Cather Studies is sponsored by the Cather Project at the University of Nebraska–Lincoln.

Library of Congress Cataloging-in-Publication Data
Names: Bintrim, Timothy W., editor. | Jaap, James A., editor. | Vanderlaan, Kimberly, editor.
Title: Willa Cather's Pittsburgh / edited by Timothy W. Bintrim, James A. Jaap, Kimberly Vanderlaan.
Description: Lincoln: University of Nebraska Press, [2021] | Series: Cather studies; 13 | Includes bibliographical references and index.
Identifiers: LCCN 2020037023
ISBN 9781496224613 (paperback)
ISBN 9781496225153 (epub)
ISBN 9781496225160 (mobi)
ISBN 9781496225177 (pdf)
Subjects: LCSH: Cather, Willa, 1873–1947—Knowledge and learning. | Pittsburgh (Pa.) | Pittsburgh (Pa.)—In literature.
Classification: LCC PS3505.A87 Z9354 2021 | DDC 813/.52—dc23
LC record available at https://lccn.loc.gov/2020037023

Frontispiece:
Willa Cather in Pittsburgh. PHO-4-RG 1951-085. WCPM Collection. Willa Cather Foundation Collections and Archives at the National Willa Cather Center in Red Cloud.

The recent passing of Angela Conrad, who finally succumbed to a long struggle with cancer in March of 2019, reminds us all of the importance of friendship within and beyond our Cather community. All who knew her will miss her sharp wit and easy humor and her dedication to excellence in teaching and scholarship. This volume of Cather Studies is dedicated to her.

CONTENTS

# ILLUSTRATIONS

# Introduction

TIMOTHY W. BINTRIM, JAMES A. JAAP,
AND KIMBERLY VANDERLAAN

Willa Cather wrote about the places and people she knew: Nebraska, of course, in so many of her most iconic works; New York in *My Mortal Enemy* and "Coming, Aphrodite!"; Virginia in *Sapphira and the Slave Girl*; and New Mexico and Arizona in, among others, *The Song of the Lark* and *Death Comes for the Archbishop*. All of these locations serve as material referents and figurative settings in both Cather's life and work, and all have received sustained critical attention. Often forgotten among these essential Cather locations has been Pittsburgh. One of the objectives of the Sixteenth International Willa Cather Seminar, held at Duquesne University in June 2017, was to explore Cather's professional activities in Pittsburgh and the artistic, professional, and personal connections she made there. During the ten years Pittsburgh was her home (1896–1906), Cather worked as an editor, journalist, teacher, and freelance writer. She mixed with all sorts and formed friendships both ephemeral and lasting. She published extensively—not just hundreds of profiles and reviews, but also a collection of poetry, *April Twilights*, and more than thirty short stories, including several collected in *The Troll Garden* that are now considered masterpieces: "'A Death in the Desert,'" "The Sculptor's Funeral," "A Wagner Matinee," and "Paul's Case" (Woodress 181).

These were years of personal growth and maturation. Having graduated from the University of Nebraska in 1895, in June 1896 she moved to Pittsburgh's East End to edit *The Home Monthly*, a new magazine appealing to middle-class families within a hundred-mile radius of Pittsburgh. She was twenty-two years old, living independently for the first time in a large, industrial city, far from the divide in central Nebraska, and earning her living through writing. She also had greater access to cultural events such as concerts and operatic and theatrical performances than she had had in Lincoln, and she could now enjoy exhibits at a large art museum and several galleries and borrow books from a massive lending library (*Selected Letters* 37). During her first five years in Pittsburgh, she would write for the *Pittsburgh Evening Leader* and contribute to the *Nebraska State Journal* and the *Lincoln Courier*, the last of which she also served as guest editor (*The World and the Parish* 502).

In spring 1900, Isabelle McClung's invitation to join her family in their new house at 1180 Murray Hill Avenue transformed Cather's personal life. Leaving boardinghouse living behind, she enjoyed greater privacy (her own bath on the third floor), more appetizing fare, and propitious social connections, as well as savings on rent, some of which she sent home to Red Cloud (Woodress 125). With her switch from journalism to teaching high school, she also had more time to work on her own material. From a sewing room converted to her study on the McClungs' third floor flowed a steady stream of stories and reviews that made their way to print, as well as occasional failures that didn't—*The Player Letters*, a collection of open letters she addressed to well-known actors, and *Fanny*, a novel she later destroyed (138, 181–82). Years after she moved to New York in 1906, she would return to that sewing room to write during long sojourns in Pittsburgh.

Cather started her Pittsburgh life with a resigned, almost fatalistic acceptance of her new home; famously, she told a Lincoln friend, "There is no God but one God and Art is his revealer; that's my creed and I'll follow it to the end, to a hotter place than Pittsburgh if need be" (*Selected Letters* 39). Nevertheless, it is safe to say that as Cather came to know Pittsburgh, she also came to love the city and its people. She immersed herself in the city's glowing social

*Introduction*

and artistic scenes, attending hundreds of musical, dramatic, and operatic performances at theaters such as the Grand Opera House, the Alvin, the Duquesne, and the Nixon, as well as the Carnegie Music Hall. She met celebrities in the dining rooms of the city's grand hotels: Fridtjof Nansen at the Hotel Henry, Ethelbert Nevin at the Hotel Schenley, and Lizzie Hudson Collier, leading lady of the Grand Opera Stock Company, at the favorite residential hotel of actors, the Lincoln. Under the pseudonym "Sibert," one of many she used at the time, she became a leading theatrical critic in Pittsburgh. While writing her articles and reviews, she rubbed elbows with the famous, including George Westinghouse, soon-to-be First Lady Ida McKinley, novelist Anthony Hope Hawkins, and a host of others; and she attended receptions for Andrew Carnegie and dined with artists such as William H. Low and Winslow Homer (Byrne and Snyder 73).

This desire to follow art would take her to New York and *McClure's* in 1906, a move that would bring the heartbreak and angst of yet another uprooting. In a 6 June 1906 letter to her students at Allegheny High School, an honest and forthright communication with them, one can detect the ambivalence in her quandary—once again moving away from a landscape, culture, and community about which she had grown fond: "The changes in my plans which will prevent my [being with you next year] have been sudden and unforeseen. . . . One always has to choose between good things it seems" (*Selected Letters* 92). Even after moving to New York, her Pittsburgh years were far from over. Cather continued to visit the McClung house until 1916, often for months at a time, revising parts of *O Pioneers!* and *The Song of the Lark* in her familiar writing room.

After Judge McClung died in November 1915, the two oldest children, Isabelle and Alfred, decided to sell the house. In a letter to her Aunt Franc, Cather expresses her sorrow upon leaving Pittsburgh:

> This kind and hospitable home which has been a home to me for fifteen years will probably be sold, as it is too large an establishment for Isabelle and her brother to keep up alone. . . . It is

very hard to see dear and familiar things pass out of one's life. I shall never feel so safe and happy in any other house, I fear. My own apartment in New York was never home in the same sense. ("Willa Cather to Frances Smith Cather")

When the engagement of Isabelle and Jan Hambourg was announced in January 1916, Cather finally left Pittsburgh for good. She was then forty-two years old and had spent nearly two decades living in and visiting the Steel City. She would not stop there again.

This volume begins to explore the myriad ways that Willa Cather's writing career was shaped during these crucial years. In "Becoming Miss Cather from Pittsburgh," Ann Romines opens with the notion that Cather's growing professionalism is analogous to Pittsburgh's transition from late-nineteenth-century industrialism to twentieth-century modernity. As Romines points out, in Pittsburgh, Cather "found the landscape that was her first love—the wooded hills and rivers of Virginia—*and* the enticements of absorbing work in a modern city" (4). Romines observes that much of Cather's writing (personal as well as professional) deals with homesickness and a desire to return to the familiar: she was "coming to realize [that] *distance* meant *loss*" (12).

The three authors of Part 1 of the volume, "East Meets West," enrich our understanding of the sophisticated politics of Cather's early works while transcending the standard platitudes. In "Bicycles and Freedom in Red Cloud and Pittsburgh," Daryl Palmer suggests that in "Tommy, the Unsentimental," a story published in the August 1896 *Home Monthly*, Cather reinvented Red Cloud. Palmer finds Cather celebrating an unprecedented kind of code for the New Woman in the American West, where she can flaunt her bicycle riding, "experiment with gender, and resist social expectations" (34) while she "race[s] imaginatively between Red Cloud and Pittsburgh, between East and West, feminine and masculine" (40). In an equally vivid analysis of the disparities between East and West (this time writ large, beyond the territorial bounds of the United States), Michael Gorman in "Where Pagodas Rise on Every Hill: Romance as Resistance in

'A Son of the Celestial'" argues that this little-studied six-page story challenges "anti-Chinese sentiments voiced by nativists in the United States" (65) at the time of the renewal of the Chinese Exclusion Acts. Specifically, Gorman argues that Cather saw America's "cultural anxiety" not rooted in "Chinese laborers," as in the fiction of Norris and London, but in "individuals who pronounce Western civilization and religion (i.e., Christianity) [to be] superior to Eastern aesthetics and systems of belief" (65). In "The Boxer Rebellion, Pittsburgh's Missionary Crisis, and 'The Conversion of Sum Loo,'" Timothy Bintrim reads a second Chinese story as a satirical response to Pittsburgh's concern for its beleaguered missionaries in north China during the 1900 Boxer Rebellion. By questioning Rudyard Kipling's claim that East and West shall never meet, these essays find that several early stories, ostensibly set in Nebraska and San Francisco, explore beliefs Cather brought to Pittsburgh from Red Cloud.

Part 2 of the volume, "Class Action: Retrying 'Paul's Case,'" brings three new approaches to the study of Cather's most famous story and her best-known work set in Pittsburgh. Mary Ruth Ryder's "Growing Pains: The City behind Cather's Pittsburgh Classroom" shows how "Paul's Case" and "The Professor's Commencement" (also set in Pittsburgh) reveal Cather's "concerns about the changes in education at the time, with commercial studies displacing the liberal arts" and "the troubling effects on her students of rapid cultural change and a consequent shift in values" (112). Drawing upon a number of new archival sources, Ryder details the many ways in which the geography of the city during Cather's five-year teaching career mapped sociological and ethnic boundaries, which in turn forced various educational reforms. Charmion Gustke's essay, "Big Steel and Class Consciousness in 'Paul's Case,'" utilizes Marxist theory to argue that Pittsburgh in the late nineteenth century "embodied the conflicts of capitalism" characterized by unequal distribution of wealth and class divisions. Three Pittsburgh landmarks referenced in the story—Central High School, the Carnegie Music Hall, and the Hotel Schenley—serve as "cultural signifiers" of a specific "class consciousness," one that drives Paul to "resist the demands of labor." His ultimate demise, Gustke argues, shows Cather expressing how this form of resistance is an "inevitable yet futile response to the inequities of a class-based society" (133). In "'The Most Exciting Attractions Are between Two Opposites That Never Meet': Willa Cather and Andy Warhol," Todd Richardson works the magic of his title—positing a number of "critical confluences" between these two artists who spent crucial parts of their lives in Pittsburgh. While acknowledging vast differences in their views on artistic representation, Richardson argues that the two share a kinship based on geography, nonheteronormativity, and their respective relationships to commercial art and modernity.

Part 3 of the volume, "Friendships, Literary and Musical," traces some of Cather's biographical associations with other Pittsburgh artists and musicians. Diane Prenatt delves into the ways Cather's experiences as a translator during her years in Pittsburgh may have influenced her practice of writing fiction. Specifically, Prenatt argues that Cather's friendship with George and Helen Seibel "played an essential role during her formative years in Pittsburgh" and that their French soirées suggest a social situation associated with "orality" (187). For Cather, translation serves "as a recurring trope for transformation," one utilized in much of her fiction. John H. Flannigan elucidates an important and lasting friendship Cather had with Ethel Herr Litchfield, a relationship which had hitherto received scant attention from Cather's biographers. The two music connoisseurs drew on one another both professionally and personally during their lifetimes, argues Flannigan, who summons fresh archival materials to mark how they shared a lifelong, spiritual kinship. Kimberly Vanderlaan makes a compelling case that Ethelbert Nevin, a great musical friend of Cather's, was likely the model for her fictional professors Godfrey St. Peter, in *The Professor's House*, and Emerson Graves, in "The Professor's Commencement." Drawing on allusions to Emersonian philosophy and other nineteenth-century artists and works, Vanderlaan further argues that Cather in both pieces "directs us to a reading steeped in the principles of Romanticism." The failed Romanticism that each academic embodies, according to Vanderlaan, makes for "a fitting tribute to her friend, Ethelbert Nevin" (231).

In Part 4, our contributors adopt new approaches to some of Cather's later stories, with a focus on how fin-de-siècle Pittsburgh contextually shaped that fiction. Kelsey Squire assesses the impact of industrialization and naturalism on Cather's stories published in *The Century Illustrated Monthly Magazine*, with a primary focus on "The Willing Muse," which Cather wrote in Pittsburgh. Squire builds on the accepted scholarly notion that Cather was an effective marketer of her own work by illustrating the ways in which Cather's writing "participates in social conversations that surrounded industrialization, labor, productivity, and leisure in the late nineteenth and early twentieth century" (238). In "Venetian Window: Pittsburgh Glass and Modernist Community in 'Double Birthday,'" Joseph Murphy reconsiders how the story's "dialectical structure," as illustrated through its central symbol, the Venetian window in the Engelhardt's family home, "serves as an entryway to Cather's depiction of modernist consciousness" (256). Described but never seen, the illustrated window, notes Murphy, "never comes fully into focus." The late Angela Conrad assesses how two Pittsburgh stories, "Paul's Case" and "Double Birthday," reflect Cather's understanding of alchemy on a symbolic level—and how that mystical process is tied to her portrayal of the strata of social class—both in Pittsburgh at the turn of the century and in these stories separated by two decades. Unlike Paul, young Albert Engelhardt recognizes that "his cultural and spiritual refinement outweighed the advantages of being wealthy" and thereby succeeds in his transformation (295).

Our volume's epilogue, written by senior Cather scholar John J. Murphy and delivered as the closing to the Sixteenth International Seminar, provides readers with a retrospective—detailing some of the reasons Cather's fiction ranks alongside the canonical greats. Through personal anecdotes drawn from a long and productive career of teaching, editing, and experiencing Cather, Murphy discusses a range of literary devices and stylistic choices that help us to understand why so many of us seek out Cather's fiction as guideposts about how to live, how to grow, and how to love in all the ways that make us human.

What we hope readers of this volume recognize is the importance the city of Pittsburgh played in Willa Cather's life and work. Her disembarking in the Steel City, on 26 June 1896, is auspicious not just for its significance in the realm of American letters, but also for its coincidence with cultural shifts closing out the nineteenth century and ushering in the twentieth. Like the narrator of "Uncle Valentine," who came to the suburb of Greenacre as an orphan, but was eagerly adopted, Cather came to Pittsburgh "at a lovely time, in a bygone period of American life; just at the incoming of this [the twentieth] century which has made all the world so different" (3). As Pittsburgh provided and developed many of the raw materials used to manufacture modern America, this volume begins the work of excavating a deep and rich vein of scholarly ore—from which we hope significant products and connections will continue to be built.

We conclude this introduction by offering thanks to the contributors of the volume, to those who answered our call to review individual essays, to the Willa Cather Foundation, the University of Nebraska Press, and the Cather Project at the University of Nebraska–Lincoln. Additionally, we are grateful to the host institution of the conference, Duquesne University, as well as the sponsoring institutions: Saint Francis University, California University of Pennsylvania, University of Nebraska–Lincoln, and Penn State–Greater Allegheny. We feature a photograph of the Smithfield Street Bridge on this book's cover to highlight the enduring strength and resilience of the structure (which was a part of Cather's cityscape as much as it is ours) and to remind us all of the analogous enduring beauty that is reflected in Cather's fiction.

## WORKS CITED

Byrne, Kathleen D., and Richard C. Snyder. *Chrysalis: Willa Cather in Pittsburgh, 1896–1906*. Historical Society of Western Pennsylvania, 1982.

Cather, Willa. #0343: Willa Cather to Frances Smith Cather, [December 25] 1915. *The Complete Letters of Willa Cather*, edited by the Willa Cather Archive team, Willa Cather Archive, 2018, www.cather.unl.edu.

——. *The Selected Letters of Willa Cather*. Edited by Andrew Jewell and Janis Stout, Knopf, 2013.

——. *Uncle Valentine and Other Stories: Willa Cather's Uncollected Short Fiction 1915–1929*. Edited by Bernice Slote, U of Nebraska P, 1975.

——. *The World and the Parish: Willa Cather's Articles and Reviews 1893–1902*. Edited by William M. Curtin, U of Nebraska P, 1970. 2 vols.

Woodress, James. *Willa Cather: A Literary Life*. U of Nebraska P, 1987.

# Willa Cather's Pittsburgh

# Prologue
## Becoming "Miss Cather from Pittsburgh"

ANN ROMINES

What happened to Willa Cather in Pittsburgh? For me, the answer begins in the location she once termed "Siberia"—her Nebraska hometown, Red Cloud. After graduating from the University of Nebraska in June 1895, Cather spent several months in Lincoln and several at home with her family. In Lincoln she continued to work as drama critic for the *Nebraska State Journal* and for three months served as associate editor for the weekly *Courier*, writing her popular "Passing Show" column and other features. And she was writing fiction, as well; her first story in a national magazine, "On the Divide," would be published in January, in *The Overland Monthly*. By the end of December, Cather at last "moved her trunk" back to her family home to Red Cloud, although she returned to Lincoln regularly to review plays and search for a full-time job.

Back in Red Cloud, Cather reluctantly celebrated the advent of 1896 by attending a "New Year's Dance" with her seven-years-younger brother, Douglass. In a letter datelined "Siberia," she reported to her close Lincoln friends, the Gere sisters: "Of all rough-house affairs, of all cake walks! . . . The refreshments consisted of ice water in a wooden pail, coffee and ham sandwitches which they <u>passed in a bushel basket</u>.... The men fell down every now and then and you had to help them up. Yet this was a dance of the elite and bon ton of Red Cloud" (*Selected Letters* 24–25). When her cousin Etta was married a few weeks later, Willa took charge of the wedding break-fast, for which she extravagantly ordered strawberries, tomatoes, and watercress from Chicago—in February!—perhaps wanting to raise the "tone" of Red Cloud social life. When she was in Lincoln, her social life seems to have been active, and her name appeared often in the society news. In the same month of her Red Cloud cousin's wed-ding, the *Lincoln Journal* noted that Miss Willa Cather had attended a fashionable masquerade ball, dressed "as folly in pink and silver, with silver bells and a harlequin hat and staff" (*Kingdom of Art* 28).

In May, Cather wrote again from Red Cloud, apologetically, to Mariel Gere, her most sympathetic Lincoln friend, who had been supportive throughout a series of undergraduate crises and crushes:

> I think I should get so disgusted with myself that I would just quietly take a dose of Prussic acid to rid myself of my own company if it were not for this one thing, that most of my idiocy has come from liking somebody or other too well.... In the years I have been away I have kind of grown away from my family and their way of looking at things.... They sort of expect something unusual of me and the Lord only knows where it's coming from for I don't. I feel all played out. How can I "do anything" here? I have'nt seen enough of the world or anything else.... There is nothing to do but quietly peg along and lie low until I get out of debt, for I haven't got the nerve to ask my family to help me out any more. Besides they cant. Hang it, I've made a sweet muddle of things for a maiden of one and twenty. (*Selected Letters* 27–29)

This letter expresses familiar postgraduate anxieties, as young Cather agonizes over recent "idiocies" (perhaps including anxieties about how to perform gender), worries about alienation from her family and their expectations, and about post-college debts. Half-jokingly, she flirts with suicidal language. However, as Bernice Slote reminds us in her commentary accompanying Cather's *The Kingdom of Art*, this anxious "maiden of one and twenty" (she was already shaving a year off her age) was already widely recognized as one of Nebraska's "chief newspaperwomen." The *Omaha World Herald* praised her "genius for literary expression. . . . If there is a woman in Nebraska newspaper work who is destined to win a reputation for herself, that woman is Willa Cather." The Beatrice, Nebraska, paper went even further: Cather was "one of the ablest writers and critics in the country, and she is improving every week." As Slote wrote, in the early months of 1896 this accomplished young woman was "in the confusing position of being a star without a firmament" (26). In June that changed. On 17 June the *Journal* reported that Miss Willa Cather would soon depart for an editorial position with *The Home Monthly* magazine, in Pittsburgh. Cather left Lincoln for Red Cloud on the very day of that announcement, and six days later, she and her trunk boarded the train for Pittsburgh.

Except for her weeklong trip to Chicago in 1895 to hear "grand opera," Cather had not returned "back East" since her family moved to Nebraska in 1883. On the train, she reported to Mariel Gere, she "began to feel good as soon as I got east of Chicago. When I got to where there were some hills and clear streams and trees the Lord planted [very much the landscape of her native Virginia, and very unlike the largely treeless Nebraska] I didn't need any mint julip. The conductor saw my look of glee and asked if I was 'gettin' back home'" (*Selected Letters* 33). After thirteen years away from her birthplace, the Shenandoah Valley was now a part of her firmament again; a few months later, she would take a bicycle trip there and visit some favorite childhood haunts.

Just a few hours after her arrival in Pittsburgh on 26 June, in another letter to Mariel, Cather christened her new home "this City of Dreadful Dirt." Pittsburgh was famous for its iron and steel mills and their noxious fumes and was also "the production and marketing heart of America's glass industry" (Rosenthal iii). The conical furnace stacks of glassworks marked the skyline and produced "dense black smoke," their ample share of "Dreadful Dirt." The local glass industry, begun in 1797, took advantage of the area's abundant supply of coal and the mobility offered by its rivers. In the ten years Cather lived in Pittsburgh, the glass industry continued to grow, taking advantage of new technologies. By 1920, 80 percent of the glass made in the United States came from the Pittsburgh area. And Cather's growing awareness of this industry, as well as the iron and steel mills, became a part of her Pittsburgh fiction.

A month later, Cather wrote to Mariel again, just back from an "excellent" evening at the opera "with a little Chicago chap." Her self-esteem is clearly in good order. She chides Mariel for considering her "bohemian." "If I haven't any regard for myself I have just a little for my family. I may go to New York sometime, but not for the express purpose of going to the bow-wows, and certainly not until I get some money ahead." She's blunt, confident, and practical—and then, in the same paragraph, we find one of her quintessential statements of artistic belief: "There is no God but one God and Art is his revealer; that's my creed and I'll follow it to the end, to a hotter place than Pittsburgh if need be" (*Selected Letters* 39). This young woman has clearly expanded her firmament. She is enjoying an active and apparently conventional social life, free from the embarrassment and self-reproach that she confessed three months before. She realizes that *The Home Monthly*, where she is writing much of the content of the next issue, is likely to be "great rot, home and fireside stuff, about babies and mince pies" (*Selected Letters* 37). But she admits, "I really like the work. . . . Its a great boon just to be of some absolute use somewhere, to be at the head of something and have work that you must do. . . . Then the town and the river and the hills would compensate for almost anything" (39). In Pittsburgh Cather has found the landscape that was her first love—the wooded hills and rivers of Virginia—*and* the enticements of absorbing work in a modern city. Here she meets "so many different kinds of people"—drama critics, actors, musicians, writers—and her head is "thumping full of new ideas. I seem . . . to be able to do better work than ever before." But then—almost as if she fears she has gone too far—she pulls back:

"I doubt if I ever do anything very good though. I seem to lack the one thing" (39–40).

The massive Carnegie Institute had just opened in Pittsburgh, and during her first month in the city, Cather wrote to another Gere sister, Ellen, full of enthusiasm for its rich resources:

We went [to] an organ recital . . . at the great Carnegie music hall Saturday night. It was great. . . . The music hall is in the same huge building with the Carnegie library and art gallery. I thought the U. of N. [Nebraska] Library was nice, but this—its marble from one end to the other and the colors and frescoes are just one artistic harmony . . . they have all the books in the world there I think. And right near it is the Casino theatre and my old friend Pauline Hall plays there all next week. I foresee alas, that I will not go to the library on matinee afternoons but will slip across to the Casino to look upon Pauline's glorious anatomy once again. The old Nick is in me . . . it's no use talking. (37)

This welcoming Pittsburgh seems the very antithesis of Siberia. But the fiction that Cather wrote for her first five issues of *Home Monthly* also suggests that her family in Red Cloud was very much on her mind. The August issue features a story for "Young Folks" to which she signed the name of a favorite brother, Charles Douglass. It is a fairy tale of sorts, "The Princess Baladina—Her Adventure." Young Baladina has been "unusually naughty that day." She has "scratched and bitten the nurse who combed her golden hair," lost her golden ball in the moat, and poured custard into the ear trumpet of her fairy godmother. Shut up in her nursery as punishment, she resolves to make her family repent by getting "enchanted by a wizard. . . . [S]ome young Prince would . . . break the spell and bear her triumphantly off to his own realm. . . . Then her unfeeling parents would never see her any more, and her sisters and brothers would have no dear sweet little princess to wait on" (1–2). This plan does not work out—the one prince she encounters calls her a "silly little girl" and says, "go home to your parents." The only friend she finds is a little miller's boy who lets her ride on his donkey, and Baladina declares him "Prince enough for me." On their way home to the palace, they meet a search party led by her father the king. "Ha there, you precious run-away.... Come here, you little baggage." Baladina demands that her prince must come too, and "'have half the kingdom'.... But the king only laughed and gave the boy a gold piece and rode away.... The miller's boy stood by his donkey, looking wistfully after them, and the Princess Baladina wept bitterly at the dearth of Princes" (5).

This tale is told with a facility that reminds us that Willa Cather had spent many years spinning such tales for her six younger siblings. An indulged and willful daughter with problematic hair and multiple siblings devises a plan to defy her family and find a life elsewhere. But she ends up, as little girls often do, being carried home by an affectionate, laughing father. This suggests that the author has been thinking about family dynamics in a large family of siblings—and of what happens when a beloved daughter decides to leave home. In the same issue, "Tommy, the Unsentimental," signed by Willa Cather, also touches on matters that were central to her Red Cloud life, with a female protagonist who wears a boy's name and clothes, and ably runs her father's banking business.[1]

One of the stories that Cather thought showed the improvement of her writing was a two-part serial, "The Count of Crow's Nest," which conveniently filled a number of pages in the September and October issues of *The Home Monthly*. She proudly told Mariel Gere that she'd been offered a hundred dollars for it by *Cosmopolitan* (*Selected Letters* 39). The protagonist, Buchanan, is just out of college, an "honor man of whom great things were expected." He is holed up in the cheapest respectable boarding house in Chicago, "Crow's Nest," trying to be a writer—or something. "He knew that he was gifted in more ways than one, but he knew equally well that he was painfully immature, and that between him and success ... lay an indefinable, intangible something which only time could dispose of" (1; pt. 1). (This paradoxical knowledge of great potential, perhaps stifled by immaturity, sounds oddly familiar.)

Buchanan makes friends with a fellow boarder, an elderly, indigent European count who is admired for his elegant style and sense of gentlemanly honor, which forbids him to make much-needed monetary profit from a cache of revealing letters written by members of European aristocracy. His daughter, also transplanted to Chicago, is an inept singer who prides herself on her practicality and modernity. She has no scruples about profiting from those revealing letters, which she steals from her father. Buchanan helps the count retrieve the letters, and honor is (somewhat) preserved. But the count finds no satisfaction in this, and the story ends abruptly with his words to Buchanan: "It is a terrible thing, this degeneration of great families. You are very happy to have nothing of it here." He is eager to die and "free the world" of the blood he carries. "When all sense of honor dies utterly out of an old stock. . . . It should be buried deep . . . blotted out like the forgotten dynasties of history" (9–10; pt. 2). What will young American Buchanan make of this tale of decline, fall, and the incipient death of honor? And, indeed, what will *Home Monthly* readers make of it? There is nothing of "babies and mince pies" here. Nevertheless, the story—Cather's longest so far—does indeed show improvement, with, as James Woodress says, "developing skill in narrative technique" (121).

The December issue of *Home Monthly* was put together as Cather was anticipating a Pittsburgh Christmas, her first far away from her family. "The Burglar's Christmas," the magazine's requisite December holiday story, is not Cather at her best and is signed with the name of her cousin in Red Cloud, Elizabeth L. Seymour. Again, the setting is Chicago, and the protagonist is a young man whose father and fond college friends once had high hopes for him. But on Christmas Eve, his birthday, he has hit rock bottom, having failed at journalism, business, and all other efforts. Wandering the festive streets, desperately hungry, he decides to attempt burglary. He slips into a house where a holiday party is in progress and begins to pocket valuable jewelry. Looking for more, he discovers a cup he recognizes: "the silver mug he used to drink from when he was a little boy" (4). At this point the door opens, and a white-haired woman enters, unafraid.

After a moment's look, she embraces the burglar, who struggles to disengage himself. She protests, "Who is it says I shall not kiss my son?" (5). He tries to confess—"I came here to rob." But she tightens her embrace and says, "How could you rob your own house?" Her jewels are (she says) "'all yours, my son, as wholly yours as my great love'. . . . He held fast to her and bowed his head on her strong shoulder." This indomitably forgiving mother surrounds the failed burglar with food, comfort, and relentless love. The story ends with a sermon-like exaltation of the mother-love that saves this failed burglar and finally suggests that the great "Potter" will offer similar Christmas salvation to all his human "Things of Clay"—in language that we are probably relieved to note is not signed by "Willa Cather" (8).

However, Cather did sign *Home Monthly*'s December story for "Young Folks," "The Strategy of the Were-Wolf Dog," illustrated with a fine portrait of Santa Claus and his helper, the White Bear. This bear, "a most gentle and kindly fellow" who loves children, is the tale's hero. His adversary is the "shaggy and monstrous" Were-Wolf Dog, who hates "good little children" and is determined to prevent Santa's Christmas Eve deliveries (13). One year he manages to entice Santa's reindeer, who are resting up for the next night's deliveries, to go out for a midnight run toward the Polar Sea. Perhaps foreshadowing *Lucy Gayheart*, the reindeer find themselves on cracking ice, and, in a horrific scene, "the black current . . . whirled them down under." Only one reindeer, Dunder, survives. "Cruelly cut and bleeding," he makes his way back to Santa's castle and awakens White Bear. "Come out, brother," he gasps, "the others are all dead and drowned. . . . [T]he treacherous Were-Wolf Dog . . . lured us to go with him toward the Pole, promising to show us the Northern lights. . . . But black Death he showed us, and the bottom of the Polar Sea." "Santa's heart will be broken," and there will be no Christmas Eve deliveries (14).

But White Bear saves the day. Riding on poor Dunder, he goes to the distant spot where "the animals of the North all gather to celebrate Christmas" (14) and entreats them to replace Santa's drowned reindeer. Only one volunteer comes forward, slightly drunk on Christmas punch—"a poor old seal" who "had fallen into the seal fishers' hands and been maimed." Nevertheless, he promises to drag "the sleigh full of presents to the World-Children." Then the reindeer all sprang forward and cried, "We will go, take us!" So the story comes to its inevitable end: "The next day ... Santa Claus ... and seven new reindeer, headed by Dunder, flew like the winged wind toward the coast of Norway. And if any of you remember getting your presents a little late that year, it was because the new reindeer were not used to their work yet, though they tried hard enough" (24).

This is a surprisingly original Christmas tale—far more so than "The Burglar's Christmas"—and it is narrated by a storyteller of considerable skill and assurance. The Were-Wolf Dog is a more murderously malicious antagonist than his twentieth-century successor, the Grinch, and his drowning of the reindeer must have fully satisfied the "Young Folks'" appetite for chills and horror, and probably generated some nightmares. Again, this may be a tale Cather told her younger siblings. She was especially attached to her youngest brother, Jack, whom she missed painfully in Pittsburgh. In "My Little Boy," a poem about him that appeared in her first *Home Monthly*, she recalled storytelling: "At the curious tales that I used to tell / His big eyes would open so wide, / And for fear of the terrible werewolf's spell / He used to creep close to my side" (*April Twilights* 39). Apparently the Were-Wolf Dog made his first appearance in the Cather home in Red Cloud. Another poem addressed to the "little boy" appeared in the October issue: "When the loneliness is heavy, / And the dark seems coming on, / Your dear eyes look out and tell me / That you're sorry I am gone" ("Thine Eyes So Blue and Tender," *April Twilights* 32–33). And in November, there he is again, in "My Horseman," as the poet's "Little boy in the West Countree," a thousand miles away, whom she implores to "jump upon your steed [a rocking horse] and ride / Across the hills to me" (*April Twilights* 35–36).

Cather's younger sister Elsie also makes an appearance in an October *Home Monthly* poem—but a far less flattering one. Elsie's family nickname was "Bobby Shafto," from the familiar nursery song. Her poem begins,

Bobby Shafto fat and fair
Would not comb her yellow hair;
Every morning just at eight
She bewailed her bitter fate.
Then the combs and brush would fly.
But one morning while she cried
Mamma found a mouse inside,
Found a mousie pink and bare,
Who had crept for warmth in there,
Right in Bobby Shafto's hair!
Pretty Bobby Shafto! (*April Twilights* 34)

This "*Jingle*," as Cather titled it, probably recalls a family story that Elsie would have preferred to forget.

Willa's own family nickname was "Willie Winkie," and the next month, Winkie also appeared in Pittsburgh in a brief story Cather wrote for the children's page she edited for another local publication, the *National Stockman and Farmer*. In "Wee Winkie's Wanderings," the little girl, tired of playing with her "sullen dolls," decides that she wants to go out and ride with her father, who is mowing the meadow. But her mother forbids this: "'I think you are tired now and need a nap more than anything else.' When Winkie wanted anything she wanted it very much, as mamma knew." She begs and pouts and threatens, "I just think I'll run away to the mountains." "Her mamma thought this was as good a time as any to cure her of the notion. . . . 'Very well, just get your hat and go.'" Mamma helps Winkie pack up cookies and dolls and puts on her hat. "Then she said, 'Hurry up, little daughter, you will have to go fast if you get to the mountains,' and shut the door." Predictably, Winkie's plan (like Princess Baladina's) does not go well; it seems to her "that the sun did not shine so brightly as it had." Reluctantly, she starts to climb up the big hill that leads to the mountain, but "someway she could not go over the brow of the hill and lose sight of the house. She sat down despondently . . . and watched the sun going down, without the heart to even eat her cookies." Watching from the window,

Mamma at last sees her daughter climb back down the hill. Tired and dusty, Winkie slips silently into the house. "Mamma washed her and gave her supper, and tucked her into her little bed and never said a word about her running away, and neither did Winkie" (18).

The wooded, mountainous farm setting of this slight story suggests the Blue Ridge, Virginia, home of Willa Cather's own early childhood. And it portrays a mother who knows well how to deal with a willful young daughter who threatens to run away, but cannot bear to lose sight of home. Cather's relationship with her own mother was complex and sometimes conflicted. However, as Edith Lewis recalled, she praised her mother's ability to leave her children alone to make their own discoveries (6–7), as Winkie does.

Cather's editorship at *The Home Monthly* lasted for less than a year. Since September of 1896 she had been writing drama criticism for the *Pittsburgh Daily Leader*, in addition to her continuing contributions to Lincoln papers. By January of 1897 she was already looking for a full-time newspaper job in Pittsburgh. By June she had either resigned or been fired from *The Home Monthly*. She enjoyed a long summer visit in Red Cloud (Byrne and Snyder 7–8, 10). In September she received a job offer from the *Pittsburgh Leader* (seventy-five dollars a month), which she accepted at once. She told her Lincoln editor that she "almost hated" to go back, since in Red Cloud she had been "writing stories . . . and getting better at it than . . . ever." "I do the society act too much in Pittsburgh . . . and can't do the hermit act one bit. But dear me there is next summer and a lot of summers ahead, and in Pittsburgh there will be . . . Bernhardt and all the rest of the great[s], so I guess I'll go" (*Selected Letters* 45).

Less than two weeks later, well started in the new job, Cather wrote to Mariel Gere that she liked it "very much" and reported with pleasure that "Five gentlemen met me at the train and every one seems really glad to see me back!" (46). In the coming months she continued to report on a dizzyingly active social life and a lengthening list of new acquaintances and friends, with composer Ethelbert Nevin the "prince and king of them all" (59). But the summer in Nebraska had intensified feelings that Cather would never entirely resolve. She told Mariel that, as her train pulled out and "I watched you all get further and further away from me . . . I had to overcome a mighty impulse to jump off the train and run back to Lincoln." As she was coming to realize, *distance* meant *loss*. A year later she would write to Mariel's sister Frances, "There is nothing I fear so much as that I may gradually drift out of your lives . . . I think nothing in life could quite make up that loss to me" (51–52). The thread of home-sickness runs through her *Home Monthly* contributions—even the family names she substituted for her own suggest an effort to keep cherished connections. This was powerfully expressed to her friend in 1897: "Mariel, I <u>will not</u> be away from Nebraska another year. Of what use are money and success if one is not happy? And I cannot be happy so far away from home." Her heart is "aching for one little lad who is asleep in his bed a thousand miles away. . . . I don't want money or fame anymore, but just my three boys always . . . life is too short for love anyway, one is a fool to be an exile" (46–47).

Cather's partner of forty-four later years, Edith Lewis, had an inti-mate understanding of this period:

> [T]he three or four years she worked on the *Leader* were, I think, her hardest years. In spite of perpetual homesickness, she would not have wanted to—she could not, in fact—go back. One does not go back. But after the first excitement of being on her own had worn off, she felt herself at a sort of standstill. She was living in cheap boardinghouses, on miserable food, and sending as much money as she could to her family in Red Cloud. . . . There were times when the sense of the best years of youth going by, and nothing to show for it, no real advance toward the kind of accomplishment she wanted, filled her with discouragement. (43)

Lewis's account must have come from hearing Cather's memories of those earlier Pittsburgh years, since she did not meet Cather until 1903. When Cather wrote to Mariel and others in 1897 and 1898, she was many years away from reaching—or at least admitting—the blunt conclusion that Lewis implies the two women shared: "One does not go back." Cather did go back to Nebraska, of course, for multiple visits—until both her parents were dead. But it was always with the knowledge that, leaving Red Cloud, she would return to a kind of exile. Lewis acknowledges the "perpetual homesickness" of which Cather must have told her.

In fact, homesickness seems to have been a constant note in Cather's life. She first experienced it at the age of nine, when she left her beloved Virginia with her family and miserably promised herself that she "would not eat much until I got back to Virginia and could get some fresh mutton" (qtd. in *Willa Cather in Person* 10). And it was still with her in 1945, two years before her death, when she wrote to her closest Red Cloud friend, Carrie Miner Sherwood, "I am not exaggerating, Carrie, when I confide to you that I would rather go home to Red Cloud than to any of the beautiful cities in Europe where I used to love to go" (*Selected Letters* 647). As a child she had imagined that she could not be fully nourished until she "got back to Virginia." And in 1945, having lived by choice in New York City for thirty-nine years, she still longs to "go home to Red Cloud"— although she has not chosen to return there since 1931, and never would again.

In *My Ántonia*, ten-year-old Jim Burden, Cather's autobiographical stand-in, well understands that homesickness can be a fatal affliction. He recognizes it as the reason for an immigrant's suicide: "I knew it was homesickness that had killed Mr. Shimerda" (97). Perhaps the only cure for such homesickness—and for Cather, obviously, it was only a partial cure—is to make a home of the place where you are. And she had already set about doing that. Her extraordinarily profuse journalistic output from those years provides ample evidence of how well she was coming to know Pittsburgh—by bicycle, streetcar, interurban railway, boat, or on foot. In one column she wrote, after a Wagner performance, that "Wagner is perhaps not so effective [here] as elsewhere, we are all so used to the noise of the iron mills" (Lewis 46), including herself in the "we" that lived with the sound of a major Pittsburgh industry. She regretfully missed one of her much-enjoyed evenings with friends George and Helen

Seibel, spent reading French and discussing literature, "because she had promised to attend a picnic of the Glassblowers' Union with the labor editor of the *Leader*" (Byrne and Snyder 44). Obviously, she was becoming familiar with the Pittsburgh-area glass industry and, since she was in the company of her newspaper's labor editor, she was also certainly becoming more aware—as most of the country was—of local labor issues. In the glass industry, child labor was a major issue. Of more than six thousand glassworkers in the Pittsburgh area, 1,470 were boys under sixteen, more than half of whom worked twelve-hour night shifts. The glass industry considered these boys an essential source of cheap labor, and thus opposed—often successfully—intensifying efforts to pass child labor laws (Madarasz 53–54).

Like the rest of the country, Cather would almost certainly have become aware of Pittsburgh-area labor issues with the news of the 1892 steelworkers' strike at Andrew Carnegie's Homestead plant. When workers went on strike to oppose lowered wages, Henry Clay Frick, who managed the plant, hired three hundred armed Pinkerton detectives to quell the strike. In the resulting conflict, nine steelworkers were killed, and the riot could only be ended by thousands of armed state militia troops. Frick, adamantly anti-union, refused to negotiate with union workers, and the widely publicized "Battle of Homestead" was a grave setback to unionization in the expanding steel industry. Soon after the riots, an assassination attempt was made on Frick. He was injured, but survived. Both the doctor who treated him and the judge who presided over the would-be assassin's trial—Samuel McClung—later became good friends of Cather's. And Cather's Pittsburgh journalism is judiciously silent about Frick, who was still very much a presence in the city during her years there.

But when she wrote for a Lincoln audience in an 1897 piece, Cather described a "little supper" Frick gave for men friends at the Duquesne Club, noting that, in Pittsburgh, "everything 'swell' . . . is called either 'Duquesne' or 'Carnegie' . . . everything that is big and expensive." The evening's entertainment was the "fair and fascinating" singer Anna Held, whom Frick paid five hundred dollars.

At first all went well, but after the champagne had been flowing freely Anna began to sing her seductive little gem, "O, Won't You Come and Play with Me?" and the crowd got so frightfully merry that mademoiselle's manager had to pick her up bodily and take her to her hotel. . . . Mr. Frick's little escapade didn't go down very well . . . Mr. Frick is a gentleman well along in years, who is a pillar in the [Presbyterian] church and directs the manifold interests of the Carnegie Steel Company, and writes didactic articles on "How to Succeed in Life" for the *Youth's Companion*, and people were surprised at him. He is the same Mr. Frick, by the way, who made all that sensation about being shot at years ago just after the Homestead strike. He wasn't shot at all, as everyone here knows, but his would-be assassin is doing time in the pen just the same. (*The World and the Parish* 505–6)

Writing for newspaper audiences in both her old hometown of Lincoln and her new city allowed Cather to maintain multiple voices and to express in Lincoln opinions about Frick and other Pittsburgh matters that she did not publish—or probably voice—in Pittsburgh. In 1905 Frick moved to New York, and his house there, with its great art collection, is now a museum. In 1943 Cather wrote in a letter that she had just taken two of her adult nieces "up to the Frick Art Gallery, we had a very jolly time" (*Selected Letters* 624–25). I can't help wondering what she told her nieces about Mr. Frick.

Lewis's appraisal of the fiction Cather wrote during her early Pittsburgh years, working for *The Home Monthly* and the *Leader*, is merciless. For her, those stories "are an indication of how valueless this sort of writing can be for a truly original writer. They were . . . a kind of practice—but practice in the wrong direction, in doing over and over the kind of thing most destructive to talent" (42). I wouldn't be quite so dismissive—those stories show tendrils of growth, and they will continue to prove revealing for Cather's biographers. But Cather's mature evaluation of them probably matched Lewis's; she never permitted any of them to be reprinted after she left Pittsburgh. In the spring of 1900, she resigned from her job at the

*Leader*, spent a few months on the staff of *The Library*—a short-lived weekly magazine—and then, in the fall, moved to Washington DC for several months, where she worked as a translator and as a Washington correspondent for Lincoln and Pittsburgh papers. Clearly, she was casting about for work that would nourish her growth as a writer. During the Washington experiment, she returned at least once to Pittsburgh, for her customary Christmas celebration with her friends the Seibels. Then, in February, she was deeply grieved by the death of another friend, composer Ethelbert Nevin, and returned to Pittsburgh two weeks after his funeral. She was now deeply committed to a web of friendships and associations that were making Pittsburgh more and more homelike to her.

The most important of these friendships was with Isabelle McClung, which began in the spring of 1899 and almost immediately became centrally important to both women. Cather spent summer 1899 in Red Cloud, and when she returned, she wrote to Dorothy Canfield that she was "studying Greek to beat the band" with "the Goddess," and "Say, do you know, it's not half bad to be back." Isabelle met her at the station, "looking as though all the frieze of the Parthenon ought to be tripping after her, and I began to have a better opinion of Pittsburgh. She's so darned good to me that she's making me positively kiddish.... We've been ... having no end of a frivolous good time" (*Selected Letters* 52–53). As their friendship deepened, Isabelle must have observed the strains of Cather's continuing newspaper job and then her efforts to find work that would allow her to become the writer she aspired to be. The move to Washington seems an especially drastic, and perhaps desperate, step when we consider that it interrupted what was becoming the most important relationship in Cather's life thus far. After several months there, Cather wrote to Preston Farrar, a friend and former suitor, for advice about finding a teaching job. In Washington, her working "headquarters" were "in a university ... and the atmosphere has appealed to me very strongly.... It seems to me to be a good time to begin to think about making the change which I have always intended to make, and my family are very anxious for me to do so." She has prospects for finding a teaching job in Washington, she thinks, "but for personal reasons I would a little rather be in Pittsburgh next year" (55–56). A few weeks later, she was back in Pittsburgh and soon accepted a job as a replacement for a teacher who had just resigned, at Central High School. She taught composition, Latin, and—for just one difficult semester—algebra. The job offered a steady (though not large) salary, regular hours, summer vacation, and—as must have pleased at least the older members of her family—it was the most conventionally respectable profession for a nineteenth-century single American woman. And Isabelle McClung—surely the most pressing of the "personal reasons" for which Cather had wanted to return to Pittsburgh—invited Cather to move in with her socially prominent family in their capacious and elegant new house on Squirrel Hill. Cather lived there, enjoying free room and board (Byrne and Snyder 41) and Isabelle's intelligent and solicitous companionship, until she left Pittsburgh five years later.

Those last five Pittsburgh years were marked by growth, discovery, and achievement. With Isabelle, she made her first, revelatory trip to Europe in 1902; in 1903, her book of poems, *April Twilights*, was published. Her stories began to be accepted by magazines with wide national circulation, such as *The Saturday Evening Post* and *Scribner's*. And she began to write of her Nebraska home in new ways. The first example of this was "The Sentimentality of William Tavener," in 1900. The story shows a subtle understanding of what it might mean to simultaneously have two home places. Tavener, who emigrated with his wife from Virginia to Nebraska, as Cather's parents, grandparents, and aunt and uncle had, is "the most prosperous farmer" in his county. His wife, Hester, a "strong" "executive woman, quick of tongue," has been a major reason for their farm's success. Their relationship is practical and businesslike, and William has become "a hard man ... even towards his sons," whom he has "worked ... hard" all summer. When they ask for a day off to go to the circus, their father refuses. Hester tries to make the sons' case: "our boys don't get to see much out here on the prairie. It was different where we were raised." She goes on to reminisce about a circus she attended as a child, in Virginia, remembering her delight in the animals, including two camels. William interjects gravely, "No, there was only one camel. The other was a dromedary" (1–2). They discover that they both attended that same circus as children, as yet unknown to each other. They draw closer and talk on, remembering "old neighbors . . . weddings, picnics, sleighing parties and baptizings." "This exchange of confidences . . . had all the miracle of romance." After years of discussing only "butter and eggs and the prices of things . . . now they had as much to say to each other as people who meet after a long separation" (4). When William finally goes off to bed, he gives Hester a ten-dollar bill for the boys to take to the circus. While waiting for the boys to come in, and thinking with renewed tenderness of her husband, Hester goes into the bedroom to check on him and finds him sleeping, but plagued by flies. She goes to the parlor where a basket of wax fruit, made by her dead sister and hand-carried from Virginia with great care, is covered by a square of protective mosquito net, which she takes to the bedroom and spreads gently over William's head. "Then she sat down by the bed and listened to his deep, regular breathing."

The Taveners, who have been so occupied with surviving and succeeding in their new home, have rediscovered, through mutual memories, the old home where their enduring love began. And Hester's repositioning of the mosquito net, so that it protects her living husband and not a lifeless relic, signals an important readjustment of priorities. When the boys come in, she gives them the circus money and, feeling "a sudden throb of allegiance to her husband . . . said sharply, 'you be careful of that an' don't waste it. Your father works hard for his money.' The boys looked at each other in astonishment and felt that they had lost a powerful ally" (5). This story articulates a fuller understanding of how an emigrant family can be sustained by both its past and present homes; it replaces the misery of homesickness with the mutual sustenance of memory. And the Taveners' Virginia is clearly the Cathers' Virginia as well, as the familiar Shenandoah Valley place names in the story confirm.

Another fine story, "A Wagner Matinee," appeared in 1904. The central character, Aunt Georgiana, is modeled on Cather's Aunt Franc, wife of her uncle, George Cather. A New England native, Georgiana is a trained musician who taught music in Boston until she impulsively married a handsome younger man and went to Nebraska to homestead with him. The story's narrator, her nephew Clark, lived with his aunt in Nebraska as a boy. Now living in Boston and enjoying the city's cultural resources, he remembers how his beloved aunt understood and shared his homesickness. When he was "ill with a fever she used to sit by my cot in the evening ... and sing 'Home to our mountains, oh, let us return!' in a way fit to break the heart of a Vermont boy nearly dead of homesickness" (4). In the Boston concert hall where Clark takes her to hear Wagner's music, Georgiana has returned to her former home and is deeply moved. When the music ended, she "burst into tears and sobbed pleadingly, 'I don't want to go, Clark, I don't want to go!'" Clark thinks he understands—that for his aunt, "just outside the door of the concert-hall" stands the ugly world of the Nebraska farm, to which Georgiana must return, with "black pond ... unpainted house," and "gaunt, moulting turkeys picking up refuse about the kitchen door" (6).

This story again explores what it means to be caught between two homes. Cather would later tell Elizabeth Sergeant, "Life began for me ... when I ceased to admire and began to remember" (117). She wrote to Witter Bynner, "[Y]ou simply can't imagine anything so bleak and desolate as a Nebraska ranch of eighteen or nineteen years ago. In 'A Wagner Matinee' I used some of the features I best remember of the one on which I lived. . . . [D]uring the first year that we spent in the West I came ... near dying from homesickness" (*Selected Letters* 88). With this great early story (which she would revise again and again before republication), Cather learned some of the possible costs of honestly writing her memories of her Nebraska home. Her Lincoln editor, Will Owen Jones, a longtime friend and advocate, rebuked her sharply for painting such a grim picture of Nebraska. She told him, "I simply used the farm house we used to live in and a few of my recollections of life there. It is so beastly true that my own family are quite insulted—they say it isn't nice to tell such things." She ended by telling Jones, "Maybe it will relieve you to know that the [story] under discussion is the only Nebraska tale" that will be included in her forthcoming book of stories, *The Troll Garden*, which appeared in 1905, through the enthusiastic support of her new mentor and publisher, S. S. McClure (*Selected Letters* 80).

In the spring of 1902, when Cather had lived in Pittsburgh for six years, the city at last became a setting for one of her stories, "The Professor's Commencement." After one year of teaching at Central High School, Cather wrote this story about a thoughtful, generous man who is retiring from high school teaching after thirty years. His sister chides him that he's been wasting his gifts teaching, and "Now it is time that you do something to justify the faith your friends have always had in you. You owe something to them and to your own name." But the Professor fears the radical change of his retirement. "It is absolutely cutting my life off at the stalk, and who knows whether it will bud again?" (2). He had planned to complete his book on modern painting, but now "his heart told him that he had no longer the strength to take up independent work" (5). The Professor is fifty-five, and Cather, when she wrote his story, was approaching her twenty-ninth birthday and realizing that teaching was something she could do well—and that might threaten her life as a writer. Would her books get written and published—or would she, like the Professor, lose the strength to do independent work?

Pittsburgh does not wear its best face in this story: "The beautiful valley, where long ago two limpid rivers met at the foot of wooded heights, had become a scorched and blackened waste ... [while] bellowing mills ... broke the silence of the night with periodic crashes of sound, [and] filled the valley with heavy carboniferous smoke." The Professor's students are the products of that environment: "boys and girls from the factories and offices, destined to return thither, and hypnotized by the glitter of yellow metal. They were practical, provident, unimaginative, and mercenary at sixteen" (3–4). This Pittsburgh seems very different from the city that had so delighted young Cather six years before, when "the town and the river and the hills would compensate for almost anything."

In March 1904 Cather wrote to Dorothy Canfield about their mutual concern that their long, close friendship had become distant:

> We have both changed. Teaching school is a quieting, settling, ageing occupation, that makes one reliable and thoughtful and conscientious, but it is not good for ones <u>disposition</u>. I think I must take it too seriously, for it seems to take out of me most of the elements that used to be most active between you and me.... I'm really alarmed, Dorothy, at the rate at which I seem to be losing the capacity for emotion.... I don't know myself.

Cather reports that Isabelle is also concerned and saddened by "this prolonged winter of discontent.... If I had left Pittsburgh when my judgment told me to, four years ago ... I might not be so far afield now." As the long letter draws to an end, she assures Canfield that "this period of hibernating will pass. I will cast my dead skin and emerge." The letter has a troubling postscript: "I can't in common decency say much about the trying and complicated household in which I live, but you must realize that such conditions do not contribute to ones being oneself. There is a continual restraint necessary" (*Selected Letters* 77–79).

When this letter was written, Cather already had her contract with McClure for the publication of *The Troll Garden* and future fiction; in 1903 she had written "with a light heart" that she was "fairly launched at last" (72–73). Through the kind help of Isabelle's father and uncle, she had a job at a better high school, in Allegheny, and had been elected head of the English Department, with shortened hours and a salary double her starting salary at Central (Byrne and Snyder 59). What triggered the letter to Canfield? Depression? Disorder in the changing McClung household? Cather had her thirtieth birthday—a traditional milestone for women then—just four months before she wrote that letter. In some ways, despite her claims of having been changed and aged by teaching, she sounds much like the new university graduate who wrote to Mariel from Red Cloud that she felt estranged from her family and "all played out," with "nothing to do but quietly peg along and lie low" (*Selected Letters* 28). The "solution" to that malaise was to leave her home in Red Cloud. Now she has a comfortable home and situation in Pittsburgh, but again, the "solution" to her loss of self seems to be to leave home behind.

When *The Troll Garden* appeared the next year, it ended with "Paul's Case," Cather's second Pittsburgh story, and one which, to the end of her life, she seems to have considered one of her very best. Adolescent Paul, whose mother is dead, has no one to understand and sympathize with his malaise, as Aunt Georgiana did with young Clark in "A Wagner Matinee." To Paul, his home in middle-class Pittsburgh, the world that most of Willa Cather's high school students inhabited, is as bleak as that naked house on the prairie that Clark remembers. This story is full of closely observed details of life on Cordelia Street, where Paul's family and neighbors spend Sunday afternoons sitting on their porches. Paul's father and the other men tell "legends of the iron kings" (109)—such as Carnegie and Frick—for whom they work. His sisters trade church gossip and, if their father is in "a jovial frame of mind," bring out lemonade "in a red-glass pitcher, ornamented with forget-me-nots in blue enamel. This the girls thought very fine" (109). The pitcher is a reminder of the special importance of glass in Pittsburgh. A pitcher almost identical to this description appears in a catalogue for a local glass company in 1904 (Madarasz 10)—the year that this story was probably written. Glass trade shows, displaying the latest merchandise, were important events in Pittsburgh, and such a fashionable pitcher might well have been considered "very fine" in a middle-class home like Paul's.

But Paul disdains such accessible pleasures as a fancy glass pitcher. He has glimpsed another Pittsburgh world at Carnegie Hall and its art gallery, the local theater and the Schenley Hotel, where "actors and singers of the better class stayed," and wealthy manufacturers spent their winters. To Paul's enchanted eyes, the hotel shines like "a lighted cardboard house under the Christmas tree." On the evenings when he ushers at Carnegie Hall, he experiences a "delicious excitement which was the only thing that could be called living at all" (106). This, of course, was a world that Cather had come to know well, and her own "delicious excitement" with it is apparent in her early letters from Pittsburgh.

When Paul is banished from this shining other world, "when they had shut him out of the theater and concert hall, when they had taken away his bone" and he was put to work at Denny and Carson's, "the whole thing was virtually determined" (114). He must steal money, take the train to New York, and briefly live in a world of beauty and luxury where he feels entirely at home, finally "at peace with himself" (117). When, after eight days, Paul reads in a Pittsburgh paper that he will not be prosecuted for his theft and that his father is on his way to New York to find his son and return him to a long, unbearable life on Cordelia Street, Paul is not homesick; he is sick of home. His suicide, leaping in front of the train that would return him to Pittsburgh, signals his refusal to return there.

Despite her anguished letter to Dorothy Canfield in 1904, Cather did not leave Pittsburgh that year or the next, although her visits to New York—often staying with Edith Lewis—became more frequent. After *The Troll Garden*'s publication in March of 1905, she spent two summer months in the West, traveling with Isabelle. They visited Cather's brothers in Wyoming and South Dakota, and, as she wrote to Mariel Gere, "we were in Red Cloud for four weeks, helping father fix up his new house." Obviously, the pull of homesickness is still real for Cather; she tells Mariel that "I think, more and more, that the West is the only place I want to live, and I am planning to get home to Red Cloud for a year before very long." But for now, she is happily returning to her Pittsburgh home and her work teaching: "I like it better every year and feel that I do it better" (*Selected Letters* 90). She did not finish that school year, however—for in March, 1906, she left Pittsburgh to become an editor of *McClure's Magazine*, based in New York.

The first story she published after the move was "The Namesake," in March 1907. The story begins with seven young American men in Paris, art students in what must have seemed the current center of the world for visual artists. One of them has suddenly been called home, and the narrator says, "we all knew what it meant to him to be called home. Each of us knew what it would mean to himself, and ... felt something of the quickened sense of opportunity which comes at seeing another man in any way counted out of the race. Never had the game seemed so enchanting, the chance to play it such a piece of unmerited, unbelievable good fortune" (3). They wait with their departing friend for his train in the studio of an older and extremely successful sculptor, Lyon Hartwell, whom they consider the quintessential American artist. "He seemed ... to mean all of it—from ocean to ocean" (2). He "had thrown up in bronze all the restless, teeming force" of iconic male figures in American history, on Western frontiers and in the Civil War. His most recent work, ready to cast for a battlefield monument, is "'The Color Sergeant' ... the figure of a young soldier running, clutching the folds of a flag, the staff of which had been shot away." The young men admire "the splendid action and feeling of the thing" (4). Moved by the student's departure, Hartwell shares an account of his own homecoming.

He was born in Italy, son of an expatriate and unsuccessful American sculptor who desired that his son "should carry on his work" and died when the boy was fourteen. Young Lyon "studied under one master after another," in Italy and then Paris, "until ... nearly thirty." Then he was called home to Pennsylvania—where he had never been—as the only remaining family member available to care for an old aunt, victim of a "cerebral disease." He planned to take her back to Paris with him, but when he met her he realized this was not possible. So he stayed with his aunt in his ancestral home for two years, until she died. The large brick house, "in the midst of a great garden," was on

the high banks of a river in Western Pennsylvania. The little town twelve miles down the stream ... had become, in two generations, one of the largest manufacturing cities in the world [Pittsburgh]. ... [T]he gentle hill slopes were honey-combed with gas wells and coal shafts, oil derricks ... the brooks were sluggish and discolored with crude petroleum. . . . The great glass and iron manufactories had come up and up the river almost to our very door . . . and their crashing was always in our ears. But, though my nerves tingled with the feverish, passionate endeavor which snapped in the very air about me, none of these great arteries seemed to feed me. (6)

Hartwell was "'never at home'" in the family house. The only link he felt was to a portrait of a young uncle, his namesake, who enlisted in the Union Army at fifteen and died at sixteen, running as he carried "the Federal flag." This uncle is the subject of Hartwell's sculpture, "The Color Sergeant." He is buried in the family garden.

On Decoration Day, the aunt insists that Hartwell put up bunting and decorate her brother's grave with flowers, and he finds some relics of the boy—toys, schoolbooks—in the attic, in a trunk marked with the name that is also his own, "Lyon Hartwell." All night he sits in the garden by his uncle's grave:

The experience of that night . . . almost rent me in pieces. It was the same feeling that artists know when we, rarely, achieve truth in our work; the feeling of union with some great force . . . of being glad that we have lived. For the first time I felt the pull of race and blood and kindred, and felt beating within me things that had not begun with me. It was as if the earth under my feet had grasped and rooted me. . . . [A]ll night long my life seemed to be pouring out of me and running into the ground. . . . And so . . . I naturally feel an interest in fellows who are going home. It's always an experience. (9)

This is not, as we might expect at this moment in Cather's career, a story about leaving Pittsburgh—but about a man who, in coming home to this place, found roots, kinship, and the sources of his own best American art. Among the student artists in Paris, we feel the competitive excitement of "the game" and the good fortune of being "a player" in Paris. "Going home," they think, means being "counted out of the race." For Cather in 1907, going to New York—then the center of "the game" for American writers—must have held the same excitement, and "going home," especially as far as Red Cloud, must have held the same potential for loss. And yet, both Lyon Hartwell and Willa Cather found the material for much of their own best work by "going home"—where they did not choose to stay.

This was the second time Cather had written "The Namesake." In the first, a poem in the 1903 *April Twilights*, a young man stands at the grave of his—and the author's—young uncle, a Confederate Civil War casualty, who is identified, in a dedication, by his initials (which Cather got wrong) and his regiment. The poem's speaker is also a namesake, who promises the dead uncle that he will "be winner at the game / Enough for two who bore the name" (*April Twilights* 84). For her story, Cather made her dead uncle a Union soldier, perhaps not wanting to be identified with the sentimental Confederate fiction that was then flooding markets. Both "Namesake" texts have male narrators and protagonists. The young artists who listen to Hartwell's story include no women. In the years to come, Cather would bring women artists to New York to play the game as well—first Thea Kronborg, then, among others, the unnamed woman writer that Jim Burden meets on the train, at the beginning of *My Ántonia*.

Going home *is*, as Hartwell says, "quite an experience." And it is one that Willa Cather wrote about, again and again, during her forty-one years in New York. After the false start of *Alexander's Bridge*, she "hit the home pasture" in *O Pioneers!* (Willa Cather to Carrie Miner Sherwood, qtd. in Stouck 283), *My Ántonia* (which ends with Jim Burden's homecoming), "Old Mrs. Harris," *Lucy Gayheart*, and—at last—*Sapphira and the Slave Girl*, in which Nancy, a free, successful, urban Canadian woman, returns to the Virginia home where she lived as an abused slave girl, and in which Willa Cather herself, in an unprecedented first-person epilogue, returned to her own first home in Virginia.

Pittsburgh belongs on that list of homecomings as well. For me, Cather's most resonant Pittsburgh story is her last one, "Double Birthday," set in the changing city of the 1920s, from which both

Cather and the now-married Isabelle McClung Hambourg had departed. It was published in 1929, just before the crash. The story celebrates the "double birthday" of an uncle and nephew, heirs of a fortune from a large Pittsburgh glass factory, who have both "squandered" that fortune through their devotion to art. The birthday celebration includes an elegant and responsive middle-aged woman friend, Marjorie, who, more than any other Cather character, resembles Isabelle McClung, and is the daughter of a conservative judge who resembles Judge McClung, Isabelle's father. And the story is lit by the memory of a radiant, glowing window made of Pittsburgh art glass. "Double Birthday" is, obviously and beautifully, Willa Cather's fond evocation of the city that was her home for ten years. For her, writing the story more than twenty years after her move from Pittsburgh to New York, it must have been a sort of homecoming.[2]

When Kathleen Byrne and Richard Snyder wrote their indispensable book *Chrysalis: Willa Cather in Pittsburgh*, they began with a chapter titled "Miss Cather from Nebraska" and ended with one titled "Miss Cather from Pittsburgh"—implying, presumably, a transformation. But I suspect that Miss Cather was both, as well as Miss Cather from Virginia and Miss Cather from New York. And I also suspect that, at moments, she was homesick for them all. The evidence is the books.

NOTES

1. For a pertinent discussion of this story, see Daryl Palmer's essay "Bicycles and Freedom in Red Cloud and Pittsburgh," pages 33–62 in this volume.

2. For a much more complete discussion of this story, see Joseph Murphy's essay "Venetian Window: Pittsburgh Glass and Modernist Community in 'Double Birthday,'" pages 255–82 in this volume.

WORKS CITED

Byrne, Kathleen D., and Richard C. Snyder. *Chrysalis: Willa Cather in Pittsburgh, 1896–1906*. Historical Society of Western Pennsylvania, 180.

Cather, Willa. *April Twilights and Other Poems*. Edited by Robert Thacker, Everyman Library, 2013.

———. "The Burglar's Christmas" [Signed "Elizabeth L. Seymour"]. *The Home Monthly*, vol. 6, December 1896, pp. 8–10, Willa Cather Archive, edited by Andrew Jewell, U of Nebraska–Lincoln.

———. "The Count of Crow's Nest" (pt. 1). *The Home Monthly*, vol. 6, September 1896, pp. 9–11, Willa Cather Archive, edited by Andrew Jewell, U of Nebraska–Lincoln.

———. "The Count of Crow's Nest" (pt. 2). *The Home Monthly*, vol. 6, October 1896, pp. 12–13, 20–23, Willa Cather Archive, edited by Andrew Jewell, U of Nebraska–Lincoln.

———. *The Kingdom of Art: Willa Cather's First Principles and Critical Statements*. Edited by Bernice Slote, U of Nebraska P, 1967.

———. *My Ántonia*. 1918. Willa Cather Scholarly Edition, historical essay and explanatory notes by James Woodress, U of Nebraska P, 1994.

———. "The Namesake." *McClure's Magazine*, vol. 28, March 1907, pp. 493–97, Willa Cather Archive, edited by Andrew Jewell, U of Nebraska–Lincoln.

———. "Paul's Case." *The Troll Garden*. A Variorum Edition, edited by James Woodress, U of Nebraska P, 1983, pp. 102–21.

———. "The Princess Baladina—Her Adventure." *The Home Monthly*, vol. 6, August 1896, pp. 20–21, Willa Cather Archive, edited by Andrew Jewell, U of Nebraska–Lincoln.

———. "The Professor's Commencement." *The New England Magazine*, vol. 26, June 1902, pp. 234–39.

———. *The Selected Letters of Willa Cather*. Edited by Andrew Jewell and Janis Stout, Knopf, 2013.

———. "The Sentimentality of William Tavener." *The Library*, vol. 1, 12 May 1900, pp. 13–14, Willa Cather Archive, edited by Andrew Jewell, U of Nebraska–Lincoln.

———. "The Strategy of the Were-Wolf Dog." *The Home Monthly*, vol. 6, December 1896, pp. 13–14, 24, Willa Cather Archive, edited by Andrew Jewell, U of Nebraska–Lincoln.

———. "A Wagner Matinee." *Everybody's Magazine*, vol. 10, March 1904, pp. 325–28, Willa Cather Archive, edited by Andrew Jewell, U of Nebraska–Lincoln.

———. "Wee Winkie's Wanderings." *The National Stockman and Farmer*, 26 November 1896, pp. 8–10, Willa Cather Archive, edited by Andrew Jewell, U of Nebraska–Lincoln.

————. *Willa Cather in Person: Interviews, Speeches, and Letters*. Edited by Brent L. Bohlke, U of Nebraska P, 1986.

————. *The World and the Parish: Willa Cather's Articles and Reviews 1893–1902*. Edited by William M. Curtin, U of Nebraska P, 1970. 2 vols.

Lewis, Edith. *Willa Cather Living: A Personal Record*. 1953. Ohio UP, 1989.

Madarasz, Anne. *Glass: Shattering Notions*. Historical Society of Western Pennsylvania, 1998.

Rosenthal, Ellen. Preface. *Glass: Shattering Notions* by Anne Madarasz, Historical Society of Western Pennsylvania, 1998, pp. iii–v.

Sergeant, Elizabeth Shepley. *Willa Cather: A Memoir*. 1953. Ohio UP, 1992.

Stouck, David. Historical Essay. *O Pioneers!* Willa Cather Scholarly Edition, edited by Susan J. Rosowski and Charles W. Mignon with Kathleen Danker, historical essay and explanatory notes by David Stouck, U of Nebraska P, 1992, pp. 283–303.

Woodress, James. *Willa Cather: A Literary Life*. U of Nebraska P, 1987.

# PART 1

# East Meets West

# 1 Bicycles and Freedom in Red Cloud and Pittsburgh

## Willa Cather's Early Transformations of Place and Gender in "Tommy, the Unsentimental"

DARYL W. PALMER

Over the years, critics and scholars have often suggested that Willa Cather needed time to come to terms with Nebraska. Perhaps because of stories such as "Peter," "On the Divide," "A Wagner Matinee," and "The Sculptor's Funeral," it has been tempting to think of "The Bohemian Girl" (1912) and *O Pioneers!* (1913) as marking the grand rapprochement of author and region.[1] But Cather's artistic trajectory is more complex than this narrative admits. As early as 1896, when she moved to Pittsburgh in order to edit *Home Monthly*, the author was more than ready to reinvent her home country in ways that would eventually inform her greatest fiction. Bernice Slote observes in her essay accompanying Cather's *The Kingdom of Art* that by "1896 Willa Cather had written nearly a half million words of criticism, self-analysis, and explorations into the principles of art and the work of the artist" (4). Marilyn Arnold points out that the seasoned author "proved herself an artist long before *O Pioneers!*

appeared in 1913. Some of her very earliest stories have the earmarks of genius, and a good many of them before *O Pioneers!* are superb" (xiii). One of these stories is "Tommy, the Unsentimental," which appeared in the August 1896 edition of *Home Monthly*. In this story, the "earmarks of genius" can be attributed to the way Pittsburgh helped Cather reinvent her hometown of Red Cloud. Eschewing early pioneer experience for her own recent memories, Cather celebrates a metropolitan town in the American West where a woman can ride bicycles, experiment with gender, and resist societal expectations. Like the cocktails that Tommy concocts for her older male friends in Southdown, the story is a heady mix of spirit and innovation that helps to explain how Red Cloud and Pittsburgh mattered to Cather's emergence as a great American writer.

Before "Tommy" appeared in *Home Monthly* in 1896, Cather had published a handful of stories set in Nebraska, the two best being "Peter" and "On the Divide." In these early works, Nebraska is a grim place of the past, marked by aridity, struggle, and futility. In "Peter," we learn that father and son had settled in "the dreariest part of south-western Nebraska" where "there was nothing but sun, and grass, and sky" (5, 6). In "On the Divide," the narrator describes the location of Canute's "shanty" on "the level Nebraska plain of long rust-red grass that undulated constantly in the wind" (8). Life in such a region is positively pathological: "Insanity and suicide are very common things on the Divide. They come on like an epidemic in the hot wind season. Those scorching dusty winds that blow up over the bluffs from Kansas seem to dry up the blood in men's veins as they do the sap in the corn leaves" (10–11). As Robert Thacker notes, "throughout these stories Cather is both direct and, apparently, embittered, seeing the prairie landscape as destroying its homesteaders' spirit through its very vastness and the loneliness it occasions" (148). Susan J. Rosowski suggests that the challenge for the young author was "how to humanize an alien world" (16).

In the months after Cather graduated from the University of Nebraska, in June 1895, she must have felt ready for any challenge. An accomplished and respected journalist, she shuttled back and

Fig. 1.1. Mary Miner, Willa Cather, and Douglass Cather, ca. 1895. Courtesy of the Willa Cather Foundation Collection, Nebraska State Historical Society.

forth between Lincoln and Red Cloud, attending parties, visiting friends, writing pieces for the local newspapers, and riding her "wheel." Cather was becoming one of the New Women who defined themselves and their freedom through what Janis Stout has called "masculinized styles" and, of course, the riding of bicycles.[2] A headline in the 31 May *Lincoln Evening Call* could have been written for the recent graduate: "The New Woman Riding into Freedom on the Bicycle" (3).

What would freedom look like for Cather? Would it, in some way, involve a bicycle? A column entitled "Literary Lincoln" in the 1 June 1895 *Courier* puts Cather "at the head of the list of the writers of Lincoln," noting that "she has ideas and knows how to express them, and to express them well. As a critic she is fearless, and has the knack of seeing things as they really are, and of writing them so that other people may see them" (5). "I find this country looking like a garden," she wrote to Ellen Gere and Frances Gere on 30 July

1895, "green and beautiful beyond words," confiding, "I had great times riding my wheel in Lincoln and Beatrice. I have a hundred adventures to tell you" (#0019 *Complete Letters*).

In August, she landed a position as associate editor at the *Lincoln Courier*. Announcing her new position, the 3 August 1895 *Courier* called her "thoroughly original and always entertaining" (1). A new life in Lincoln was taking shape, but the fearless critic seems to have been unable to resist waging war against political corruption in the city. Fed up with the way the federal court was handing (or mishandling) the R. C. Outcalt embezzlement scandal at the Capital National Bank, the *Courier*'s fiery editorializing ran afoul of the presiding judge. The 13 December 1895 *Lincoln Herald* reported the finale for the editors:

> Col. W. Morton Smith has been fined $50 and fifteen days in jail by the federal court at Omaha, for the naughty things he said about the Outcalt case in his valuable paper. Miss Sarah Harris one of the editors was subpoenaed as a witness and Miss Willa Cather the third and best looking of the trio, quietly resigned her position and left the city. (1)

Cather's new professional life in Nebraska had fallen apart almost as quickly as it had begun. On 2 January 1896, writing to friends back in Lincoln, she headed the letter "Siberia," offering a jaunty and satiric report of a New Year's dance that included "the elite and bon ton of Red Cloud" before concluding that "one of the charms of the Province is that one gets indifferent toward everything, even suicide" (#0021 *Complete Letters*). The Nebraska Cather knew so well had become "Siberia," an alien world that the ambitious young journalist could not civilize.

Fate, looking very much like publisher James Axtell, provided the answer. When Axtell offered her the position of managing editor of *Home Monthly* in Pittsburgh, she seized the opportunity. After feeling trapped in "Siberia," she could save face by escaping to a world that held more opportunities than the one she was leaving. She had all the skills necessary for the job and the opportunity to go east seemed especially attractive. When she arrived in Pittsburgh on 26 June 1896, Cather wrote to Mariel Gere, noting the hills, "clear streams," and trees east of Chicago (#0025 *Complete Letters*). "The conductor saw my look of glee," Cather wrote, "and asked if I was 'gettin' back home.'" Describing Pittsburgh as the "City of Dreadful Dirt," she quickly realized that fate had carried her far beyond Nebraska.

But the conductor had spoken prophetically. As the days passed, Cather quickly discovered that Red Cloud and Pittsburgh echoed each other with a precision guaranteed to fuel the writer's imaginative conceptions of home. Cather was making a momentous discovery, which would shape her best work for decades to come. Years later in a 1921 *Nebraska State Journal* interview, she explained, "When in big cities or other lands, I have sometimes found types and conditions which particularly interested me, and then after returning to Nebraska, discovered the same types right at home, only I had not recognized their special value until seen thru another environment" (*Willa Cather in Person* 40). In 1896 Cather looked about and identified a shared fascination with rivers, trolleys, manufacturing, musical culture, brick buildings, bridges, bicycles, and New Women. To an author already inclined to write fiction set in Nebraska, Pittsburgh materialized before her eyes as a kind of looking glass, a magic mirror that made it possible for Cather to look at the new world of Pittsburgh, dream of Red Cloud, and write "Tommy, the Unsentimental."

As she surveyed her new home, the author studied a formidable metropolis of manufacturing. The impressive trolley system that had "carried more than 23 million passengers" in 1888 was expanding (Tarr 31). Electric power had illuminated the city since 1887, thanks to George Westinghouse's Allegheny County Electric Company (Tarr 34).

City Attorney Clarence Burleigh spoke rhapsodically about the city's metropolitan accomplishments in the 14 April 1896 *Pittsburgh Press*:

I come from that great human hive of industry and invention standing at Pennsylvania's western gate, whose ground is sacred with our country's history and glutted with nature's richest wealth; whose manufactories are gigantic and legion with furnaces; whose never-quenched fires transform night into day; the hum of whose wheels is incessant, and whose finished products reach to every clime; a city with no industrial goal but perfection. (2)

There is no doubt that Cather's imagination was stirred by the "great human hive," but she must have been surprised by the way recollections of Red Cloud could mingle with her experiences of Pittsburgh.

Although Pittsburghers would probably have laughed at the notion, Cather knew that Red Cloud newspapers often invoked the terms "metropolis" and "metropolitan" when they discussed local progress in Webster County.[3] She would have recognized that Burleigh's vision of Pittsburgh "standing at Pennsylvania's western gate" echoed an oft-used epithet from back home. As the 28 August 1885 *Chief* explained, Red Cloud held "the proud distinction of being the metropolis of the Great Republican Valley and the Gate city thereto" (5). When Cather noted the many examples of progress in one "gate city," she could easily summon up echoes in the other "gate city." Red Cloud newspapers had made the case for metropolitan progress time and again as she was growing up. Cather would certainly recall the rhetoric of the 20 April 1888 *Chief*:

> Red Cloud is going to be a mighty live town this year, and is already putting on signs of great activity. Two new railroads, a street railway, a creamery and several manufacturing institutions will go far to make her the beau ideal city of the valley and don't you forget it. No other city or town in the valley can boast of a street railway, electric lights and numerous other enterprises. (1)

Only eight years after New York City first installed electric lights and nearly fifty years *before* the Rural Electrification Act, the *Chief* could boast justifiably of the town's electrified illumination, an undeniable sign of metropolitan progress. Well aware that such declarations about a town of some three thousand citizens on the Great Plains would never impress citizens from large American cities back East, the editors liked to season their prose with bursts of jocular bluster. "Whoop-la," the 20 July 1888 *Chief* declared, "who says Red Cloud isn't metropolitan. Water works, street cars, electric lights, five weeklies and one daily. Come to Red Cloud and be happy" (1).

Having left Red Cloud because she was most unhappy, Cather had good reason to reconsider her feelings about her Nebraska home. Growing up surrounded by civic boosting that was part reality and part myth, with a touch of hokum added for good measure, the ambitious young editor was ready to experience a new sense of pride in Red Cloud. Although much has been made of the way Cather's earliest fiction laments the hard life of the pioneers, this emergent pride played a vital role in transforming the author's personal and artistic relationship to Nebraska. After spending time in Pittsburgh, Cather was prepared to set aside the pioneer past and write a story set in a version of *metropolitan* Red Cloud.

Settling into her editorial position in the eastern metropolis, she returned to her beloved wheel and must have felt that her emergence as a New Woman was complete. On 4 August 1896, she reported to Mariel Gere that the work was hard but life in Pittsburgh offered distinct pleasures: "The only form of excitement I indulge in is racing with the electric [street] cars on my bicycle. I may get killed at that, but certainly nothing more" (#0028 *Complete Letters*).[4] In risking life and limb on her wheel, Cather embodied the modern ambition of the New Woman while adapting to her new urban life. As Virgil Albertini explains, Cather "was astride her own private machine, which gave her the opportunity to travel cheaply, to enjoy the exhilarating freedom of mobility, to have exercise and possible camaraderie, and to test her stamina and speed with the electric cars" (14).

Later that fall, Cather set out on a cycling trip through the Shenandoah Valley that allowed her to explore what would become an abiding disposition. James Woodress comments on this cycling adventure: "Among the several polarities that pulled at Cather all her life was the attraction of the eastern mountains against the tug of

the prairie of her adopted state" (112). By the summer of 1896, Cather
the cyclist was beginning to race imaginatively between Red Cloud
and Pittsburgh, between East and West, feminine and masculine. The
New Woman had discovered a new kind of freedom.

Needless to say, Cather was part of a global phenomenon. In 1896
Londoners were celebrating the ten-year anniversary of the invention
of the safety bicycle. From London to Estonia to Red Cloud and
Pittsburgh, people were forming bicycle clubs.[5] In the United States,
ordinary riders joined the League of American Wheelmen. Readers
of the *New York Times* saw regular features on the sport—"Among
the Wheelmen" and "Gossip of the Cyclers"—that were replicated all
over the country in places like Red Cloud, Lincoln, and Pittsburgh.

There was much to talk about, but the subject of women and
bicycles inspired the most debate. Annie Kopchavsky, known to the
world as Annie Londonderry, embodied the conversation for many
people when she completed an around-the-world cycling trip in 1895.
Married with three children at the time, Londonderry was rewriting
the Victorian narrative of female ambition and hardiness. Evan Friss
observes, "The debates about female cyclists spiraled into a national
discussion, encompassing a range of issues such as femininity, Victorian respectability, and physical health" (161). In the midst of this "discussion," as Ellen Gruber Garvey points out, "advertising-dependent
magazines asserted a version of women's bicycling that reframed
its apparent social risks as benefits" (67). Sarah Hallenbeck notes
that these "magazines provided an effective vehicle for promoting
not only women's bicycling in general but also a distinctly modern
model of heterosexual desire, courtship, and domesticity" (xxiv).

No one in this debate was more dynamic than Frances Willard,
president of the Women's Christian Temperance Union. In *How
I Learned to Ride the Bicycle*, she told the story of learning to ride
after the age of fifty and described her particular relationship with
"Gladys," her bicycle. Willard had a powerful message: "She who
succeeds in gaining the mastery of such an animal as Gladys, will
gain the mastery of life, and by exactly the same methods and characteristics" (28). The reviewer in the 18 May 1895 *New York Times*

Fig. 1.2. Frances Willard and Gladys, her bicycle. Photograph from her book, *How I Learned to Ride the Bicycle*, Fleming H. Revell, 1895.

called it a "spicy little book" and praised Willard's admonition: "all
failure is from a wobbling will rather than a wobbling wheel" (3).
With this admonition in mind, Hallenbeck suggests that Willard is
"reinforcing her indirect claim that women need only confidence
and persistence to achieve personal or social success in life" (117).

In the 1890s, women and bicycles were nothing short of revolutionary. As Gruber Garvey observes, "the new mobility the bicycle allowed
offered freer movement in new spheres, outside the family and
home—heady new freedoms that feminists celebrated" (72). Susan
B. Anthony spoke to the fact directly in 1898: "Let me tell you what
I think of bicycling. I think it has done more to emancipate women
than anything else in the world. I stand and rejoice every time I see
a woman ride by on a wheel" (qtd. in Sher 277). Admitting a prefer-
ence for his horse but his delight in mounting a bicycle, Owen Wister
claimed, "More than the trolley does the bicycle promise to fulfill for
us the Declaration of Independence; women are become the equals
of men, and the black and the Chinaman speed with them across
the pleasant levels of Democracy" (qtd. in "Authors on the Wheel"
226–27). Writing from her own experience in the early 1890s, Grace
E. Denison remembered the derision she and other female riders had
experienced, but Denison declared a combat victory: "We lived down,
or rather rode down, our enemies" (52). By the time Cather arrived in
Pittsburgh in 1896, she was caught up in this revolutionary spirit.

She certainly came to the right place. Pittsburgh in the 1890s was
positively buzzing about bicycles. Cyclists were everywhere. In 1898,
as Friss points out, Pittsburgh had one bicycle shop for every "5,300
people (still more shops per capita than present-day Amsterdam).
Pittsburgh was also home to a half dozen bicycle liveries, renting
out bicycles" (25). The city's newspapers were crammed with stories about bicycle races, clubs, riding apparel, winter riding, the
dangers of cycling, proper pedaling instructions, famous cyclists,
and the ongoing controversy over women cyclists. The *Pittsburgh
Dispatch* offered "Gossip of the Cyclers" on a regular basis. A week
or so after arriving in Pittsburgh, Cather could have read in the 11
July 1896 *Pittsburgh Daily Post* about James Hoar's agonizing death

AROUND THE WORLD
WITH WHEEL AND CAMERA

BY FRANK G. LENZ.

Fig. 1.3. Cover of *Outing Magazine*, August 1892.

from *scorching*, the popular practice of cyclists riding extremely fast
(4). A couple of weeks later, the newcomer could have experienced
the "Sunday Scenes at Schenley Park," where, according to the 27
July 1896 *Pittsburgh Gazette*, "bicycles, single and tandem, shot in
between the larger rigs, dodging like swallows just before a rain
storm" (5). The popularity of such stories can be gauged by the
announcement in the 14 August 1896 *Pittsburgh Press*: "WHEELMEN!
Everything of interest and importance concerning cycling is to be
found in THE PRESS" (II).

In 1890s Pittsburgh the most compelling cycling stories of the day
were about Pittsburgher Frank Lenz, arguably the most famous cyclist
in the world by the time Cather arrived in the city. In the pages of *Outing* magazine, Lenz linked his ambition to his Pittsburgh origins: "My
wheel and I had become familiar with all routes within reach of Pitts-

burgh" (xx). Lenz had advertised his civic pride by setting out from the Smithfield Street Bridge on 15 May 1892 to pedal around the world.[6]

Completed in 1883, the same year the Cather family moved to Nebraska, the bridge symbolized Pittsburgh's metropolitan status but must have conjured up memories of Red Cloud in Cather's mind. In her youth, the local newspapers had campaigned for a substantial bridge over the Republican River that would symbolize the town's prosperity. The writer who loved Shakespeare must have recollected how the *Chief* produced headlines such as "To Bridge or Not to Bridge" and "My Kingdom for a Bridge."[7] By 13 April 1888, the newspaper was calling the town "one of the bright and shining lights among Western Nebraska cities," boasting that "four years ago nothing but an old wooden bridge spanned the great Republican river south of the city, to-day one of the finest iron bridges in the west stretches across its placid waters, a monument to the enterprise of our city and county" (1). When Cather gathered her childhood friends to build a play-town in the backyard, her first project as mayor and editor of the enterprise was the construction of a bridge (Bennett 172–73). Now in Pittsburgh, her imagination already stirred by bicycles, Cather discovered more reflections of Red Cloud.

Famous or not, wheelmen were everywhere in Pittsburgh, but wheelwomen attracted the most critical attention. A steady stream of articles offered advice to women cyclists. Typical of the genre is "For the Fair Cyclist," appearing in the 16 August 1896 *Pittsburgh Press*, which admonishes, "The very first 'do' is, do dress appropriately" (11). More than anything else, women cyclists should be concerned about appearances, or so many commentators suggested (Hallenbeck 43–52). As Cather worked at *Home Monthly*, the 30 July 1896 *Pittsburgh Press* reported, "A Chicago new woman ran down a man with her wheel. No gentleman would run down a woman, no matter who she is" (1). Women cyclists could be dangerous. Days later, in the 9 August 1896 *Daily Post*, Helen Ward described the battle between Charlotte Smith, president of the Woman's Rescue League and crusader against the bicycle, and Willard, who "found her health in the revolutions of the two little wheels" (11). Six days later, a poem in the

Fig. 1.4. Smithfield Street Bridge, Pittsburgh, Pennsylvania, ca. 1900. Detroit Publishing Company photograph collection, Library of Congress Prints and Photographs Division, LC-DIG-DET-4A09244.

15 August 1896 *Pittsburgh Daily Post* entitled "Sectional Characteristics" identified regional types of women based on what they carried when they rode their bicycles:

> That the cycling girl of Texas
>    As she rides is not afraid—
> She provides a pistol pocket
>    When she has her bloomers made;
> That the bloomer girl of Boston
>    Always cool and wisely frowning,
> Has a pocket in her bloomers
>    Where she carries Robert Browning;
> That the Daisy Bell of Kansas,

DARYL W. PALMER

Fig. 1.5. Red Cloud Bridge, ca. 1883. Courtesy of the Willa Cather Foundation
Collection, Nebraska State Historical Society.

> Who has donned the cycling breeches,
> Has a pocket in her bloomers
> Full of woman suffrage speeches. (4)

While in no danger of rivaling the verses of Dickinson or Whitman, the poem does reveal the way cycling and women were
linked in the popular imagination. Women cyclists were dynamic,
often unconventional, perhaps dangerous. Types were real. Eastern
women carried poetry. Western women carried pistols and fought
for equality. Cather may or may not have read these particular
newspaper items, but they help us appreciate the cycling conversation she was joining as she wrote "Tommy." The New Woman
from Nebraska who indulged in racing street cars in Pittsburgh
was right at home.

Back in Nebraska, newspapers in both Red Cloud and Lincoln had given Cather ample opportunities to keep up with the latest cycling advice, news of clubs and races, stories of celebrity cyclists and local enthusiasts, and the ongoing debate over women and bicycles.[8] An article in the 2 October 1891 *Chief* proclaimed cycling "The Queen of Sports" (3). The 29 June 1894 *Chief* described the adventures and misadventures of the young men from the Bladen Bicycle Club who rode down to Red Cloud on a Sunday morning: "The boys all report a good time and are highly pleased with the way in which Red Cloud entertained them" (4). The 25 October 1895 *Chief* reported that Cather's brother Roscoe was "recovering from a bicycle fall" (8). "American women are not walkers," an article in the 19 July 1895 *Chief* declared, "but the cycle is perhaps even better suited to woman's use than man's and seems destined to add an outdoor element to the life of woman the world over" (2). An article in the 31 May 1896 *Nebraska State Journal* invoked Willard while arguing that the bicycle had helped "women" displace "ladies": "Women and the bicycle now swarm the world over" (18).

A fine student and accomplished athlete, Louise Pound was one of these women. Early in her college career in Lincoln, Cather had been infatuated (perhaps in love) with Pound, who was also, among many other things, a remarkable cyclist (Lindemann 17). Albertini observes: "It was not uncommon for her as a member of a Century Club to ride one hundred continuous miles in one day. This active, ambitious, and talented woman earned her first Century Road Club bar in 1895 and her second in 1896, and in 1896 she received the Rambler Gold Medal for riding five thousand miles in one year" (13; Yost 484; Cochran 82). The 27 April 1895 *Courier* provides a sense of the athlete's standing in the community after she set a single-day, long distance record: "On Saturday last, with an escort, Miss Louise Pound of this city, added another laurel to her reputation as one of the best lady athletes in the state by making a run of 111 miles on a bicycle" (12; Cochran 80–82). In 1896, as she contemplated a cycling heroine, Cather's thoughts would have turned to the Lincoln celebrity she knew so well. As Albertini suggests, "If Tommy indeed does have a prototype, Louise Pound is a solid candidate" (16).

DARYL W. PALMER

Fig. 1.6. Louise Pound with her Rambler bicycle, ca. 1893. Courtesy of the Willa Cather Foundation Collection, Nebraska State Historical Society.

Well aware that the summer was flashing by, the new editor of *Home Monthly* had good reason to be thinking about prototypes. She needed material for her publication and a story of her own seemed like the obvious course of action. Given her existing body of work and the focus of the magazine, a story of pioneer domesticity on the Nebraskan prairie would have been appropriate, but Cather's thoughts shifted to Red Cloud in the 1890s. It was a career-changing discovery. From "Tommy" to *The Song of the Lark* and *My Ántonia* and on to "The Best Years," written near the end of the author's life, Cather's reinventions of Red Cloud would be central to her vision.

Fascinated by the way that Pittsburgh is triggering this discovery, Cather explores her own awakening in the opening pages of "Tommy, the Unsentimental." Having moved "back East," Cather firmly locates the fictional town of Southdown in "the West" (473). The narrator implies a certain metropolitan vibe by placing Southdown in the context of "live western towns" inhabited by "active young business men and sturdy ranchers" who enjoy "cocktails" and "billiards" (474). Perhaps merging herself and Louise Pound in a composite prototype, Cather invents a professional heroine who works in the Southdown National Bank, occasionally needs to take a run "on her wheel," and has recently spent a year in school back East where "she distinguished herself in athletics" (475). Tommy could easily be speaking for the author as she describes her recent epiphany:

> It's all very fine down East there, and the hills are great, but one gets mighty homesick for this sky, the old intense blue of it, you know. Down there the skies are all pale and smoky. And this wind, this hateful, dear, old everlasting wind that comes down like the sweep of cavalry and is never tamed or broken. O Joe, I used to get hungry for this wind! I couldn't sleep in that lifeless stillness down there. (475–76)

Writing from the hills of Pittsburgh, Cather is being proleptic here, already imagining a homecoming in which she will share her new vision with "everyone." The author of "On the Divide" was ready to praise the sky and the wind of Nebraska, a region now firmly located in the American West.

The resulting shifts in Cather's artistic consciousness were radical indeed. In these moments, Cather was recasting her vision of Nebraska while realizing that remaking Red Cloud could be endlessly diverting. More theoretically, Cather was discovering the power of the *palimpsest*, a term referring to the ancient practice of scraping words from a piece of vellum and writing over the traces of the old text. As Sarah Dillon explains, the fact that the old writing often showed through the new led Thomas De Quincey to use the term in a figurative way to describe

> the way in which "our deepest thoughts and feelings pass to us through perplexed combinations of concrete objects. . . ." The adjective "involuted" describes the relationship between the texts that inhabit the palimpsest as a result of the process of palimpsesting and subsequent textual reappearance. The palimpsest is an involuted phenomenon where otherwise unrelated texts are involved and entangled, intricately interwoven, interrupting and inhabiting each other. Another word that describes this structure is the neologism "palimpsestuous." (245)

In "Tommy," Southdown comes into view as an "involuted phenomenon," a palimpsest that mingles bits of Pittsburgh and Red Cloud. Tommy's enthusiasm for life in this live western town echoes the author's awakened feelings. Indeed, Cather seems to have experienced a new and piquant pleasure in writing about Nebraska that would carry her through the rest of her career.

This palimpsestuous pleasure is on display as Cather maps the story's setting. The narrator identifies the little town of "Red Willow, some twenty-five miles north, upon the Divide" (475). Twenty-five miles north of Red Cloud was Blue Hill. In creating this little palimpsest, Cather playfully exchanges Blue for Red. Hill becomes Will-ow, perhaps with a wink at "Willie and Willwese," as Cather's little sister Elsie dubbed the two women (Lindemann 24). Instead of a grim parsing of a pathological landscape, Cather becomes a "territorial colorist" while creating monikers for familiar places (Palmer 34–37). Over the years, many of the author's readers have shared precisely this pleasure as they explore Cather's involuted topographies.

In this mood, the narrator explains that Tommy's "best friends were her father's old business friends, elderly men who had seen a good deal of the world, and who were very proud and fond of Tommy" (474). Cather is here creating another sort of palimpsest, recasting for the first time in her fiction a group of adult friends from childhood that included Gilbert Einstein McKeeby, J. L. Miner, and Charles Wiener. Mildred Bennett points out "that every one of these gentlemen appeared later as important characters in Willa Cather stories" (24). Although Tommy does not show any hetero-sexual interest in the available men of Southdown, she finds genu-ine friendship with these "elderly" men. As the narrator goes on to explain, "She was just one of them; she played whist and billiards with them, and made their cocktails for them, not scorning to take one herself, occasionally" (474). Cather, of course, was writing from personal experience, making a case for a young woman's freedom to enjoy male friendship. In 1896 the author was already beginning to sketch the *involuted* world of Thea Kronborg in *The Song of the Lark*.

Although Cather's domestic partner, Edith Lewis, concluded that the stories written during this period "are an indication, I think, of how valueless this sort of writing can be," scholars, when they discuss "Tommy" in any detail, have found value in the story's approach to gender and sexuality (Lewis 42). Sharon O'Brien rightly concludes that the story "mocks the Victorian ideal of womanhood to which the *Home Monthly* was supposedly dedicated" (229). For Judith Butler, the central character is trapped in a Lacanian matrix "of prohibition, propriety, and cross-gender appropriations" (156). Gruber Garvey cogently argues that the story "plays out the bicycling woman's threat to gender definition" and even offers "an alternative model of gender" (92). Noting Cather's fondness for the work of J. M. Barrie and the short story's obvious allusion to Barrie's recent and popular novel *Sentimental Tommy*, Michelle Ann Abate explores the ways in which both works "present central characters who possess nonheteronor-mative sexualities" (470). Abate persuasively nudges the conversa-tion away from binary categories and toward "emerging modernist forms of queer sexuality" (470). As Debra J. Seivert notes, "Tommy" is also a "literary 'conversation' about romanticism, sentimentality, and realism that would become fundamental to her own art" (104).

The notion of the palimpsest offers another way of moving this conversation forward. Some years ago, Sandra M. Gilbert and Susan

Gubar argued that the great women writers of the nineteenth century "produced literary works that are in some sense palimpsestic" (73). In this vision, which at first glance seems applicable to Cather's "Tommy," an essential truth of gender might be glimpsed by the astute critic, but Dillon counters that

> the palimpsest is not simply a layered structure which contains a hidden text to be revealed. Rather it is a queer structure in which are intertwined multiple and varying inscriptions, in this instance both male and female. Whereas the traditional understanding of the palimpsest corresponds to a reading approach that seeks only to uncover or reveal, this more complex understanding ... requires a more radical queer palimpsestuous reading. (257)

"Tommy" invites such a reading in remarkable ways by offering the bicycle as an interpretive key in a palimpsestuous vision of Nebraska. The surprising thing for readers today and perhaps for Cather at the time is that the creation of the involuted topography helped the author begin to explore her own involuted and evolving notions of gender, sexuality, and identity.

With its opening paragraphs, "Tommy" drops the reader into this more complex vision. The central character is a strong-willed woman of business who has, according to the narrator, a "peculiar" relationship with Jay Harper, a relationship less than romantic, and something more exotic than mere friendship (474). Tommy and Miss Jessica discuss Jay, but most readers are probably still trying to determine who is talking about whom when the narrator declares, "Needless to say, Tommy was not a boy, although her keen gray eyes and wide forehead were scarcely girlish, and she had the lank figure of an active half grown lad" (473). As Butler observes, the "needless to say" is disingenuous (155). No reader would have suspected that Tommy is a woman, but many would have recognized that slang versions of "Tommy" in the 1890s could suggest everything from unruliness to prostitution to lesbian desire (Butler 154–55; Abate 478). In this bold way, Cather was introducing her *Home Monthly* readers to a world where gender is open to inquiry and experimentation.

What, after all, defines *boys* and *girls*? Eyes? Forehead? Figure? Sentiment? Clothing? Journalists in the 1890s were particularly fond of asking these sorts of questions. Typical of the genre is the aforementioned poem in the *Pittsburgh Daily Post* that proposed *sectional characteristics*. In the 19 July 1896 *Pittsburgh Daily Post*, Helen Ward offered an example of this genre that either uncannily anticipated or actually inspired Cather's initial paragraphs and her description of Tommy's eyes. An "old beau" opens Ward's article by declaring, "Girls are known for their eyes" (20). After this gambit, Ward's speaker proceeds to sketch different types of girls, moving from "the flirt" to "the sentimental type" to "the chum girl" (20). The old beau confesses he used to like the latter sort:

> She is the girl who is a match for you on all your expeditions.
> "Will you go cycling, my pretty maid?"
> "Can you do a mile in 2:10?" she said. (20)

It would be tempting to suggest that Tommy is a "chum girl" until the speaker describes "the talented girl," who can do everything from sports to "setting a broken arm," who "has kept wide awake and knows a little of everything" (20). The talented girl "goes in for sports," but will not focus on them because she realizes there "are so many real things in the world for her" (20). This latter description comes closer to describing Cather's wide-awake heroine, but it could never stand in for the complexity of Tommy's evolving position over the course of the story.

Indeed, after examining this sort of popular journalism, readers of "Tommy" are better able to appreciate the way the author is questioning rather than applying contemporary gender types. The eastern girl, Jessica, is "a dainty, white, languid bit of a thing, who used violet perfumes and carried a sunshade" (476). In this initial description, Cather's story seems to confirm that gender "types" are rooted in region, but readers quickly realize that it would be a mistake to assume that such "types" are stable. A little later, the narrator ostensibly explains why people call Theodosia "Tommy": "That blunt sort of familiarity is not unfrequent in the West, and is meant well enough. People rather expect some business ability in a girl there, and they respect it immensely" (473). Is the narrator implying that gender is, in some senses, attained? Jay's masculinity is certainly diminished in such a system. Tommy dismisses him as "a baby in business" (473). Further complicating Jay's position in the story as a potential partner for either Tommy or Jessica is his carnation, which, Abate suggests, may highlight his "status as a queer character" (481).

At this juncture, Cather has set the stage for her cycling story, which ultimately illustrates Hallenbeck's notion that women in the 1890s *"drew from* the bicycle in constructing new identities and arguments for and about themselves" (xiii). That Cather embraces this agenda is evident if one surveys the cycling stories published during the period. As Hallenbeck observes, "much fiction about bicycling—written by both men and women—simply emphasized heroines' youth, beauty, appropriate femininity, and suitability for a match with a dashing male bicyclist" (79). Writing from Pittsburgh while looking back to Nebraska, Cather was aiming for "new identities and new arguments" as she introduced the story's crisis.

Tommy gets a telegram from Harper, pleading with her to help him save his failing bank. The clock ticking, Tommy must figure out a way to get funds to Harper in time. Cather's good humor shines through as Tommy declares, "There is nothing left but to wheel for it" (477). In this palimpsestuous moment, Cather was compressing her final summer days in Red Cloud and her thrilling rides through Pittsburgh streets. She may also have had in mind the (possibly apocryphal) story Roger Welsch rehearses of Louise Pound racing on her Rambler to rescue her brother Roscoe:

> At any rate, the story, which I treasure as the truth, goes that Pound jumped on her bicycle and pedaled as fast as she could to the den of iniquity to warn her brother before the arrival of the police, only to find when she arrived that Roscoe had already left the establishment. But she herself did not leave in time to escape being detained by the police, who would probably have been amazed and even scandalized to find a woman present. (x)

Part mythmaking, part experiment, Cather's palimpsestuous rescue scene invites the reader to reconsider the emergence of the New Woman in the 1890s.

At the same time, Cather was ready to engage the larger conversations about women and cycling that were going on everywhere from Red Cloud to Pittsburgh and, more particularly, the pages of *Home Monthly*. As Jennifer Bradley points out, Cather published nine articles about cycling during her tenure at the magazine, covering such concerns as damaged digestion, improved complexion, safe riding techniques, and the danger (for women) of unintended arousal.[9] With "Tommy" Cather was offering her own more complex and even radical contribution to the conversation.

Tommy's ride is, as Albertini points out, "heroic" and "arguably possible even if she is burdened with abundant handicaps" (18). The narrator explains, "The road from Southdown to Red Willow is not by any means a favorite bicycle road; it is rough, hilly and climbs from the river bottoms up to the big Divide by a steady up grade, running white and hot through the scorched corn fields and grazing lands" (477). If we imagine Tommy riding a Rambler after the fashion of Louise Pound, completing the ride of twenty-five miles in less than seventy-five minutes, the feat seems worthy of notice in the local newspapers under "Wheel Notes." Needless to say, Jessica does not measure up to this standard of heroism.

Tommy sums up her triumph in a fascinating rumination that expands on the inquiry into gender types: "Poor Jess.... Well, your kind have the best of it generally, but in little affairs of this sort my kind come out rather strongly. We're rather better at them than at dancing. It's only fair, one side shouldn't have all" (478). Cather's heroine believes in multiple "kinds" and "sides" expressed in the difference between cycling and dancing, West and East, the New Woman and the traditional lady, women who desire men and women who do not, and so on.

Cather was also, at this crucial juncture, reworking some of her Nebraska journalism from earlier that summer. Discussing the actress

Emma Calvé, Cather had declared in her "Passing Show" column in the 7 June 1896 *Nebraska State Journal*:

> Volcanic emotions are all right on the stage, but they don't go on a bicycle. Bicycles are for the age of steel in which Carmens and Calves belong not. Bicycles are not to be wooed by languorous glances or guitars or the Spanish melodies of Bizet; they are stiff and formal and uncompromising; they stand for the age of steel in which Carmens and Calves belong not. A bicycle insists upon being treated coolly and respectfully and bitterly resents arduous advance. (13)

Perhaps we should think of Tommy as a new sort of heroine of the West invented for an age of steel perfected in Pittsburgh.

But this passage also raises provocative questions about the place of sexuality in Cather's story. In the newspapers and magazines of the day, critics of women cyclists were concerned about the potential for arousal. As Hallenbeck observes, pundits fretted over "friction," implying that "both the high pommel and any contact between the rider's body and her saddle might signify a female rider's depravity" (54). Sue Macy points out that the November 1896 *Medical Record* was more than ready to consider cycling "a means of gratifying unholy and bestial desire" (44). In this context, Cather's notion of the bicycle resenting "arduous advance" may be juxtaposed with Tommy's choice of the bicycle over dance. Perhaps Tommy, as she identifies with bicycles, is rebelling against any imposed notions of sexuality?

Even staid Pittsburgh housewives, familiar with popular cycling stories, might have been able to overlook such radical ideas if the story had ended in the "proper" engagement of Tommy and the rescued Jay. Fans of Annie Londonderry would have noted that her extraordinary cycling adventures did not preclude her from embracing marriage and children. But Cather offers no such consolation. Tommy is firm with Jay: "I wish you'd marry her and be done with it, I want to get this thing off my mind" (479). Thinking in terms of gender, Jay feels like a failure. "You almost made a man of even me," he declares (479). Tommy questions the quality of her own life:

"Since I have known you, I have not been at all good, in any sense of the word, and I suspect I have been anything but clever" (480). The statement is probably more epiphany than confession. A kind of reckoning has occurred.

What to make of such an ending? Scholars have offered a variety of interpretations. Arnold, with good reason, sees "emerging in this story the pattern of the strong female and the weaker male that appears in several of Cather's novels" (10). Butler argues that "Tommy's cycling becomes the argument by which Jessica's desire, if it was ever for Tommy, becomes successfully deflected" (158). In this reading, the story culminates in "the reflexive sacrifice of desire, a double-directional misogyny that culminates in the degradation of lesbian love" (161). Abate concludes that Tommy's resistance to sentiment marks "a movement closer to the more outwardly reserved but also self-consciously erotic form of lesbian identity that would emerge in the twentieth century" (479).

The story's ending may be even more rebellious than these readings suggest. Bradley identifies a clear message "that those women willing to sacrifice relationships with men can find new independence" (58). Why, after all, would any reader want to see talented Tommy attached to Jay? But what if Cather is also suggesting that women willing to sacrifice certain relationships with women can find new independence? Why, for instance, would any reader want to see talented Tommy attached to Jessica? Far from deflecting desire as Butler suggests, the cycling adventure may serve to clarify Tommy's independence. Gruber Garvey puts it well: "A life of fast riding in the larger sphere of action and Westernness is clearly superior to either Jay's world of incompetence or Miss Jessica's adjoining world of decorum" (94). Perhaps Tommy will find a partner, or perhaps she will determine that she needs no partner. In any event, her character and abilities suggest a future that looks less like a settled life in Southdown and more like the life of Louise Pound, who became an accomplished scholar, the first woman to serve as president of the Modern Language Association, and the first woman to be inducted into the Nebraska Sports Hall of Fame.

In fact, a closer examination of the final scene between Tommy and Jay reveals Cather's explicit—and even moral—framework for this finale. Tommy's explanation to Jay that Jessica is "your kind" is palimpsestuous, suggesting (simultaneously) something about "types" of women and men, mental and physical capabilities, ambition, and, of course, sexuality. In so doing, the story offers an early glimpse of what Marilee Lindemann has called Cather's "queering of America," "a process of making and unmaking, settling and unsettling that operates at times on the surfaces and at times on the deep structures of her fiction" (4). Tommy is emphatic about her part in this process: "We have been playing a nice little game, and now it's time to quit. One must grow up sometime" (479). In Barrie's *Sentimental Tommy*, the young man is unwilling to grow up. In Cather's story, the young woman has grown up, does not claim the man, and argues that maturity is all about self-knowledge and an honest response to the complexities of gender and sexuality.

At the end of the story, Tommy embodies an independence more radical than Anthony and Wister could have imagined for women who ride bicycles. Like Denison, Tommy seems ready to "ride down" her adversaries, having discovered what it means for a woman to grow up at the end of the nineteenth century. Cather could have come across the notion in Red Cloud just before she left for Pittsburgh. The 8 May 1896 *Chief* "Wheel Notes" counselled: "Learn how to ride correctly, and afterwards ride to gain your own approbation. Never mind what others think about it" (7). Here, in the author's first palimpsestuous recasting of life in Nebraska inspired by her arrival in Pittsburgh, Tommy discovers what it means to gain her own approbation, a revelation Cather was anxious to claim for herself and endorse as maturity.

## NOTES

With thanks to the publishers and the editors of this volume, I adapt and expand upon portions of this essay that appear in my book *Becoming Willa Cather*.

1. In 1928 T. K. Whipple articulated an early and antagonistic version of this notion: "Her triumph over Nebraska implies that Miss Cather has also conquered the Nebraska in herself" (193). For later versions of this argument, see, among others, Edward Bloom and Lillian Bloom (3, 58); Quantic (7); Gross (106); Rosowski (18); and Lee (38).

2. Stout (16, 321, n. 7). For more on bicycles and the New Woman, see also Sims (125–45); Friss (176); and Hallenbeck (70–71).

3. See, for example, *Chief*, 21 March 1884, p. 5; *Argus*, 9 July 1885, p. 3; *Chief*, 20 July 1885, p. 5; *Chief*, 1 March 1889, p. 5; *Chief*, 2 August 1889, p. 4; *Chief*, 18 March 1892, p. 5; *Chief*, 17 November 1893, p. 5.

4. A 7 March 1896 *Pittsburgh Press* article presaged the Nebraskan's derring-do: "Bloomers and bicycle faces still may be the insignia of the new woman . . . but unless she can 'bounce' a cable car [leap on a moving car] her talents might just as well be wrapped up in a napkin and her ambitions blighted under a bushel" (7).

5. For a contemporary account of the celebration in London, see *The House Furnishing Review*, 8, Jan.–June, 1896, p. 25. For more about bicycle clubs in Estonia, see Kylliäinen (295).

6. Readers around the globe followed the Pittsburgher's exploits until he disappeared in Armenia in 1894. See, for instance, the *Pittsburgh Dispatch*, 12 June 1892, p. 16. Eventually, the newspapers reported his murder by Kurdish bandits: "The Murder of Bicycle Rider Lenz," *New York Times*, 30 September 1895. In Red Cloud, the *Chief* (like many other newspapers) was still updating his story in 1895. See the *Red Cloud Chief*, 1 February 1895, p. 8. When it came to bicycles, Red Cloud and Pittsburgh were, in many ways, on the same page.

7. *Chief*, 17 April 1885, p. 5; *Chief*, 19 June 1885, p. 5.

8. See, for example, the *Nebraska State Journal*, 30 August 1891, p. 15; *Nebraska State Journal*, 31 May 1896, p. 19.

9. Bradley (55). On the presumed sexuality of bicycle riding, see, among others, Macy (44).

## WORKS CITED

Abate, Michelle Ann. "Constructing Modernist Lesbian Affect from Late Victorian Masculine Emotionalism: Willa Cather's 'Tommy, the Unsentimental' and J. M. Barrie's *Sentimental Tommy.*" *Women's Writing*, vol. 18, no. 4, 2014, pp. 468–85, http://dx.doi.org/10.1080/09699082.2011.600044.

Albertini, Virgil. "Willa Cather and the Bicycle." *Platte Valley Review*, vol. 15, no. 1, 1987, pp. 12–22.

Arnold, Marilyn. *Willa Cather's Short Fiction*. Ohio UP, 1984.

"Authors on the Wheel." *The Critic*, vol. 27, no. 712, 12 October 1895, pp. 225–28.

Bennett, Mildred. *The World of Willa Cather*. 1951. U of Nebraska P, 1961.

Bloom, Edward, and Lillian Bloom. *Willa Cather's Gift of Sympathy*. Southern Illinois UP, 1964.

Bradley, Jennifer. "To Entertain, To Educate, To Elevate: Cather and the Commodification of Manners at the *Home Monthly*." *Willa Cather and Material Culture: Real-World Writing, Writing the Real World*, edited by Janis P. Stout, U of Alabama P, 2005, pp. 37–65.

Butler, Judith. "'Dangerous Crossing': Willa Cather's Masculine Names." *Bodies that Matter: On the Discursive Limits of Sex*, Routledge, 1993.

Cather, Willa. *The Complete Letters of Willa Cather*, edited by the Willa Cather Archive team, Willa Cather Archive, 2018, www.cather.unl.edu.

——. *The Kingdom of Art: Willa Cather's First Principles and Critical Statements, 1893–1896*. Edited with two essays and a commentary by Bernice Slote, U of Nebraska P, 1967.

——. "On the Divide." *Willa Cather's Collected Short Fiction, 1892–1912*, edited by Virginia Faulkner, introduction by Mildred R. Bennett. 1965. U of Nebraska P, 1970.

——. "Peter." *Willa Cather's Collected Short Fiction, 1892–1912*, edited by Virginia Faulkner, introduction by Mildred R. Bennett. 1965. U of Nebraska P, 1970.

——. "Tommy, the Unsentimental." *Willa Cather's Collected Short Fiction, 1892–1912*, edited by Virginia Faulkner, introduction by Mildred R. Bennett. 1965. U of Nebraska P, 1970, pp. 473–80.

——. *Willa Cather in Person: Interviews, Speeches, Letters*. Edited by Brent L. Bohlke, U of Nebraska P, 1986.

Cochran, Robert. *Louise Pound: Scholar, Athlete, Feminist Pioneer*. U of Nebraska P, 2009.

Denison, Grace E. "How We Ride Our Wheels." *Outing*, vol. 19, no. 1, 1891, pp. 52–54.

Dillon, Sarah. "Reinscribing De Quincey's Palimpsest: The Significance of the Palimpsest in Contemporary Literary and Cultural Studies." *Textual Practice*, vol. 19, no. 3, 2005, pp. 243–63.

Friss, Evan. *The Cycling City: Bicycles and Urban America in the 1890s*. U of Chicago P, 2015.

Gilbert, Sandra M., and Susan Gubar. *The Madwoman in the Attic: The Woman Writer and the Nineteenth-Century Literary Imagination*. 1979. Yale UP, 2000.

Gross, Barry. "In Another Country: The Revolt from the Village." *Midamerica*, vol. 4, no. 4, 1977, pp. 101–11.

Gruber Garvey, Ellen. "Reframing the Bicycle: Advertising-Supported Magazines and Scorching Women." *American Quarterly*, vol. 47, no. 1, 1995, pp. 66–101.

Hallenbeck, Sarah. *Claiming the Bicycle: Women, Rhetoric, and Technology in Nineteenth-Century America*. Southern Illinois UP, 2016.

Kylliäinen, Mikko. "Riding toward the Civil Society: Bicycles in Nineteenth-Century Estonia." *Baltic Journal of European Studies*, vol. 1, no. 1, 2013, pp. 294–306.

Lee, Hermione. *Willa Cather: Double Lives*. Pantheon Books, 1989.

Lenz, Frank. "Around the World with Wheel and Camera." *Outing*, vol. 20, no. 5, August 1892, pp. 339–48, 482–87.

Lewis, Edith. *Willa Cather Living: A Personal Record*. 1953. Bison Books, 2000.

Lindemann, Marilee. *Willa Cather: Queering America*. Columbia UP, 1999.

Macy, Sue. "The Devil's Advance Agent." *American History*, vol. 46, no. 4, 2011, pp. 42–45.

O'Brien, Sharon. *Willa Cather: The Emerging Voice*. Fawcett Columbine, 1987.

Palmer, Daryl W. *Becoming Willa Cather: Creation and Career*. U of Nevada P, 2019.

Quantic, Diane Dufva. "The Revolt from the Village and Middle Western Fiction, 1870–1915." *The Kansas Quarterly*, vol. 5, no. 6, 1973, pp. 5–16.

Rosowski, Susan J. *The Voyage Perilous*. U of Nebraska P, 1986.

Seivert, Debra. "Responding to Romance with Realism in Cather's 'Tommy, the Unsentimental.'" *American Literary Realism*, vol. 33, no. 2, 2001, pp. 104–9.

Sher, Lynn. *Failure Is Impossible: Susan B. Anthony in Her Own Words*. Random House, 1995.

Sims, Sally. "The Bicycle, the Bloomer and Dress Reform in the 1890s." *Dress and Popular Culture*, edited by Patricia A. Cunningham and Susan Voso Lals, Bowling Green State UP Press, 1991, pp. 125–45.

Stout, Janis P. *Willa Cather: The Writer and Her World*. UP of Virginia, 2000.

Tarr, Joel A. "Framing the City at the Point: The Development of Pittsburgh's Infrastructure in the 19th Century." *Western Pennsylvania History*, vol. 85, no. 1, 2002, pp. 28–35.

Thacker, Robert. *The Great Prairie Fact and Literary Imagination*. U of New Mexico P, 1989.

Welsch, Roger. Introduction. *Nebraska Folklore*, by Louise Pound. 1959. U of Nebraska P, 2006, pp. v–xvi.

Whipple, T. K. "Willa Cather." *Willa Cather: Critical Assessments*, edited by Guy Reynolds, vol. 1, Helm Information, 2003.

Willard, Frances. *How I Learned to Ride the Bicycle*. Fleming H. Revell, 1895.

Woodress, James. *Willa Cather: A Literary Life*. U of Nebraska P, 1987.

Yost, Nellie Snyder. "Nebraska's Scholarly Athlete: Louise Pound, 1872–1958." *Nebraska History*, vol. 64, no. 4, 1983, pp. 477–90.

## 2 Where Pagodas Rise on Every Hill

Romance as Resistance in "A Son of the Celestial"

MICHAEL GORMAN

### BEFORE AND BEYOND PITTSBURGH

On 29 May 1900, the front page of the *Pittsburg Press* declared, "Reign of Anarchy Is Threatened in China." The report beneath that headline noted the systematic killing of Christian missionaries and the "imminent peril" facing the foreigners who remained. When Pittsburgh's leading afternoon daily printed that story, Willa Cather was living in the city, working as a journalist and aspiring to be a novelist. As the turmoil in China escalated over the summer, newspapers in Pittsburgh and across the United States enthralled readers with sensational accounts of the Boxer Rebellion.[1] For a wannabe writer of fiction, the headlines from China were ripe for exploitation, and Cather seized the moment. Before the insurgency concluded in September, she had published two thematically related compositions in *The Library*. The July issue included "A Chinese View of the Chinese Situation," presented as an interview with a Pittsburgh-based Cantonese importer. Cather followed that up in August with "The

Conversion of Sum Loo," a short story revolving around a Protestant mission's attempt to convert the family of a Chinese importer living in San Francisco.

The alacrity of Cather's response in print to the Chinese unrest is impressive, but specious—she brought the seeds for these Pittsburgh publications with her from the Great Plains. In other words, Cather's back-to-back write-ups in *The Library* during the Boxer Rebellion were products of a longstanding fascination with China, a preoccupation that began during her childhood and found literary expression in "A Son of the Celestial," a short story she published in 1893 while a student at the University of Nebraska. To fully appreciate "A Chinese View of the Chinese Situation" and "The Conversion of Sum Loo," therefore, demands reading them alongside the story Cather conceived seven years earlier in an entirely different region of the country.[2]

In *Willa Cather: A Literary Life*, James Woodress reduces "A Son of the Celestial" to "a covert attack on some of Cather's own teachers" and dismisses it as "of no real importance" (79). To be sure, the text does not appeal to twenty-first-century sensibilities. Its racialized portraits and preposterous diction are abhorrent, and, in these respects, the story resembles the work of Frank Norris and Jack London, two of Cather's notoriously nativist contemporaries. In light of these facts, it is tempting to condemn "A Son of the Celestial" as a piece of Orientalist juvenilia. Doing so, however, is shortsighted.

"A Son of the Celestial" is culturally and literarily important because of its anticipation of issues addressed by Cather in later—and more accomplished—works, its resistance to the xenophobia and anti-Chinese politics common in the American West at the end of the nineteenth century, and its international scope. This early story touches on concerns, historical and political circumstances, themes, and literary tastes that Cather continued to address in her correspondence, essays, fiction, and journalism for decades. It reflects, for instance, her fascination with empire and the influence Romanticism exercised on her artistic vision even as naturalism came to dominate the American literary scene.

In "A Son of the Celestial" Cather challenges the anti-Chinese sentiments voiced by nativists in the United States and traces the source of America's cultural anxiety not to Chinese laborers but to individuals who pronounce Western civilization and religion (i.e., Christianity) to be superior to Eastern aesthetics and systems of belief. The critical and pluralist tone of "A Son of the Celestial" is echoed in "A Chinese View of the Chinese Situation" (1900) and "The Conversion of Sum Loo" (1900), pieces she published from Pittsburgh during the Boxer Rebellion.[3] Cather's enduring sympathy for Chinese subjects and values in the 1893 and 1900 publications—despite changing political circumstances—is especially intriguing and warrants further investigation into "A Son of the Celestial."

### KIPLING'S AMERICAN APPRENTICE

By the final decade of the nineteenth century, the United States had achieved its "Manifest Destiny" by using European immigrants to spread Western civilization and Christianity across the continent.[4] With the frontier no longer available for unrestricted settlement, expansionists had to look elsewhere to extend U.S. political and cultural influence. Elsewhere became the Far East and the Pacific.[5]

The turning of America's colonial gaze overseas was aided by British adventure writers such as Robert Louis Stevenson, Rudyard Kipling, and H. Rider Haggard. The exotic settings and imperial themes in their writing reinforced Britannia's global mission and inspired similar notions in readers living in America. Owing to the popularity of such writers in the United States, Americans were well-versed in the discourse of imperialism before their nation actually became a global power. Among the Americans enchanted by stories and poems set in British India, the Far East, and the Pacific was Willa Cather. Rudyard Kipling was a particular favorite of hers. Against the growing popularity of naturalism, she championed his exotic subject matter and Romantic approach, and he left a discernable mark on her first stories, including "A Son of the Celestial."[6]

Cather came to professional maturity amid the global upheaval occurring between America's involvement in the Spanish-American War and World War I. In her early career as a journalist, she directly invoked imperial discourse and themes, especially in discussions of her literary tastes.[7] For instance, in a December 1894 article in the *Nebraska State Journal*, Willa Cather called on Rudyard Kipling (then living with his American wife in Brattleboro, Vermont) to return to the imperial themes of his earlier work:

> Go back to the east [i.e., the Far East], Mr. Kipling.... Tell us of things new and strange and novel as you used to do. Tell us of love and war and action that thrills us because we know it not.... Go back where there are temples and jungles and all manner of unknown things, where there are mountains whose summits have never been scaled, rivers whose sources have never been reached, deserts whose sands have never been crossed. "Back to the land where the great sun is born." You need fierce color and we have not got it to give you; you need wild action and you will not find it here [in the United States]. In your younger and better days, Mr. Kipling, you would not have missed this great war [the Sino-Japanese War, 1894–95] in the east. You would be doing something better than writing stories for the holiday magazines. (qtd. in *Kingdom of Art* 317–18)

This impertinent column captures the spirit of the age in which it was written and conveys the young columnist's ennui with post-frontier American life, when the nation's "fierce color" had faded and its "wild action" had been tamed. A devotee of British adventure fiction, Cather encourages Rudyard Kipling to further the Romantic legacy of the recently deceased Robert Louis Stevenson (who had died on 3 December 1894) by returning to the exotic locales and daring themes reflected in his earlier poetry and prose like *Plain Tales from the Hills* (1888), *Soldiers Three* (1888), and *Barrack-Room Ballads* (1892).

By the close of the century, Rudyard Kipling had unquestioningly returned to the subject matter and settings Cather outlines above. With the February 1899 publication in *McClure's Magazine* of his poem "The White Man's Burden: The United States and the Philippine Islands," Kipling became forever associated with the idea of empire. Although this controversial ballad explicitly warns readers about the dangers attending imperialism and the responsibility colonizing powers have to better the economic, political, and social conditions in the territories they rule (e.g., "seek another's profit / And work another's gain" ll. 15–16), "The White Man's Burden" incensed American anti-imperialists who read it as an exhortation for the United States to join European powers in empire building.

Despite the virulent reaction of antiexpansionists to Kipling's sentiment, he remained highly popular in the United States—and for good reason. Like the Anglo-Indian poet, by 1899 the United States had deepened its association with colonialism. Between the 1893 coup in Hawaii and the publication of Kipling's "The White Man's Burden," the United States formally annexed the Hawaiian Islands, fought and concluded a war with Spain, and assumed control of former Spanish possessions in the Caribbean and in the Pacific.

As her reviews of Kipling's work from 1896 to 1899 suggest, Cather never figured among the critics of America's "friend from India" or his subject matter (qtd. in *World and the Parish* 555).[8] On the contrary, in the wake of U.S. military successes in the Spanish-American War of 1898 and the Boxer Rebellion of 1900, Cather celebrated his prophetic vision. In a column written from Pittsburgh for the *Lincoln Courier* on 24 August 1901, Cather reflected on the increasing relevance of Kipling's work to Americans, particularly to the U.S. troops battling insurgents in Philippine jungles:

> It is rather strange, when one comes to think of it, now that the eyes of all the world are turned upon Asia and the nations of the Orient, that the man who most nearly speaks the voice of the [American] people and the spirit of the times first called our attention to the old East ten or twelve years ago. Rudyard Kipling set the song of the East humming in a million brains, and long before he knew that bungalows and punkahs would

ever figure in [U.S.] government expense bills, we began to use the names of them. Before Kipling's day we knew as little about the mixed religions and mixed nations of the Orient as we knew about the etiquette of Tibet, and cared as little. (qtd. in *World and the Parish* 853–54)

From Cather's perspective, the events Kipling had been describing in relation to British India, an enormous territory stretching from present-day Pakistan to Myanmar (Burma), provided a ready frame of reference for U.S. activities in Asia. At the very least, the challenges depicted in his work reflected the complications facing American troops in the Philippines.

While Cather valued Kipling's insights, it is doubtful that he would have captivated her for very long had he been simply an apologist for imperialism, rather than a writer of romances and poetry. She respected several realist writers but firmly believed the naturalism in vogue at the fin de siècle was a passing trend. In 1895 she claimed, "Romance is the highest form of fiction, and it will never desert us. If Stevenson did not accomplish its revival, some other man will. It will come back to us in all its radiance and eternal freshness in some one of the dawning seasons of Time. Ibsens and Zolas are great, but they are temporary. Children, the sea, the sun, God himself are all romanticists" (*Courier*, 2 November 1895, qtd. in *Kingdom of Art* 232–33). Despite realist aspects of Kipling's writing and the prescience of his ideas, it is clear that Willa Cather prized him as a master of fiction's "highest form" and sought to emulate him.

Cather introduces "A Son of the Celestial: A Character" with four ballad stanzas: sixteen lines of verse written from the perspective of Yung Le Ho, the titular "Character." The introductory poem foreshadows events that will occur in the story. In addition to providing readers a hint of what will follow in the narrative, the epigraph calls attention to the exotic nature of the story, à la Rudyard Kipling. The ballad was a literary form intimately associated with the Anglo-Indian poet by the 1890s. Kipling was celebrated by his peers for his mastery of the ballad and for the range of meters he deftly employed. According to J. K. Buda, Kipling "took the ballad back to its roots and produced a hybrid form whose appeal transcended barriers of class, education, and cultivated taste" ("Kipling's 'The Ballad of East and West'"). Therefore, by simply choosing to open her short story with a ballad, Cather evoked Kipling. She reinforces the association to Kipling by sprinkling clichéd images of "the Orient"—"sunrise land," "camels," "Hwang-Ho," "pagodas," "idols"—liberally throughout the brief poem.

The tone and content of Cather's introductory poem closely resemble those of Kipling's "A Ballad of Burial" (1887, 1892). The speakers in each poem, for instance, instruct listeners where to take their corpses after they die. In Kipling's verse, a soldier serving in the desert "Plains" of British India asks a favor of his audience: "If down here I chance to die, / Solemnly I beg you take / All that is left of 'I' / To the Hills for old sake's sake" (ll. 1–4). Cather's poem begins with a similar request:

> Ah lie me dead in the sunrise land
> Where the sky is blue and the hills are gray,
> Where the camels doze in the desert sun,
> And the sea gulls scream o'er the big blue bay.

> Where the Hwang-Ho glides through the golden sand,
> And the Herons play in the rushes tall,
> Where pagodas rise upon every hill
> And the peach trees bloom by the Chinese Wall. (ll. 1–8)[9]

Kipling's influence upon Cather is manifest in the imagery she employs. Her poem reveals a sketchy but romanticized picture of China as she depicts the Yellow River (Hwang-Ho) flowing through deserts, under hilltop pagodas, and past trees blossoming within sight of the Great Wall. Almost two years after publishing these lines, Cather recycled several of the poem's images for use in the aforementioned December 1894 column urging Kipling to abandon his American wife and return to the Far East. By adding a dash of hyperbole, Cather recast "sunrise land," "desert sun," "golden sand," and "pagodas" from the poem as "the land where the sun is born," "deserts whose sands have never been crossed," and "temples and jungles and all manner of unknown things" in her open letter to Kipling.

## SAN FRANCISCO AND ALL MANNER OF UNKNOWN THINGS

In 1893 Willa Cather had yet to realize the potential of the midwestern landscape and its people, a lesson she would learn in a conversation with Sarah Orne Jewett thirteen years later. So, desirous of "things new and strange" and with Kipling's "song of the East" humming in her own brain, she searched for an Asian setting for a story. Cather naturally trained her eyes on San Francisco, the most exotic (i.e., "Oriental") city in North America.[10] As a city built by proceeds from the 1849 Gold Rush and defined in the 1890s not only by its proximity to the Pacific and Asian markets but also as home to a famed Chinese community, San Francisco embodied America's transition from pursuing its Manifest Destiny to performing the White Man's Burden, the program of American imperialism that President McKinley described as "benevolent assimilation."

Cather cast a wayfarer named Yung Le Ho as the protagonist of the tale. Yung is an eclectic, as unique as the city he lives in. Cather describes him as "one of the few white-haired Chinamen . . . seen about the streets of San Francisco" who sat cross-legged in his stall "silent like the gods of his country, carving his ivory into strange images" (523, 524). In his dotage he sits speechless and still like a Buddhist statue, but in his youth Yung Le Ho meandered across much of Asia before heading to sea, like the Yellow River to which Cather alludes in the epigraph to the story. Though born and educated in "Nanking, the oldest city in the oldest empire," Yung moved on to Soutcheofou where he lived among "the most beautiful [maidens] in the Middle Kingdom" (525). After Soutcheofou, he traversed Tibet and crossed into India, where he devoted ten years to studying sacred Hindu texts before falling in with "some high caste Indian magicians" (525). What he learned from them, Cather never reveals.

In San Francisco, Yung leads a furtive existence. Chinese by birth, Yung is a global citizen and a Renaissance man who knows "Sanskrit as thoroughly as his own tongue" (524). He is esteemed for his knowledge of Indian philosophy and is occasionally sought out by local scholars for his insights. While academics request his aid in interpreting esoteric texts, they never credit him for his intellectual assistance. When consulted about Sanskrit, Yung answers their questions, but finds "American schoolmen distasteful" pedants whom he feels are "Too muchee good to know muchee" (524). Dismissed by Californians as "a heathen Chinee who bowed down to wood and stone" (524), Yung is never invited to teach at a university. He is obliged, therefore, to earn his livelihood with his hands. As a craftsman, he makes a good living "carving . . . ivory into strange images and . . . sandalwood into shapes of foliage and birds" (524). Cather compares Yung's talent for working with ebony, ivory, and silk to the skills of Michelangelo, but his creations never achieve the same spiritual or cultural status as Michelangelo's *Pietà* or *David*. Rather than being displayed in cathedrals and other public sites, Yung's work is purchased by wealthy homemakers in San Francisco "to adorn their drawing rooms" (524). His pieces are regarded as ornaments rather than treasured as art, and the artist receives little or no recognition. Yung is admired for his intellect and is paid whatever price he demands for his carvings, yet without acknowledgment of his expertise in Sanskrit or his talent as a sculptor, he remains essentially anonymous.

Despite generally disliking American academics, Yung befriends a former college professor known only as Ponter, who, to an extent, serves as Yung's American doppelgänger. Like Yung, he is mysterious and peripatetic with a deep knowledge of Sanskrit. "Ponter was one of the most learned men who ever drifted into 'Frisco, but his best days were over before he came. He had held the chair of Sanskrit in a western university for years, but he could drink too much beer and was too good a shot at billiards to keep that place forever, so the college had requested his resignation" (525). Cather reveals to readers even less about Ponter than she does of Yung. After being driven out of an unspecified university, he bounced "from place to place until at last he drifted into San Francisco where he stayed" (525). In the story, Ponter is left to himself and ekes out a modest living. Exactly "[h]ow he lived," Cather writes, "no one knew. He did some copying for the lawyers, and he waited on the table in a third-rate boarding house, and he smoked a great deal of opium" (525). It is, in fact, the opium that draws Ponter and Yung together:

> Yung, too, loved the Smoke; perhaps it was that as much as Sanskrit that drew the men together. At any rate, as soon as Yung's bazaar was closed, they went together down to his dark little den in the Chinese quarters, and there they then talked Buddha and Confucius and Lau-tsz [*sic*] till midnight. Then they went across the hall to the Seven Portals of Paradise. There they each took a mat and each his own sweet pipe with bowls of jade and mouthpieces of amber ... and pulled a few steady puffs and were in bliss till morning. (525)

In the preceding passage, Cather draws upon exotic associations with opium, a narcotic closely associated with the British Empire's activities in the Orient.

Opium was the most profitable internationally traded product in the 1800s, particularly for the British Crown. According to historian James Bradley, "opium accounted for 15–20 percent of the British Empire's revenue" in the nineteenth century (*The Imperial Cruise* 274). Opium raised and harvested in British India was processed and then transported by British merchants to consumers in China. Policymakers in Europe had known of opium's ill effects on human health since the sixteenth century (Derks 713), but the opium trade in China was too lucrative to abandon. As Bradley notes, Britain "grew fat on Chinese silver drained from the formerly richest country in the world. The sums were so enormous that Queen Victoria stands as history's largest drug dealer" (*The Imperial Cruise* 276).

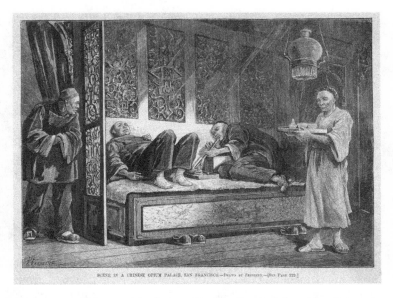

Fig. 2.1. Paul Frenzeny, *Scene in a Chinese Opium Palace, San Francisco,* *Harper's Weekly,* 3 April 1880, p. 221, Online Archive of California, www.oac.cdlib.org.

As a principal commodity in the nineteenth century, opium was a common motif in literature and art. Kipling addressed the opium trade in several of his works, and in the passage quoted above Cather appears to have drawn upon one of his tales for inspiration. The name—"the Seven Portals of Paradise"—that Cather gives the opium den frequented by Yung and Ponter echoes "The Gate of the Hundred Sorrows," a story Kipling wrote about an opium den in British India and included in his 1888 collection *Plain Tales from the Hills.*

In the 1890s opium was big business in San Francisco. Chinese immigrants to California brought opium with them, and it soon became popular with people of all persuasions. In 1875 San Francisco had made operating and frequenting opium dens a misdemeanor, but the law had little impact on the opium trade since importing it into the United States remained legal until 1905. In fact, as Chris

Roberts notes for the *San Francisco Examiner*, at one point in the 1890s there were reported to be no fewer than three hundred opium dens in Chinatown ("The Country's First War on Drugs," 11 June 2015).

## EURO-AMERICAN CULTURAL ANXIETY AND CHINESE EXCLUSION

At the time Cather imagined the cross-cultural friendship between Yung and Ponter, relations between Californians of Chinese and European heritage were severely strained. In the contrasting profitabilities of Yung's and Ponter's employment, Cather embeds a source of anxiety among Californians in the 1880s and 1890s: the fear that cheaper Chinese labor would supplant European workers. The antagonism between these two groups in the nineteenth century led to negative depictions of Chinese in newspaper exposés and other publications, including Bret Harte's 1870 poem "Plain Language from Truthful James," popularly known as "The Heathen Chinee." Visual representations of the tension were also plentiful (see figure 2.2).[11]

The anti-Chinese sentiment of the period was not limited to popular literature and magazine illustrations. In "American Naturalism and Asiatic Racial Form," Colleen Lye notes that it "pervaded almost every social reform and radical movement in the late nineteenth and twentieth centuries—organized labor, Populism, Progressivism, and socialism" (76). Leaders of trade unions and anti-immigrant groups like the American Protective Association lobbied Congress to prevent Chinese laborers' entry into the United States. The pressure resulted in the Chinese Treaty of 1880, which seriously curtailed the immigration of Chinese laborers, and eventual passage of the 1882 Chinese Exclusion Act, which completely prevented unskilled Chinese laborers from entering the country.

As James Bradley explains with intended irony, the Chinese Exclusion Act was unprecedented in its intentions and scope:

From America's inception in 1783 to 1882, a period of ninety-nine years, there had been no concept of illegal immigrants in

THE COMING MAN—JOHN CHINAMAN.
Uncle Sam introduces Eastern Barbarism to Western Civilization.

Fig. 2.2. *The Coming Man—John Chinaman.* Cartoon from *Harper's Weekly Magazine* depicting hostilities between Irish and Chinese immigrants in California, 1869. The Miriam and Ira D. Wallach Division of Art, Prints and Photographs: Picture Collection, the New York Public Library, New York Public Library Digital Collections.

the United States. That changed with the Chinese Exclusion Act of 1882. For the first time in U.S. history, an immigration gate was erected with the specific goal of blocking non-Whites. Senator George Hoar of Massachusetts described the Chinese Exclusion Act as "nothing less than the legalization of racial discrimination." But because of the dire race threat presented by the yellow men, most Americans had no problem with the new legislation. Twenty-four years old and just out of Harvard, Theodore Roosevelt proclaimed in 1882, "No greater calamity could now befall the United States than to have the Pacific slope fill up with a Mongolian population." (282)

As Senator Hoar recognized—and Theodore Roosevelt explicitly demonstrated—economic motives played a lesser role in passing the Chinese Exclusion Act than racism did. Like Senator Hoar, Cather perceives discrimination at work behind the passage of the anti-Chinese legislation. Accordingly, in "A Son of the Celestial," she traces the reason for the legislation not to fears for the economic livelihood of native-born Americans, but to cultural motives:

> Wise Yung! It was not because of the cheapness of Chinese labor that the Chinese bill was enacted. It was because the church and state feared this people who went about unproselyting and unproselyted. Who had printed centuries before Gutenberg was born, who had used anesthetics before chloroform was ever dreamed of. Who, in the new west, settled down and ate and drank and dressed as men had done in the days of the flood. Their terrible antiquity weighed upon us like a dead hand upon a living heart. (526)

In this political aside, Cather ascribes the motivations behind the anti-Chinese legislation to a national inferiority complex and suggests that government agencies and the Protestant Church view the history of technological innovation and cultural advances in China as threats to the core cultural framework in the United States. Cather recognizes that American racists regard Chinese immigrants' customs—their ways of eating, dressing, and worshipping—as threats to Western European identity and ways of thinking. In the story, she uses Ponter to illustrate this cultural anxiety.

A key ingredient to the turn-of-the-century anti-Chinese sentiment was the "notion of Chinese unassimilability ... the notion of persistent difference" (Lye 74). In the passage above from "A Son of the Celestial," Cather toys with this notion, implying that the fear is not simply that Asian immigrants will not assimilate to American customs, but that Chinese cultural traditions may corrupt America's identification with European culture and threaten the predominance of the Judeo-Christian tradition.

Beyond worrying that Chinese immigrants will take jobs from Euro-Americans or that they will resist assimilating to Euro-American culture, illustrious Americans at the turn of the century feared that the United States would eventually become an Asian nation culturally. Lye discusses the prevalence of this paranoia in academic circles. Typical of the pseudoscientific reasoning popular at the time was an argument proffered by Stanford University sociologist Edward Ross who warned in "The Causes of Race Superiority" (1901) that Asian efficiency would manifest itself economically, reproductively, and culturally and would eventually wipe out Western European thought and culture. Asian organization and efficiency, the "efficiency of average units," as Ross words it, "will trump inventive genius" associated with the Anglo Saxon (qtd. in Lye 75). As troubling as Ross's generalization is, it was a widespread conviction in the United States at the fin de siècle.

In a telling passage, Cather's fictional academic in "A Son of the Celestial" voices biases similar to those expressed eight years later by the actual professor, Edward Ross. Despite being described as "one of the most learned men who ever drifted into 'Frisco" (525), Ponter subscribes to absurd prejudices about the lack of Chinese creativity and feeling. Although he was a scholar of Sanskrit with a cursory knowledge of Chinese, Ponter regards William Shakespeare's *Hamlet* as the paragon of literary genius and attempts to share it with Yung Le Ho. After Ponter read the "whole of *Hamlet*" to Yung one night, Yung replied, "[I]t is a great book, but I do not understand. If I were a young man I might try, but it is different. We [Chinese] cut our trees into shape, we bind our women into shape, we make our books into shape by rule. Your trees and women and books just grow, and yet they have shape. I do not understand" (526). Ponter reacts violently to Yung's unenthusiastic response: "[D]—n you! You are a terrible people! I have come as near losing all human feeling . . . as ever a white man did, but you make me shudder, every one of you. . . . You ought to be a feeling, passionate people, but you are as heartless and devilish as your accursed stone gods. . . . You are dead things that move!" (526–27).

With Ponter labeling all Chinese as zombies incapable of appreciating the genius of William Shakespeare, Cather evokes the paranoid rhetoric associated with the anti-Chinese movements and social Darwinists like Theodore Roosevelt and Edward Ross. She does so by touching on two facets of the complex discourse of "the Asiatic" figure: plurality and inhumanity.

In the age of the "Yellow Peril," Chinese and other Asians were vilified and labeled "Mongolians" or "Asiatics." In the latter nineteenth and early twentieth centuries, the stereotypical "Asiatic" in the United States was "the coolie," the indentured laborer from China who was typically imagined en masse rather than individually. Lye explains: "The coolie is a figural variant of modernity's economic masses; by definition, the coolie lacks individuality. Asiatic racial form is indissociably plural" (75). In his anger precipitated by Yung's dispassionate reaction to *Hamlet*, Ponter does not simply berate Yung, but all Chinese: "[Y]ou are a terrible people" (527). Yung concedes that his own difficulty to fully appreciate *Hamlet* is due to his age rather than his ethnicity. Nevertheless, based on a single man's response to his reading of *Hamlet*, Ponter criticizes an entire people. He refuses to consider the possibility that he may be at fault, that his translation of *Hamlet* into "doggerel Chinese" (526) may be deficient.

The journalism and literature of the late nineteenth and early twentieth centuries imagined Chinese as inhuman or villainous. Colleen Lye points out that, unlike "savage" brutes (e.g., Magua in James Fenimore Cooper's *The Last of the Mohicans*) depicted in earlier American literature, "the coolie signifies a different kind of monstrous presence, not the ambivalent pleasure of the body's libidinal release but the efficient prospect of its mechanical abstraction" (76). In his tirade, Ponter expresses a notion similar to the monstrous mechanical abstraction Lye describes. By labeling Yung and all Chinese, as "dead things that move," he insists that Chinese are automatons incapable of feeling.

Although Ponter gets the "last word" in the story by virtue of outliving Yung, Cather's narration does not support his racist generalizations. By the end of the story, she emphasizes Yung's individuality and shows that he *is* capable of feeling even though he may not articulate his emotions as passionately as Ponter would like.[12] Immediately following Ponter's diatribe (526–27), Yung smiles and takes up his opium pipe and drifts off to vivid dreams of his homeland, which then haunt him the rest of the day (527). Yung's "dreams of the sea and the mountains and forests and the slopes of sunny land" betray a profound, but unexpressed, attachment to his home country, a land he left in his youth and can only imagine returning to after death. His deep affection for his homeland serves to silently refute Ponter's nativist attack, as does the similarity between the content of his dream (i.e., sun and sea) and Cather's linkage of these universal subjects to Romanticism (see "On Nature and Romance" 233). In Cather's world, Yung's affection for nature proves him to be a Romanticist.

## "A SON OF THE CELESTIAL" AS POLITICAL RESISTANCE

Today Willa Cather is celebrated for her fiction set on the Great Plains, but early in her career she was unmindful of the creative possibilities of her homeland.[13] As reflected in the 1894 plea for Kipling to return to writing about Asian subject matter, she preferred "things new and strange" to the familiar landscape of her childhood. So, inspired by British adventure writers, this daughter of the landlocked American prairie (who had yet to make her first intercontinental voyage) turned her imaginative gaze to San Francisco—North America's gateway to Asia, where Manifest Destiny would soon make way for Benevolent Assimilation.

"A Son of the Celestial" is not merely an attempt to capitalize on America's growing appetite for the exotic. It is a seminal act of resistance—an urtext condemning the racist ideology and cultural anxiety informing U.S. politics. With this story, Cather uses Romanticism to counter bigoted notions of Chinese otherness and to deconstruct the justifications for Chinese exclusion. While living in Pittsburgh at the height of the Boxer Rebellion, she drew once more from that text and its ideas to challenge essentialist narratives of Chinese cruelty and duplicity circulated in the American press and seized upon by American politicians to justify hegemonic foreign policies in China and the Philippines.

NOTES

An earlier version of this article (entitled "Willa Cather's Imperial Apprenticeship: Rudyard Kipling, the Celestial Empire, and San Francisco") was published in Japan in *Studies in English Language and Literature*, vol. 20, March 2012. The revised article is the result of research supported by the Japan Society for the Promotion of Science, Grants-in-Aid for Scientific Research (Kakenhi) number 16K02501.

1. According to Judy Crichton in *America 1900: The Sweeping Story of a Pivotal Year in the Life of a Nation*, over three hundred foreigners were killed in China during 1900, and missionaries accounted for the majority of these victims (180).

2. Cather reuses several images and passages from "A Son of the Celestial" in "The Conversion of Sum Loo." Less obvious are the ways the 1900 pieces from *The Library* echo the sentiment and tone of the 1893 story, which I explore in "Willa Cather, Cultural Imperialism, and 'The Coming Man.'"

3. In "The Chinese Connection: Cather and Pittsburgh's Chinatown," Li Zhu and Tim Bintrim discuss the significance (and journalistic rarity) of Cather's sympathetic characterization of Yee Chin in the 1900 interview and a 1902 profile titled "Pittsburgh's Richest Chinaman." In chapter 3 of this volume ("The Boxer Rebellion, Pittsburgh's Missionary Crisis, and 'The Conversion of Sum Loo'"), Bintrim revises this estimate, arguing that the 1900 interview was staged and questioning Cather's motivations for the 1902 profile, which erroneously claimed Yee Chin's wife died in 1900.

4. In 1889, when he published *The Winning of the West*, Theodore Roosevelt already referred to the matter of continental expansion in the past tense (24). Six months after Cather published "A Son of the Celestial," Frederick Jackson Turner conclusively "settled" the matter of Manifest Destiny. With an eye on the 1890 Census data, the University of Wisconsin historian declared the American frontier closed in "The Significance of the Frontier in American History," a lecture delivered to the American Historical Association on 12 July 1893, during the World's Columbian Exposition in Chicago.

5. The first step in expanding American hegemony overseas was inventing an argument for it. As Edward Said notes in *Culture and Imperialism*, ideologies of expansion and "the cultural correlatives well precede the actual accumulation of imperial territories world-wide" (58). Imperialism is rooted in the imagination, and material culture responds to the call.

6. Her surviving correspondence reveals a lasting fondness for the Anglo-Indian writer as well as a marked distaste for the poetry of Edgar Lee Mas-

ters, a noted anti-imperialist. Cather disparages Masters in letters to Robert Frost; see Cather to Frost, 17 December 1915 (*Selected Letters* 213) and Cather to Frost, 20 January [1936] (*Selected Letters* 214). In a 9 April 1937 letter to E. K. Brown, Cather likens Kipling's 1897 novel *Captains Courageous* to his early stories (*Selected Letters* 213–14, 530).

7. There are surprisingly few overt references to imperialism in Cather's mature fiction. As Deborah Karush recognizes in *Innocent Voyages*, direct commentary on imperialism in Cather's fiction is fairly limited and relegated to the "margins of her narratives" (24–25).

8. In a 4 August 1896 letter to Mariel Gere from Pittsburgh, Cather claims, "I have talked 46 minutes with Rudyard Kipling, which alone was worth coming here for" (*Selected Letters* 39). Based on Kipling's situation at the time, Bintrim doubts that this conversation could have taken place, which he argues in an unpublished conference paper of June 2017, "Her First Fibs: There Were Two." Thomas Pinney, the editor of Kipling's letters, confirmed Bintrim's suspicion by email, "So far as I can tell, Kipling never went west of the Hudson during the four years of his Vermont residence" (email to Bintrim, 8 November 2015). Nor could the conversation have occurred over the telephone. According to conservator Kelly Carlin of the Landmark Trust, which curates Kipling's Vermont estate today, there was no telephone at Naulakha in 1896. She explained that the Kiplings "apparently did not like telephones and banned them from their houses" (email to Bintrim, 12 November 2015).

9. In "The Chinese Mortuary Tradition in San Francisco Chinatown," Linda Sun Crowder notes that it was common for Chinese living in California to have their remains shipped back to China (where they would be venerated according to Chinese belief) for permanent burial (197–98). Exactly how Cather came to learn of this custom is unclear, but Western American publications that Cather is known to have read, such as *The Overland Monthly*, referred to this practice.

10. As James Woodress notes, however, Cather had not yet visited San Francisco before writing this story (146).

11. For an illuminating overview of the imagery relating to Chinese Exclusion, see Michele Walfred's website *Illustrating Chinese Exclusion*.

12. Early in the story, Ponter is introduced in the following sentence: "There was one American whom Yung took to his heart and loved, if a Chinaman can love, and that was old Ponter" (524–25). I view the phrase "if a Chinaman can love" in this sentence to be an intentionally ironic aside by the narrator. This prejudiced statement—to which Ponter seems

to subscribe—is refuted near the end of the story when Yung dreams of the "sunny land" of his home, immediately after Ponter criticizes him for being unable to feel the sun's fire (526–27).

13. Nebraska and the rural Midwest play little role in Cather's literary production before she moved to Pittsburgh. This began to change after "Eric Hermannson's Soul" was published in 1900.

## WORKS CITED

Bradley, James. *The Imperial Cruise: A Secret History of Empire and War*. Little, 2009.

Buda, J. K. "Kipling's 'The Ballad of East and West.'" *Waseda University Faculty Publications*, f.waseda.jp/buda/texts/ballad. *Otsuma Women's University Faculty of Literature Annual Report*, vol. 18, no. 19, 1986.

Cather, Willa. "A Chinese View of the Chinese Situation." *The Library*, 28 July 1900, pp. 16–17.

———. "The Conversion of Sum Loo." *Willa Cather's Collected Short Fiction, 1892–1912*, edited by Virginia Faulkner. 1965. U of Nebraska P, 1970, pp. 323–31.

———. "Go Back, Mr. Kipling." 1894. *The Kingdom of Art: Willa Cather's First Principles and Critical Statements*, edited by Bernice Slote, U of Nebraska P, 1967, pp. 316–18.

———. *The Kingdom of Art: Willa Cather's First Principles and Critical Statements, 1893–1896*. Edited by Bernice Slote, U of Nebraska P, 1967.

———. "Kipling: 'a force to be reckoned with.'" *The World and the Parish: Willa Cather's Articles and Reviews, 1893–1902*, vol. 2, edited by William M. Curtin, U of Nebraska P, 1970, pp. 554–61.

———. "Literary Notes." *The World and the Parish: Willa Cather's Articles and Reviews, 1893–1902*, vol. 2, edited by William M. Curtin, U of Nebraska P, 1970, pp. 851–54.

———. "On Nature and Romance." *The Kingdom of Art: Willa Cather's First Principles and Critical Statements*, edited by Bernice Slote, U of Nebraska P, 1967, pp. 231–33. First published in the *Lincoln Courier*, 2 November 1895, p. 2.

———. *The Selected Letters of Willa Cather*. Edited by Andrew Jewell and Janis Stout, Knopf, 2013.

———. "A Son of the Celestial." *Willa Cather's Collected Short Fiction, 1892–1912*, edited by Virginia Faulkner. 1965. U of Nebraska P, 1970, pp. 523–28.

———. *Willa Cather's Collected Short Fiction, 1892–1912.* Edited by Virginia Faulkner. 1965. U of Nebraska P, 1970.

———. *The World and the Parish: Willa Cather's Articles and Reviews, 1893–1902.* Edited by William M. Curtin, U of Nebraska P, 1970. 2 vols.

Crichton, Judy. *America 1900: The Sweeping Story of a Pivotal Year in the Life of a Nation.* Holt, 2000.

Crowder, Linda Sun. "The Chinese Mortuary Tradition in San Francisco Chinatown," *Chinese American Death Rituals: Respecting the Ancestors,* edited by Sue Fawn Chung and Priscilla Weggars, Altamira P, 2005, pp. 195–240.

Derks, Hans. "The Story of the Snake and Its Tail." *History of the Opium Problem: The Assault on the East, ca. 1600–1950,* edited by Hans Derks, Brill, 2012, pp. 711–32.

Doré, Hunk E. [Pseudonym]. "The Coming Man—John Chinaman: Uncle Sam Introduces Eastern Barbarism to Western Civilization." *Harper's Weekly,* n.d. 1869, The New York Public Library Digital Collections, 2014, www.digitalcollections.nypl.org.

Frenzeny, Paul. *Scene in a Chinese Opium Palace, San Francisco. Harper's Weekly,* 3 April 1880, p. 221, Online Archive of California, www.oac.cdlib.org.

Gorman, Michael. "Willa Cather, Cultural Imperialism, and 'The Coming Man.'" *Fukusuu no "kankaku gengo bunka" no intaafeisu* [Diverse Interfaces of "Sense, Language, and Culture"], Suiseisha, 2019, pp. 97–109.

———. "Willa Cather's Imperial Apprenticeship: Rudyard Kipling, the Celestial Empire, and San Francisco." *Studies in English Language and Literature* [Japan], vol. 20, March 2012, pp. 41–67.

Harte, Bret. "Plain Language from Truthful James" ["The Heathen Chinee"]. *Overland Monthly and Out West Magazine,* September 1870, p. 287.

Karush, Deborah. *Innocent Voyages: Fictions of United States Expansion in Cather, Stevens and Hurston.* 1997. Yale U, PhD dissertation.

Kipling, Rudyard. "A Ballad of Burial." *Departmental Ditties and Ballads and Barrack-Room Ballads.* 1892. Kessinger, 2004, pp. 63–65.

Lye, Colleen. "American Naturalism and Asiatic Racial Form: Frank Norris's *The Octopus* and 'Moran of the *Lady Letty.*'" *Representations,* vol. 84, 2003, pp. 73–99.

"Reign of Anarchy Is Threatened in China." *Pittsburg Press,* 29 May 1900, front page.

Roberts, Chris. "The Country's First War on Drugs: SF vs. Opium." *San Francisco Examiner,* 11 June 2015, http://sfexaminer.com.

Roosevelt, Theodore. *The Winning of the West*, vol. 1, 1889. Presidential Edition, Putnam's, 1900.

Said, Edward. *Culture and Imperialism*. 1993. Vintage, 1994.

Walfred, Michele. *Illustrating Chinese Exclusion*. Thomas Nast cartoons, http://thomasnastcartoons.com, 2014.

Woodress, James. *Willa Cather: A Literary Life*. U of Nebraska P, 1987.

Zhu, Li, and Tim Bintrim. "The Chinese Connection: Cather and Pittsburgh's Chinatown." *Willa Cather Pioneer Memorial Newsletter & Review*, vol. 27, no. 1, 1998, pp. 1–5.

## 3 The Boxer Rebellion, Pittsburgh's Missionary Crisis, and "The Conversion of Sum Loo"

TIMOTHY W. BINTRIM

Sweeping across northern China like a prairie fire during the summer of 1900, the Boxer Rebellion became a story no journalist of Willa Cather's ambition could ignore.[1] With more than two dozen missionaries stationed in districts where the Boxers were determined to kill or expel all foreigners, Pittsburgh congregations were justifiably worried. That summer, Cather published three pieces about the rebellion in Pittsburgh's new arts and opinion weekly, *The Library*, writings that confirm her opposition to Christian missionaries proselytizing the Chinese, a belief formed during her teen years in Red Cloud.

Scholars have explored her contributions to Pittsburgh's *Home Monthly* as both writer and editor in a number of articles, dissertations, and book chapters.[2] Her role at *The Library*, by contrast, remains little studied. This essay will examine Cather's writings about the Boxers in the context of an extended debate over Chinese missions in *The Library* and the city press. More than two decades later, individuals who linked Pittsburgh with north China at the time of the uprising inform her depictions of Enid Wheeler and Arthur Weldon in *One of Ours* and shape key passages of that novel. Enid's father, Jason Royce, approximates Cather's mature estimate of the missionary enterprise when he tells Claude, "I don't believe in one people trying to force their ways or their religion on another ... [China] seems like a long way to go to hunt for trouble, don't it?" (*One of Ours* 292). I argue that Cather reached this conclusion as early as August 1900, when "The Conversion of Sum Loo," her final contribution to *The Library*, charged that the missionaries of Pittsburgh deserved much of the trouble they received at the hands of the Boxers.

The Boxer Rebellion grew out of a number of environmental and cultural stressors. Catastrophic floods and a three-year drought had left the farmers of Shantung Province facing starvation. Thousands more lost their livelihoods when the new railway built by the Germans coopted freight traditionally carried by carters and boatmen (Silbey 39). Among foreigners in Shantung, the Germans were particularly unwelcome because Kaiser Wilhelm II had ordered his subjects to impress on the Chinese the superiority of Teutonic civilization (Silbey 14). Having claimed Shantung as a "sphere of influence" in 1897, the Germans, backed by their formidable navy, acted as if they already owned the country. German diplomats, railroad engineers, and missionaries bullied officials, from the Manchu elite in Peking down to local magistrates. Railroad engineers inundated farm fields and desecrated graveyards and holy sites, ignoring local protests. With one crop killed in the fields and no rain to grow another, the people of Shantung were left hungry, idle, and increasingly resentful of foreign impositions on their land and traditions.

At first, the people's anger was directed toward Chinese converts to Christianity, but on the last night of 1899 it was vented on a European. According to historian Norman Cliff, the first Western casualty of the rebellion was twenty-four-year-old Sidney Brooks, a novice working for the British Society for the Propagation of the Gospel. On 31 December, after dining with his sister in Tiana, Shantung Province, "[Brooks] was waylaid by a band of young toughs. He tried to run ahead of them, but men on horseback chased after him, and he was beheaded." Brooks's murder and mutilation was attributed to a secret society called the "Righteous and Harmonious Fists" or the "Big Knives." Western journalists dubbed the group Boxers for the callisthenic exercises adherents were told would equip them with "iron shirts" impervious to bullets (Silbey 7). Though armed with little more than knives, swords, and tridents, the Boxers became a formidable militia, murdering Chinese Christians and missionaries, burning churches and railroad stations, and routing professionally trained European troops. The Boxers' promises to drive the foreigners from Chinese soil, restore stolen lands, and propitiate the ancestors so that the rains would commence appealed to a hungry and desperate people (Silbey 74).

Initially, Dowager Empress Cixi denounced Boxerism, but in mid-June, when German and Japanese diplomats were assassinated in Peking, it became clear that Cixi and her nephew, Prince Tuan, had formed a secret alliance with the rebels. When the railway was sabotaged by the Boxers in early June, trapping foreign nationals inland, the Allied Powers grew alarmed and ordered their gunboats at the mouth of the Han River to reduce the Taku forts in preparation for landing troops (see figure 3.1). The conflict escalated when thousands of Boxers, supported by Imperial Guards, besieged the Foreign Legation Quarter of Peking, within whose walls five hundred Western and Japanese civilians, four hundred marines, and twenty-eight hundred Chinese Christians sought refuge. On 10 June, the Allies launched an Expeditionary Force of nearly two thousand men, led by British Vice Admiral Edward Seymour, but guerilla attacks were so relentless that Seymour was forced to retreat and await reinforcements. Allied arms and strategy eventually prevailed, but before hostilities ceased in September, one hundred thousand Chinese combatants and civilians and two hundred and fifty foreign missionaries had been killed. Atrocities abounded on both sides. Libraries and cathedrals were burned by the Boxers during the siege of the legations, and the Allied army responded by thoroughly sacking Peking, earning international condemnation for pillage, rape, and murder of Chinese civilians.

Halfway around the world, in Pittsburgh, a smart new current-events magazine named *The Library* debuted on 10 March 1900.

TIMOTHY W. BINTRIM

# FROM THE PEI-HO TO PEKIN
## *A Bird's-eye View of the Disturbed Area in China.*

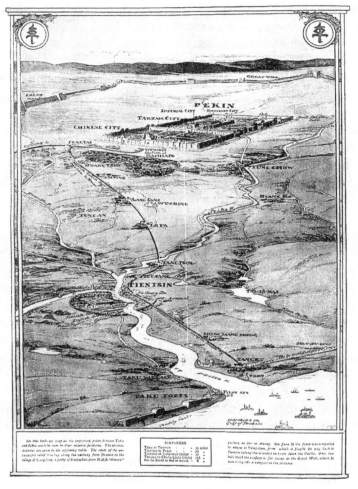

Fig. 3.1. An illustration, originally from *Leslie's Illustrated Weekly*, ca. 1900, shows the rail line by which the Seymour Expedition tried to reach the Foreign Legations at Peking. Seymour's mission was stymied by Boxers tearing up the rails between the city of Tientsin and the village of Lang Fang, at center. Similar illustrations in the city papers taught Pittsburghers the geopolitics of northern China (Martin 9).

Freshly detached from the *Pittsburgh Leader*, Cather began contributing with the magazine's second issue. William Curtin doubts she was on staff, but he judges she had an "inside track," meaning that managing editor Ewan Macpherson would publish anything she and George Seibel submitted (*World and the Parish* 753; Seibel 205). Born in Jamaica and educated at Stonyhurst, the premier Jesuit college in England, Macpherson, like Cather, was a cultural outsider and an outspoken critic of Pittsburgh Presbyterianism (Lewis 147; Seibel 205). Several years after Cather made fun of local divines protesting classical music concerts on Sunday, Macpherson mocked the same cadre for imposing their Sabbath on the entire city (Cather, "The Passing Show," 17 January 1897, in *World and the Parish* 2: 507; Macpherson, "For Our Country's Good," *The Library*, 11 August 1900, 13).

Initially at least, both Macpherson and Cather sided with the Boxers. In the 14 July *Library*, Macpherson exclaimed with mock horror, "What a villainous horde of ruffians those Boxers must be" and then proceeded to demonstrate that Americans would behave exactly like Chinese Boxers if faced with similar threats to their liberty. In another column, he introduced his favorite figure of speech—analogy—proclaiming, "Now it is always good to put oneself in the mind of others if this can be done." While Pittsburgh's Independence Day fireworks were yet a recent memory, Macpherson offered, in his *Library* article "For Our Country's Good," a thought experiment comparing the Chinese custom of ancestor worship to America's veneration of its Founding Fathers:

> There seems to me to be a striking analogy between [Chinese ancestral rites] and certain celebrations in which Americans delight. And suppose that Chinese settlers should come into America in large numbers and all smile pityingly at our idolatrous fireworks, whereby we think we honor the memory of a number of persons and deeds long since dead and done—suppose they jeered at Washington's Birthday and called Thanksgiving Day a piece of antiquated poppycock—would there not be here and there an American Boxer to deal with

them? And suppose they had a fleet, stronger than ours, scattered up and down our coast, and perhaps they were largely represented at Washington and there constantly bulldozed the President, pointing out to him that American ideas were preposterous and threatening him with their formidable displeasure if he did not become enlightened with light from China—might not a Ku Klux Klan, or a Vigilance Committee, or a Whitecap Society arise even in Washington? But that would be an American patriotic movement, not a movement of Chinese Boxers, who, as I have said above, are a villainous horde of ruffians. (14 July 1900)

Macpherson's analogies probably amused Cather, but more importantly they influenced the way she understood the Boxer movement, for several weeks later, adopting the voice of Pittsburgh Cantonese importer "Lee Chin," she, too, imagined the tables turned. In "A Chinese View of the Chinese Situation," she envisioned China joining America's former colonial powers to partition the United States: "Suppose China should decide she wanted San Francisco and take it, and France should take New Orleans and the Mississippi, and Germany New York; what would your people do?" (17). Her appeal to readers' historical imagination is a clear echo of Macpherson's assertion that American patriots would not tolerate the indignities imposed by the Allied Powers. Cather found Macpherson's editorials refreshingly combative and *The Library*'s pay scale agreeable.[3] Most of the remaining twenty-five numbers contain a poem or short story with her byline and a second piece signed with a pseudonym (*World and the Parish* 2: 754; Seibel 205).

Not all contributors to *The Library* sympathized with the Boxers. Defending the foreign missions were the coeditors of the "Pittsburgh People and Doings" department, "E.O.D." and "C.W.S."[4] Filling their two pages each week with photos and letters from local missionaries, most often they used the correspondence of Charlotte Elizabeth Hawes, a member of the Nevin publishing family. Hawes had for the past three years taught women's Bible and kindergarten classes from

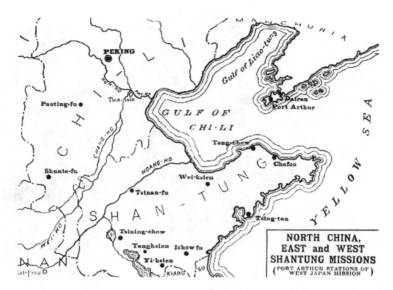

Fig. 3.2. A map of the Presbyterian missions in north China shows Wei Hsien's central location, about two hundred miles from the coast. Source: *Sixty-Fourth Annual Report* of the Board of Foreign Missions of the Presbyterian Church of the United States, May 1901, p. 111, Google Books.

Wei Hsien mission, the oldest and largest Presbyterian station in north China (see figure 3.2). Wei Hsien was largely financed by Pittsburghers, as reflected in its boys' high school, Point Breeze Academy, named for the elite East End enclave where lived Frick, Carnegie, and fellow industrialists. In addition to the boys' high school, the high perimeter wall of Wei Hsien contained ten missionary residences, a girls' high school, a kindergarten, two hospitals and dispensaries, two churches, and a chapel (Presbyterian Church).

Charlotte Hawes's correspondence was supplied by her elder sister, Mrs. Eleanor (Nellie) Nevin, the widow of John I. Nevin, co-founder of the *Pittsburgh Leader*.[5] Having worked for three years as assistant telegraph news editor of the *Leader*, Cather could not have helped knowing Mrs. Nevin, nor could she have missed reading Miss Hawes's dispatches from Wei Hsien. The 30 June issue of *The*

TIMOTHY W. BINTRIM

Fig. 3.3. One of two photographs of Charlotte Hawes's kindergarten students that appeared in the 30 June 1900 issue of *The Library* (6–7). The setting appears to be the Wei Hsien mission.

*Library*, for example, placed Cather's own poem, "Broncho Bill's Valedictory" opposite two photographs of "Miss Hawes and Her Chinese Lambs" and a seven-inch selection from one of Charlotte's letters (see figure 3.3).

In this particular excerpt, Charlotte assured her sister, "We are all well here and around Wei Hsien is peaceful, so don't worry about me. I can go anywhere except in an easterly district, which I have never visited anyhow" (7). But rioting outpaced her letters from China. On 25 June, five days before these assurances appeared in the 30 June *Library*, a mob of about five hundred burned Wei Hsien. Informed by cable of the attack on 26 June, churchgoing Pittsburgh obsessed about the three missionaries who had not yet evacuated—the Rev. Frank Chalfant, Miss Emma F. Boughton of Buffalo, and Miss Charlotte Hawes. Their fate would not be known stateside for eleven days.

Cather tapped Pittsburgh's interest in the Boxer Rebellion thrice. Her first effort, co-written with her brother Douglass, was "The Affair at Grover Station," serialized in *The Library*'s 16 and 23 June issues. The Cather siblings imbued Freymark, their half-Chinese, half-French villain, with stereotypes used by newspaper journalists to malign the Boxers. According to the focal character Terrapin Rogers, Freymark's Chinese blood "explained everything" nefarious about him (342). He is a "rat eater" who, although just thirty, possesses the "yellow, wrinkled hands of an old man." He is addicted to gambling, has trafficked opium in London, and proves a "clam-blooded" killer who, after shooting Larry Donovan fatally through the mouth, sadistically shot Larry's spaniel, Duke, through the side (339–43). The story probably dates from early June 1900, when Willa and Douglass would have been reading in newspapers about the sabotage of rail lines and arson of railroad stations around the city of Tientsin. But it is curious that Freymark's revenge is accomplished using an insider's knowledge of railroad logistics and telegraphy, for in her own journalism, Cather insisted that the Chinese psyche could not adapt to European modernity.[6] Presumably, Freymark's paternal blood—his father was a French military officer—countered the "amphibious" blood of his Chinese slave-girl mother (343) so that he could exploit the railroad's flaws in security.

Mildred Bennett finds it remarkable that barely a month after the Cather siblings subjected Freymark to racist invective in "The Affair at Grover Station," Cather treated Pittsburgh Cantonese importer Yee Chin with greater sympathy when asking him about the causes of the Boxer Rebellion (*Early Short Stories* 245). Although Bennett and others have assumed "A Chinese View of the Chinese Situation" is a legitimate interview with Yee, I conclude from its timing and many inaccuracies that Cather faked the encounter (*Recovering the Extra-Literary* 164–209). Writing as her man-about-town persona Henry Nicklemann, Cather claimed that "when I stopped at [Yee's] shop last Friday afternoon he was busy making preparations to take his wife to San Francisco" because "loneliness, lack of exercise, and homesickness [had] brought on a [life-threatening] mental disorder." Cather offers no reason why Yee would pause in the midst of such an emergency to sit down with a reporter he did not know. The day before the presumed "interview," both the morning *Pittsburgh Gazette-Times* and the afternoon *Pittsburgh Press* had announced that Mrs. Yee had suffered a nervous breakdown. Both papers noted that the Yees would depart the next day for San Francisco in the hope that some time with her family would restore Mrs. Yee's mental equilibrium ("Chinese Woman May Be Insane" 20 July 1900; "Going to California: The Wife of Yee Chin is Suffering from Mental Disease" 20 July 1900). But internal evidence suggests Cather began writing only after the couple were safely on their way to California on 21 July.[7]

Cather-as-Nicklemann found Yee (or as she misnamed him, "Lee" Chin) reluctant to talk about the unrest in China, yet with little prompting she extracted a suspiciously coherent explication of the Boxer conflict. "Lee" Chin claimed the common Chinese did not care who ruled them as long as taxes were bearable and their nominal rulers left them alone. The current empress was Manchu, one of the Tatar people who had ruled the Chinese for generations after wars of corresponding length. Cather expounded on the history of the Qing Dynasty, facts near at hand from her *Leader* work embellishing cabled news. The Chinese people cared little for the Manchus, and the Manchus even less for the people they ruled, but Empress Cixi was determined to remain in power, even if doing so meant appeasing the Western powers with concessions of land. It was this "sacrifice of land to foreigners for purposes that [they] cannot understand" that had turned the common Chinese against Europeans. The Boxer insurgency was less a religious confrontation than a territorial struggle, not a revolt against Christianity but against Western imperialism. The attacks upon missionaries puzzled "Lee": the common Chinese did not dislike missionaries, and "there was no general revolt when European missionaries went to China." Thirty years before, when "Lee" lived in China, "all missionaries who were gentlemen were well liked, and all who were not were detested." What the Chinese could not abide was the greed of the European politicians, their intolerance of other religions, and their attacks on the age-old practices that formed the very fabric of Chinese culture. The Chinese commoner was "wedded to his traditions and institutions, and with these the [Manchus] have never interfered, though the Europeans have" (Zhu and Bintrim 4).

Under pressure from the European powers, Cixi "[began] cutting off slices of the Empire and giving them to Europe"; consequently, the peasants were "maddened at the prospect of losing the land they have held since two thousand years before Christ." Germany, particularly, had used the killings of Europeans as pretense for extorting more territory. The common Chinese, meanwhile, suspected that "the railroad, the telegraph, [and] Christianity were only the forerunners of this wholesale theft of land—means to facilitate the division of the Empire among Western nations," Cather wrote in "A Chinese View."

Two weeks after this "interview," Cather placed in *The Library*'s 11 August issue a third, clearly fictional commentary, blending her experience of real missionaries in Red Cloud and Pittsburgh and her imaginings about those in Shantung. Advertised on the masthead as "A Sketch of Native Chinese Life" and ostensibly set in San Francisco, "The Conversion of Sum Loo" had roots elsewhere. According to Mildred Bennett, Cather's aversion to Chinese missions began in Red Cloud. A young townswoman she particularly disliked traveled with her husband, physician L. D. Denny, to Peking in 1884, where the two briefly served the Methodist mission. The Dennys wrote "effusive letters home that were published in the local newspaper" but before the year was out, the couple came home "with a large collection of curios, linens, and objets d'art," which they took on the lecture circuit. "Willa suspected [Laura Denny] had acquired these treasures by some sort of mis-dealing with the natives," Bennett continues, and "could not endure the exploitation of possessions and experiences when this woman charged for her lectures." Cather's aversion to the Dennys' cultural appropriation, concludes Bennett, became a conviction that "the ancient civilization of China could get along quite well without our . . . interference" (*World of Willa Cather* 136).

Though Willa probably did not collaborate with Douglass on "The Conversion of Sum Loo," she seems to have had her siblings in mind as a target audience.[8] Just two missionaries in the story are given names: Sister Hannah—a name derived from Red Cloud and her youth, a name that would have delighted her siblings—and Norman Girrard, described as the "pale eyed theological student" torn between serving art and the church. Like the early, tolerant Jesuit missionaries, Girrard (his name suggesting French ancestry) befriends Cantonese importer Sum Chin without trying to change him. Sketching Sum Chin in the backroom of his shop, Girrard draws inspiration from this exotic space (324). Initially, these "séances" are mutually helpful: Sum's stories and surroundings excite Girrard's imagination, and Girrard arranges through "the Rescue Society" the immigration of Sum's Chinese bride, circumventing the Chinese Exclusion Act. Eventually Girrard accepts a large bankers' check for services rendered on behalf of Sum's infant son, but does not pressure Sum to convert to Christianity. Sister Hannah's ministrations, by contrast, are calculated and pecuniary; she covets Sum Chin's influence among his people and the souls of his wife and child. In her eyes, the merchant equates to a literal sum: "a convert worth a hundred of the coolie people" (323). Hannah labors to convince the rich man's wife, Sum Loo, of the value of Christianity, for "above all things [Hannah] desired to have the [infant Sum Wing] baptized" (328).

The title of the story promises the conversion of a pagan Chinese family to Christianity in the manner of Sunday-school fiction. But the rug is pulled out as the healthy toddler is killed by holy water, the premature "joy at the Mission of the Heavenly Rest ... [is] turned to weeping," and the grieving parents reject Christianity (329). Abandoned by his domestic gods and mocked by the priest of the Joss House (Taoist temple) across the street, Sum Chin changes from a model husband to a "broken old man" who shuns his friends and demands that his wife "cleanse herself from the impurities of the Foreign Devils" (330), a clear allusion to the Boxers' cry to "extirpate the foreigner." Without a son to pray for the repose of his ancestors, Sum Chin expects eternal torment.[9] His wife is changed from a joyous mother to a depressed penitent, spending her days atoning for childlessness in the Taoist temple.

Not just the Chinese couple but also the erstwhile missionaries are transformed by the catastrophe. Girrard quits church and country

to "become an absinthe drinking, lady-killing, and needlessly profane painter of oriental subjects and marines on the other side of
the water" (324). And in the story's last paragraph, even stolid Sister
Hannah is touched after pursuing Sum Loo into the Joss House,
having been barred from the Sums' home. Within the temple, Hannah beholds Sum Loo kneeling before the altar of the goddess of
childbirth, burning tapers made from folded pages of the Chinese
New Testament. Hannah retreats in terror, all her verities gone up
in smoke, and that night withdraws her application to the Board of
Foreign Missions (331).

The fictional Sister Hannah had but to cross the street to disrupt
the Sum fortunes, but an actual Episcopal deaconess named Sister
Hannah, known to the Cather siblings, literally held together the
Grace Church of Red Cloud (Bennett, "Cather and Religion"). Bennett explains that as the Baptist congregation declined in numbers,
the Cathers began attending Grace Church in the 1880s and joined
in the 1920s, by which time Grace had become the town's "elegant
church" (11). But throughout Cather's childhood, Grace had been a
struggling mission, ill-served by a succession of itinerant priests who
rode a hundred-mile circuit preaching to congregations in fourteen
other towns. Surveying the church's many incarnations in Cather's
fiction, Brent Bohlke recalls that Grace suffered "false starts, . . . disappointments, and much travail" until Sister Hannah arrived and
took "charge . . . as the licensed lay reader" (6). Finding the church
building badly twisted by a tornado, the tireless Sister had its frame
"brace[d] . . . with iron rods," had the structure moved to a more
central lot in town, and had its shattered plaster walls replaced. She
held fundraisers to pay for the renovations and doubled the church's
membership before she departed Red Cloud in March 1893 (Bennett,
"Cather and Religion" 11; Bohlke, "Grace Church, Red Cloud" 7).

While few outside of Red Cloud would have appreciated her satire
on the real Sister Hannah, Cather took a greater risk in making her
fictional deaconess flee from the sight of fire, for the near-martyrdom
of Charlotte Hawes and her companions was fresh in the collective
memory of Pittsburghers. The public learned on 7 July that the fugi-

tives from Wei Hsien had reached safety, but the days between the arson and the first telegram from Frank Chalfant must have been agony for family, friends, and congregational sponsors. Nellie Nevin told *The Library* she was "besieged with questions" regarding Charlotte's safety, perhaps unconscious of comparing her own ordeal to the ongoing siege of the legations.[10] On 24 July, almost a month after the event, the first accounts of the Pittsburgh missionaries' flight from the Boxers appeared in the city newspapers.

Frank Chalfant explained that when he learned of the Allies firing on the Taku forts, he and the other minister at Wei Hsien, C. S. Fitch, anticipated trouble. It was decided that Reverend Fitch should escort the fourteen American women and children to a steamer waiting at the coastal city of Chefoo, about two hundred miles distant. The Fitch party left on 23 June, while Frank Chalfant would remain until the two women who were teaching Bible classes in the off stations—Miss Emma Boughton and Miss Charlotte Hawes—could be warned and recalled. Miss Boughton was not far afield, but Miss Hawes had to travel fifty miles nonstop by mule litter so did not reach Wei Hsien until the early morning of 25 June. The three missionaries crated their belongings and reserved carts to depart early the next morning, but by 5:00 p.m., hundreds of rioters had gathered outside the mission walls. Armed with a revolver, Frank Chalfant mounted the wall and ordered the crowd to disperse, but his commands were answered with jeers and a hail of bricks. In a later interview, Charlotte Hawes described what transpired:

> [Reverend Chalfant] said he would shoot [only if] absolutely necessary, and he did fire over their heads several times. These shots were met with the cry, "Big Knife society don't fear guns." He finally came in [to his residence] after killing one Boxer and injuring several more, and told us that the crowd was getting stronger and an attack was imminent ... The Boxers in the meantime had come in at the south gate ... We did not know exactly what was to be the method employed in our death until suddenly a little [child] cried out, "See, they are picking up fire-

Fig. 3.4. The ruins of Wei Hsien mission, rebuilt the following year. From *The Sixty-Fourth Annual Report* of the Board of Foreign Missions of the Presbyterian Church of the United States, May 1901, p. 102, Google Books.

wood." We pulled open the curtains on the east of the house and saw that the chapel was on fire and on the other side my house could be seen in flames. We supposed that the flames would soon be applied to the building we were in and that we would be burned to death. ("Escaped the Boxers," *Pittsburgh Commercial Gazette*, 14 August 1900, p. 3)

As the mob broke into the rear of the residence and paused to examine the crated belongings piled in the study, the Americans realized the front yard was deserted. Separated from the Boxers by only a sliding door, they stole out of the residence and used a ladder to cross the twelve-foot wall. While helping one of the female servants to clamber over, Frank Chalfant dropped his revolver; thereafter, their only defense was a hammer that Miss Hawes had carried away from her packing. Crossing fields to avoid villages and roads, the fugitives reached the German coal mines at Fangtze, about ten miles away, around midnight. There they were taken in by the German mining engineers who afterward provided a military escort to the coast.[11]

Fig. 3.5. *The Library* published "the first photograph of [Miss Hawes] since her return from China, taken . . . on the day after her arrival in Pittsburgh," 18 August 1900, p. 3.

News of the attack reached Pittsburgh via cable on 26 June. Reverend Fitch's party was known to have reached Chefoo safely, but nothing had been heard from Frank Chalfant, Emma Boughton, and Charlotte Hawes as rumors flew that all of the missionaries in the province had been killed. Finally, on 7 July, a cablegram from Frank

Chalfant reached the Board of Foreign Missions in New York, who forwarded his message to his minister father in Pittsburgh. In the next day's newspapers, Dr. George Chalfant confirmed that the three were safe ("Chalfants Are Believed Safe," *Pittsburgh Daily Post*, 6 July 1900, p. 8).[12] Two days after the publication of "The Conversion of Sum Loo" in *The Library*, Charlotte Hawes arrived in Pittsburgh on the steamer *Empress of Japan*, escorting eleven-year-old Margaret Chalfant, one of Reverend Fitch's evacuees ("Escaped the Boxers," *Pittsburgh Commercial Gazette*, 14 August 1900, p. 3).[13] That day, Charlotte granted the city press several interviews. One titled "The Home-coming of Miss Hawes" appeared in the 18 August issue of *The Library* (see figure 3.5).[14]

By making Sister Hannah withdraw her application to the Board of Foreign Missions, Cather seems to have anticipated Nellie Nevin's reaction to her sister's peril. Charlotte told *The Library* that she intended to return to China "as soon as it was advisable" ("The Home-coming of Miss Hawes"), but the 1901 annual report to the Presbyterian Board of Foreign Missions confirms that "on account of need in her home" Miss Hawes had resigned (102). It appears Charlotte took a furlough at the insistence of her sister who had been so proud of her service earlier that summer.

If, when Cather left Red Cloud for Pittsburgh, she assumed she had escaped small-town showboating, she may have resented Nellie Nevin colonizing with her sister's letters the magazine Cather made her own. Two decades later, a small scene in *One of Ours* appears to reference Nellie Nevin indirectly. After a shopping date in Hastings, Enid asks Claude to accompany her on a social visit to Brother Weldon. Seated in Mrs. Gleason's parlor, Weldon reads Carrie Royce's letters from China aloud, "without being asked to do so," to Enid's great delight and Claude's intense disgust (180). Enid seeks Weldon's counsel about whether she ought to follow her sister to China, but like Nellie Nevin or the fictional Sister Hannah, Weldon equivocates. Claude observes that Weldon is "careful not to commit himself, not to advise anything unconditionally, except prayer" (181). Instead of encouraging Enid's missionary ambitions, Weldon urges her to do her duty on the home front and "reclaim" Claude through marriage, for, Weldon says, "the most important service devout girls could perform for the church was to bring promising young men to its support" (242). The adjective "devout" links Enid to the "devout deaconess" Sister Hannah, who Cather wrote, "should have had her own children to bother about" ("Conversion of Sum Loo" 328)—which sentiment a younger Cather may have applied to Miss Hawes and her Chinese lambs.

In the same issue of *The Library* that contained "The Conversion of Sum Loo" (11 August), Ewan Macpherson addressed the latest wrinkle in the debate over who was to blame for the Boxer trouble. The week before, the Reverend Regis Canevin, rector of Saint Paul's Roman Catholic Cathedral in Pittsburgh's East End, offended many Presbyterians when he told a newsman that Protestant missionaries in China should not demand invading armies rescue them but should instead, like their Catholic brethren, be prepared to die as martyrs. "I am not opposed to the deliverance of legations and Europeans whose lives are imperiled by the attacks of the Chinese," Bishop Canevin clarified the next day, "but I am opposed to the sending of a single regiment to protect or assist the missionaries who are engaged in preaching the Gospel of peace" ("Rev. Canevin on China," *Pittsburgh Commercial Gazette*, 4 August 1900, p. 4). Making converts at rifle point, Canevin insisted, was incompatible with Christian principles; further, he suspected that the European powers were using the missionary crisis as an excuse to further their imperialist agenda:

> There are missionaries and missionaries ... The first cabled message has yet to come from one of my faith asking for soldiers. They will die as they have lived, without a murmur, without the shriek for protection. The press teems with the plaints of ... the Protestant workers grouped here and there in the disturbed districts ... I am opposed to the [Allied military] advance on China ... Better ... the death of every missionary ... than the landing of thousands of soldiers and the infliction of all the horrors and evils of war on [China's] shores. ("Rev. Canevin on China," p. 4)

Canevin denied that Catholic missionaries were any more resolute than their Protestant counterparts, but pointed out that most of his faith were unmarried, whereas Protestant missionaries were commonly accompanied by their wives and children. If Protestant ministers were willing to die for Christ, they were less willing to sacrifice their loved ones. As a member of the Catholic minority in Pittsburgh, Ewan Macpherson seemed embarrassed by the so-called Canevin controversy; his column in *The Library* urged Christians of all persuasions to close ranks, asking, "Would it not be to [the clergy's] general advantage to show a solid front not only against Prince Tuan and the Boxers, but also to the thousands of angry critics among Christian nations who recent events have stirred up against them?" ("For Our Country's Good," 11 August 1900, p. 14).

Cather seems to have been one of those angry critics who believed the Chinese should be allowed to work out their own salvation. As "Lee" Chin maintained in "A Chinese View," she thought "the Chinese were very well satisfied with their own religion and they think their Empire a dear price to pay for a new one" (17). Two decades later, Cather alluded to the Bishop Canevin controversy when Enid asks Brother Weldon if her own chilly personality may have been ordained by Providence to hold her "in reserve for the foreign field—by not making personal ties" (*One of Ours* 181). Although married and an evangelical Protestant, Enid prefers to live as a chaste bride of Christ, like a Catholic sister. Claude remarks on her willingness to separate, "It's not only your going . . . It's because you want to go. You are glad of the chance to get away among all those preachers, with their smooth talk and make-believe" (297).

Claude conceded that "when [Enid] made up her mind, there was no turning her" (294), and Charlotte Hawes proved just as indomitable. By 1903, Miss Hawes was back at Wei Hsien, where she remained for more than twenty years, except for an occasional furlough, through revolutions, outbreaks of pneumonic plague, and terror campaigns against Christian missionaries ("Pittsburg Missionary is in the Danger Zone"). Defying contagious disease and violence, she lived to be eighty-five, dying in Pittsburgh on 25 November 1944 ("Miss Charlotte Hawes," *Pittsburgh Press*, 26 November 1944, p. 36).

Whether Miss Hawes's many Pittsburgh friends took offense at "The Conversion of Sum Loo" is difficult to determine. I have located no outraged letters in the city press. The story was Cather's last word in *The Library* and may have signaled her temporary leave-taking from the city. *The Library* failed in September (as anticipated by Seibel and Cather), about the time she left Pittsburgh to assist her cousin Howard Gore in Washington DC (Seibel, "Miss Willa Cather," *World and the Parish* 2: 755). If the story did give offense, the damage was not lasting, for beginning in January she published a Washington letter in *The Index of Pittsburg Life*, which had absorbed some of *The Library*'s staff (*World and the Parish* 2: 793).

Though Cather's association with *The Library* lasted just six months, we should not discount its importance. The spring and summer of 1900 that proved so calamitous for the Chinese was for her a time of intense productivity and high spirits. She wrote to Will Owen Jones at the end of September that the year had been "the happiest of her life so far" (Woodress 147). And although *The Library* was no more, in later years her friendship with Ewan Macpherson resumed. Edith Lewis remembered Macpherson as "a fine scholar, with a thorough knowledge of Catholic tradition," who had intended to become a priest, but abandoned this vocation to marry (147). From 1905 to 1912, Macpherson worked for the *Catholic Encyclopedia* in New York, where he and Cather met for conversation. Lewis credits these "long talks," in part, for giving Cather confidence to attempt another missionary story, *Death Comes for the Archbishop* (148), which, like *One of Ours*, may have long tendrils stretching back to Pittsburgh.[15]

## NOTES

1. Two months after she quit the *Leader*, Cather could have seen this analogy to a prairie fire on the paper's front page in a letter from missionary William Chalfant to his father, Dr. George W. Chalfant, of the Park Avenue Presbyterian Church. William described "anti-foreign demonstrations [that erupted] with a suddenness and fury which I can only liken to the devastating prairie fires of our own western states" (see "In Great Danger. Pittsburg[h]ers and Western Pennsylvanians in China. Most are Missionaries,"

in the *Pittsburgh Leader* of 31 May 1900, p. 1). William was interviewed in California, where his wife was being treated for a serious illness contracted in China. The next month, William's younger brother, Frank, Frank's family, and their Pittsburgh neighbor, Charlotte Elizabeth Hawes, would feature in what I call "Pittsburgh's missionary crisis."

2. Peter Benson's "Willa Cather at *Home Monthly*" claimed to provide "the first careful, systemic account" of Cather's contributions but introduced careless errors, the most persistent of which was identifying fashion editor Mildred Beardslee as one of Cather's pseudonyms. Becky Roorda was the first to identify Beardslee conclusively as a Boston-based contributor to *Vogue*, among other magazines; but even before Roorda made this identification, careful readers would hardly mistake Beardslee's tortured prose for Willa Cather's (email to the author, 5 Sept. 2016). A more careful account is Jennifer Bradley's "To Entertain, To Educate, To Elevate: Cather and the Commodification of Manners at the *Home Monthly*," which expands upon William Curtin's valuable notes in *The World and the Parish*. My own 2004 dissertation, *Recovering the Extra-Literary: The Pittsburgh Writings of Willa Cather*, is also worth consulting, especially pp. 27–163.

3. George Seibel recalled that Macpherson paid between fifteen and forty dollars for his writings, helping the Seibels to burn the mortgage from their new home on Giffin Street in the Mount Oliver neighborhood on Pittsburgh's South Side ("Miss Willa Cather").

4. C. W. S. was surely Clara Wood Shipman, who signed her full name to other features in the magazine. E. O. D. has not been identified.

5. Colonel John I. Nevin, a Civil War veteran, died in 1884, at age forty-seven, from Bright's disease, a kidney ailment he contracted in a Confederate prison camp. His widow, Eleanor, lived until 1941. For more than fifty years, Nellie Nevin published her poems, sketches, and memoirs of her late husband in the *Pittsburgh Leader* and other city papers (Adelaide Nevin 153). The *Leader* indulged Mrs. Nevin because it was literally a family paper: all of its officers and most of its editors shared her surname; composer Ethelbert Nevin was one of the few who escaped working there. Cather generally liked the Nevin family, but she may have bridled at Eleanor constantly making news of her sister's adventures in China.

6. Although she did not succeed in interviewing Minister Wu Ti'ang Fang in Washington DC, in January 1901, Cather told readers of *The Index of Pittsburg Life* that she had heard enough about Wu to disprove reports published in Pittsburgh that he was "that impossible thing, a completely Europeanized Chinaman" (*World and the Parish* 2: 803). In what may be the

most explicit statement of her Orientalism, she added, "The Chinaman has held his identity through too many centuries of adverse conditions to lose it in a few years of European culture; his nerves, his brain stuff, and even his emotional instincts are totally different from the nations of the West" (803).

7. Numerous discrepancies with more reliable sources suggest that Cather did not interview Yee Chin. For example, Cather used free indirect discourse, claiming that "Lee" Chin's "circumlocutions" would "make rather difficult reading," but other journalists quoted Yee at length and praised his fluent English. Cather has "Lee" Chin protest against "steam, electricity and Christianity" costing the Chinese their empire, but Yee Chin invested in modernization efforts in China, including a joint stock company "to start towboats and passenger steamers" on the Yellow River. In November 1900, after securing an audience with Minister Wu Ti'ang Fang after the Carnegie Institute's Founder's Day ceremonies, Yee reluctantly gave up his steamboat plan and refunded money to his partners ("Boxers Stopped a Local Project," *Pittsburgh Daily Post*, 5 Nov. 1900, p. 3). Tellingly, when two years later she reworked "A Chinese View" as a profile of "Pittsburgh's Richest Chinaman," writing as Henry Nicklemann (*Pittsburg Gazette*, 15 June 1902, p. 5), Cather erroneously asserted that Mrs. Yee had died in San Francisco in 1900. Anyone who knew the Yees or their friends could have learned that Mrs. Yee had in fact made a speedy and complete recovery from her nervous breakdown, as was reported in the *Leader* on 17 Aug. and the *Post* on 18 Aug. 1900 ("Yee Chin's Wife Is Quite Well Again" 7; "Local Chinese Boycott" 19). Finally, in the 1902 piece, Cather asserted that Yee's adult son had never visited the United States, a claim contradicted by other sources.

8. The week before, Cather had dedicated a poem, "Are You Sleeping Little Brother?" to her brother Jack. That summer she probably continued her early habit of mailing clippings from Pittsburgh periodicals to her siblings, as Bernice Slote noted in "The Secret Web."

9. As Bennett and others have observed, the fictional Chinese couple is loosely based on sixty-year-old Yee Chin and his twentysomething wife, Yee Oi, of Pittsburgh (Bintrim and Zhu 1–5).

10. See E. O. D., "Pittsburgh People and Doings," *The Library*, 30 June 1900, p. 7.

11. See "Narrow Escape from the Boxers. Rev. Frank Chalfant Had All-Afternoon Fight with Yellow Savages," *Pittsburgh Daily Post*, 14 Aug. 1900, p. 1, and "Yellow Fiends Slain by a Pittsburgh Man: Rev. F. H. Chalfant Fought to Save Lives of His Co-Workers. The Story of Attack and Flight," *Pittsburgh Commercial Gazette*, 11 Aug. 1900, p. 2.

12. See Clara Wood Shipman (as C. W. S.), confirming that Frank Chalfant and Misses Hawes and Boughton were safe, in "Pittsburgh People and Doings" *The Library*, 14 July 1900, p. 7.

13. On the arrival of Miss Hawes in Pittsburgh, see "Pittsburgh People and Doings" *The Library*, 11 Aug. 1900, p. 11.

14. See also "Their Escape was Miraculous. Miss Charlotte Hawes Tells of Her Horrible Experience with Boxers. Expected to Be Massacred. Chinese Thought They Were Bullet-Proof," *Pittsburgh Daily Post*, 14 Aug. 1900, p. 6.

15. I am indebted to William Gonch, a PhD candidate at the University of Maryland, for informing me of Lewis's account of the continued friendship of Cather and Macpherson in New York City. I look forward to Bill Gonch's investigation of Macpherson's influence on *Death Comes for the Archbishop* (Gonch, "Re: Research Questions about Cather's Pittsburgh Years," email to the author, 21 Aug. 2018).

## WORKS CITED

Bennett, Mildred R. "Cather and Religion." *Literature and Belief*, vol. 8, 1988, pp. 5–13.

———. *Early Short Stories of Willa Cather*. Dodd, Mead, 1957.

———. *The World of Willa Cather*. 1951. Revised edition with notes and index, U of Nebraska P, 1961.

Benson, Peter. "Willa Cather at *Home Monthly*." *Biography*, vol. 4, no. 3, Summer 1981, pp. 227–48.

Bintrim, Timothy. *Recovering the Extra-Literary: Cather's Pittsburgh Writings*. 2004. Duquesne University, PhD dissertation.

Bintrim, Timothy, and Li Zhu. "The Chinese Connection: Cather and Pittsburgh's Chinatown." *Willa Cather Pioneer Memorial Newsletter and Review*, vol. 42, no. 1, Summer 1998, pp. 1–5, Willa Cather Foundation, www.willacather.org/willa-cather-review.

Bohlke, Brent. "Grace Church, Red Cloud—A 'True Story' of the Midwest." *Willa Cather Pioneer Memorial Newsletter*, vol. 27, issues 1 and 2, 1983, pp. 1–8, Willa Cather Foundation, www.willacather.org/willa-cather-review.

Bradley, Jennifer L. "To Entertain, to Educate, to Elevate: Cather and the Commodification of Manners at *The Home Monthly*." *Willa Cather and Material Culture*, edited by Janis P. Stout, U of Alabama P, 2005, pp. 37–65.

Cather, Willa. "The Affair at Grover Station." *Collected Short Fiction 1892–1912*, edited by Virginia Faulkner, introduced by Mildred R. Bennett, U of Nebraska P, 1965.

————— [Henry Nicklemann, pseud.]. "A Chinese View of the Chinese Situation," *The Library*, 28 July 1900, pp. 16–17.

—————. "The Conversion of Sum Loo." *Collected Short Fiction 1892–1912*, edited by Virginia Faulkner, introduced by Mildred R. Bennett, U of Nebraska P, 1965.

—————. *One of Ours*. Willa Cather Edition, historical essay and explanatory notes by Richard Harris, with textual essay and editing by Frederick M. Link, with Kari A. Ronning, U of Nebraska P, 2007.

—————. *Willa Cather in Person: Interviews, Speeches, Letters*. Edited by Brent Bohlke, U of Nebraska P, 1986.

—————. *The World and the Parish: Willa Cather's Articles and Reviews 1893–1902*. Edited by William M. Curtin, U of Nebraska P, 1970. 2 vols.

Cliff, Norman. "The Boxer Rebellion." December 1999, *Wei Hsien Paintings*, www.weihsien-paintings.org/NormanCliff/history/boxer/txt_boxer.htm.

Lewis, Edith. *Willa Cather Living: A Personal Record*. 1953. U of Nebraska P, 1976.

Macpherson, Ewan. "For Our Country's Good." *The Library*, 14 July, 11 Aug. 1900, p. 13.

Martin, William Alexander Parsons. "From the Pei-Ho to Peking, a Bird's-Eye View of the Disturbed Area in China." *The Siege in Peking: China against the World*, 1900, p. 9, Hathitrust, www.catalog.hathitrust.org/Record/100335177.

Nevin, Adelaide Mellier. "Mrs. Nellie Nevin" and "Miss Charlotte Hawes." *The Social Mirror: A Character Sketch of the Women of Pittsburg and Vicinity*, T. W. Nevin, 1888, p. 153.

Presbyterian Church in the USA (Old School). Board of Foreign Missions. *Sixty-Fourth Annual Report of the Board of Foreign Missions of the Presbyterian Church, in the United States of America*, Board of Foreign Missions, 1900–1903, 146–47, Hathitrust, www.catalog.hathitrust.org/Record/005909213.

Seibel, George. "Miss Willa Cather from Nebraska." *New Colophon*, vol. 2, no. 7, Sept. 1949, 195–208.

Silbey, David S. *The Boxer Rebellion and the Great Game in China*. Hill and Wang, 2012.

Slote, Bernice. "Willa Cather: The Secret Web." *Five Essays on Willa Cather: The Merrimack Symposium*, edited by John Murphy, Merrimack College, 1974, pp. 1–19.

Woodress, James. *Willa Cather: A Literary Life*. U of Nebraska P, 1987.

# PART 2

# Class Action

Retrying "Paul's Case"

# 4 Growing Pains
## The City behind Cather's Pittsburgh Classroom

MARY RUTH RYDER

As a small-town, midwestern girl of twenty-two settling into the foreign environs of the rapidly developing Pittsburgh of 1896, Willa Cather was understandably homesick. She was, though, equally entranced and excited by the energies and cultural opportunities that lay before her in the bustling industrial complex known as "Steel Town." Within five years of arriving, she entered the classrooms of that city, and her experiences there have been recounted as completely as possible, based on available sources. But, as all teachers know, teaching experiences are shaped by far more than just the students in the classroom and textbooks from which they learn.

In 1901, when Cather began teaching, Pittsburgh was a changing tableau, suffering from adolescent growing pains of trying to determine its direction and identity. Thick with the noise of industry, the city projected a vibrancy and energy that bespoke its shifting face as immigrants poured in, wealthy capitalists contributed to civic improvements and public works, and concerned citizens agitated for beautification of the cityscape. Education was a priority for its civic leaders and captains of industry and for the ordinary workers who sought the American dream for their children. During the five years in which Cather was a part of Pittsburgh's educational system (1901–6) significant changes took place in the city's schools, changes propelled by shifting cultural demographics and by the demands of a city trying to establish itself as a leading commercial and cultural center. Not unlike the city itself, Cather, as a beginning teacher, was experiencing growing pains and learning about a world beyond the plains of Nebraska. The pulse of the city was that of the teenagers whom she taught, beating with energy, excitement, and hopeful expectations—with just a shadow of fear. Cather's response to these sometimes painful changes is reflected in two of her stories written during her teaching years, "The Professor's Commencement" and "Paul's Case." These works not only reveal her concerns about the changes in education at the time, with commercial studies displacing the liberal arts, but also show the troubling effects on her students of rapid cultural change and a consequent shift in values.

Hired in March of 1901 to teach at Central High School, the academic curriculum–based school of the city, Cather was immersed in this rapid change. Between 1902 and 1908, the population of Greater Pittsburgh swelled from about 950,000 to 2.2 million (Nevin 8–9; White 31). In 1902 manufacturers were handling ten million tons of cargo and producing 450 million dollars annually in revenue (Nevin 8–9). "The millionaire springs up in Pittsburgh like a weed," one commentator wrote, and an estimated 250 millionaires called the city home (Nevin 42, 46).

But Pittsburghers were not all of the moneyed class. Carnegie alone employed about forty thousand workers, with Westinghouse hiring ten thousand more (Nevin 34, 38). Whereas the early entrepreneurs and settlers of the area who had built this wealth had come largely from Germany and the British Isles, this new crop of workers were "colored and foreign" (Nevin 53), with the largest number from eastern and southeastern Europe. While Cather, who had known and admired the Bohemians back home in Nebraska, would, no doubt, have been delighted to see some students from this latter ethnic group in her classes, that was not to be the case. The high schools of the city had been divided by areas of study, with Central High School, Cather's first education employer, hosting the classic, academic program. By the time Cather began work at Central, three high schools existed in the city. The Commercial Department left Central High School in 1896 for its own building on Fifth Avenue, where for some time the Normal School was also housed. During the 1890s over a thousand teenagers from the families of manual workers entered the Commercial Department of Pittsburgh's public high schools (DeVault 7). Their largely unskilled working parents sought for their children an education that would propel the young people into jobs beyond the manual trades. They and their families recognized that an academic program that included studying works in English literature, Latin, and ancient history placed their children at a disadvantage in the job market, leaving them with no specific job skills. Meanwhile, the Commercial School boomed. Records show that in 1901, the year in which Cather first taught, sixty-eight graduated from Central High School, while fifty-three matriculated at the Normal School and eighty-nine at the Commercial High School (Fleming 223).

The students in Cather's Central High classrooms were not the sons and daughters of the barons of industry, most of whom by the 1890s were attending prestigious preparatory schools elsewhere (Couvares 100). Nor were they part of the most recent wave of immigrants; rather, they were the children of established, skilled workers who had carved out a place of rising social prominence for themselves as "native" Pittsburghers, having their roots in the first wave of British and German immigration. A glance at her class lists reveals names like Lovelace, Forester, Hutchinson, Kelly, Miller, Soffel, Otte, Klingensmith, Merker (Kvasnicka 160, 162). Conspicuously absent from these rolls are eastern European surnames, or even Italian. The Italian residents of Pittsburgh had become, next to the Germans, "the largest and the most prosperous foreign element" of the city, numbering over forty thousand in the Greater Pittsburgh area (Nevin 57). Although the district known as "Little Italy" was not far from Central High School (Nevin 58), Italian youth generally did not attend the public school but attended parochial schools, perhaps not feeling welcomed at Central High, which was in 1871 said to be "one of the finest, if not the finest [high school] in the state" (qtd. in Kristufek 21). By the time of Cather's arrival, however, Central had lost some of its prestige as the school for children of the rising middle classes. Early on, Central had, after some contentious struggle, integrated, and in 1872 listed three African Americans among its students (Morris). As it continued to grow more diverse, greater pressure came to change its educational mission.

Until 1909, though, the schools continued to be governed under the ward system, limiting the ethnic makeup of the students because of their place of residence. Even labor policies, Francis Couvares writes, "encouraged this 'Balkanization' of the population" with ethnic communities lying primarily between the river and the railroad. "Beyond the tracks," Couvares continues, "steep bluffs sharply marked off the zone of settlement" (89). In "The Professor's Commencement," Cather pointedly refers to these bluffs on Mount Washington, a geologic and social line of demarcation:

> To the west, across the river, rose the steep bluffs, faintly etched through the brown smoke, rising five hundred feet, almost as sheer as a precipice, traversed by cranes and inclines and checkered by winding yellow paths like sheep trails which led to the wretched habitations clinging to the face of the cliff, the lairs of the vicious and the poor, miserable rodents of civilization. (484)

Cather recognized that geography was a sociological demographic and that the students beneath the bluffs were like the Cyclopean exiles of Ulysses's adventure. Atop an opposite bluff that overlooked the clamoring Union Station sat Central High School. Professor Graves, in "The Professor's Commencement," describes the school as "a fortress set upon the dominant acclivity of that great manufacturing city" and commanding its heart (483). That world outside sometimes threatened learning as the "puffing of the engines in the switch yard at the foot of the hill" would drown out the voices of students as they recited (484).

This is not to say that Cather was fully dissatisfied with the place in which she taught or the quality and type of student whom she was teaching. The majority were from the now established and comfortable middle class. Their fathers were physicians, musicians, railroad conductors, and hotel managers (Kvasnicka 160). The high school prided itself in the academic achievements of its students and regularly published in local papers pictures and stories of its honor students. (See, for example, *Pittsburgh Weekly Gazette*, 21 March 1902). In such an atmosphere of success, one can imagine how the faculty would have reacted to a student like Paul in "Paul's Case." Paul's flippant attitude and contempt for his teachers, if not for the entire education system, go undisguised. Kvasnicka notes that Cather recalled one young man, likely the model for Paul, who was the "only student she never could seem to reach" (165). Cather would have participated in faculty disciplinary hearings, perhaps even for her one unreachable student. Central High School was known to apply discipline policies rigidly, especially since a long history of student pranks was a tradition at the school (Morris). The almost inquis-itorial atmosphere of Paul's suspension hearing leaves his teach-ers "dissatisfied and unhappy; humiliated to have felt so vindictive toward a mere boy" (217). Cather's empathetic tone points to her dichotomous view of the educational system, a view perhaps reflec-tive of the city's culture itself (Morris). Echoing Caesar's *Gallic Wars*, she had written in a 10 January 1897 article for the *Nebraska State Journal*, "Now all Pittsburgh is divided into two parts. Presbyteria and Bohemia, the former is much the larger and more influential kingdom of the two" ("Presbyteria and Bohemia" 505). At Central, Cather taught students from both kingdoms. While the number of Bohemian Pauls was likely smaller than the sons and daughters of Presbyteria, perhaps they better matched her own sentiments. She was enthusiastic about her profession, though, commenting to the astonishment of interviewers that she taught Latin because she liked it (Bloom 103). Teaching, she said, "suited her" (Robinson 106). Cather was known to have invited favorite students to her lodgings on Sunday afternoons for tea, and they recalled the warmth with which she entertained them. They recognized and appreciated her interest in them as an endorsement of their potential both as scholars and as young people of social refinement.

Still, we know that she had an interest in those "other" students in her classes and those who made up the classes in competing high schools. Cather realized that the city's schools were not serving just students of the established middle class. In an 8 December 1901 column for the *Pittsburgh Gazette*, Cather described her experiences on Mulberry Street, an ethnically diverse area of the city where she did research for her column. There she observed the contrasting lives of Italians, Germans, Hebrews, and African Americans ("Pittsburgh's Mulberry Street" 871). Between 1901 and 1902, Cather also wrote for the *Gazette* a series of "investigative reports" on the city's ethnic communities, including Pittsburgh's Chinatown (Zhu and Bintrim 4). As a champion of immigrants she had known in Nebraska, how chagrined she must have been to have read the 1905 thirty-seventh annual report of the Pittsburgh Board of Education, indicating that the board was turning attention to the "education of the masses" and considered their teaching staff a "great standing army of peace, maintained to fight foreignism, illiteracy, and vice" (qtd. in DeVault 39). The fight against illiteracy Cather would have embraced, but she would not have seen herself as a teacher-soldier fighting against "foreignism" and its compatriot "vice." At the time, the term "foreignism" connoted fear of recent working-class immigrants who chose not to assimilate or to embrace Americanism in language and religion but to retain their cultural identity and customs. Such "foreigners" were often cited in the press as involved in corruption and criminal activities, as well.

As a result, Pittsburgh schools were undergoing growing pains, grasping at ways to deal with the city's burgeoning diversity while trying desperately to provide workers to feed the maw of their industrial complex. Truancy was a problem, something Cather recounts in "Paul's Case." In 1895 a state law made public school attendance compulsory for ages eight to thirteen, yet only five years later, although attendance levels were steadily rising, Pittsburgh still had "one of

the lowest high school attendance rates of large U.S. cities" (Kleinberg 125, 131). Paul is a product of the rising middle class that, while
sending its children to high school, often in the rigorous academic
program, valued money-making over the liberal and fine arts.

In response to these crises and other problems, the Pittsburgh
School Board took action. In 1904 the teachers launched a petition
campaigning for higher wages, merit pay increases, and retirement
programs. Whether or not Cather signed those petitions is unknown.
The school board, however, responded to the teachers' concerns by
establishing a Teachers' Salary Commission, raising yearly salaries,
setting up a class system based on experience and training, and
putting in place a graduated salary scale (Greenwald 42–43). These
reforms would have been welcome news to women teachers like
Cather whose wages had been "tailored to meet the needs of single
women, not career-minded professionals" (Greenwald 42). Salary levels for women teachers had been depressed as the number of women
attending normal schools increased and as the number of graduates
exceeded the number of available entry-level teaching positions.
This situation led to "higher unemployment rates for teachers than
of other women workers at the turn of the century" (Kleinberg 153).

The school board also faced the perpetual problem of money
management. Charles Reisfar, father of a Central High student in
Cather's classes and secretary of the board, presented the financial
case for the high schools on February 1, 1902. Asking for a $861,280
outlay of monies, Reisfar earmarked $700,000 for teachers' salaries,
$3,000 for repairs to the high school's physical plant, $1,000 for fuel,
$2,500 for janitor services, $100 for the library, $2,300 for furniture,
$600 for books, and $1,000 for high school athletics (*Municipal Record*
402). Reflecting social interests of the day, athletics was now a bud-
geted line item. The popular annual exposition in Exposition Park
is evidence of those interests. What had once been an event to draw
the huge working class had, by 1890, "become an event of 'high culture,'" denying its original purpose of providing "popular" (i.e., for
the people) entertainment and instead appealing to the "aspiring
bourgeois spirit" of the rising middle class (Couvares 101). By the

turn of the century, sport therefore became central to reinvigorating the exposition's original purpose. Sports clubs sprouted up throughout the city in "revolt against bourgeois gentility and Protestant repression" (Couvares 102), the latter of which Cather commented on critically, but amusedly, during her stay at the Axtells' home (see her letter to Ellen Gere of 29 June 1896).[1]

For the rising middle class of Pittsburgh, Sunday afternoons were often their sole opportunity to encounter the arts or to engage in sport. Sport, like music, offered relief from the humdrum work place, and boys and girls alike were strongly encouraged to "exert themselves physically." All this led to a trend toward "middle-class sport" (Couvares 102–3), something the schools were forced to acknowledge and embrace. In 1880 team sports flourished at Central High School, including football, baseball, hockey, and girls' basketball. By 1889 the school had "standardized cheers, colors, mottoes, and insignia" (Couvares 103). One can imagine Cather being pleased with this organized display of physical vigor at the school. After all, she had pumped hand cars, ridden horses, and raced Pittsburgh street cars on her bicycle (*Selected Letters* 39). Her interest in sport even appears in an early story, "The Fear That Walks by Noonday," published in the University of Nebraska *Sombrero* in 1895. Not only did Cather attend university games, but she also knew something about football, naming positions and play strategies. She recognized the energy of youth, whether on the playing fields of Lincoln or in the vigorous environs of Pittsburgh and knew that such energy demanded an outlet. Pittsburgh had growing pains and was, like Chicago, "proud to be alive and coarse and strong and cunning. / . . . Laughing the stormy, husky, brawling laughter of / Youth" (Sandburg 3–4).

Cather's students, male students in particular, were caught up in this cultural emphasis on hale and hearty physical activity and were attuned to the Teddy Roosevelt Rough Rider mentality that was sweeping the nation. For her teenage readers, the *American Boy* magazine was the gospel, something of which Cather, as a budding journalist, must have been aware. Just as athletic clubs began springing up throughout the Pittsburgh area, so did American Boy

Clubs draw the preteens and teens. Like nearly every major city and small town in America, Pittsburgh sported a number of clubs of the "Great American Boy Army," groups devoted to developing "manliness in muscle, mind and morals" ("Great American" 120–21). The May 1903 issue sported a Young Rough Rider on its cover and included a photo of the Pittsburgh "Rough Riders," a troop of boys ages eight to twelve, wearing full western regalia and on horseback ("Pittsburg 'Rough'" 219). This spirit of sport, play, athleticism, and daring was a strong attraction for Cather's students. When Cather created her protagonist in "Paul's Case," though, she drew a portrait of a teenager who was an antithesis to this cultural norm. Paul is a misfit among his peers; he is drawn to the theater, not the playing field. Music, not touchdowns, fires his imagination. He stands apart from the prototype of the American Boy.

The magazine also reflected the values that shaped the shift in education from classical to so-called practical learning. Each issue profiled the boyhood of a successful man such as Rockefeller, Carnegie, Heinz, or Chicago meatpacker Armour. Often quoting their advice, even if posthumously, the magazine offered models of success who told youth that "this is the country of the young. We can't help the past, but we can look out for the future" ("Sayings" 224). Carnegie is lauded for his "good penmanship" and "knowledge of arithmetic" that "gave him a chance to secure a clerical position, and this was given up that he might learn telegraphy" (Harbour 211). Articles stressed that a boy should seek work in railroading, engineering, telegraphy, electricity, bookkeeping, printing, or drafting. Regular monthly columns were titled "Boys as Money Makers, Money Savers," "Boys in Games and Sport," and "The Boy Photographer." America was on the move, away from traditional courses of learning and toward reading and study that would make businessmen and athletes of the younger generation. In such a climate, most of Cather's students would prefer to become an Alexander Bartley, successful engineer even if failed man, to being Horatius at the Bridge. In "Paul's Case," Cather describes the neighborhood fathers who embrace this gospel of progress and recount to one another "legends of the iron kings [punctuated] with remarks about their sons' progress at school, their grades in arithmetic, and the amounts they had saved in their toy banks" (227). While Paul "rather like[s] to hear these legends . . . that were told and retold on Sundays and holidays," he has no interest in struggling through the "cash-boy stage" to reach the pinnacle of success in business (229).

In 1905, Cather's last year of teaching, the *American Boy* had garnered its place in the national consciousness, along with all the accompanying values of hard work, physical hardiness, and inventive genius. The American boy was destined to become a Tom Edison, Andrew Carnegie, Cy Young, or Richard Byrd. Little if any mention is made in any issue of the *American Boy* at this time of finishing school so as to become a liberally educated man. Rather, the goal of getting an education was to become a respected businessman and subsequently to become wealthy enough to embrace Carnegie's directive to share with others the "sacred trust" of one's wealth. Paul's defiant attitude in school results in his being "taken out of school and put to work" (235), the accepted solution to setting him on the right path to becoming like the young man whom his father held up as a model—a previously slightly "dissipated" youth who was now a "clerk to one of the magnates of a great steel corporation" (228).

Cather would later attack these changes in education through the words of Professor Godfrey St. Peter in *The Professor's House*. He is dismayed at the commercialization of education and is exhausted by the "old fight to keep up the standard of scholarship, to prevent the younger professors . . . from farming the whole institution out to athletics, and to the agricultural and commercial schools favoured and fostered by the State Legislature" (58). Professor St. Peter comments to his younger colleague Professor Langtry that "there have been many changes" at the college in recent years, "and not all of them are good" (54). The incredulous Langtry can't grasp what the Professor means when saying that the current crop of students is different from those of earlier years, a more "common sort" (54). This shift occurred in Central High's and later Allegheny High's population, as well. While supportive of the city's effort to offer educational opportunities to the working class, and particularly to immigrant families, Cather knew the Commercial High School on Fifth Avenue competed with her own, attracting capable young minds to the god of Mammon rather than to Apollo and the Muses. In "The Professor's Commencement" Professor Graves, an early sketch of Professor St. Peter, knows what Cather knows. She saw the lure of Mammon pulling especially immigrant youth from the liberal arts that would free them, that would, as the Professor says, "secure [for them] the rights of youth; the right to be generous, to dream, to enjoy" ("Professor's Commencement" 484). "They were boys and girls from the factories and offices, destined to return thither, and hypnotized by the glitter of yellow metal"; they were "practical, provident, unimaginative, and mercenary at sixteen" (484). He hopes and believes that he has over the years given to at least some of his students "a vital element that their environment failed to give them." But, the Professor admits, "[T]his city is a disputed strategic point. . . . It controls a vast manufacturing region given over to sordid and materialistic ideals. . . . I suppose we shall win in the end, but the reign of Mammon has been long and oppressive" (483).

The flood of students to the Commercial Department of the Pittsburgh high schools also resulted in a decline of program quality during Cather's tenure. Students who failed the entrance exams were often admitted simply to meet the demand of filling office jobs in the city (DeVault 33). By 1903, the ten skyscrapers in the city skyline (DeVault 144) were full of bookkeepers, typists, and stenographers. Fourth Avenue was called "the Wall Street of Pittsburgh," and there were in 1905 more typewriters in Pittsburgh than in any other American city, except New York (DeVault 144, 1). One instantly recalls the picture of Cather herself hunched over her typewriter as she worked, sometimes feverishly, to meet deadlines for columns in the *Pittsburgh Leader* or *The Home Monthly*.

Both Cather and some of her colleagues were caught in this transition from classical education, as that which distinguished the learned and professional class from the working class, to commercial education, as the only course for success in turn-of-the-century Amer-

Fig. 4.1. *Prof. Frederick Merrick*, from *My High School Days* by George Thornton Fleming, Press of William G. Johnston, 1904.

ica. Professor Frederick Merrick was one such colleague.[2] He was a legend when Cather arrived at Central High School in the spring of 1901. Hired first in 1871 to teach Latin, Professor Merrick eventually chaired the Math Department and served thirty years before resigning in December of 1900. Cather likely replaced him, at least with part of her teaching load, notably the course in algebra, which was a trial for her.

Professor Emerson Graves, as Cather describes him in "The Professor's Commencement," embodies many of the characteristics of the beloved Professor Frederick Merrick, to whom the Class of 1880 paid tribute in their twenty-fifth reunion class book. Like Professor Graves, who feels "distraught and weary" ("Professor's Commencement" 482), the aging Professor Merrick resigned "on account of the need of rest from mental labors" (Fleming 205). He is remembered as a "courtly professor—ever gentlemanly and kind" (Fleming 207), a "very dignified man of fine fibre" (Bingham 17). His photograph shows a silver-haired man with kind and expressive eyes, not unlike his literary counterpart whose slight build and silver-white hair made him memorable to this students "long after they had forgotten the things he endeavored to teach them" ("Professor's Commencement" 481). As Professor Graves looks back on his teaching career so similar to Professor Merrick's, he uses the language of battle to describe the struggle he has undergone for the sake of the young people in his classroom. On his last morning at the school he feels the call of duty as he has never before felt it, on the very day "he was to lay down his arms" (484). At his farewell dinner he sees his colleagues not as just old men but as "spent warriors" (487), and he ironically stumbles once more in an effort to recite the story of "Horatius at the Bridge."

While Cather could not have read the Class of 1880 reunion book from 1905 prior to writing "The Professor's Commencement" (published 1902), included in that class book is an open letter from the retired Professor Merrick. In response to his students' inquiries, he, in words akin to Professor Graves's, responds that he had fought the good fight. He says that he is flattered by their praises but is conscious of "the weak and trembling battle that I have sometimes, as the boys say, put up" (Bingham 97). Like Cather's Professor Graves, Merrick labored "in the garden of youth" for "motives Quixotic to an absurdity" ("Professor's Commencement" 483, 482).

Cather likely did not know Professor Merrick personally since after retiring he removed to his hometown in Massachusetts. His reputation, though, remained, and some of his former students still attended Central and likely were in Cather's classes. Many of his former colleagues were also still on staff. How much of Merrick appears in Cather's portrait of the Professor in "The Professor's Commencement" is arguable, but the Professor's case presents a sense of what surrounded Cather as she held her first teaching position. She experienced education shifting toward acquiring "mechanical skills and the making of money" rather than "to an examination of moral values and the traditional liberal arts" (Bloom 102). She viewed education as "the last refuge of traditional values" and felt that "in the secondary schools attention to the classics was probably even more perfunctory" than in the universities (103).

Cather was apparently not alone in worrying about the loss of traditional areas of study and culture for both the youth and the residents of her adopted home. This was a major growing pain for the city itself: How could it provide more than just jobs and money for its people? From where would exposure to the arts come? How could Pittsburgh compete with Eastern Seaboard cities in culture, music, and the arts? Pittsburgh already had more money. In the lingo of the day, the oft-used phrase "He's a 'Pittsburgh man'" evoked at once an image of wealth and power (DeVault 168). The captains of industry, though, were not the only ones who worried. Cather found herself surrounded by civic-minded women of Pittsburgh whose goal was to address these questions and to promote civic and sociological advancement "in every possible way" (Civic Club iv).

Groups like the Civic Club of Allegheny County (CCAC) committed themselves to "moral environmentalism" as well as to "urban progressivism" (Bauman and Spratt 153). Moral uplift of the rapidly changing, cosmopolitan city was sorely needed, and the women envisioned themselves as the ones to do it. The Education Department of this group "led a move to open several school playgrounds for the public use," including one at Central High School (Bauman and Spratt 177); they established recreational parks throughout the city, and in conjunction with the Central School Board built public libraries, gyms, baths, and game rooms. The Civic Club "open[ed] the school yards as playgrounds" and provided swings and sandboxes; they employed teachers to direct games, conduct story time, and watch over free play. The Civic Club also initiated reform policies for everything from child labor laws and juvenile courts to pure water and smoke ordinances. But the arts were not a major player in their agenda, and not all their projects achieved the hoped-for success. Both playground workers and librarians "paid little more than 'lip service'" (Couvares 115) to the goal of moral uplift. Many librarians did "little more than read stories and fairy tales to children," turning the libraries themselves into "pleasant place[s] staffed by pleasant people into whose hands children could be safely deposited for a few hours on weekends" (Couvares 115). Cather, who as a girl had entertained her younger siblings with fanciful stories, knew that stories alone would not launch children into a lifelong love of learning and literary appreciation.

Three amusement parks built between 1900 and 1910 (Couvares 222), dance halls, skating rinks, and public parks all proved more enticing to youth than did playgrounds and libraries. Theaters, including at least one that featured a local acting troupe, were sprouting up throughout the city and were equally alluring, as Cather knew and described in "Paul's Case." In his position as an usher at Carnegie Hall, Paul becomes "vivacious and animated" (219), a far cry from his cynical and flippant schoolboy self: The "first sigh of the instruments seemed to free some hilarious and potent spirit within him.... He felt a sudden zest of life" (220). The "delicious excitement" that comes to him in the concert hall is, he muses, "the only thing that could be called living at all" (221). In what Cather describes as the twelve-story Schenley Hotel, looming across the street, he imagines a life of ease and exotic beauty, and the stage entrance becomes for him "the actual portal of Romance" (232). After being backstage, he finds "the school-room more than ever repulsive" (233). The trivial question in his Latin class of prepositions that govern the dative is meaningless to him. Many of Cather's students came from homes like Paul's on other Cordelia Streets and longed for escape into a world of romance and beauty, something theater could offer them, even if temporarily. But local theater companies were being sorely taxed by their competition. By the late 1880s "impressive touring shows of the New York and Philadelphia syndicates" had smothered local stock companies as the rising middle class demanded more spectacle and glamor (Couvares 121). Bourgeois patrons "demanded more exclusive fare," while "poor alien audiences, unfamiliar with the conventions of theatrical comedy and melodrama" (Couvares 121), preferred the comedy of vaudeville. Paul was of the first class, lured by the splendor of professional touring troupes and befriending stock company players like Charley Edwards. The less cultured gravitated to the burlesque and variety shows springing up throughout the city.

Both these forms of entertainment, however, were under threat. In 1905 John Harris, proprietor of highly successful ten-cent houses in Pittsburgh, built the "first all-motion picture theater" in America (Couvares 122). But the moving picture had by then already made its presence known in the city. As early as 1896, the year that Cather arrived in Pittsburgh, theaters like the Bijou, as well as smaller venues, were experimenting with showing cinematic clips, using either Edison's "Marvelous Vitascope" or the French Cinèmatographe (Aronson 28). By the time Cather left Pittsburgh in 1906, forty-five, full-fledged "nickel theaters were paying for annual city operating licenses" (212). While the allure of the moving picture may not have yet been widespread among her students, fascination with the movies had begun. Costing only a nickel, this new form of entertainment offered equitable access to youth of all classes, and even reformers of the day, concerned about the moral and cultural impact of this new phenomenon, generally considered the movies "less socially problematic" than the saloon and pool halls that lined areas like the Strip District (Aronson 13).

For teenagers in her classrooms, the imminent arrival of the nickelodeon was, no doubt, like that of the iPhone for today's youth. But for sensitive culturalists like Paul, the movies signaled the death of all that was marvelous about live theater. Nonetheless, the Saturday evening picture show provided escape and consolation, a place to glimpse a side of life that many young people felt had been denied them (Couvares 122). In her 1929 letter to Harvey Newbranch, a friend since her university days and editor of the *Omaha World Her-ald*, Cather lauded the "old traveling companies" who put on "cred-itable performance[s]," and she expressed regret that that they had come to an end (*Willa Cather in Person* 185). She concedes, though, that the "screen drama [has] a great deal to be said in its favor" but is a very different thing from a play (186). She concludes that mov-ies are "a fine kind of 'entertainment' and are an ideal diversion for the tired business man" but that only "real people speaking the lines can give us that feeling of living along with them" (187). The mov-ies were, however, here to stay, and the students in Cather's classes had embarked upon a new way of learning about the world, one devoid, perhaps, of deep emotions and the firing of the imagination that mark us as human.

Like the movies, the three amusement parks of the city continued to attract large audiences, particularly young people and working-class crowds. When Dream City, "the larger of the two East End parks, opened on Memorial Day, 1906," thirty-seven thousand people poured in (Couvares 122). But, neither the cinema nor the parks were venues for the arts. Whereas Pittsburgh had long boasted museums where students could expand their appreciation of fine art, it would take Carnegie himself to put Pittsburgh on the map as a center of the arts equal to the larger, Eastern Seaboard cities. Embracing an Arnoldian "Gospel of Art," Carnegie established his International Exhibitions in 1895, encouraging artists to display their works in Pittsburgh in competition with one another and promoting a national American art (Neal 9, 14). His was an experiment in "cultural uplift" with hopes of "spiritualiz[ing] the local populace" (Neal 14). Concerned that the young people had little access to great art, Carnegie organized and encouraged visits by secondary school classes, and within one year of the institute's opening, "such field trips were common and there were even visits from public schools in which art formed no special part of the curriculum" (Neal 47–48). A survey of curricular offerings at Central High School shows, though, that freshmen in the academic course were required to take drawing (Fleming 219). Paul of "Paul's Case" is one such student. Cather recounts his drawing master's frustration over this boy whom he could neither understand nor reach. Paul dozes at his drawing board, and his art teacher's despair is evident in the declaration that "there is something wrong about the fellow" (217). Not all students could be reached by the opportunity to engage in the arts, as Cather well knew. Problem students did exist, and a teacher's life—whether Cather's, Paul's instructor's, or Professor Graves's—was sometimes rife with disappointments. The city, however, was ready and eager to prove itself a place of culture and refinement. Coupled with a thriving venue of concert halls and professional musicians, Pittsburgh came into its own as a city that knew and loved the arts, and not just the smell of money. As Joseph Murphy points out, "Carnegie's concert hall, museum, and library in Pittsburgh's Oakland section" became an "important refuge for Cather on the ground as for her protagonist in 'Paul's Case'" (6).

In this atmosphere of a city struggling to find itself, Cather began her teaching career. We are a part of all that we have met, the Professor remarks in "The Professor's Commencement," alluding to a line from Tennyson's "Ulysses" (481). Like the Professor, Cather persisted in teaching the classics to her students and insisted on their importance in shaping a liberally educated person. As late as 1939, in a letter to the editor of the College English Association, Cather noted that unless American boys "read the great English classics in high school and in college, they never find time to read them" (*Willa Cather in Person* 190–91). She then asserts, "I think we should all, in our school days, be given a chance at [the classics]" (191). Like her students, though, she found herself strolling in the parks of a vibrant city, seeing beyond the smoke and clamor, preparing herself for a world much different from that of her parents. In her Pittsburgh teaching years, Cather observed the effects on her students of rapid social and cultural changes and the corresponding effect on public education itself. But she, like Pittsburgh, forged ahead. She would continue in her later works, like *My Ántonia*, to embrace otherness and diversity, to defend classical education through the voice of Professor Godfrey St. Peter, to criticize rampant materialism in *One of Ours* and *A Lost Lady*, and to champion the arts in works like *The Song of the Lark* and "Uncle Valentine" (1925). The direction for Cather's body of fiction was thus shaped, in part, by both her early experiences in a city where change proved inevitable and by her time in a classroom, the training ground not only for her students but also for herself.

## NOTES

1. The dating of this letter as June 29, 1896, rather than July 27, 1896, as shown in Jewell and Stout's *The Selected Letters of Willa Cather*, follows the revisionist timeline discovery of Kimberly and Brett Vanderlaan in regard to Cather's arrival in Pittsburgh (see Bintrim et al.). Jewell, in the same article, approves and endorses this date as accurate.

2. Cather may have drawn on Professor Merrick's name for her character's surname in "The Sculptor's Funeral" (1905). The deceased Harvey Merrick of that story was, like Professor Merrick, a sensitive and gentle man who confronted a culture that did not embrace the values he espoused. Like Professor Merrick, Harvey is a "master" ("Sculptor's Funeral" 69, 78) to his students and faced in his hometown "a desert of newness and ugliness and sordidness, for all that is chastened and old, and noble with traditions" (73). Like Professor Merrick's literary counterpart, Professor Graves in "The Professor's Commencement," Harvey Merrick confronted pressures to learn business rather than to pursue art, to discard the classics for profit-making, much as did Professor Graves's students in Pittsburgh.

## WORKS CITED

Aronson, Michael. *Nickelodeon City: Pittsburgh at the Movies 1905–1929*. U of Pittsburgh P, 2008.

Bauman, John F., and Margaret Spratt. "Civic Leaders and Environmental Reform: The Pittsburgh Survey and Urban Planning." *Pittsburgh Surveyed: Social Science and Social Reform in the Early Twentieth Century*, edited by Maurine W. Greenwald and Margo Anderson, U of Pittsburgh P, 1996, pp. 153–69.

Bingham, John, ed. *Class Book, the Class of 1880, Pittsburgh Central High School, Academical Department*. Murdoch, Kerr, 1906, http://books.google.com.

Bintrim, Timothy, et al. "'Beginning a New Life': Discovering the Exact Date of Cather's Arrival in Pittsburgh." *Willa Cather Newsletter and Review*, vol. 58, no. 3, 2016, pp. 31–36.

Bloom, Edward A., and Lillian D. Bloom. *Willa Cather's Gift of Sympathy*. Southern Illinois UP, 1962.

Cather, Willa. "Paul's Case: A Study in Temperament." *The Troll Garden*, McClure, Phillips, 1905, pp. 213–52.

———. "Pittsburgh's Mulberry Street." *The World and the Parish: Willa Cather's Articles and Reviews, 1893–1902*, edited by William M. Curtin, U of Nebraska P, 1970, pp. 2: 869–74.

———. "Presbyteria and Bohemia." *The World and the Parish: Willa Cather's Articles and Reviews, 1893–1902*, edited by William M. Curtin, U of Nebraska P, 1970. pp. 2: 504–6.

———. "The Professor's Commencement." *New England Magazine*, vol. 26, June 1902, pp. 481–88.

———. *The Professor's House*. Willa Cather Scholarly Edition, edited by James Woodress, Kari A. Ronning, and Frederick M. Link, U of Nebraska P, 2002.

———. "The Sculptor's Funeral." *The Troll Garden*, McClure, Phillips, 1905, pp. 57–84.

———. *The Selected Letters of Willa Cather*. Edited by Andrew Jewell and Janis Stout, Knopf, 2013.

———. *Willa Cather in Person: Interviews, Speeches, and Letters*. Edited by L. Brent Bohlke, U of Nebraska P, 1986.

Civic Club of Allegheny County, Pittsburgh, Pennsylvania. *Fifteen Years of Civic History, October 1895-December 1910*. Nicholson Printing, 1910, HathiTrust Digital Library, www.babel.hathitrust.org/cgi/pt?id=hvd .32044019964089.

Couvares, Francis G. *The Remaking of Pittsburgh: Class and Culture in an Industrializing City, 1877–1919*. State U of New York P, 1984.

DeVault, Ileen A. *Sons and Daughters of Labor: Class and Clerical Work in Turn-of-the-Century Pittsburgh*. Cornell UP, 1991.

Fleming, George Thornton. *My High School Days: Including a Brief History of Pittsburgh Central High School from 1855–1871 and Addenda*. Press of William G. Johnston, 1904, http://www.books.google.com.

"The Great American Boy Army." *The American Boy*, vol. 4, no. 4, 1903, pp. 120–21.

Greenwald, Maurine Weimer. "Women and Class in Pittsburgh, 1850–1920." *City at the Point: Essays on the Social History of Pittsburgh*, edited by Samuel P. Hays, U of Pittsburgh P, 1989, pp. 33–67.

Harbour, J. L. "A Great Giver and His Home." *The American Boy*, vol. 6, no. 7, 1905, p. 211.

Kleinberg, S. J. *The Shadow of the Mills: Working-Class Families in Pittsburgh, 1870–1907*. U of Pittsburgh P, 1989.

Kristufek, Richard. *The Immigrant and the Pittsburgh Public Schools: 1870–1940*. 1975. U of Pittsburgh, PhD dissertation. ProQuest Dissertations and Theses Publishing.

Kvasnicka, Mellanee. *Education in the Parish/Preparation for the World: The Educational Tradition in the Life and Works of Willa Cather*. 1997. U of Nebraska, PhD dissertation. ProQuest Dissertations and Theses Publishing.

Morris, Sue. "The Historical Dilettante: Pittsburgh's Central High School." *Blogger*, 3 March 2017, www.historicaldilettante.blogspot.com/2017/03/things-that-arent-there-any-more.html.

*Municipal Record, Proceedings of Common Council of the City of Pittsburgh*, vol. 34, no. 24, 1902, http://www.books.google.com.

Murphy, Joseph C. "The Dialectics of Seeing in Cather's Pittsburgh: 'Double Birthday' and Urban Allegory." *Cather Studies 7: Willa Cather as Cultural Icon*, edited by Guy Reynolds, U of Nebraska P, 2007, pp. 253–68.

Neal, Kenneth. *A Wise Extravagance: The Founding of the Carnegie International Exhibitions, 1895–1901*. U of Pittsburgh P, 1996.

Nevin, Theodore W. *Pittsburg and the Men Who Made It*. 1904. HathiTrust Digital Library, www.babel.hathitrust.org/cgi/pt?id=nyp.334330818188878;view=1up;seq=7.

"Pittsburg 'Rough Riders.'" *The American Boy*, vol. 4, no. 7, 1903, p. 219.

Robinson, Phyllis C. *Willa: The Life of Willa Cather*. Doubleday, 1983.

Sandburg, Carl. "Chicago." *Chicago Poems*, U of Illinois P, 1992, pp. 3–4.

"Sayings of the Late P. D. Armour." *The American Boy*, vol. 4, no. 7, 1903, p. 224.

White, Edward, editor. *150 Years of Unparalleled Thrift: Pittsburgh Sesqui-Centennial Chronicling a Development from a Frontier Camp to a Mighty City: Official History and Programme*. Issued by Executive Committee, 1908. HathiTrust Digital Library, www.babel.hathitrust.org/ cgi/pt?id=loc.arlc/13960/t9p27pk73,view=1up;seq-9.

Zhu, Li, and Timothy Bintrim. "The Chinese Connection: Cather and Pittsburgh's Chinatown." *Willa Cather Pioneer Memorial Newsletter and Review*, vol. 42, no. 1, 1998, pp. 1–5.

## 5  Big Steel and Class Consciousness in "Paul's Case"

CHARMION GUSTKE

Class consciousness, George Lukács proposes, is a systematic practice governing the whole of life. As the driving force behind capitalism, class consciousness guides individuals in their day-to-day activities as they navigate class distinctions and the materiality of history. From the beginning of his analysis, Lukács emphasizes, as did Karl Marx, that class consciousness is constructed in relation to economic conditions and the social institutions created by these conditions, which combine to form the ideological struggles of a profit-driven society.[1] This ideology, made visible through the public structures it creates, is a product of power and embodies the aesthetic appeal and illusory attraction of any philosophy or work of art. "Regarded abstractly and formally, then, class consciousness implies a class-conditioned *unconsciousness* of one's own socio-historical and economic condition" (Lukács 52). Producing an ongoing contradiction between our (un)conscious thoughts and actions and the interests of capital, capitalism depends on class signifiers for order and control in a world where, as the Pittsburgh teenager Paul comes to realize, "money was everything, the wall that stood between all he loathed and all he wanted" (232). While class consciousness may inspire the individual to strive to achieve success, it may also have the reverse effect, as it does in "Paul's Case," causing the subject not only to resist the demands of labor, but to rebel against them in an attempt to disrupt the directives constituted by capitalism. "Paul's Case," entrenched in the social economy of turn-of-the-century Pittsburgh, is a study of the ways in which this latter form of resistance, this "revolt against the homilies by which the world is run" (234), is an inevitable yet futile response to the inequities of a class-based society.

Although all U.S. cities faced the divergences of capitalism at the end of the nineteenth century, Pittsburgh, due to its unparalleled success in the steel industry and the philanthropic influence of tycoons such as Andrew Carnegie and Henry Clay Frick, embodied the conflicts of capitalism in a way few other industrialized cities did, permitting the inherent disparities of class to play out against the backdrop of a fin-de-siècle aestheticism propagated by privilege and exclusion. I examine these contradictions through an analysis of three landmarks essential to the development of Cather's experience of the American class system: Pittsburgh's Central High School, the Carnegie Music Hall, and the Hotel Schenley. These places and their economic histories, when read in relation to Paul's class consciousness, delineate the impact Cather's time in Pittsburgh had in forming her early understanding of the dynamics of wealth and social mobility.

Upon moving to Pittsburgh in 1896, Cather saw firsthand how the "City of Dreadful Dirt" (*Selected Letters* 33) was transformed into a cultured, yet conflict-ridden metropolis with elastic class divisions and a thriving art scene. The city's transformation was due in large part to the reform efforts of the urban elite living in Pittsburgh's East End neighborhoods, which, by 1900, were among the world's richest suburbs (Skrabec 9). Unlike the aristocracy of New York's Fifth Avenue, many of whom inherited their place in the world, the majority of Pittsburgh's ruling class was from Scottish and Irish immigrant families who earned their wealth through hard work, industry, and inventiveness. According to Edward K. Muller and John F. Bauman, prosperous Pittsburgh families, inspired by the City Beautiful Movement of the late nineteenth century, "espoused a philosophy that equated environmental quality with elevated moral behavior" (132). Disgusted by the tangle of "streets, mills, department stores, rail yards, warehouses, courthouses, jails" and the web of slum housing in the central city, these reformers embarked on a crusade for municipal improvement, creating parks, removing billboards, and installing public baths to better represent the standards of good taste and to extend the order of the East End to downtown Pittsburgh (Muller 123).[2] These developments were accompanied by the continued efforts of the glass, steel, coal, oil, and banking giants to create a sophisticated city in which their industries could thrive. As Francis G. Couvares states, Pittsburgh capitalists understood that "civic improvement was just good business" (95). These benefits, however, were not extended into the community judiciously. Localized renewal ultimately functioned to isolate workers living in increasingly sectionalized boroughs, deepening the divide between the suburban neighborhoods and the proletarian districts.

The city's inequitable distribution of wealth, as the *Pittsburgh Survey* revealed, was magnified by its topography, with its hills, ravines, floodplains and bluffs, making it difficult for immigrant families to fully engage in civic life (18). This geographical exclusion was mirrored in the workplace, where capital controlled labor by pitting workers in competition with one another, successfully instilling segregation and discrimination into the fabric of the community. Carnegie's introduction of cost-saving technologies further split laborers into skilled and unskilled categories, spreading friction and hostility among workers, departments, and neighborhoods. The Homestead plant and town, which Cather visited in 1898 and wrote about as the guest editor of the *Courier* in 1901, illustrates the alarming consequences of these advancements and the social hierarchies they produced. In her article "The Real Homestead," Cather discusses the wage and living discrepancies between the skilled chemists and draftsmen on one hand, and the unskilled day laborers on the other, who suffer the greatest of indignities during the notorious "double turn": "There are plenty of cases on record where a substitute stood his ground for sixty-four hours without sleep and with few breathing spells. It would seem that Mr. Carnegie's sense of humor must be deficient when he supplies Herbert Spencer and Wagner for these men" (857). Referring to the opulent Carnegie Library of Homestead, outfitted with a music hall, swimming pool, and billiard room, Cather is pinpointing one of the essential incongruencies generated by the "benevolence" of the industrial elite who exhibit art and present music in elaborate spaces when the majority of their workers are overworked and underpaid. She plainly states that the men and women working at the plant and raising families at Homestead have no "margin left" in their lives for social relaxation. Due to the stress and demands on their labor, their free time is so limited "that clubs and libraries established in their interests seem almost absurdities" (856).

From the perspective of the union workers, the challenging working conditions at Homestead went well beyond the unevenly distributed luxuries of the library and began when Carnegie introduced the open-hearth facility. Although this innovation brought incomparable commercial success, the low placement of the furnaces was a "return to some of the most nightmarish concepts and consequences" of plant and pit work (Kobus 173). The nation received a detailed account of the hazardous "man-killing" working conditions at Homestead through an article published in *McClure's* in 1894 by an anonymous workman who painstakingly exposed life in the "frightfully hot pit," in which the laborers' "clothes smoke" and "the skin contracts and seems about to burst" (qtd. in Kobus 177–78). The increased mechanization of the steel industry brought "jobs so physically demanding that the work was nearly impossible to accomplish without an extremely low-paid crew that quickly became depleted by the brutal conditions" (Kobus 179). As the labor force continued to be populated by men with fewer skills, the unions, representing generations of craftsmen, lost power while management and employers gained the financial dominance of increased productivity.

The tension between laborers and bosses culminated in the Homestead Strike of 1892, during which the Amalgamated Association of Iron and Steel Workers fought against the Carnegie Steel Company, led by the formidable Henry Clay Frick. The drama and violence of the strike, exacerbated by Carnegie's use of Pinkertons and then National Guardsmen to break the union, greatly weakened labor organization in the mills and forever changed the contour of working-class neighborhoods. Most notably, as more immigrants with distinct languages and cultures took these jobs, steel masters further segregated the city by playing groups against one another in order to squelch organizing across ethnic lines. While Big Steel continued to expand, metropolitan Pittsburgh became demarcated by new configurations of class and ethnicity as Slavs, Italians, and African Americans from the South replaced the Irish, German, Welsh, and English who had moved up the ranks of the work force and established themselves in the streetcar suburbs as middle-class Americans. With a rising leisure class and a vast and alienated polyglot work force, turn-of-the-century Pittsburgh became a capitalists' haven motivated by the logic of labor surplus.

Moving easily between classes, Cather witnessed these vicissitudes and the imbalances they created, observing the way in which Pittsburgh's dominant members influenced everything from the city's culture and revenue to its politics and entertainment. Cather's initial experience of the city was "cut up between" long hours as the editor of *The Home Monthly* magazine and "the craziest possible diversions" such as bicycling and attending the local stock company productions at the New Grand Opera House Theater (*Selected Letters* 49). She spent many nights at the Carnegie Music Hall and the Casino Summer Theatre across the avenue during her first summer, and her life was, by her own account, more socially "pleasant than it ever" had been (*Selected Letters* 44). Nevertheless, she was often preoccupied by financial concerns and the need to balance her own sense of freedom with her work and personal commitments. In a letter to Mariel Gere, in 1898, Cather writes: "O I have grown enamoured of liberty! To be wholly free . . . to do with one's money what one likes, to help those

Fig. 5.1. *Central High School*, 1916, Pittsburgh Public Schools. Courtesy of Detre Library & Archives Division, Senator John Heinz History Center, Pittsburgh, Pennsylvania.

who have helped me, to pay the debts of one's loves and one's hates!" (*Selected Letters* 49). Cather's salient enthusiasm for the independence she gained in Pittsburgh is thus shadowed by the worrisome feeling that she owed her family and needed to send money home, placing fiscal strain on what was otherwise a happy period of her life.

Although Cather's financial burdens decreased in 1901 when she moved from a boardinghouse into the well-heeled home of Isabelle McClung and her parents, the social dichotomies of her life were magnified by her new teaching job at Central High School. Splitting her time between the affluent Squirrel Hill neighborhood and the densely populated Hill District in which Central was located, Cather's daily life was marked by both the economic boundaries of the city and a challenging work environment. The school, originally founded in 1855 as an exclusive "People's College," was once known, as Jake Oresick explains, for sending graduates to elite universities and was resented by the "working-class" public as a haven for wealthy students studying Roman mythology and Greek grammar while "their own children went to work at age fourteen" (6). By the time Cather began teaching there, however, the upper middle class were sending their sons to elite prep schools while immigrant families began to see the value of their children's extended education, causing the poorly maintained Bedford Avenue building to become overcrowded (Oresick 11), with every room having at least one-third more pupils than normal capacity (Oresick 171). The school's injurious facilities, cramped classrooms, and demanding curriculum exhausted Cather physically and mentally. As she tells George Seibel, she was so worn out by the "year's hard work," the horror of final exams, and the stifling heat that she was twenty pounds thinner and was left with that "good for nothing feeling" (*Selected Letters* 60).

The congested atmosphere of the decaying building was directly related to the astonishing evolution of capitalism in Pittsburgh and its contiguous growing population; more jobs lured more laborers and lowered wages, resulting in higher profits and hardened social hierarchies. As the population swelled and the downtown neighborhoods became increasingly dense, a new social geography was created; tensions between these classes and ethnicities were inevitable. The character of everyday life was thus experienced in relation to the pyramids structuring one's position and place in the mill, plant, or office. Neighborhoods like East Liberty, which is featured in "Paul's Case," were inhabited by like-minded families whose lives centered on productivity and gain. Accordingly, homogeneity and separation shape Paul's Pittsburgh, where each subdivision is clearly distinguished from the other. Take for example, Cordelia Street, modeled after Aurelia Street, which was made up of a "solid wall of elaborate Queen Anne homes" (Toker 250) with identical dormers:

> It was a highly respectable street, where all the houses were exactly alike, and where businessmen of moderate means

begot and reared large families of children, all of whom went
to Sabbath-school and learned the shorter catechism, and were
interested in arithmetic; all of whom were as exactly alike as
their homes, and of a piece with the monotony in which they
lived. (209)

There are no boundaries here among home, work, or church, as all
are appendages of capital, preparing children, with mathematical
precision and mechanical uniformity, to follow their fathers into
business; to produce is therefore also to reproduce. From the perspective of Paul, the lack of variation among the houses highlights
the uninteresting lives of the businessmen and their offspring who
stand in stark contrast to the local stock company and its colorful
performers.

    This distinction is exaggerated in the loathsome characteristics
Paul gives to his home and to his father: after a late night working
as an usher at the Carnegie Music Hall, Paul dreads returning to his
"ugly sleeping chamber; the cold bath-room with the grimy zinc
tub, the cracked mirror, the dripping spigots; his father at the top of
the stairs, his hairy legs sticking out from his nightshirt" (211). Paul's
heightened sensitivity to decay parallels his fear of middle-class masculinity as he chooses to sleep in the basement despite being wet,
cold, and "horribly afraid of rats" (210) so as to avoid his father's
questions about his late arrival home. This self-induced exile fuels
Paul's fear of potential violence as he envisions his father mistaking
him for an intruder and regretting "that there had been no warning cry to stay his hand" (211). Paul is simultaneously repulsed and
crudely fascinated with the brawny power of his father and extends
these conflicted feelings to the men of Cordelia Street, whom he
perceives as suffocating examples of the ethics of big business and
hard work: on a Sunday afternoon, paunchy men sit on their stoops
discussing prices and sharing tales of their wise "chiefs and over-
lords" (212). Intertwining "legends of the iron kings with remarks
about their sons' progress at school, their grades in arithmetic, and
the amounts they saved in their toy banks," the "burghers" of Cor-

delia Street fill their day of leisure with talk of work and the hope that their children, already attuned to the logic of numbers and the benefits of durable employment, will grow to surpass their fathers in wealth and status.

Like his neighbors, Paul's father is not poor, but has a "worthy ambition to come up in the world" (212) and wants his son to do the same. Paul's father hopes he will pattern himself in the footsteps of a young neighbor who is a clerk "to one of the magnates of a great steel corporation and was looked upon in Cordelia Street as a young man with a future" (213). Clerks were an essential part of the growing steel economy, replacing craftsmen as key players in the modern mill, with direct ties to management, resources, and production (Couvares 88). Carnegie claimed that "nothing was more profitable than clerks" for keeping track of workers in the mills, taking note of "who saved material, who wasted it, and who produced the best results" (qtd. in Couvares 88). At once bookkeeper and informant, Paul's neighbor represents everything Paul does not want to be: a "mere rivet in the machine" (226). Having sired children with an unattractive wife, the young man abdicated the rights of youth to devote himself to his career and his boss, who is currently cruising on a yacht in the Mediterranean, heroically working as much on his vacation as he does at home (213). While Paul finds his father's "wholesome advice as to how to succeed in life" tedious (216), he is charmed by the "triumphs of cash boys who had become famous," savoring the "high play at Monte Carlo," while having "no mind for the cash-boy stage" (214).[3] These stories of luxury and excess fuse with Paul's vivid imagination, intensified by the stimuli of Carnegie Hall, to create Paul's sense of himself as distinct from the practical men of Cordelia Street.

This aversion to middle-class authority is most striking at school, where Paul's class consciousness proves to be the governing force of his temperament. After all, Cather establishes Paul's character not in the streets of Pittsburgh but in the principal's office of Pittsburgh High School where he is being reprimanded for "various misdemeanours" (199). From the moment the story opens, there is a disconnect between the insurgent Paul, who disrupts the seriousness of the occasion with his suave demeanor and theatrical dress, and the rigidity of the authorities who state their concerns with "rancour and aggrievedness" (200). Paul responds to the charges as he does to all confrontations not just by lying, but also by brandishing his flamboyant disregard for rules and regulations: "he seemingly made not the least effort to conceal" his condescension; his "physical aversion" to his teachers was "involuntary and definitely personal" (200–201). The instructors are so disturbed by Paul's lack of contrition and by his impertinence that they leave the "inquisition" in despair and humiliation, unable to fully "put into words the real cause of the trouble" (200). While the thing not named here may allude to Paul's adolescent sexual indeterminacy, as Chang-Hao Ku maintains, or the "gender liminality" betraying his homosexuality, as Eve Sedgwick suggests, it is also Paul's disruption of class-based logic, I propose, that makes his behavior uncanny. His style and mannerisms are unintelligible to his teachers because they violate the expectations and authorized codes through which capital gains authority and compliance. His teachers lack the language to successfully normalize his "hysterically defiant manner" (200), as the discourse surrounding Paul's interrogation is confined by the heteronormative systems and uneven superstructures, both economic and linguistic, enforced by Pittsburgh High School.

Disrupting conventional protocol, Paul's protest against mediocrity is embodied by his perverse costuming, which allows him to move freely between ranks with a smug feeling of superiority. His scandalous red carnation, opal pin, and outgrown, velvet-collared overcoat, distressed and shabby, symbolize his flippant attitude toward propriety, merging bourgeoisie signifiers in unpredictable ways. Although Terrell Scott Herring sees Paul as "a well-dressed vagabond" who engages in "a queer form of slumming," Timothy Bintrim reads Paul as a dandy, flaunting "convention and academic censure by adorning himself with jaunty neckwear" (4). Noting Cather's opening description of Paul who has, despite his worn-out vestments, "something of the dandy about him" (199), Bintrim employs Charles Baudelaire's genealogy of the dandy to inform his analysis of Paul's combative attitude and perpetual ennui. Paul is both stylized and mockingly self-assured, his very body, his "forced animation" (201), and sly smirk deployed as signs of aversion to all that is commonplace. Incorporating Dick Hebdige's punk semiotics, I regard Paul's attire as a form of bricolage which consciously juxtaposes previously unconnected commodities. For Hebdige, subcultures like punks and mods style themselves in "*obviously* fabricated" ways, displaying, abusing, and modifying codes to "go against the grain of mainstream culture" (101–2). Parodying the lifestyle and bourgeoisie beliefs of his accusers, Paul undermines authoritative discourse with his defiant gestures and punk apparel, which combine, in the language of Hebdige, to signal a "[r]efusal" (3) to participate in the status quo.

If Pittsburgh High School represents the smothering and dull values of a striving middle class, Carnegie Music Hall in the city's Oakland neighborhood epitomizes the infinite possibilities of class mobility for Paul; it is "his secret temple, his wishing carpet," transporting him, "blue league after blue league" (217) away from "all the stupid and ugly things" (216–17). Built in 1895, the Carnegie complex had an "explicit social agenda: to define, create and disseminate the highest culture" (Couvares 105). The Music Hall, Carnegie insisted, was for the masses who had an appreciation and love for the music which the "prosperous already enjoyed" and was built by a man who himself was a wage-earner and who had "the good of that class greatly at heart" (Nasaw 502). Its location in the Oakland section of the city, midway between downtown and the streetcar suburbs it abuts, served to establish Oakland as a "pivot for the middle class," a frontier of East End culture, and a "*staging* ground for new efforts" to elevate and civilize working-class sensibilities (Couvares 105–6). Not surprisingly, labor organizers were critical of the endeavor and would continue to associate the Carnegie complex with the antilabor rhetoric of the Homestead Strike and its ensuing trials.[4] Although "this cluster of enlightened agencies," as the *Pittsburgh Survey* notes, magnified the economic inequalities of the city, the Carnegie campus, specifically the Music Hall with free weekly organ recitals, also gave coherence and shape to the spirit of citizenship (18); Paul's connection with the Music Hall exemplifies this schism alongside an exaggerated awareness of cultural exclusion to fabricate a chain of contradictions characteristic of class consciousness.

As Sara Nadal-Melsió emphasizes, class consciousness is not an end in itself, but the beginning of a series of oppositions manufactured by bourgeois thought, where the subject, unaware of her agency, is always at odds with the objects around her (74). Cather captures the institutional conflicts inherent in the Music Hall in the decisive scene in which Paul's English teacher unexpectedly appears in the aisles to be seated by Paul. The teacher's trespass, "with checks for the seats which a prominent manufacturer had taken for the season," exposes the uneven social structure of the Carnegie Music Hall by making a statement about belonging and patronage (205). Although Paul ultimately concludes she has "about as much right to sit there as he had," he must first define himself in opposition to her as the gatekeeper of the people in his section (205). The arrogance feigned by both participants here attests to the fallacy of identity politics, which is a fetishistic form of bourgeoisie thought having nothing to do with the subject or object they claim to represent and are "an expression of the reproductive potential of ideology" (Nadal-Melsió 71). Making palpable what was previously an unconscious abstraction, both Paul and the teacher are made suddenly aware of their place by seeing each other out of context. In the Music Hall, which Paul envisions as a utopia, he can pretend to be who he is not: a "charming boy" hosting a "great reception" (204–5). Similarly, the teacher, with tickets most likely "sent to her out of kindness" for seats she cannot afford, is assuming a position outside her class with "a hauteur" that will embarrass her later (205). The teacher's reaction to Paul makes her "feel very foolish," leaving Paul with the upper hand as he looks her over critically, deciding she is a fool to be sitting "downstairs with such togs" (205). As a conduit of capital enterprise, the Carnegie Music Hall is a place where the "masses" come to enjoy the rewards of their labor, yet, as this scene reveals, pleasure is employed by and for the bourgeoisie as an ideological apparatus sustaining the economic divisions and interests of the Carnegie class.

Paul is caught between the reality of this division and the fantasy of escape until the music begins and he is able to lose himself, freeing "some hilarious spirit within him; something that struggled there like the Genius in the bottle found by the Arab fisherman" (205). For David Carter, Cather's reference to the fairy tale here "serves to undercut any possible evaluation of [Paul] as artistically serious or mature" (602). Unable to appreciate the work and skill inherent in the creative process, Paul is trapped within a myth of his own making and wants nothing more than the imaginative possibilities, "the indiscernible thrill" he obtains from the music (217). The allusion to the "Genius in the bottle," I suggest, doubles as a reference to Carnegie Hall, "Paul's fairy tale," and to his unfulfilled wish of "doing or saying splendid, brilliant things" (215). Without any substantial interest in the artistic merit of the symphony, Paul simply admires the instruments as they fuse together to create a blaze of "unimaginable splendor," disconnecting him from the actual work of the performers (206). Paul's limited imagination, as Claude Summers suggests, "distorts his capacity to perceive clearly his relationship to society and others" (113). The dancing lights and energy of the performers permit Paul to feel a "zest for life," but he is incapable of transferring this experience to the world beyond the stage. Dependent upon the intoxication and stimuli of Carnegie Music Hall, the "delicious excitement which was the only thing that could be called living at all," Paul is "irritable and wretched" once the concert is over and hurriedly changes out of his uniform in pursuit of his next distraction (206).

"Pacing rapidly up and down the walk" like a stage-door Johnny, Paul refuses to let the night come to an end and quickly channels his energy into catching a glimpse of the soloist coming out of the Music Hall. But the singer receives little attention here, as the real star is the Hotel Schenley:

Fig. 5.2. *Hotel Schenley*, 1910. Courtesy of University of Pittsburgh Archives Photograph Collection, 1810–2006, UA. Photos, University Archives, Archives & Special Collections, University of Pittsburgh Library System.

> big and square through the fine rain, the windows of its twelve stories glowing like those of a lighted card-board house under a Christmas tree. All the actors and singers of any importance stayed there when they were in the city, and a number of the big manufacturers of the place lived there in the winter. (206–7)

Cather conveys the regal presence of the hotel by delineating the way in which Paul, always an outsider waiting and watching, accesses the hotel as both an idea and concrete, lived experience, as if his knowledge of who goes in and goes out allows him to be a witness as well as a participant of privilege. Yet the reader, unlike the naïve Paul, is aware that this establishment epitomizes yet another wish that will never come true; analogous to the miniature house under the Christmas tree, the hotel projects an image of an ideal that Paul cannot attain. Off-limits to Paul, the Hotel Schenley, with its "glistening surfaces and basking ease," enkindles Paul's appetite for wealth in a way no other Pittsburgh site does. Although his imagination failed him earlier in the evening, it does not fail him here, as Paul imagines himself entering the hotel and going up the steps "into the warm lighted building, into an exotic tropical world" (207). Inspired by his longing to transcend the boundaries of his class, Paul follows his fantasy further into the dining room, picturing the "mysterious dishes" and "green bottles in buckets of ice, as he had seen them in the supper-party picture of the Sunday supplement" (207). Hunger permeates this imagined reflection, which serves to enhance Paul's fictional sense of belonging while simultaneously differentiating him as an interloper. Drawing on the work of Raymond Tallis, this palpable hunger for food, for the satisfaction of a fine meal in a beautiful warm room, leads to other hungers, namely the intoxicating desire for money, which promises limitless possibilities and is the "most potent agent of insatiable consumption" (68). Paul is so seduced by the infinite variety of pleasures shining through the window that he is shocked to find himself "still outside in the slush of the gravel driveway" (208). With the rain beating down on his face, Paul's trance is temporarily broken; still, his desire for the "fairy world" of the Hotel Schenley and the indulgences it affords is affirmed "tangibly before him" (208).

The hotel's majestic allure reflected Edward Manning Bigelow's City Beautiful vision of the Schenley Park area as a retreat from the "mechanized, brutal world of the city" (Muller and Bauman 132). Bigelow, who was appointed by his cousin, politician Christopher Lyman Magee, to be the director of the Department of Public Works in 1888, created Pittsburgh's first park by convincing Mary Elizabeth Croghan Schenley to donate three hundred acres of land to the city on the condition that the park be named after her ("Schenley Plaza" 1–2).[5] He then hired British landscape architect William Falconer to design a "romantic landscape," introducing Pittsburgh to the most "advanced and modern botanical standards of botany, horticulture, and landscape architecture" ("Schenley Plaza" 2). The park would expand over time to include bridle paths, a lake for boating, a lily pond, a music pavilion, and the hotel, which was built in 1898. With the financial backing of the industrial elite, Franklin Niccola, a member of the Civic Club of Allegheny County, conceived of the Hotel Schenley "as a cornerstone of his design for a Pittsburgh 'White City' in Oakland" (Muller and Bauman 133). To this end, the hotel served as a towering example of fin-de-siècle architecture, combining the Beaux Arts ethos of an exquisite estate with a cosmopolitan passion for urban environmentalism. Landscaped by the Olmsted brothers, whose father was the renowned designer of New York's Central Park, the circumference of the hotel featured formal and informal pathways, an ordered assembly of trees, and a hedge of closely planted shrubs protecting the lawn and serving as a barrier between the communal sidewalk and the more regulated entrances of the hotel. At once a private and public institution, the hotel exemplified the paradoxes of the reform movement that, fearful of social disorder, pushed the boundaries of concern for beauty and safety into larger, shared social spaces, which were nonetheless off-limits to the majority of Pittsburghers.

The restrictedness of the hotel, as well as its connection to Big Steel, was underscored on January 9, 1901, when eighty-nine executives of Carnegie companies gathered in the Schenley Hotel ballroom on the eve of the formation of the United States Steel Corporation. Worried that the steel industry "was facing a potentially ruinous crisis of overproduction" that would lead to "lower prices and vanishing profits" (Nasaw 584), Charles M. Schwab worked diligently to smooth negotiations between Carnegie and Pierpont Morgan, pleading "industrial peace and growth through consolidation" (Pittsburgh Post-Gazette and Carnegie Library of Pittsburgh, *Pittsburgh: 1758–2008* 54). Although Carnegie did not initially want to do business with Morgan, he eventually changed his mind and sold his company for $480 million, establishing U.S. Steel as the first corporation in the United States worth more than one billion dollars, a deal that would make several dozen attendees millionaires and grant Carnegie the status of being the richest man in the world.[6] The much anticipated "Meal of Millionaires," a celebration of private accumulation and corporate dominance, showcases the exclusivity of the Hotel

CHARMION GUSTKE

Fig. 5.3. R. W. Johnston, Carnegie executive dinner, Schenley Hotel Ballroom, where guests sit at tables arranged in the shape of a railroad rail cross section, 9 January 1901. Courtesy of University of Pittsburgh Archives Photograph Collection, 1810–2006, UA. University Archives, Archives & Special Collections, University of Pittsburgh Library System.

Schenley and its entitled guests. Cather underscores this connection in the 1905 version of "Paul's Case" in which Paul perceives the hotel doormen as "mocking spirits" forbidding his entry.[7] Magnifying the foreboding omnipotence of wealth alongside Paul's fascination with his own exclusion, these ghostly figures correlate to the unpredictable mutations that occur within the historical evolution of capital whenever massive financial power is assembled.

With or without these taunting guards, the looming presence of the hotel operates as a material marker of Paul's class consciousness as it moves imperceptibly from the present to the future: "Tangibly before him, like the fairy world of a Christmas pantomime" (208), the hotel represents the immeasurable, embellished affluence of the elite—and is as unreal and enticing to Paul as a Christmas pageant. This childlike wonder is accompanied by Paul's dread of a future in which he is destined "always to shiver in the black night outside, looking up at it" (208). While in one sense, the "it" here is the opulence of capital, represented by the Hotel Schenley, "it" also refers to the destination to which Paul aspires, foreshadowing his transition from standing outside the "Waldorf of Pittsburgh" to residing, however temporarily, in the Waldorf-Astoria in New York City, where Paul, now a fugitive, will wonder how "there were honest men in the world at all" (226). This maneuver and the criminality it entails were inspired by a story in the Pittsburgh newspapers, in which a nineteen-year-old clerk, James J. Wilson, stole between fifteen hundred and two thousand dollars from the Denny Estate. Wilson fled to Chicago with his friend Harold Orr; once there, the young men indulged in "aristocratic" extravagances, buying designer clothes and jewelry and staying in high-priced hotels (Bintrim and Madigan 112). Similarly, Paul uses the money he steals from Denny & Carson to immerse himself in the lavish lifestyle he feels he deserves, replete with the accoutrements of shiny trinkets and gourmand meals. Feeling "a good deal more manly, more honest," Paul may now "dress the part" without remorse for his crime or the need for "boastful pretensions" (228–29). But these illusions quickly evaporate once news of the heist is circulated in the Pittsburgh papers and Paul spends the last of his money in a frantic, drunken haze.

When Wilson was caught by the police on 17 November 1902, the *Pittsburgh Chronicle-Telegraph* quoted him as saying, "I cannot explain why I took the money. I seemed to be in the power of some unforeseen force" (Bintrim and Madigan 113). This indescribable "force" corresponds to the magical thinking, "the childish belief in miracles" (230), that buoys Paul along the shores of disillusionment until he is no longer capable of manufacturing the images necessary to sustain him: "the picture-making mechanism was crushed" (234). Paul's decision to commit suicide raises questions regarding values and how the choices we make establish our values, our design for living. As David Harvey notes, Marx maintained "that there is a certain kind and measure of value which is being determined by a process that we do not understand and which is not necessarily directed by our conscious choice" (21). Unpacking the manner in which these standards are being imposed is crucial if we are to comprehend where we are in "this maelstrom of churning values" (Harvey 21). Cather's ten years in Pittsburgh gave her the opportunity to witness how these values and the aesthetic ideals they create are fueled by inequality and the establishment of a ruling, leisure class. In "Paul's Case," Cather has exposed the historical geography and economic development of Pittsburgh to underscore the influence of institutions in the construction of a class consciousness that relies on the problematic relationship between the materiality of Cordelia Street and "the glaring affirmation of the omnipotence of wealth" (225), leaving the reader to decide if the price is worth the cost.

NOTES

1. For Lukács, capitalism creates societies with "a purely economic articulation," which allows class consciousness, previously concealed in precapitalist periods, to emerge as the driving force of history and production (58–59).

2. Many of these reformers, like Isabelle McClung, were members of the Civic Club of Allegheny County, which was founded in 1895.

3. On 12 January 1902, the *New York Sun*, under the headline "Schwab Breaks the Bank," reported that Charles M. Schwab, president of the U.S. Steel Corporation, had been seen playing roulette in Monte Carlo, winning "75,000 francs on two successive coups" and dropping several thousand dollars. Carnegie was shocked by the news of Schwab's gambling and wrote a letter to J. P. Morgan suggesting Schwab resign from his position; however, "Morgan made light of the matter" (Nasaw 638). (See John A. Garraty, "When the Headlines Said: Charlie Schwab Breaks the Bank," *Heritage*, vol. 8, no. 3, 1957). Carnegie felt personally betrayed, as he had spent a lifetime trying to dispel the image of capitalists as gamblers. The fact that "his chief protégé had been caught red-handed" was his "worst nightmare" (Nasaw 638).

4. Judge Samuel A. McClung, Isabelle McClung's father, presided over the trial of Alexander Berkman who had tried to assassinate Henry Clay Frick a week following the Battle of Homestead; the judge gave Berkman the most extreme sentence allowed under law (Lewis 52).

5. Heiress Mary Elizabeth Croghan Schenley inherited a thousand acres of choice land in Pittsburgh from her grandfather but chose not to live there. Eloping with a captain in the British navy when she was fifteen, she lived the rest of her sixty-two years in France and England (Toker 80). Although she remained loyal to Pittsburgh, she never returned to the city and was unpopular "with most Pittsburghers, who regarded her estate as a 'parasite'" (Oresick 16). Oresick claims that the modern myth of her popularity is a symptom of historical forgetfulness (16).

6. An immediate success, the company made two-thirds of the country's steel, controlling every aspect of the steelmaking process, from the materials to the ships carrying the steel.

7. As Carpenter and Woodress discuss, Cather revised "Paul's Case" extensively between its 1905 publication in *The Troll Garden* and its later appearance in *Youth and the Bright Medusa* in 1920.

## WORKS CITED

Bintrim, Timothy W. "Exit Smiling: The Case for Paul's Dandyism." *Willa Cather and Aestheticism*, edited by Sarah Cheney Watson and Ann Mosely, Fairleigh Dickinson UP, 2012, pp. 17–28.

Bintrim, Timothy W., and Mark J. Madigan. "From Larceny to Suicide: The Denny Case and 'Paul's Case.'" *Violence, the Arts and Willa Cather*, edited by Joseph R. Urgo and Merrill Maguire Skaggs, Fairleigh Dickinson UP, 2007, pp. 109–23.

Carpenter, David A. "Why Willa Cather Revised 'Paul's Case': The Work in Art and Those Sunday Afternoons." *American Literature*, vol. 59, no. 4, December 1987, pp. 590–608.

Cather, Willa. "Paul's Case." *Youth and the Bright Medusa*. 1920. Willa Cather Scholarly Edition, historical essay and explanatory notes by Mark J. Madigan, textual essay and editing by Frederick M. Link, Charles W. Mignon, Judith Boss, and Kari A. Ronning, U of Nebraska P, 2009, pp. 199–234.

———. "The Real Homestead." *The World and the Parish: Willa Cather's Articles and Reviews, 1893–1902*, edited by William M. Curtin, U of Nebraska P, 1970, pp. 2: 854–59.

———. *The Selected Letters of Willa Cather*. Edited by Andrew Jewell and Janis Stout, Knopf, 2013.

Couvares, Francis G. *The Remaking of Pittsburgh: Class and Culture in an Industrializing City (1877–1919)*. State U of New York P, 1984.

Harvey, David. *A Companion to Marx's Capital*. Verso, 2010.

Hedbige, Dick. *Subculture: The Meaning of Style*. Routledge, 2008.

Kobus, Ken. *City of Steel: How Pittsburgh Became the World's Steelmaking Capital during the Carnegie Era*. Rowman and Littlefield, 2015.

Ku, Chung-Hao. "A Boy under the Ban of Suspension: Renouncing Maturity in Willa Cather's 'Paul's Case.'" *Modern Fiction Studies*, vol. 61, no. 1, Spring 2015, pp. 69–89.

Lewis, Edith. *Willa Cather Living: A Personal Record*. 1953. U of Nebraska P, 2000.

Lukács, Georg. *History and Class Consciousness: Studies in Marxist Dialectics*. Translated by Rodney Livingston, MIT Press, 1971.

Muller, Edward K., and John F. Bauman. "The Olmsteds in Pittsburgh: (Part I) Landscaping and the Private City." *Pittsburgh History*, vol. 76, no. 3, Fall 1993, pp. 122–40.

Nadal-Melsió, Sara. "Georg Lukács: Magus Realismus?" *Diacritics*, vol. 34, no. 2, 2004, pp. 62–84.

Nasaw, David. *Andrew Carnegie*. Penguin, 2006.

Oresick, Jake. *The Schenley Experiment: A Social History of Pittsburgh First Public High School*. Pennsylvania State UP, 2017.

Pittsburgh Post-Gazette and Carnegie Library of Pittsburgh. *Pittsburgh, 1758–2008* (Images of America: Pennsylvania), Arcadia Publishing, 2008.

*The Pittsburgh Survey*. Edited by Paul Underwood Kellogg, Press of Wm. F. Fell, 1914.

"Schenley Plaza, Schenley Park and Environs." Frick Fine Arts Library, Library Guide Series, no. 11, www.haa.pitt.edu/sites/default/files/other-research-guides/Schenley-Park.pdf.

Skrabec, Quentin. *The World's Richest Neighborhood: How Pittsburgh's East Enders Forged American Industry*. Algora Publishing, 2010.

Tallis, Raymond. *Hunger*. Acumen Publishing, 2008.

Toker, Franklin. *Pittsburgh: An Urban Portrait*. U of Pittsburgh P, 1986.

Woodress, James. *Willa Cather: A Literary Life*. U of Nebraska P, 1987.

## 6 "The Most Exciting Attractions Are between Two Opposites That Never Meet"

Willa Cather and Andy Warhol

TODD RICHARDSON

Comparing Willa Cather and Andy Warhol is like comparing apples and amphetamines. Within her lifetime, Cather crafted twelve novels, novels that feel less written than carved, full of precisely controlled prose that illuminates the nobility and fragility of human experience in a manner both timeless and intimate. Warhol, conversely, might make as many as twelve paintings an hour, obliterating craft altogether through a silk-screening process he was drawn to because it was "quick and chancy," adjectives never attached to anything Cather created. Had she survived long enough, Cather would likely have hated Warhol's work.[1] In "The Novel Démeublé," she insisted, "One does not wish the egg one eats for breakfast, or the morning paper, to be made of the stuff of immortality" (44), yet such insubstantial phenomena were Warhol's preferred subjects, and, in *A Boy for Meg* (1961), *129 Die in Jet (Plane Crash)* (1962), and *Tunafish Disaster* (1963), he literally made high art from the morning paper. Throughout his career and via a multitude of media, Warhol approached the disposable as if it were immortal, goading audiences into pondering the significance of cheap, low-quality culture that Cather dismissed as, at best, mere amusement. Fundamentally, the two artists had opposite views on artistic representation: whereas Cather promoted meaning over things, Warhol, whose aesthetic trademark was serialization of the same, strove for the inverse, insisting, "The more you look at the same things, the more the meaning goes away, and the better and emptier you feel" (*Popism* 50).

The epochal distance between them is not so much because of their different places in time—their lives actually overlapped—but because of their very different vantages on time. Cather's aesthetic affinities ran backward, exemplified by the line she drew with the title of her 1936 collection of essays *Not Under Forty*. For Cather, there was, temporally speaking, a right side of history and it was the other side of 1922 (or thereabouts). "It's for the backwards," Cather insists in the book's prefatory note, "and by one of their number, that these sketches were written" (v). In no way am I suggesting that Cather was anachronistic, outdated, or otherwise fusty, only that her gaze drifted rearward, looking to the past in order to make sense of the present. Warhol, conversely, looked to the future: "We were seeing the future and we knew it for sure." He says in *Popism*, his memoir of the 1960s, "We saw people walking around in it without knowing it, because they were still thinking in the past, in the references of the past. But all you had to do was know you were in the future, and that's what put you there" (40). Unlike Cather, who was suspicious of technological progress, Warhol's work embraced it as an ideal, from the silver walls of his New York studio, known as the Factory, which he said were the same color as the space program, to the mass-production methods he emulated through his painting process.

Despite the aesthetic chasm separating Andy Warhol and Willa Cather, they share a surprising number of critical confluences. Some, such as the renegade "a" at the end of their names that both dropped during adolescence—Cather picked hers up again, but Warhol never went back to being Andrew Warhola—are more curious than profound, whereas others can be quite revealing. Consider, for example, their complicated relationships to gay identity. While both artists maintained decades-long same-sex partnerships, Warhol with Jed Johnson and Cather with Edith Lewis, their queerness is frequently debated if not discounted altogether. With Cather, it's due to an absence of any public proclamation of her lesbianism; Warhol's gayness, on the other hand, gets lost in too many contradictory signs. Contending that Warhol was asexual, biographers and critics frequently point to statements like, "Fantasy love is much better than reality love. Never doing it is very exciting. The most exciting attractions are between two opposites that never meet" (*Philosophy* 44). Such assessments, however, are misguided as they confuse a discomfort with sex for an absence of sexuality and, more significantly, ignore the fact that Warhol habitually lied. The important point is that gay desire permeates Warhol's life and work, yet his queerness, like Cather's, remains somehow simultaneously both obvious and opaque.

Putting Willa Cather and Andy Warhol in conversation with one another reveals an infrathin kinship, "infrathin" being Marcel Duchamp's word for the meaningful absences shared by distinct but related phenomena, the warmth of a seat recently vacated, for instance, or the affinity between two items made from the same mold.[2] It's a goofy, quasi-mystical concept offered up by an artistic charlatan, but it's useful here as the correlations between Cather and Warhol, two vastly different artists, are so eye-opening and, frankly, fun to ponder, they should not be dismissed as mere coincidence. Indeed, considering Cather in a Warholian context, and vice versa, offers new perspectives on two canonical and hyperanalyzed artists. Cather's closeness in time to Warhol, for example, shows that she was within spitting distance of postmodernity—a direction in which she would have happily spit—and Warhol's closeness to Cather expands his artistic lineage in surprising ways. While I do not promise the ideas that emerge for this exercise will always be useful in a scholarly sense, I am convinced they are always worth pondering.

Of the correlations between them, the easiest to discern is geographic as both Cather and Warhol spent crucial years in Pittsburgh. Cather's Pittsburgh experiences are on display throughout this volume, but Warhol's Pittsburgh roots warrant some explanation as, in many ways, they have been effaced by his close association with New York (just as Cather's Pittsburgh experiences are frequently overshadowed by her association with Nebraska).[3] Warhol's parents, Andrej and Julia Warhola, moved to Pittsburgh from Slovakia in 1914 and 1921 respectively, settling in a Rusyn immigrant neighborhood. Born Andrew Warhola on 6 August 1928, Warhol was the youngest of three boys—a sister died before his parents moved to the United States—and it was clear from the first that he was different. A hypersensitive child who preferred the company of girls, his sensitive nature was made even more so by a traumatic bout with Syndenham's Chorea, which struck in third grade. Also known as St. Vitus' Dance, the condition causes uncontrollable jerking movements of the limbs, and it rendered Andy bedridden for long stretches of time, further alienating him from peers while strengthening his connection with his mother. About this time and perhaps accentuated by the Chorea, Warhol's skin lost pigmentation, leaving him with patchy spots on his face and initiating a lifelong belief in his own ugliness.[4] Throughout his years in Pittsburgh, Warhol went to mass, conducted in Slovakian at St. John Chrysostom Byzantine Catholic Church, multiple times a week with his mother. He routinely attended mass throughout his life, often sneaking away from the debauchery of the Factory to attend mass at St. Vincent Ferrer Parish on Manhattan's Upper East Side, again with his mother, who moved to New York in 1951 to live with him. He attended Schenley High School in Pittsburgh's North Oakland neighborhood, and while he said he was completely ostracized in high school, peers remembered Andrew Warhola as an eccentric-but-well-liked classmate. He graduated in 1945, his senior yearbook photo captioned "genuine as a finger print." He went on to study commercial art at Carnegie Tech, earning a pictorial design degree in 1949 and moving to New York less than a week after his graduation.

Cather's Pittsburgh doesn't often dovetail with Warhol's largely working-class experience of the city, but they both felt a strong connection to the Carnegie Institute complex. Cather was enamored with the Carnegie Library—"they have all the books in the world there I think," she wrote to Ellen Gere—and she frequently discussed the Carnegie Museum and its exhibits in *Home Monthly* and the *Pittsburgh Leader*. As for Warhol, when he was six, his father bought a house in a middle-class, Lower Oakland neighborhood about a mile from the Carnegie Museum and Library, and Andy often spent his days there, thumbing through books or roaming the museum's galleries—he was especially fond of the Hall of Casts and its replicas of famous statues. It was the Music Hall, however, that was especially important to both of them. Being a music lover, Cather frequented the Carnegie Music Hall, going there on her second night in Pittsburgh and later using the space for a setting in "Paul's Case." "[Cather] put a little of herself into the title character in 'Paul's Case,'" James Woodress suggests in *Willa Cather: A Literary Life*, "whose spirits were released by the first strains of the symphony orchestra when he ushered at Carnegie Hall" (46). And it was in that same Carnegie Music Hall that Andrew Warhola took his first art class. Every Saturday from the 1930s up through the 1980s, three hundred Pittsburgh children streamed into the Carnegie Music Hall to take art classes with Joseph Fitzpatrick, a local artist and flamboyant character. As part of the class, students drew what they had seen earlier that week on Masonite board with crayons, after which Fitzpatrick invited ten exceptional students on stage to share their work with the auditorium. Andrew Warhola, a fixture in the class in the late 1930s, was frequently one of the ten chosen to share their work on the Carnegie Music Hall stage, his first encounters with artistic recognition, at least outside of his family, in a lifetime full of them. The influence of Joseph Fitzpatrick's classes on Warhol cannot be overstated.

Isabelle Collin Dufresne, better known as Factory Superstar Ultra Violet, suggested Warhol learned other, extra-artistic lessons at those Saturday morning classes in Carnegie Music Hall: "Several times he

mentioned two youngsters who arrived in limousines, one in a long
maroon Packard and the other in a Pierce-Arrow. He remembered
the mother who wore expensively tailored clothes and sumptuous
furs. In the 1930s, before television and with no glossy magazines
for poor families like Andy's and few trips to the movies, the art
classes opened a peephole for Andy to the world of the rich and
successful. He never forgot what he saw" (qtd. in Bockris 50). Cather,
too, learned something about wealth and wealthy people while living in Pittsburgh. She had known rich people in Red Cloud, but
their fortunes were meager when compared to the Fricks, Carn-
egies, and Mellons of Pittsburgh, and, like Warhol, making sense
of such unearthly fortunes affected her greatly. Ultimately, the two
artists came to similar conclusions about the importance of money
while placing very different values on the conclusions they came to:
Cather ruefully acknowledged the importance of money while Warhol gleefully painted dollar bills when told he should paint what he
loves. In each instance and despite the contrary values placed upon
it, money played a significant role in their aesthetic worldviews. For
Cather, money complicated artistic endeavors.[5] "Economics and art
are strangers," she said. Whereas for Warhol, money was the point:
"Making money is art and working is art and good business is the
best art" (Cather, *On Writing* 27; Warhol, *Philosophy* 92).

While they expressed contradictory ideas about the value of com-
mercialism, Cather and Warhol's career trajectories follow a similar
arc in that both became "fine artists" after first achieving success in
the commercial world. Warhol relocated to New York in 1949 to
work as a freelance illustrator and draughtsman, and his success in
advertising over the next decade was considerable, becoming the
most highly sought-after illustrator on Madison Avenue and earning more than one hundred thousand dollars annually. In addition
to illustrations for *Glamour* and other high-profile fashion magazines, Warhol designed Christmas cards, book jackets, and numerous album covers for Columbia Records, but his most lucrative and
notable work during the 1950s was for the shoe company I. Miller.
While Warhol had "high art" aspirations from the beginning, com-

mercial work occupied most of his time during his first decade in New York, and his personal work, which employed the same blotted-line technique that was his trademark in the advertising world, was rarely exhibited and even more rarely purchased. Nevertheless, these years were crucial for Warhol as he built a professional infrastructure that would later support his outsized notoriety and productivity. On the one hand, he developed a network of influential people, always being careful to make the right impression on them, whether in his performance of self—in the advertising world, Warhol was known as "Andy Paperbag" due to his deliberately quirky habit of carrying his work in cheap paper bags—or by leaving little gifts with people so they would better remember him, a trick he picked up from his Slovakian mother. Just as important, Warhol developed professional routines during these years and learned how to meet deadlines and be productive when he did not feel like it. Indeed, the relentless creativity that characterizes his later fine art career was rooted in his early commercial work.

Cather had earlier made the same move from Pittsburgh to New York, but that move was preceded by her great relocation—there were a few—from Nebraska to Pittsburgh a decade earlier, an event that more closely resembles Warhol's relocation to New York. Like Warhol, Cather was a young twentysomething with high art aspirations, but her work as an editor with *The Home Monthly* and other publications occupied most of her time and energy. Regardless, these years, as they were for Warhol, were crucial to her later high art success, as Katherine Byrne and Richard Snyder suggest in *Chrysalis: Willa Cather in Pittsburgh*: "Through her journalistic work, as she involved herself in the busy social and cultural life of Pittsburgh, she began to widen her horizons and to acquire the necessary discipline for writing daily" (ix). Of those horizons being widened, Cather's growing collection of influential associates, people who would be instrumental to her success as an author, was an especially important development during her Pittsburgh years, almost as important as the work ethic and marketing acumen she acquired and refined while working for commercial periodicals. Cather, like Warhol, became a successful and highly regarded artist only after first learning how to make a living (while also acquiring a taste for personal comfort with a dash of luxury).

Working for *The Home Monthly* and other popular publications gave Cather, in the words of Peter Benson, "practical experience in the tough business of writing for the popular taste" (246). As disdainful of popular literature as she was, Willa Cather was keenly aware of, and, at least on occasion, enjoyed the business of being Willa Cather. She wanted to be successful and she wanted to be known, no matter how strongly she may have insisted otherwise. Nowhere is this clearer than in her switch from Houghton Mifflin to Knopf as the publisher of her work. In "'As the Result of Many Solicitations': Ferris Greenslet, Houghton Mifflin, and Cather's Career," Robert Thacker shows that while with Houghton Mifflin, Cather was deeply involved in the presentation and promotion of her novels, that "she both asserted the worth of her writing and concurrently offered advice on matters of marketing, defining possibilities, pursuing reviewers, building upon the attention her work had received and was continuing to attract during the 1910s" (375). And the move to Knopf was, fundamentally, driven by advertising concerns, Cather feeling that Houghton Mifflin never sufficiently distinguished her from their other authors and offerings. In a telling moment in a letter to Greenslet, Cather writes, "I think the recognition of the public and reviewers has outstripped that of my publishers" (*Selected Letters* 275), a statement that demonstrates her awareness that not only was she in the publishing business, she was herself a *business* (or, in more contemporary terms, a brand).

Working for *McClure's* and working for I. Miller shoes respectively, Cather and Warhol learned the importance of meeting deadlines, reading markets, and generating content even if the mood didn't strike. They developed creative routines and a sophisticated appreciation for audience by expressing themselves professionally at the behest of other people. The artist with great ideas and no discipline is a cliché, one that both Cather and Warhol managed to avoid. Yet neither "sold out," which happens the other way around, when fine artists compromise their vision for commercial reasons. Cather and Warhol, rather, bought in, developing professionalism and discipline before pursuing an artistic vision. Instead of thinking of them as commercial artists turned high artists, perhaps it would be better to think of them as employees transformed into artistic executives, wholly in control of their products and promotion. Contrary to the romantic notion of the transcendent artist separate from market concerns and popular opinions, Cather and Warhol learned how the real world operated and then fit their respective talents into it.

Had Cather and Warhol ever met, their echoing experiences as commercial artists would have given them much to talk about, much more than their mature work as fine artists. And the idea of them meeting is not so absurd as it seems. As mentioned earlier, Andy Warhol and Willa Cather's lives did overlap, which means, for a short while at least, they read and responded to the same headlines. "The atomic bomb has sent a shudder of horror (and fear) through all the world," Cather wrote in August of 1945, "and one's own affairs seem scarcely worth thinking about" (*Selected Letters* 652). The same day that first atomic bomb was dropped on Hiroshima, Andy Warhol celebrated his seventeenth birthday. All told, Willa Cather and Andy Warhol were alive simultaneously for just short of two decades— when Cather, fifty-four years older than Warhol, died in her Park Avenue home in April of 1947, eighteen-year-old Andrew Warhola was a student at Carnegie Tech planning his first visit to New York City. However briefly, Cather and Warhol were, in the most generous possible sense of the word, contemporaries.[6]

Willa Cather and Andy Warhol's temporal proximity is best illustrated through their separate and truly fantastic encounters with Truman Capote, who is a sort of missing link between them. According to an essay Capote began writing the day before he died, he first met Willa Cather one snowy day around 1945 in the New York Society Library ("Willa, Truman. Truman, Willa"). Unable to hail a taxi, Capote went for tea with "the blue-eyed lady"—he did not yet know it was Cather—whom he had seen at the library before, and, after expressing his love for *My Mortal Enemy*, Cather informed him that she was its author. Previously, in the "Conversational Portraits" portion of his 1980 collection *Music for Chameleons*, Capote mentioned his relationship with Cather and her partner, Edith Lewis, reminiscing, "I often sat in front of their fireplace and drank Bristol Cream and observed the firelight enflame the pale prairie blue of Miss Cather's serene genius-eyes" (161). Even earlier, in a 1967 interview with Gloria Steinem, Capote identified his encounter with Cather as a true *frisson* in his life, calling Cather "one of my first intellectual friends . . . the first person I'd ever met who was an artist as I defined the term, someone I respected and could talk to" (97).

Had Cather lived another year, Truman Capote surely would have told his friend Willa about the strange fan mail he was receiving from an Andrew Warhola of Pittsburgh. During his first trip to New York in 1948, Warhol encountered a blown-up version of Truman Capote's curiously erotic jacket photo for *Other Voices, Other Rooms*: "Twenty-year-old Andy was instantly taken with the image of the 23-year-old Truman." Warhol biographer Victor Bockris wrote, "He was everything Andy wanted to be. He lived in New York and gave dinner parties for Greta Garbo and Cecil Beaton in his boyfriend's apartment. He was young, attractive, talented, glamorous, rich and famous" (73). Andy became obsessed. (See figure 6.1 of Truman Capote by Andy Warhol.) According to the painter Philip Pearlstein, who attended Carnegie Tech with Warhol and was his first roommate in New York, "Every few days for several weeks Andy would put a drawing with a note expressing his wish for a meeting [with Capote] in an envelope filled with 'fairy dust,' sparkling bits of colored foil that flew out when the envelope was opened." When Warhol moved to New York a year later, he loitered outside Capote's apartment, hoping to "accidentally" run into the writer, and at one point, actually finagled his way into Capote's home, getting the author's mother to let him in. She, however, simply wanted someone to drink with. When Capote came home to the scene—Andy sharing his troubles with an inebriated Mrs. Capote—he humored Warhol because, in Capote's words, "He seemed one of those helpless people that you just know nothing's ever going to happen to, just a hopeless born

Fig. 6.1. Andy Warhol (American painter, printmaker, and filmmaker, 1928–1987), *Truman Capote*, ink on printing paper, ca. 1954. © 2019 The Andy Warhol Foundation for the Visual Arts, Inc. / Licensed by Artists Rights Society (ARS), New York.

loser, the loneliest, most friendless person I'd ever seen in my life" (qtd. in Bockris 91).

All this time, Warhol had been sending Capote illustrations, illustrations that would provide the basis for Warhol's first solo show in New York, "Fifteen Drawings Based on the Writings of Truman Capote." The show opened at the Hugo Gallery on 16 June 1952, and in an *Art Digest* review James Fitzsimmons claimed, "[T]he work has an air of preciosity, of carefully studied perversity. Boys, tomboys and butterflies are drawn in pale outline with magenta or violet splashed here and there—rather arbitrarily it seems." According to the gallery owner, David Mann, Capote and his mother did come to look at the work, but they made sure Warhol was not there when they did. Mann remembered that both had nice things to say about the drawings, yet Capote did not buy any pieces, nor did he commission Warhol to illustrate any of his future work, which was what Warhol had really wanted to accomplish through this show. Ultimately, none of the drawings sold, and the show was mostly ignored as this was still the era of Abstract Expressionism, and Andy's "sissy" drawings did not conform to the prevailing macho aesthetic.

That Warhol's first solo show drew on literary inspiration makes sense because drawing scenes from books was familiar to him. Robert Lepper, one of his instructors at Carnegie Tech, frequently had students read and illustrate significant literary works. "Andy excelled at the task." Bockris writes, "He began to draw and paint a series of large blotted-line pictures that showed an intelligent understanding of what the books were really about, and a star ability to go straight to the heart of them and choose an image that would capture their essence" (70). One such illustration, Warhol's drawing of the Huey Long character in *All the King's Men*, still hangs in the Carnegie Library in Pittsburgh. It was another instructor, however, who asked Warhol, sometime in 1947 or '48, to read and illustrate Willa Cather's "Paul's Case."[7] Howard Worner, according to Warhol's classmate Bennard Perlman, emphasized the practical aspects of drawing and, toward that end, moved the story's climax from Newark to nearby Panther Hollow Bridge, so that students might study the site and represent it from different angles. Perlman recollected:

> When the completed illustrations were tacked up on the wall for a critique, there were numerous examples showing the figure of Paul silhouetted in the dazzling headlight of an onrushing locomotive, of his body in midair as the train sped by, of his lifeless form sprawled on the ground below. And then there was Andy's illustration—a striking red blob of tempera paint. Standing before it, Professor Worner turned to the class and observed: "It could be catsup," to which Andy replied, in a nearly inaudible voice, "It's supposed to be blood." (157)

Truman Capote surely would have loved this story, and had Warhol known about his obsession's affection for Willa Cather, he surely would have shared it with him. Perhaps then it would not have taken until 1972, when *Rolling Stone* magazine hired Andy Warhol to interview Truman Capote, for the two to become the close friends they became.

As fun as the near miss is to ponder, Warhol's reaction to "Paul's Case" is worth considering on its own terms. Warhol grew up on middle-class Dawson Street in the Oakland neighborhood of Pittsburgh, which bears a striking resemblance to Cordelia Street in "Paul's Case," and, like Paul, Warhol shared a desire to escape the mundane circumstances of his Pittsburgh upbringing: turning onto Cordelia Street, Paul felt "a shuddering repulsion for the flavourless, colorlessness mass of every-day existence," and Dawson Street was the sort of place Warhol was talking about when he said "being born is like being kidnapped. And then sold into slavery" (*Philosophy* 96). Paul and Andy also shared numerous traits, such as their aversion to physical contact, their fascination with fame, and their belief in the redemptive power of money. Paul and Andy were a pair of dandies, valuing experience for the degree of its artifice rather than the depth of its authenticity—like Andy, Paul believed "the natural nearly always wore the guise of ugliness, that a certain element of artificiality seemed to him necessary in beauty" (179). And all this is in addition to the geographic concurrence, from their shared interest in the Carnegie's Hall of Casts to the Music Hall where Paul found aesthetic release and young Andrew Warhola's love of painting incubated. And, finally, Warhol also wanted to escape Pittsburgh and pursue beauty and glamour in New York, only he was afraid tragedy would eventually get him there, too, his mother warning Andy whenever he talked about moving to New York that he would wind up "dead in a gutter" (Bockris 77).

Assuming Andy actually read "Paul's Case," his severe depiction of the story's conclusion was much more than a stunt, was likely a response to the unsettling biographical similarities between him and Paul. That's only if he actually read the story. It is entirely likely, however, that Warhol never read "Paul's Case," that another student told him what happened at the story's end and Andy went from there. Much like Warhol's overall intelligence—Gore Vidal allegedly once said Warhol was "the only genius with an I.Q. of 60"—Andy's reading habits are highly disputed. Bockris claims Warhol "read voraciously," yet is quick to add that the artist paid "particular attention to the photographs" (57). In his biography of Warhol, Wayne Koestenbaum contends Warhol was an undiagnosed dyslexic—the children of working-class immigrants were not often diagnosed with dyslexia in Depression-era America—because what little of his actual handwriting survives is full of transpositions like "scrpit" for "script," and "herion" for "heroin." While Warhol did write numerous books, which suggests high literacy, they were all transcribed from recordings.[8] Warhol, in fact, used ghostwriters at least since his Carnegie Tech days when Andy and his friends Ellie Simon and Gretchen Schmertz would "get together after class and ask [Warhol] what he thought about the book or play in question. Gretchen would put his thoughts, which she remembered as always interesting, into literary English, then the three of them would go over the paper to make sure it sounded as if Andy had written it" (Bockris 61). Despite their best efforts, Warhol failed out of Carnegie Tech his freshman year because he was unable to pass a writing-intensive course called "Thought and Expression"—he was readmitted after passing the course when it was taught by a more forgiving professor over the summer. And while the written word, always in the same spritely and angular script, features prominently in Warhol's art, particularly his earlier commercial works, that distinctive handwriting was actually his mother's, whom he routinely got to help him with any illustration that required words—when his mother wasn't up for it, Warhol's longtime assistant Nathan Gluck could ably forge Warhol's mother's handwriting.[9]

Yet Andy did have a college degree, and he did graduate fifty-first in a class of 278 at Schenley High School. The art critic Blake Gopnik's forthcoming biography of Warhol emphasizes the artist's deep and wide reading habits and their effect on his work. Warhol was certainly capable of reading—he had a special fondness for "Page Six" of the *New York Post*—so it makes sense that he would have read "Paul's Case" when it was assigned. And, assuming he did, he does cut to the core of the story with his severe depiction of Paul's demise. Fatalist Andy, who followed up his Campbell's Soup paintings with the Death and Disaster series, who made a walking corpse of himself with his white wig and pale skin, distilled "Paul's Case" to its essence: death. Andy was obsessed with death, devoting an entire chapter to the subject in *The Philosophy of Andy Warhol*, albeit a chapter of only two sentences: "I don't believe in it, because you're not around to know that it's happened. I can't say anything about it because I'm not prepared for it" (123). In Andy's estimation, death was meaningless, as meaningless as a smear of red paint.[10]

The ambiguity surrounding Andy Warhol's reading habits reflects a larger ambiguity that accompanies all assessments of his life and work: despite being the embodiment of fame and as "overexposed" as a person can be, little can be said definitively about him. Warhol believed everything, even the stuff that contradicted. When asked if Pop Art criticized capitalism, he said it did. When asked if Pop Art celebrated capitalism, he said it did. In interviews, he agreed with whatever the interviewer said; in one famous instance, Warhol said it would be much easier if his interviewer simply told him what to say so he could repeat it back verbatim. Moreover, not only did Warhol say everything, he recorded and catalogued all of it. He composed three memoirs during his lifetime and tape-recorded almost all of his interactions. His diaries, which he started keeping at the suggestion of his accountant following an IRS audit, maintain a record of everything he bought, everyone he met and everything he did over the last decade of his life. His grandest project, the *Time Capsules* project, even preserved the detritus of his life. Starting sometime around 1974, Warhol began to collect the miscellany of his existence—personal correspondence, magazines, source materials, ticket stubs, partially eaten food and whatever else landed on his desk—in cardboard boxes. When he died, Warhol left behind roughly six hundred of these boxes, each an intimate and disjointed chronicle of the day-today goings-on of an artist and his community. Now housed in the Andy Warhol Museum in Pittsburgh, the *Time Capsules* have only recently attracted serious critical attention, largely because so few knew what Warhol had been up to. Add it all up and it becomes clear that due to his profligate signification, there is an effectively limitless amount of information available about Andy Warhol, information that can be arranged in whatever way the consumer prefers.

Contrast this with Cather, a fiercely private individual who was always circumspect in the execution of her public self, evidenced, obviously, by the exacting demands regarding the posthumous life of her words and the prohibition on publication of her letters. She offered a precisely calibrated "Catherness" in interviews, always keeping her identification with things, the West for instance, a little bit incomplete—when asked in 1921 about the inspiration Nebraska gave her, Cather told the *Lincoln Journal Star*, "Everywhere is a storehouse of literary material. If a true artist was born in a pigpen and raised in a sty, he would still find plenty of inspiration for his work" (Hinman 46). Nonetheless, like Warhol, Cather wanted to be known and was not afraid to court attention—shrinking violets, as a rule, do not wear such fabulous hats—a situation Brent Bohlke summed up wonderfully: "Willa Cather courted and enjoyed public notice, yet she loved anonymity and seclusion. She was enamored of the notice of the press and deeply resentful of the intrusions the press made upon her time and energies. She sought fame but disliked attention" (xxi).

Perhaps if Cather had adopted a cartoonish persona and worn a fright wig, she, too, could have achieved the difficult mix of fame and anonymity that Warhol managed. After all, the challenge of postmodernity—and Warhol, regardless of his IQ, understood postmodernity better than most—is not too little meaning: it is too damn much meaning. Consequently, as the eras have changed, Cather's strategy of keeping information about herself to a minimum only makes the clues she did leave behind more valuable and profound. Warhol, on the other hand, could have provided a skeleton key to unlock his entire being—a violent red smear of paint in response to a morbid story that felt far too autobiographical, perhaps—only to have it lost forever in the debris of his semiotic promiscuity. More than anything else, this is what I have learned from the infrathin kinship of these vastly different figures: a puzzle can confound by providing too few pieces, or too many.

## NOTES

1. I do not suggest that Cather was old-fashioned in her artistic taste. For a more complete assessment of Cather's open-mindedness when it came to visual art, please read Janis Stout's "'The Nude Had Descended the Staircase': Katherine Anne Porter Looks at Willa Cather Looking at Modern Art" (2011).

2. Marcel Duchamp insisted "infrathin" could be demonstrated but never defined, but the French art critic Hector Obalk provided something of a specific definition when he described it as an "infinitesimal thickness" shared by distinct but identical objects, such as the urinal Duchamp selected for exhibition and those urinals he did not ("The Unfindable Readymade").

3. Warhol's life is difficult to piece together because there's so much conflicting information out there, which I discuss later in this article. For the biographical information in this article, I rely primarily on Wayne Koestenbaum's *Andy Warhol*, Victor Bockris's *Warhol: The Biography*, and the Warholstars, a site maintained by Gary Comenas.

4. In an 1893 letter to Mariel Gere, a late-adolescent Cather also comments on her perceived physical attractiveness: "By the way I must tell you about that aunt of mine some time, she is one of the ugliest, smartest, and most eccentric of human kind—they say I am like her in ugliness and eccentricity" (20).

5. Cather struggled with the importance of money both in her life and through her work. For a deeper investigation of how Cather tried to resolve her concern with money and status through her work, please see Kimberly Vanderlaan's "Sacred Spaces, Profane 'Manufactories': Willa Cather's Split Artist in *The Professor's House* and *My Mortal Enemy*" (2011).

6. David Bowie, Iggy Pop, Elton John, Kareem Abdul-Jabbar, Farrah Fawcett, and David Letterman, all of whom were born in early 1947, are also, in this most generous sense of the word, "contemporaries" of Cather. Hillary Clinton, Arnold Schwarzenegger, Danielle Steele and Stephen King just miss being "contemporaries" of Cather, all being born in 1947 but after Cather's death on April 24th.

7. I am deeply indebted to Timothy Bintrim, who had been gifted a copy of this article by a senior colleague, Kirk Weixel, for proof of this. That something like this might have happened was first suggested to me when I presented an earlier version of this paper at the Willa Cather International Seminar in Pittsburgh in 2017. Tim then led me to Bennard Perlman's essay about Andy Warhol's educational experiences, in which Perlman relates this story, unfortunately misidentifying "Paul's Case" as "Paul's Place." It was an exhilarating find.

8. Warhol loved the idea of transcription, and, for this reason, he would have adored Cather's short story "Her Boss" and the erotics of transcription within it.

9. In 1958 the Art Director's Club of New York gave her an award for her work on an album cover for the musician Moondog, the certificate officially made out to "Andy Warhol's Mother."

10. Sometimes it really is best to take Andy at his word: "If you want to know all about Andy Warhol, just look at the surface of my paintings and films and me, and there I am. There's nothing behind it."

## WORKS CITED

Benson, Peter. "Willa Cather at 'Home Monthly.'" *Biography*, vol. 4, no. 3, 1981, pp. 227–48.

Bockris, Victor. *Warhol: The Biography.* Da Capo, 2003.

Bohlke, L. Brent. Introduction. *Willa Cather in Person: Interviews, Speeches, and Letters*, edited by L. Brent Bohlke. U of Nebraska Press, 1986, pp. xxi–xxx.

Byrne, Kathleen D., and Richard C. Snyder. *Chrysalis: Willa Cather in Pittsburgh, 1896–1906.* Historical Society of Western Pennsylvania, 1980.

Capote, Truman. *Conversations.* Edited by M. Thomas Inge. University Press of Mississippi, 1987.

———. *Music for Chameleons.* Random House, 1980.

———. "Willa, Truman. Truman, Willa." *Vanity Fair*, November 2006.

Cather, Willa. "#0027: Willa Cather to Ellen Gere [June 29, 1896]." *The Complete Letters of Willa Cather*, edited by the Willa Cather Archive team, Willa Cather Archive, 2018, www.cather.unl.edu.

———. *Not Under Forty.* U of Nebraska P, 1988.

———. "Paul's Case." *Youth and the Bright Medusa.* 1920. Willa Cather Scholarly Edition, edited by Mark J. Madigan, Frederick M. Link, Charles W. Mignon, and Kari A. Ronning, U of Nebraska P, 2009, pp. 199–234.

———. *The Selected Letters of Willa Cather.* Edited by Andrew Jewell and Janis Stout, Knopf, 2013.

————. *Willa Cather on Writing: Critical Studies on Writing as an Art.* Knopf, 1949.

Comenas, Gary. Warholstars, www.warholstars.org.

Fitzsimmons, James. "Irving Sherman, Andy Warhol." *Art Digest*, vol. 26, no. 18, July 1952, p. 19.

Gopnik, Blake. *Warhol.* Ecco, 2020.

Hinman, Eleanor. "Willa Cather, Famous Nebraska Novelist, Says Pioneer Mother Held Greatest Appreciation of Art—Raps Women Who Devote Themselves to Culture Clubs," *Lincoln Journal Star*, 6 November 1921. Republished in *Willa Cather in Person: Interviews, Speeches, and Letters*, edited by L. Brent Bohlke, U of Nebraska P, 1986, pp. 42–49.

Koestenbaum, Wayne. *Andy Warhol.* Penguin, 2001.

Obalk, Hector. "The Unfindable Readymade." *Tout-Fait: The Marcel Duchamp Studies Online Journal*, vol. 1, no. 2, May 2000, www.tout-fait.com.

Pearlstein, Philip. "Watching Warhola Become Warhol." ARTnews, April 2014, p. 74.

Perlman, Bennard. "The Education of Andy Warhol." *The Andy Warhol Museum: The Inaugural Publication*, Andy Warhol Museum, 1994, pp. 146–65.

Stout, Janis. "'The Nude Had Descended the Staircase': Katherine Anne Porter Looks at Willa Cather Looking at Modern Art." *Cather Studies 9: Willa Cather and Modern Cultures*, edited by Melissa J. Homestead and Guy J. Reynolds, U of Nebraska P, 2011, pp. 225–43.

Thacker, Robert. "'As the Result of Many Solicitations': Ferris Greenslet, Houghton Mifflin, and Cather's Career." *Studies in the Novel*, vol. 45, no. 3, 2013, pp. 369–86.

Ultra Violet. *Famous For 15 Minutes: My Years with Andy Warhol*, 2004, www.backinprint.com.

Vanderlaan, Kimberly. "Sacred Spaces, Profane 'Manufactories': Willa Cather's Split Artist in *The Professor's House* and *My Mortal Enemy.*" *Western American Literature*, vol. 46, no. 1, 2011, pp. 4–24.

Warhol, Andy. *The Philosophy of Andy Warhol (From A to B and Back Again).* Harcourt, 1975.

Warhol, Andy, and Pat Hackett. *Popism: The Warhol Sixties.* Harcourt, 1980.

Woodress, James. *Willa Cather: A Literary Life.* U of Nebraska P, 1987.

# PART 3

# Friendships, Literary and Musical

# 7 Willa Cather as Translator
## The Pittsburgh "French Soirées"

DIANE PRENATT

In 1949 George Seibel published in *The New Colophon* a reminiscence of his Pittsburgh friendship with Willa Cather, someone "few people knew" by the time of her death, he believes, because she shunned publicity and was "so shy" as to have become reclusive (195). In the essay, Seibel describes the Cather of 1896–1906 as a smart, energetic, ambitious young professional woman and a warm and fun-loving friend with whom he and his wife, Helen, spent considerable time during that decade in Pittsburgh. Notably, Cather came "to the Seibel home once or twice a week to 'read French'" at what Seibel calls their "French soirées" (196, 198). The French soirées lasted for years, perhaps for most of the time Cather was in Pittsburgh, and Seibel's list of the group's readings is extensive, representing something of a romp through nineteenth-century French literature. Midway through her Pittsburgh decade, Cather spent a winter in Washington DC, translating French documents from the 1900 Paris International Universal Exposition to assist her cousin Howard Gore in compiling his report as the chief American juror. That was the winter of 1900–1901, and when she returned to Pittsburgh in March, it was to teach Latin—among other subjects—at Central High School, where she was touted as "an accomplished linguist" (Southwick 160). This essay attempts to reframe these three separate references to translation during Cather's Pittsburgh years, to amplify the connection among them, in order to consider what her experience of translation might have contributed to Cather's practice as a fiction writer.

In the Seibels, Cather found allies for her own literary and cultural interests and for her creative energy. The 1922 *History of Pittsburgh and Environs* identifies George Seibel as the "widely known speaker and writer, editor and playwright" (314). Born the year before Cather, he was "educated in the public schools" and had little advantage but "his own native powers and the overwhelming demand for self-expression" (314); in other words, like Cather, he made himself born as a writer. He began his career in 1893 as editor of *The Youth Journal*, a one-person operation much like *The Home Monthly*; from 1896 to 1922, he was editor of the *Pittsburgh Gazette-Times*; from 1912 to 1925 (notice the overlap), editor of the German-language *Volksblatt und Freiheits Freund*; from 1927 to 1936, dramatic and literary editor of the *Pittsburgh Sun-Telegraph*; and from 1939 until his retirement in 1954, director of the Carnegie Free Library of Allegheny, to which he donated ten thousand books. For some time during these years, he also taught as a professor of poetry and drama at the Fillion Music School and broadcast a weekly radio program of book reviews. From 1923 to 1937, he was also national president of the American Turnerbund, the association of German American athletic clubs headquartered in Pittsburgh, in which capacity he had the honor of being censored by the German government during a 1933 international radio broadcast when he described Adolf Hitler as "a messianic harlequin" ("George Seibel Dies at 85," *Pittsburgh Post-Gazette*, 26 July 1958, p. 3). Throughout his career, he regularly contributed reviews and cultural commentary to a variety of journals and newspapers including *The Home Monthly*, which Cather edited, and *The Library*, to which she also contributed, and published at least one play and several works of nonfiction. Helen Seibel was a member of the Pittsburgh Women's City Club and, along with such distinguished women as Jane Addams and eventually Eleanor Roosevelt, a member of the Women's International League for Peace and Freedom. Helen hosted salon-style Sunday afternoon teas, which were attended by culturally active residents of Pittsburgh and well-known performers and artists who were visiting the city. George and Helen had a daughter, Erna, born just a few months after Cather arrived in Pittsburgh, who was no small part of the appeal the Seibel home held for Cather (Byrne and Snyder 22).

Cather enjoyed the simple and gracious domestic routine of the Seibel family, who claimed their German heritage through food as well as literature and music. She joined them every year in trimming their Christmas tree with ornaments that had been handed down in the Seibel family (suggesting, perhaps, a model for the Austrian ornaments Otto Fuchs contributes to the Burden tree in *My Ántonia* [1918]). The Seibel apartment Cather knew was located in a house that still stands at 114 Seventeenth Street and is the model for the Engelhardts' shabby-genteel apartment in "Double Birthday": "only four rooms" in "a workingman's house" in "a queer part of the city," offering a "snug sitting room" with a fire, a piano, and a "large and very personal" collection of books.[1] This was a home like the Weiners' in Red Cloud—like the Rosens' in "Old Mrs. Harris" and the Erlichs' in *One of Ours*—not grand in any way but enriched by its unpretentious familiarity with European high culture. Politically, the Seibels were nineteenth-century-style, liberal free thinkers, neither radical nor parochial; Seibel states that they believed, as Cather did, "in Santa Claus and the Golden Rule" (204).

Cather and the Seibels constituted the entire membership of the French soirées, and they did not—as one might have thought—come together to discuss a French text they had all read in common but, rather, they each "held a copy of the French text" while Seibel orally delivered a "rough and ready" English translation of that text (Seibel 197). His fellow readers might interrupt him to challenge its accuracy, and "[s]ometimes there was a what-the-hell-does-that-mean pause" (197). The energy and intensity with which the Seibels and

DIANE PRENATT

Willa Cather translated French literature is evident in the partial list of authors Seibel provides: Alphonse Daudet, Alfred de Musset, Edmond About, Pierre Loti, Émile Souvestre, Anatole France, Théophile Gautier, Victor Hugo, Paul Verlaine, Charles Baudelaire, Paul Bourget, Joris-Karl Huysmans, and, of course, "our adored Flaubert" (197)—and Honoré de Balzac, George Sand, Prosper Mérimée, Guy de Maupassant, Alexandre Dumas (*fils*), Edouard Rod, Jean Richepin, and Edmond Rostand (203). Their selection was guided in part by Henry James's essays on French literature in *French Poets and Novelists* (1878) and *Partial Portraits* (1888); at the time, Seibel writes, Cather thought Henry James "was the last word—and I hoped it was" (203). We might pause a moment here to register the number of volumes Cather translated with the Seibels. To translate a French text as Seibel describes it might be accomplished with varying degrees of fluency, but at the very least, with a list this extensive, it means that Cather was intensely preoccupied with making meaning of French at the most fundamental level—word and sentence—over a rather long period of time. Building on her reading of Latin and French as a student, translation became something of a natural mode for her at this time.

In the middle of the Pittsburgh years—and the French soirées—Cather went to Washington DC to translate French documents from the Paris Exposition of 1900 for her cousin Howard Gore, the chief American juror. This was, of course, the same Paris Exposition at which the paradigm shifted so violently from virgin to dynamo that Henry Adams "found himself lying in the Gallery of Machines . . . his historical neck broken by the sudden irruption of forces totally new" (382).[2] Her work on the Paris Exposition report hardly figures in most biographical accounts of Cather's early years: neither E. K. Brown, Edith Lewis, nor Elizabeth Shepley Sergeant mentions it; James Woodress states in a single sentence that during the winter of 1900–1901, Cather "stayed with her cousin Howard Gore and found a job translating letters and documents for the United States commission to the Paris Exposition of 1900" (147), not clarifying Gore's connection to the work; Kathleen D. Byrne and Richard C. Snyder report in *Chrysalis* that Cather intended to establish herself in Washington, taking a job as government translator but that "[c]ircumstances ... drew her back to Pittsburgh in the spring" (89). In a 1982 essay for *The Western Pennsylvania Historical Magazine*, however, Cather's niece, Helen Cather Southwick, explains that Cather translated "French documents and letters" relating to the exposition, "assisting her cousin, James Howard Gore, juror-in-chief of the exposition in the preparation of the jury's report to the United States government" (159). Southwick goes on to state that two of the six volumes of the 1901 report "bear the name of Gore as author" but that "[i]t is probable that those volumes were largely the work of Cather," Gore being completely preoccupied by his duties as professor of mathematics at Columbian (now George Washington) University (159).

The two volumes that bear Gore's name total almost twelve hundred pages. They are principally a compilation of the reports of the American jurors (of whom there were 95, as compared to the 1,421 French jurors). The encyclopedic range of these reports is staggering. There were more than eighty-five thousand exhibits in the exposition, including W. E. B. Du Bois's landmark collection of photographs, "The American Negro," and a fine arts exhibit that included the work of such American artists as Thomas Eakins and Winslow Homer, as well as Childe Hassam and other painters Cather may later have become acquainted with during a 1902 stay in Cos Cob.[3] Gore's volumes, however, are largely concerned with the products of industry, scientific research, agriculture, and education that defined material progress at the turn of the century. The report on Class 59, "Sugars, Teas, Confectionary, Condiments and Stimulants," alone runs to 104 pages (including not only the cultivation and marketing of sugar and tea, but the process of candying fruit in Auvergne, the production of chocolate in Belgium and Holland, the cultivation of vanilla, and the roasting of chicory—with notes on national preferences for licorice and the excellence of Colman's mustard). Undoubtedly, there were "letters and documents" to translate, but the American jurors' reports included in Gore's volumes were originally written in English. It seems impossible to know how much of Cather's work was actual translation and how much was transcribing and editing—although that cannot have been any small thing. There is no discernible trace of Cather's voice in these volumes of the report. We might imagine the future writer of "The Novel Démeublé" (1922) contemplating the hundreds of thousands of objects that were the subject of the jurors' reports, from escalators to Lalique glass to American popcorn—all of them lacking emotional penumbrae— but we have no record of it.[4] What we do know is that while she was in Washington, Cather attended performances by Sarah Bernhardt, in French, on four successive days.

When Cather returned to Pittsburgh, she took a position teaching Latin (as well as algebra and English composition) at Central High School, where the *High School Journal* reported that "Miss Cather is ... an accomplished linguist" (Southwick 160). Cather left jour- nalism for teaching apparently in order to free up time for writing; perhaps, momentarily, the freelance work of translation—if that is indeed the way the exposition work was represented to her—may have looked as if it would offer her a similar kind of flexibility. She had already published "experiments in translation" in her newspa- per pieces and *The Home Monthly* in the 1890s, and during her uni- versity years in Lincoln, she had read widely in classical and French literature and had begun translating "lines from Greek or Latin and then poems from modern Continental writers" (Slote, "Willa Cather and Her First Book" xii). At this time, there were notable examples of women making a career of translation, among them Constance Garnett (1862–1946), who translated more than seventy works of Russian literature beginning in the early 1890s, and Ellen Marriage (1865–1946), who translated the complete works of Bal- zac for Dent (1895–98). Dorothy Canfield, whose fluency in French Cather so admired, had begun her doctoral studies at Columbia Uni- versity by the time Cather went to Washington; perhaps her work with Corneille and Racine suggested such a possibility. In the end, however, Cather abandoned whatever plans she might have had for herself as a translator in Washington DC, although the high school newspaper piece indicates that she wanted others to know she had done such work. The "circumstances" that called her back to Pittsburgh were related to her new friendship with Isabelle McClung, for when she returned, she took up residence in the McClung home in Squirrel Hill, her teaching position possibly secured by Isabelle's father, Judge Samuel McClung (Woodress 150). Fred Otte, a student in Cather's English class at Central High, remembers being assigned short works by Loti, Felix Gras, Maupassant, and Daudet, translated from the French (45); another student, Phyllis Martin Hutchinson, recalls that Cather "was steeped in the classics, and her knowledge of Latin was always evident in class. Invariably [Cather] tried to show us how to derive the meaning of English words from their Latin roots" (50).

How might Cather's interest in translation, such as it was, have affected the fiction she would later write? In some ways, very literally. It is remarkable how often the act of translation is depicted in the novels she would write after the Pittsburgh years. It is not unusual for novels, appealing to middle-class literacy, to depict characters in the act of reading. But Cather's fiction repeatedly depicts characters in the act of translating texts. To select only a few examples: in *The Song of the Lark*, Professor Wunsch translates, for Thea, Ovid's line "Lente currite, lente currite, noctis equi" ("Go slowly, go slowly, ye steeds of the night"; 25); in a similar scene, Mr. Rosen in "Old Mrs. Harris" gives Vickie her first French lesson by translating Michelet's "Le but n'est rien; le chemin, c'est tout" ("The end is nothing; the road is all"; 158); on the range, Tom Outland translates one hundred lines of Caesar a day and he reads Lucretius with Professor St. Peter, while the Professor, of course, has spent virtually a lifetime translating the accounts of the Spanish explorers for his history; Jim Burden of *My Ántonia* translates Virgil and reads Dante's *Commedia* with his tutor; Claude Wheeler of *One of Ours* reads the transcript of Joan of Arc's trial in English translation but with "the French text at his elbow, and some of her replies haunted him in the language in which they were spoken" (91).

The act of translation also figures in Cather's fiction as a recurrent trope for personal transformation. As an immigrant, for example,

Ántonia Shimerda learns to translate Bohemian words into English
as she learns to translate her Bohemian mother's inadequate domestic practices into the "nice ways" of American wives and mothers like
Mrs. Burden and Mrs. Harling.[5] In *Shadows on the Rock* (1931), Cécile
Auclair translates the refined French domestic rituals she learned
from her mother into a rough Canadian vocabulary, musing over a
sentence of schoolgirl French as her father analyzes the difference
between French and Québecois gooseberries (18). Vickie Templeton's
French lesson and Thea Kronborg's Latin lesson mark points in the
*bildung* arc of the young women's lives. Translating Virgil's *Georgics*,
Jim Burden has the "inestimably precious" "revelation" that without
the hired girls of Black Hawk, "there would be no poetry" (262). In
the New World, Jean Marie Latour of *Death Comes for the Archbishop*
(1927) learns to speak English and Spanish and is transformed from
a young French missionary priest into a venerable American archbishop. Professor St. Peter has translated the stubborn soil of Hamilton into a French garden but resists translating himself into his wife's
construct of the successful middle-aged man. In Pittsburgh, Cather
herself was in the process of personal transformation, which Seibel
in his essay reads as a translation: referring to intellectual discoveries Cather made in those years (i.e., Nietzsche, Richard Strauss, A. E.
Housman), he notes that "other new planets swam into Willa's ken"
(202), a deft appropriation of Keats's metaphor in "On First Looking
into Chapman's Homer"—a poem about the way a translation can
transform the imagination.

Cather not only depicted characters performing translation, both
literal and figurative; she used translation as a narrative strategy,
lending authenticity to such works as *Death Comes for the Archbishop*
and *Shadows on the Rock*. Françoise Palleau-Papin has demonstrated
that Cather's grammatical constructions of English in these two
novels imitate recognizable French constructions like the alexan-
drine line, bringing "English closer to the French rhythm and syntax" so that the French language resonates throughout in a version
of Gilles Deleuze's "ghost language" (53). Essentially, Palleau-Papin
describes Cather as a translator in these two novels, "passing from

one language to another" (57), "submit[ting] her use of English to the restraint of a foreign language" (61), setting her English, as Deleuze would say, "to a minor key" (52) so that the French vocabulary and syntax resonate. "Cather seems to have thought and felt in this language," Palleau-Papin concludes, "midway between French and English" (61).

In her wide-ranging study of the influence of French writers on Cather's fiction, Stéphanie Durrans sees the interpolation of French words and passages in *Shadows on the Rock* as an expression of the "interaction of antagonistic cultures" that is the subject of the novel (223). Unlike the "free interplay of languages" in *Death Comes for the Archbishop*, *Shadows on the Rock* displays "Cather's reluctance to translate" that echoes "the resistance of the French settlers to the indigenous culture and the resistance of the French language itself to all attempts at assimilation" (224). Durrans sees translation as a writing strategy for Cather, "whose acute awareness of language issues led her to investigate the potentialities of multilingual discourse" (233). This translated and multilingual discourse is also evident in *One of Ours*, in Claude Wheeler's awkward French rendered side by side with the French-inflected English dialogue of such French characters as Madame Joubert and Mademoiselle de Courcy.

Delineated in this "language midway between French and English" is a construction we might call "Cather's French imaginary," the particular ideation of a cultural and historical France that Cather had begun to form through her earliest reading of French literature, a personal France that the Romantic texts of the French soirées surely affirmed. In a 1974 essay, the Aixois scholar Michel Gervaud wonders whether "[t]he France she loved may represent just a myth"; nevertheless, "it fecundated and nourished her creativeness" and "played [a part] in the shaping of her genius and the orientation of her inventive powers" (66). "There seemed to be a natural affinity between her mind and French forms of art," Dorothy Canfield Fisher remembered (93). More recently, Marc Chénetier, who has translated nine of Cather's works into French, states that Cather aspired "to a set of aesthetic and intellectual ideals that French . . . had come to stand for," and that the French language "provided her with new modes of apprehension and aesthetic perception" (39). Discerning the presence of the French language even "in works that do not referentially need it," which he calls the "ghost in translation" (32), Chénetier writes that Cather's use of French "is less a direct matter of language than a frame of mind" (37). In other words, Cather writes as a translator, in constant reference to an idiom that is not native to her, to a culture in which she is a privileged foreigner.

Cather's imagined France filled an empty space on her personal map. In *French Lessons*, the remarkable 1993 memoir chronicling her own acquisition of French, Alice Kaplan asks, "Why do people want to adopt another culture? Because there's something in their own they don't like, that doesn't *name* them" (209; original emphasis). Cather's biography indicates how deeply she felt at times unnamed by Red Cloud, Pittsburgh, and even New York—how she chafed at the normative social constructs for women's lives, for example, and at the banality of American consumer culture. Her early reading of nineteenth-century French *romanciers* like Daudet, Dumas, and Loti led her into a historical world of adventure, eccentricity, and sensuality. The texts of the French soirées, many of them in the same genre, affirmed that world. The grammatical apparatus of the French language itself, like that of Latin, was a model of the kind of intellectual rigor that informs Cather's early critical statements. In her later novels, we can observe with Michel Gervaud "the sheer delight she found in handling an idiom she loved" (70).

What Cather sought in French literature and the French language was *affiliation*, membership in a community that nurtured her creativity, a relationship to a tradition that offered her models of great artistic achievement. She was a "hero-worshipper," as Elizabeth Shepley Sergeant realized, "amaze[d]" at Cather's awestruck description of Mrs. Fields's "literary Elysium," the Charles Street parlor haunted by the ghosts of Hawthorne and Dickens (41). A quarter of a century later, "A Chance Meeting" (1933) conveys Cather's thrill at a similar proximity to greatness—discovering that the elderly woman she has been chatting with at Aix-les-Bains is the niece of Gustave Flaubert.

French was the idiom of the world to which Cather felt deeply affiliated and in which she longed to feel at ease. Her desire to be fluent in that world can be measured by the humiliation she felt during her first visit to France, in 1902, unable to make her way in French and outshone by her friend Dorothy Canfield's fluency. Dorothy Canfield probably knew better than any of Cather's friends the world in which French language proficiency was a mark of cultural privilege, acquired through childhood trips to Europe, French governesses, and finishing schools. As Mark Madigan has shown, Cather "felt a certain inferiority in comparison with the more cosmopolitan [Canfield]" ("Willa Cather and Dorothy Canfield Fisher" 116). In Paris in 1902, Cather was abashed by her failure to translate into the world she had claimed through her study of French and her prodigious reading of French literature. She had wanted to feel as Canfield did, "completely French" (Madigan, "Regarding" 3). Devastated and envious, she behaved so badly that almost two years later, she wrote an abject letter of apology to Canfield, acknowledging that "I was ill-tempered and ungrateful and . . . I behaved very childishly," explaining that "I didn't understand French and . . . I felt very provincial and helpless and ignorant. It makes me ill to think of it, it surely does" (*Selected Letters* 76). So deep was her frustration and sadness at being excluded that Cather tried to explain it again, eighteen years later, when she wrote to Canfield, who was reading the proofs of *One of Ours*, that Claude Wheeler's feeling of cultural inferiority to David Gerhardt *"was the way you made me feel when we were in France together that time"* (316; original emphasis); she now realizes that she herself had made her cousin G. P. Cather feel that way, "the way helpless ignorance always feels" (316). In "A Chance Meeting," the 1933 essay about her conversations with Flaubert's niece, Cather—a generation older and a little less brash than the "accomplished linguist" of Pittsburgh—writes of herself, "I am a poor linguist" (5).

But translating with the Seibels, in the French soirées occurring both before and after the 1902 European trip, Cather did not feel provincial and helpless and ignorant; she felt knowledgeable and included; she felt affiliated. As collaborative oral performances, the soirées were, on the one hand, very familiar to Cather, of a piece with the oral performances by which turn-of-the-century middle America was entertained and edified. Cather grew up in a time when family members and friends regularly read aloud at home for entertainment, and schoolchildren learned by reciting orally. Her own talents led her to community theatricals in which, as young as eleven, she "electrified the audience with elocutionary powers" (Woodress 57); she delivered an oration at her high school graduation (58). She and Isabelle McClung read aloud together when Cather lived at 1180 Murray Hill Avenue, and they later read Michelet together when Cather visited from New York; her countless newspaper reviews attest to her fervent love for theatrical performance; even "her apparent interest in music," George Seibel observed, "was really always confined to performers of music or to music connected to theatricals, as in the opera" (Bennett 152).

In addition, Cather already had almost fifteen years' experience listening to the nonnative speakers of English in and around Red Cloud. Later, as a fiction writer, she represents realistically the broken English of immigrants who are between two linguistic worlds: not only Mrs. Shimerda (a prime example) but Crazy Ivar and old Mrs. Lee from *O Pioneers!*, Jacinto from *Death Comes for the Archbishop*, the German Mrs. Vogt and the French villagers of *One of Ours*. She demonstrates sensitivity to the physical sound of language as it was represented on the page: when she met Flaubert's niece, Mme. Franklin Grout, and they talked about Flaubert's work, Cather referred to the last line of Flaubert's *Herodias*, with its rhythm so suggestive of the physical act it described. She reproduces the last word phonetically, syllable by syllable, separated by hyphens: "Comme elle était très lourde, ils la portaient al-ter-na-tiv-e-ment" ("As [John the Baptist's head] was very heavy, they took turns carrying it"; 22). Michel Gervaud confirms that Cather "had a keen perception of the cadence and musicality of French" (although he points out ["Willa Cather and France" 69] that the last word in Flaubert's sentence should be divided as "al-ter-na-ti-ve-ment").[6] Cécile Auclair's concern over her mother's pot of parsley—"Papa, j'ai peur pour le persil"—might be an exercise in the pronunciation of the French *p* and French diphthongs.

On the other hand, the soirées conferred the kind of inclusion and cultural privilege Cather longed for during her 1902 visit to France. By its very nature, the translating project necessarily restricted membership and created a sense of intimacy, even secrecy. Seibel's essay conveys the interiority of the French soirées: that snug sitting room warmed by a fire, well-fed friends chatting over books and music, the baby finally in bed, the lamp refilled so as to prolong the evening. The interiority is emphasized by the sense these young friends had that they were banded together, out from under the watchful eye of Pittsburgh's stern Presbyterians, conspiring to do something a tiny bit wicked—reading Daudet's short stories "bubbling with malicious delight in feminine foibles" (196). And Balzac! Right here in River City! At fifty, Cather would write, "It is scarcely exaggeration to say that if one is not a little mad about Balzac at twenty, one will never live" ("Chance Meeting" 24). But the fact is that there was serious censorship—at least, bowdlerizing—of some of this literature at the time Cather and the Seibels were meeting. The American and British translations of Balzac at this time, for example, were never "completely complete" even at forty volumes; at least five novels "were discreetly dropped on grounds . . . of lesbianism, cynicism, bestiality, and general 'morbidity'" (Lesser 346). Henry James described the first American translator of the (almost) complete Balzac—Katharine Prescott Wormley, a friend of Sarah Orne Jewett's—as "a New England old maid, unacquainted with French—and other badnesses—mistranslating Balzac" (Lesser 344). Ellen Marriage, Balzac's British translator for Dent, assumed a male pseudonym to tackle his more salacious novels.

The orality of the translation project is enhanced by the sociability of the French soirées, suggested by the Seibels' generous hospitality. Food figures prominently in Seibel's account of the French soirées—no surprise to anyone who belongs to a book group—and contributes a Pickwick-like conviviality to their gatherings. (Indeed, both George and Helen later became members of the Dickens Fellowship, when the Pittsburgh branch was founded in 1925.) Seibel reminisces about those days "before ... calories or vitamins" when they would sit down to a simple supper of noodle soup, potato salad "larded with delicious slices of cucumber," and "crisp and crackling" cookies (198). Erna, growing up through the years of the French soirées, horrified her mother at the supper table once by commanding Willa to "look!" as she picked up a bowl of berries and slurped the juice. At Christmas time, Cather "crunched her share of anise cakes and *pfeffernüsse*" and chewed on needles from the Christmas tree (199). A young Dorothy Canfield, who visited with Cather one Christmas, was given a second cup of coffee—considered quite an adult treat for a girl of sixteen. The Seibels' cat was named Hasenpfeffer, after the traditional German rabbit stew. Seibel uses food and drink as a metaphor for the text as well. The three friends devoured "pleasant [French] pastry" like Souvestre's *Philosophe sous les Toits* (*An Attic Philosopher*, 1854), "indulged oftener in devil's food like Anatole France's *Le Lys Rouge*" (*The Red Lily*, 1897), and drank "deep draughts of young Rostand's ruby wine" (197, 203). He describes two of Cather's *April Twilights* poems as "sugared sonnets" and others with "a drop of absinthe from Verlaine" (199–200). Seibel's delighted memories of the French soirées correspond to what Marc Chénetier identifies in Cather as "an orality variously illustrated by her love for food and cooking and her delight in conversation" (40) linked to her "abstract sensuous quest for the feel of an ideal French language" (39).

As Seibel recounts them, the social circumstances of the French soirées provide a frame for the orally translated literature. As Cather and the Seibels devour the nineteenth-century French canon, the Pittsburgh frame tells its own changing story. Erna grows from an infant who is put to bed before the evening begins, to a toddler who argues about being put to bed, to a girl who is allowed to sit at the supper table with the adults. Cather publishes *April Twilights* and the stories of *The Troll Garden*, the Seibels among their very first readers. Cather meets Isabelle McClung. Seibel and Cather contribute to "another forlorn hope of literature" (205), the short-lived journal *The Library*, and Seibel's poetic style, he writes, shifts from Sir John

Suckling to Austin Dobson. The social frame of the French soirées allowed Cather to listen to the translation of stories as she would have listened to any orally recited tale; although Cather and the Seibels were translating written texts, the performative aspect of their project was more like the oral storytelling and oratory of Cather's childhood than her reading of French literature as a university student. Additionally, the literature of the French soirées, so much of it nineteenth-century romances and tales, makes conspicuous use of the framed narrative itself. Daudet's *Femmes d'artistes* (*Artists' Wives*, 1874) and Edmond About's *Roi des montagnes* (*The King of the Mountains*, 1856), both on Seibel's list, are framed narratives, as are many of Balzac's shorter pieces (e.g., "Ficino Cane" and "A Passion in the Desert"). The French soirées contributed to Cather's use of storytelling scenes and framed narrative structures in novels from *O Pioneers!* through *Shadows on the Rock*.

Cather's friendship with the Seibels played an essential role during her formative years in Pittsburgh, and she maintained a friendly correspondence with the couple for some years after she moved to New York, as indicated by the thirty letters from Cather to her parents that Erna Seibel Yorke donated to the Willa Cather Pioneer Memorial, now the Willa Cather Archive, in 1970. During visits with Isabelle McClung in Pittsburgh, Cather called upon the Seibels, now moved to a more spacious house in Mount Oliver. In response to Helen Seibel's enthusiasm for *The Song of the Lark*, Cather wrote in 1916 that Mr. Kohler's "piece-picture" described in that novel "hung in the fitting room of a German 'Ladies Tailor' in the East End [of Pittsburgh], long and long ago" (*Selected Letters* 215). "I'm glad you still like those old simple things we used to laugh about and enjoy," Cather continues and closes warmly, "Please come to visit me when you are in New York" (216). When *My Mortal Enemy* was published in 1926, Cather wrote to George Seibel that she "had a premonition [he] would understand [the novel]— and that most people wouldn't" (Seibel 207). But by 1933, when Cather wrote to Dorothy Canfield Fisher to look for "A Chance Meeting" in the February *Atlantic*, she refers to Seibel, with whom

"I dug through *Salammbô* and all the Letters [from Flaubert to his niece]" as "the German proofreader in Pittsburgh" (*Selected Letters* 481), unkindly diminishing the standing of her old friend who was then a published author and the dramatic and literary editor of the *Pittsburgh Sun-Times*. In 1937 she wrote to Meta Cather asking that she forward to her any mail from Seibel (who must not have had her Park Avenue address), inexplicably adding, "This George Seibel is a Pittsburgh editor, and is one of the most persistent and tormenting of all my many curses" (527).

Cather's final disdain for George Seibel is difficult to reconcile with the mutual regard and sheer joy of their earlier friendship. Her changed attitude may have been symptomatic of the increasingly withdrawn social behavior that Elizabeth Shepley Sergeant, for one, noticed in Cather's later years and to which Seibel himself alludes in his *New Colophon* essay. Cather may have feared that Seibel, journalist and critic, would presume upon their personal friendship to write something about her for publication. As the world moved toward a declaration of war against Germany, she may have grown wary of the political discourse in which Seibel was sometimes engaged. She may not have wanted to revisit her years in Pittsburgh, a time of struggle and vulnerability. Whatever the case, the French soirées had run their day and, like the East End tailor's piece-picture, had become one of "those old simple things we used to laugh about and enjoy." They leave their mark, however, on Cather's fiction, in which translation functions as a narrative strategy, as a plot device, and as enduring evidence of the deep meaning Willa Cather found in a language, a literature, and a culture not her own.

## NOTES

1. "Double Birthday" in *Uncle Valentine* (45–46). In her introduction, Bernice Slote states, "The [Engelhardts'] apartment itself is in every detail that of the George Seibels, so the late Mrs. Seibel once told me" (xxviii). Byrne and Snyder concur: "Two letters written by Helen Seibel agree that the Engelhardt home described in ... 'Double Birthday' is a fair representation of the Seibel home" (21).

2. "Langley," who serves as Adams's guide to the exposition, is Samuel Pierpont Langley (1834–1906), who taught astronomy at the Western University of Pennsylvania (now University of Pittsburgh) and directed the Allegheny Observatory in Pittsburgh, where he developed the Allegheny Time System, a prototype for the Standard Time Zones. In 1887 he became director of the Smithsonian, an institution that figures importantly in Cather's novel *The Professor's House* (1925).

3. Painters Cather may have met at Cos Cob who exhibited at the Paris Exposition include Childe Hassam, Leonard Ochtman, and J. Francis Murphy. Merrill Maguire Skaggs has proposed that Cather visited Cos Cob between October 1902 and April 1903, after returning to her teaching job in Pittsburgh from the European trip with Isabelle McClung and that, although "she carefully obfuscated this interlude ... it significantly affected her career" (43).

4. Hélène Trocmé reports that Americans at the Paris Exposition were regarded like "les sauvages de l'exposition des Colonies" (39). They were thought self-important (they insisted that the minaret on the nearby Turkish pavilion be reduced so as not to outdo an American cupola), crude (they spat and they were seen enjoying popcorn and corn on the cob, considered food for swine in France), and deplorably Puritanical (the American pavilion was closed on Sundays) (38–39).

5. For an extended discussion of translation as a trope for ethnic and national assimilation, see my essay, "Ántonia's Mother Tongue: Reading and Translating (in) *My Ántonia*."

6. Gervaud notes that the young Cather "took little interest in French grammar and was bored by exercises" (68) but that we can assume "her understanding of written French was very good" (69). He points out that the French phrases in her novels "are correct most of the time though they occasionally contain a few mistakes (or misprints?) and even may look clumsy" (69).

## WORKS CITED

Adams, Henry. *The Education of Henry Adams.* 1907. Modern Library, 1931.

Bennett, Mildred. *The World of Willa Cather.* U of Nebraska P, 1951.

Byrne, Kathleen D., and Richard C. Snyder. *Chrysalis: Willa Cather in Pittsburgh, 1896–1906.* Historical Society of Western Pennsylvania, 1980.

Cather, Willa. "A Chance Meeting." 1933. *Not Under Forty,* U of Nebraska P, 1988, pp. 3–42.

———. "Double Birthday." *Uncle Valentine and Other Stories: Willa Cather's Uncollected Short Fiction, 1915–1929*, edited by Bernice Slote, U of Nebraska P, 1973, pp. 39–63.

———. *My Ántonia*. 1918. Willa Cather Scholarly Edition, historical essay by James Woodress, explanatory notes by Woodress with Kari A. Ronning, Kathleen Danker, and Emily Levine, textual commentary and editing by Charles Mignon with Ronning, U of Nebraska P, 1994.

———. "Old Mrs. Harris." *Obscure Destinies*. 1932. Willa Cather Scholarly Edition, historical essay and explanatory notes by Kari A. Ronning, textual essay by Frederick M. Link with Kari A. Ronning and Mark Kamrath, U of Nebraska P, 1998, pp. 63–157.

———. *One of Ours*. 1922. Willa Cather Scholarly Edition, historical essay and explanatory notes by Richard C. Harris, textual editing by Frederick M. Link with Kari A. Ronning, U of Nebraska P, 2006.

———. *The Selected Letters of Willa Cather*. Edited by Andrew Jewell and Janis Stout, Knopf, 2016.

———. *Shadows on the Rock*. 1931. Willa Cather Scholarly Edition, historical essay and explanatory notes by John J. Murphy and David Stouck, textual editing by Frederick M. Link, U of Nebraska P, 2005.

———. *The Song of the Lark*. 1915. Willa Cather Scholarly Edition, historical essay and explanatory notes by Ann Moseley, textual essay and editing by Kari A. Ronning, U of Nebraska P, 2012.

Chénetier, Marc. "Shadows of a Rock: Translating Willa Cather." *Cather Studies 8: Willa Cather; A Writer's Worlds*, edited by John J. Murphy, Françoise Palleau-Papin, and Robert Thacker, U of Nebraska P, 2010, pp. 23–45.

Durrans, Stéphanie. *The Influence of French Culture on Willa Cather: Intertextual References and Resonances*. Edwin Mellen P, 2007.

Fisher, Dorothy Canfield. "Willa Cather, Daughter of the Frontier." 1933. *Willa Cather Remembered*, edited by Sharon Hoover, U of Nebraska P, 2002, pp. 90–96.

Gervaud, Michel. "Willa Cather and France: Elective Affinities." *The Art of Willa Cather*, edited by Bernice Slote and Virginia Faulkner, U of Nebraska P, 1974, pp. 65–83.

*History of Pittsburgh and Environs*. Vol. 5. American Historical Society, 1922.

Hutchinson, Phyllis Martin. "Reminiscences of Willa Cather as a Teacher." 1956. *Willa Cather Remembered*, edited by Sharon Hoover, U of Nebraska P, 2002, pp. 48–51.

Kaplan, Alice. *French Lessons*. U of Chicago P, 1993.

Lesser, Margaret. "Ellen Marriage and the Translation of Balzac." *Translation and Literature*, vol. 21, 2012, pp. 343–63.

Madigan, Mark. "Regarding Willa Cather's 'The Profile' and Evelyn Osborne." *Willa Cather Pioneer Memorial and Educational Foundation Newsletter and Review*, vol. 44, no. 1, 2000, pp. 1–5.

———. "Willa Cather and Dorothy Canfield Fisher: Rift, Reconciliation, and *One of Ours*." *Cather Studies 1*, edited by Susan J. Rosowski, U of Nebraska P, 1990, pp. 115–29.

Otte, Fred. "The Willa Cather I Knew." c. 1940. *Willa Cather Remembered*, edited by Sharon Hoover, U of Nebraska P, 2002, pp. 42–49.

Palleau-Papin, Françoise. "The Hidden French in Willa Cather's English." *Cather Studies 4: Willa Cather's Canadian and Old World Connections*, edited by Robert Thacker and Michael A. Peterman, U of Nebraska P, 1999, pp. 45–65.

Prenatt, Diane. "Ántonia's Mother Tongue: Reading and Translating (in) *My Ántonia*." *Something Complete and Great: The Centennial Study of "My Ántonia,"* edited by Holly Blackford, Fairleigh Dickinson UP, 2018, pp. 63–80.

*Report of the Commissioner-General for the United States to the International Universal Exposition, Paris*. 1900. Government Printing Office, 1901. Vols. 5 and 6.

Seibel, George. "Miss Willa Cather from Nebraska." *The New Colophon*, vol. 2, 1949, pp. 195–207.

Sergeant, Elizabeth Shepley. *Willa Cather: A Memoir*. 1953. U of Nebraska P, 1963.

Skaggs, Merrill Maguire. "Young Willa Cather and the Road to Cos Cob." *Willa Cather's New York: New Essays on Cather in the City*, edited by Merrill Maguire Skaggs, Fairleigh Dickinson UP, 2000, pp. 43–59.

Slote, Bernice. Introduction. *Uncle Valentine and Other Stories: Willa Cather's Uncollected Short Fiction, 1915–1929*, edited by Bernice Slote, U of Nebraska P, 1973, pp. ix–xxx.

———. Introduction. "Willa Cather and Her First Book." *April Twilights (1903)* by Willa Cather, edited by Bernice Slote, U of Nebraska P, 1976, pp. ix–xlv.

Southwick, Helen C. "Willa Cather's Early Career: Origins of a Legend." 1982. *Willa Cather Remembered*, edited by Sharon Hoover, U of Nebraska P, 2002, pp. 156–70.

Trocmé, Hélène. "1900: Les Américains à l'exposition universelle de Paris." *Revue française d'études américaines*, vol. 59, 1994, pp. 35–44.

Woodress, James. *Willa Cather: A Literary Life*. U of Nebraska P, 1987.

# 8  A Collegial Friendship
## Willa Cather and Ethel Herr Litchfield

JOHN H. FLANNIGAN

In November 1912, an esteemed Pittsburgh pianist published an essay, "Why Should Our Children Study Music?," alerting readers to "the absolute necessity in the human life for a leavening proportion of happiness."[1] The author, Ethel Herr Litchfield, advised that children should study the arts and sciences because the "intellectual enjoyment" of such studies would "help them through the times of depression or monotony or loneliness that are sure to come later" ("Why Should"). For support, Litchfield turned to an essay on education by Harvard psychologist Hugo Münsterberg, who, as a boy, had eagerly studied botany but years later was unable to "discriminate a mushroom from an apple tree" (Münsterberg 49). "But what matter?" asked Litchfield. "The enthusiasm for botany served its purpose at the time; it stimulated and brought into play the capacities of the young mind" ("Why Should").

Litchfield may have known of Münsterberg through her friend, Willa Cather, under whose guidance his essays appeared in *McClure's Magazine* beginning in 1907 (Woodress 208; Urgo 62–64). However Litchfield discovered Münsterberg, her essay, full of observations

Cather likely would have endorsed, supports the claim Cather made late in her life that she and Litchfield "melted together" early in their friendship (*Selected Letters* 602). Yet Litchfield has received little attention from Cather's biographers beyond token references to her abandonment of a music career after marriage to a distinguished physician (Woodress 119; Byrne and Snyder 49–50; Lee 49). Questions of who Litchfield was or what drew her to Cather and vice versa have remained unanswered in Cather studies.

In fact, Cather and Litchfield grew close because they had followed similar paths. Enormously gifted and precocious music lovers, both had attracted critical notice early in adolescence and appeared destined for success, but they became trapped in long apprenticeships and artistic doldrums. Both sought reinvigorated careers at the same time, and both discovered distinguished mentors to guide them. With so much shared history between them, it is not surprising that the two remained close friends for life.

Furthermore, David Porter's claim that Cather saw painters Earl and Achsah Brewster "not just as friends but as fellow artists," even as "colleagues," applies to the Cather-Litchfield friendship, too (Marks and Porter 94). In fact, Cather likely borrowed from Litchfield's extensive musical knowledge and experience for her fiction, and Litchfield in turn relied on Cather's skill in poetry, as evidenced by the song "The Swedish Mother" that unexpectedly surfaced in 2001 (Ford and Bybee).[2] Moreover, "The Swedish Mother" was not Litchfield's only composition. According to newspaper coverage of Litchfield's performances, discussed later in this essay, Litchfield composed other works, some of them vocal settings of unattributed texts, and I suggest the titles of these song texts reflect Cather's influence or authorship. Therefore, exploring Litchfield's life and career not only will illuminate an important, collegial friendship between two successful artists but also may encourage a reexamination of the interplay between the personal and the professional throughout Cather's friendships.

Ethel Herr Jones was born 2 April 1876 in New Brighton, Pennsylvania.[3] She was the seventh of eight children of Sarah Ada Herr

(1835–1930) and David Jones (1835–1920), the Welsh-born pastor of Pittsburgh's Fifth Avenue Methodist Protestant Church and later president of Adrian College ("Obituary News—Rev. David Jones"). Jones began piano studies at age ten with Joseph H. Gittings (1848–1920), and, in December 1889, when she was only thirteen, Gittings showcased her at the convention of the Pennsylvania State Music Teachers' Association in Philadelphia ("The Music World"). Critics there praised her "strength of mind and grasping power of intricate musical forms" in performances that were "a natural outburst of young genius. . . . Her manner was devoid of all affectation, natural and child-like, yet not in the least childish. . . . We predict for this young talent a brilliant future" ("The Music World").

Billed as "the wonderful child pianist," Jones toured Ohio, Illinois, Wisconsin, and Minnesota in January and February 1891 with Chicago oratorio soprano Genevra Johnstone-Bishop (1857–1923) and received excellent reviews ("Congregational Church"; "Mrs. Bishop Cheered by 800"). Jones's pièce de résistance, the solo part of Mendelssohn's G Minor Concerto, shared programs with shorter works, including a ballade for solo piano by Carl Reinecke and the aria "I Know that My Redeemer Liveth" from Handel's *Messiah*, the same pieces that young Thea Kronborg plays in *The Song of the Lark* ("Music in St. Paul"; "Among the Musicians"; *Song of the Lark* 67, 296).

Stories of Jones's successful tour would have impressed Cather, a prodigy herself whose earliest writing exhibited "the range, felicity, and braggadocio of the music reviews" she would later write (Porter 254). Cather would have remembered Jones's touring partner, too. On 18 April 1895, Cather heard Johnstone-Bishop, accompanied by Theodore Thomas and the Chicago Symphony Orchestra, sing selections by Gounod, Weber, and Chaminade at Lincoln's Funke Opera House. Cather long remembered the occasion as "a great day," too, for Thomas's program that evening also included the Lincoln premiere of Dvořák's *New World Symphony* (*Selected Letters* 216; "Theatre").

Seemingly unbeknownst to Cather's biographers, Jones studied in New York in 1895–96 with Hungarian pianist Rafael Joseffy (1852–1915) and was one of his favorite pupils ("Music"). Perhaps Cather drew on Jones's memories for the story "Double Birthday" (1929), in which Pittsburgher Albert Englehardt, a former protégé of Joseffy, speaks warmly of him (*Uncle Valentine* 55; 61–62). Another pianist friend of Jones's from this period aided the mature Cather in more tangible ways. On her way to Vienna in August 1896 to study with renowned teacher Theodor Leschetizky (1830–1915), Jones traveled with his prospective pupil Lucy Parsons Hine ("Society"). Twenty-one years later, while renting Woodbine Farm (High Mowing) near Jaffrey, New Hampshire, Hine and her partner, Ethel Buchanan Acheson, loaned a tent and the use of a meadow to Cather where she wrote much of *My Ántonia* (1918) (Byrne and Snyder 112; Lewis 104–5; *Selected Letters* 619).[4]

Jones enjoyed life in Vienna and extended her stay to two years ("In Society"). In spring 1897 she wrote to colleagues at Pittsburgh's Tuesday Musical Club, sharing amusing accounts of learning German and of Leschetizky's habits, and expressed the hope that chamber music would become popular in America, "for it is one of the most enjoyable forms of concert music" (Harding, "In the Realm of Women's Clubs"). (Later, this hope would become a driving force in Jones's life.) Jones's postponed return home induced her suitor, Dr. Lawrence Litchfield (1861–1930), to sail for Europe, and, on 9 June 1898, Leschetizky gave the bride away as Litchfield and Jones were married at the American legation in Vienna ("In Society"). The *Pittsburgh Post* reported that the wedding had been expected and concluded with the laconic—and unprophetic—comment, "The marriage presumably ends further European study" ("In Society").

In April 1899 the Litchfields settled in Pittsburgh's Shadyside neighborhood at 5431 Fifth Avenue, the house outside which Cather, before she knew its owner, often stood "listening to the music that streamed from it at all hours of the day and night" ("Real Estate"; Byrne and Snyder 49–50; Lewis 49). Litchfield and Cather met in 1902, and the latter discovered "something intimate, congenial, and extremely enriching" in her friend's family that influenced the short story "The Garden Lodge" (1905) and its characters Howard Noble and his pianist wife, Caroline (Byrne and Snyder 49–50; Lewis 49;

Woodress 178). The Nobles' sixteen-year age difference mirrors the nearly fifteen-year gap between Litchfield and her husband (*Troll Garden* 49). And the Litchfields, who invited French artist Edmond Aman-Jean (1858–1936) to rest at their home for six weeks in March and April 1903 while he painted his *Portrait of Mrs. Lawrence Litchfield*, clearly prefigured the Nobles, who host French tenor Raymond d'Esquerré for a month's rest before his London opera engagement ("A Distinguished Visitor"; *Troll Garden* 49, 46).[5]

Beginning in 1902, her responsibilities as president and vice president of the Tuesday Musical Club allowed Litchfield limited opportunities to concertize (Harding, "The Club Woman's World"; "The Week's Doings"). And the births of three children, Ethel Carver (1899–1976), Lawrence Jr. (1900–1967), and Margaret (1903–90), all of whom received lessons in the arts, further restricted her appearances.[6] When she did perform, it was usually at private musicales and club meetings, of which the program for 14 January 1902 is typical: salon pieces, light songs, and truncated versions of the standard repertoire, on this occasion Litchfield's performance of the first movement only of Chopin's B-flat Minor Sonata, followed by tea and ices ("Happenings in Society's Realm").

Litchfield's dissatisfaction with this pattern would soon become apparent. A harbinger of change came in April 1907 when she appeared at the National Arts Club in New York with composer and pianist Giuseppe Ferrata (1865–1928) of the Beaver College and Musical Institute and others in an unusual concert devoted entirely to Ferrata's works ("Notes of Musical Events"). It was Litchfield's only known New York appearance and probably a welcome opportunity for ensemble playing. Another event around this time had far greater importance for her: meeting Russian pianists Josef Lhevinne (1874–1944) and his wife, Rosina (1880–1976), who visited Pittsburgh in March 1907, became her teachers, mentors, and lifelong friends, and, as will be seen, broke the mold of Litchfield's musical life. Although both Lhevinnes had been gold medalists at the Moscow Conservatory, Rosina abandoned a solo career to avoid competing with her husband (Wallace 50–51, 61). They both so impressed Litchfield, however, that, shortly after Josef's Pittsburgh debut, she helped arrange a joint recital for the couple on 2 May 1907 ("Lhevinne Wins Triumph"; Suydam).

Both gifted teachers, the Lhevinnes attracted many American students to their home in Wannsee, near Berlin (Wallace 120), and among them were Litchfield's friends Lucy Hine and Ethel Acheson, who traveled there in 1908 (*U.S. Consular*). Litchfield, too, moved to Germany in October 1908 with her children, and the latter attended schools in Berlin and Lausanne, Switzerland (*U.S. Passport [Ethel Herr Litchfield]*; *U.S. Passport [Margaret Litchfield]*; Tudor). Her activities around this time are unknown, but she did not immediately begin studies with the Lhevinnes, for, the same month she arrived in Europe, they began another American tour and were away from Wannsee until May 1909 (Wallace 116).

Very likely, Litchfield's plan to study overseas was negotiated amicably with Dr. Lawrence Litchfield, who pursued his own professional interests in spring and summer 1909 surveying venereal disease clinics in European cities, including Berlin, for a paper he later published ("A Plea for the Establishment"). The entire Litchfield family reassembled in Pittsburgh in September 1909, but Ethel and her children were in Europe again between June and October 1910 and made a final sojourn between June 1911 and September 1912 (*Hamburg Passenger Lists*; *U.S. Passport [Margaret Litchfield]*; *New York Passenger Lists*). Pittsburgh's newspapers were silent about her absences except for a May 1913 advertisement for piano rolls touting her as "one of Josef Lhevinne's most prominent pupils, having spent four years under the tutelage of this master in Berlin" ("The S. Hamilton Company").[7] The ad writer exaggerated her time overseas, for she probably was in Berlin for no more than twenty-eight months between 1908 and 1912.

But there is no exaggerating her gratitude to the Lhevinnes for their assistance during some crisis around this time. The timing of her article "Why Should Our Children Study Music?," quoted at the beginning of this essay and published only weeks after she returned to Pittsburgh in September 1912, indicates that recent experiences had opened her eyes. The article, too, alludes to a possible loss of her confidence, claiming that the happiness yielded by the arts "is ours to keep if we wish.... But it is necessary to reach out and seize and hold it, for it will not come unbidden and will not stay without cherishing" ("Why Should"). Having juggled family, social, and musical responsibilities in the years after her marriage, she may have forgotten to "cherish" the happiness that concertizing gave her and paid a high price for her neglect.

In any event, as late as 1954—ten years after Josef's death—Litchfield still recalled her debt to the Lhevinnes in one of two surviving letters to Rosina and borrowed language from her 1912 essay to describe their legacy: "I owe so much to you and Josef, I'm glad to tell you again how much you enriched and broadened my musical experience. You both came into my life at a time when I felt rather starved musically and what I learned from you both is a cherished possession" (letter to Rosina Lhevinne, 6 December 1954).

Interestingly, around the same time that Litchfield was "starved musically," Willa Cather was hungry, too. She complained to Sarah Orne Jewett in a December 1908 letter that her irritating editorship at *McClure's* had given her "as much food to live by as elaborate mental arithmetic would be" (*Selected Letters* 119). And echoing Litchfield's apparent frustration with a life that consumed energy formerly devoted to music-making, Cather told Jewett, "Everything leaks out as the power does in a broken circuit" (*Selected Letters* 119).

At almost simultaneous junctures in Cather's and Litchfield's lives, Jewett and the Lhevinnes intervened in their respective mentees' stalled careers. By inviting Cather to "find [her] own quiet centre of life, and write from that to the world," Jewett helped point her away from magazine work toward a life devoted to writing fiction (Lewis 66–67). And shortly after returning from Berlin, Litchfield embarked on a successful career as concert arranger, chamber artist, and vocal accompanist while occasionally studying under both Lhevinnes after they moved to New York in October 1919 ("The Fillion Violin Studios"; Wallace 167).

No correspondence between Cather and Litchfield has surfaced, but surely two friends who had "melted together" would have known of each other's artistic roadblock and breakthrough. Such knowledge would explain, too, why Litchfield introduced Josef Lhevinne to Cather and why the latter "hardly ever missed one of his concerts" (Lewis 173). She may well have attended the gala Carnegie Hall performance of Saturday afternoon, 14 January 1939, at which both Lhevinnes, by then distinguished professors at the Juilliard School, celebrated their fortieth wedding anniversary (Wallace 242–44). Cather perhaps sat with Litchfield, who went backstage afterward to offer congratulations.[8] Cather would have understood, too, the exhilaration Litchfield felt and expressed again a few days later in a letter to Rosina: "I was as proud as if we were blood relations or something. I always feel like saying to everybody, 'Listen to them! *Those* are *my* people!' Wonderful people, you two. . . . Thank you again for all you have meant to me and been to me" (Litchfield's emphasis; letter to Rosina Lhevinne, 16 January 1939).

Litchfield also studied with the brilliant virtuoso Leopold Godowsky (1870–1938), probably around March 1913, and occasionally performed his famously difficult piano transcriptions ("The Fillion Violin Studios"; "Members Give Program"). In fact, Litchfield never entirely gave up performing solo works, but she clearly preferred playing in ensembles. And in January 1914, her career as a chamber artist took off in earnest when she combined the roles of impresario and performer and launched a series of chamber concerts ("Mrs. Litchfield's Concerts"). Her intelligent programming and booking of local talent were lauded by critic Glendinning Keeble, who reminded Pittsburghers that "we only rarely had opportunity to hear chamber music of any sort" before these performances (Keeble, "Music").

Keeble, whom Cather trusted to read proofs for *The Song of the Lark*, admired Litchfield and encouraged her venture into composition (*Selected Letters* 204). At her second chamber concert at the Schenley Hotel, on 16 March 1914, Litchfield premiered her trio, Romanza in D Major, with violinist Vera Barstow (1891–1975) and cellist Sara Gurowitsch (1889–1981), earning Keeble's praise: "We do not as a rule look forward with any particular degree of pleasure to the 'Opus 1' of a composer, especially of a fellow citizen perhaps, nor have we usually much reason to do so. This 'Romanza,' then, must be called an exception." Keeble found the work "an excellent and very enjoyable composition which promises well for other things to come from this writer" (Keeble, "Mrs. Litchfield's Trio a Musicianly Work"). But despite Keeble's encouragement, she composed few, if any, chamber compositions besides the Romanza and instead composed songs and transcriptions while exploring the chamber repertoire and frequently accompanying singers' recitals.

A famous vocal collaborator of hers, too, left his mark on a late Cather novel. On 14 May 1915, Litchfield performed solo works and played accompaniments for the distinguished American baritone David Bispham (1857–1921) at a concert at the Schenley Hotel celebrating the inauguration of the president of the Pennsylvania College for Women ("Music News of the Week"). Jane Dressler recently identified Bispham as the likely model for baritone Clement Sebastian in *Lucy Gayheart* (1935), and Bispham's hitherto unknown connection to Litchfield suggests that the latter's firsthand recollections of rehearsing with and accompanying Bispham could have influenced Cather's portrayal of Sebastian's rehearsals with Lucy (Dressler).

Furthermore, Cather probably inserted into *Lucy Gayheart* a song from Bispham and Litchfield's May 1915 concert. At that event, Bispham had sung "Lungi dal caro bene," a melancholy song by Antonio Secchi (1761–1833), in an English translation as "When Two That Love Are Parted" (Secchi; "Music News of the Week"). In the novel, Sebastian sings an encore, "When We Two Parted," "a sad simple old air which required little from the singer, yet probably no one who heard it that night will ever forget it" (*Lucy Gayheart* 34). The resemblance between the titles of Secchi's song and Sebastian's encore seems too close to be coincidental, implying that the haunting effect on Lucy of Sebastian's singing, too, may have had its source in Litchfield's memories (34).[9]

Perhaps Cather drew on Litchfield for other details as well. The sole pianist among Cather's main characters, Lucy is thwarted by a taboo that lingered well into the 1960s and of which her teacher, Paul Auerbach, reminds her: "For the platform, they always have a man" (Katz 4–5; *Lucy Gayheart* 141). Lucy would have faced this insurmountable obstacle even had Sebastian lived, but Litchfield conquered it with the Bispham recital. It appears that, by emphasizing Lucy's restricted opportunities, Cather is gesturing toward both Litchfield's landmark achievement and the futility of Lucy's desire for the same distinction.

The turn to chamber music fostered new musical friendships for Litchfield, one of which intertwined with Cather. Vera Barstow, the violinist in the Romanza's premiere, had known Litchfield for several years, and, after 1913, became her longtime collaborator. In 1914, Litchfield invited Barstow and cellist Boris Hambourg (1885–1954) to her family's summer home on Lake Erie to rehearse as a trio for the coming season ("Music of the Week—Chamber Music Concert"). The following summer, she hosted Hambourg and his violinist brother, Jan (1882–1947), and that autumn the three announced the formation of the Litchfield-Hambourg Trio ("Music of the Week—Notable Trio Coming").

The trio's first performance, featuring works by Handel, Mozart, and Rachmaninoff, took place at the Twentieth Century Club on 15 November 1915 (Keeble, "Music—The Litchfield-Hambourg Trio"). Cather was in Pittsburgh that day for the funeral of Isabelle McClung's father, Judge Samuel McClung, and may well have attended the performance (Woodress 276). It was enthusiastically reviewed by Keeble, who praised Litchfield's "admirable control of rhythmic and dynamic values," a skill no doubt contributing to her distinction as "an ideal interpreter of chamber music" (Keeble, "Music—The Litchfield-Hambourg Trio"; "Vera Barstow"). Later that week, the trio performed in Indianapolis and, on 21 November, in Chicago at the Fine Arts Building, a venue well-known to readers of *The Song of the Lark* and *Lucy Gayheart* ("Trio Will Give First People's Concert"; "Concert Calendar").

Litchfield may have assisted the romance between Jan Hambourg and Isabelle McClung, as Byrne and Snyder posit (51). Certainly, Litchfield shared Rosina Lhevinne's well-known penchant for matchmaking, for, in the 1939 letter quoted above, Litchfield asks Lhevinne for help finding "a nice husband" for a mutual friend (Wallace 309–10; letter to Rosina Lhevinne, 16 January 1939). The Litchfields probably attended the Hambourgs' wedding on 3 April 1916 in New York, too, and Ethel Litchfield remained close to the Hambourgs and to Jan's brother Boris, but if Litchfield encouraged the marriage, there is no evidence that Cather held it against her ("Jottings About People").

In fact, soon after the Hambourgs' marriage, Litchfield resumed composing and probably asked Cather's advice about poetry and perhaps even tapped Cather's texts for material. During a concert on 5 April 1917 at the Twentieth Century Club, Litchfield played her own transcription of "Dixie" and premiered two songs, "The Bankrupt Bunnies" for four women's voices and "The Land of Lost Content" sung by Helen Horne House ("Twentieth Century Club"). No author for the text of "The Bankrupt Bunnies" has been identified, nor has a manuscript copy of either song been located. But given that Litchfield's concert took place three days before Easter and that Cather once had penned a whimsical poem "The Easter Rabbit" (1896) that remained unpublished in her lifetime, the possibility exists that the lyrics for "The Bankrupt Bunnies" are Cather's (*April Twilights* 153). Surely, Cather influenced Litchfield's choice of A. E. Housman's evocative poem "The Land of Lost Content" for the companion song of the April 1917 concert. Cather's "worshipful" admiration of Housman's poetry would have been well-known to Litchfield, and she certainly would have known from the earliest days of her friendship with Cather of the latter's awkward 1902 meeting with Housman (Nettels 285–86).

At the 3 February 1920 meeting of the Tuesday Musical Club, Litchfield, Margaret Horne (violin), and Hubert Conover (cello) reprised Litchfield's Romanza, and Litchfield accompanied her two-part songs, "Bankrupt" (perhaps a revised version of "The Bankrupt

Fig. 8.1. Mrs. Lawrence Litchfield, pianist, Carnegie Library of Pittsburgh—Music Department, *The Musical Forecast*, vol. 16, no. 4, June 1929, p. 8.

Bunnies") and "The Purple Cows" (*Tuesday Musical Club Members Book 1920–1921* 35). Three songs unveiled 5 February 1924 by Litchfield and soprano Genevieve Elliott Marshall (1893–1988) during a Woman's City Club musicale at the William Penn Hotel most strongly suggest collaboration with Cather ("Woman's City Club").[10] The first song's title, "The Sea Is Very Kind to Me," resembles Cather's claim that she did not suffer from seasickness when traveling (*Selected Letters* 507). The second song title, "The Shropshire Lad," recalls Housman again and repeats Cather's misquote in a 1908 letter to Jewett of the title of Housman's 1896 *A Shropshire Lad* (*Selected Letters* 112). And the third, "To Edith," written for soprano and addressed to a woman, invites speculation that its text is an unpublished poem dedicated to her partner, Edith Lewis.

In fall 1926, Litchfield joined the piano faculty of the Fillion Music Studios and taught there until she and her husband moved to Northwest Philadelphia in December 1929 (see figure 8.1) ("The Fillion Violin Studios"). Dr. Litchfield died the following month, and, within a few years, she relocated to Manhattan's East Side, where her daughter-in-law and son, later president of Alcoa Corporation, lived after their marriage ("Dr. Litchfield Dies in East"; *U.S. City Directories*; Byrne and Snyder 102n66). Her eldest child, Baroness Ethel van Boetzelaer, had married a Dutch diplomat in a June 1923 Paris wedding attended by Cather and Isabelle Hambourg, and, during a visit to the van Boetzelaers in summer 1936, Litchfield also spent a week in Paris with the Hambourgs ("Pittsburgh Girl Marries Baron van Boetzelaer in Paris"; Hambourg). Isabelle wrote to Cather that August and believed Litchfield was adapting well to widowhood: "It seems to me that Ethel loves to be entirely alone, or, with whom she deems good company. . . . Having real freedom and being able to feel and appreciate it seems to make Ethel young" (Hambourg).[11] Apparently solitude was as essential to Litchfield as it was to Cather characters Godfrey St. Peter and Myra Henshawe and to Cather herself (Porter 281).

In November 1938, Litchfield attended the Tuesday Musical Club's fiftieth anniversary celebrations and played Mozart's Sonata in F Major, K. 332, at the University of Pittsburgh's Stephen Foster Memorial, perhaps her last public recital (*Tuesday Musical Club Members Book 1939–1940* 41). In the 1930s and '40s, she "dined . . . nearly every week" with Cather and Lewis in New York and enjoyed listening to Cather's phonograph records (Lewis 173). Litchfield and Cather also met regularly in the winter of 1946–47 for meals and brief walks in Central Park (Brown 328–29). And when Cather died in April 1947, Litchfield traveled from Philadelphia to New York to attend the funeral service at Cather and Lewis's apartment (*Selected Letters* 674).

After their mutual friend May Willard's death in April 1941, Litchfield had begged Cather not to die first, claiming she could not endure another death, feelings that Cather reciprocated (*Selected Letters* 602). Nevertheless, Litchfield survived Cather by twenty-eight years. In the 1950s, she lived at 200 East Sixty-sixth Street, very near Edith Lewis, and Cather would have been pleased to know that

Lewis and Litchfield remained good friends, too, as the inscription in a copy of Lewis's 1953 Cather biography indicates: to "Ethel— dearest and truest of friend[s]—with love from E. L." (letter to Rosina Lhevinne, 6 December 1954; Ford and Bybee 33). Litchfield's only known letter to Lewis, written from Arnhem, Holland, in July 1955, is similarly heartfelt, containing the same salutation—"My darling Edith"—that Cather had used in October 1936 in her one surviving letter to Lewis (letter to Edith Lewis; *Selected Letters* 519). In her letter, Litchfield asks Lewis to address mail to the American embassy because she "couldn't bear it if all of your letters failed to reach me" and wonders if Cather and Lewis's friend Stephen Tennant has visited recently. She concludes, "We will have much to say to each other when we meet," indicating that the two saw each other in New York (letter to Edith Lewis). Around 1960, she moved to the home of her daughter Margaret Denton in Bethesda, Maryland. Litchfield died there on 31 May 1975, two months after her ninety-ninth birthday and almost three years after Lewis's death, and is buried with her husband at Marshfield, Massachusetts ("Litchfield Obituary").

Throughout her life, Cather surrounded herself with accomplished people—musicians, artists, journalists, authors, playwrights, critics, booksellers, publishers, and so on—but many of these friends proved transitory. Some, such as George Seibel, Elizabeth Shepley Sergeant, and Olive Fremstad, drifted away over time. Much-loved friends, including Ethelbert Nevin, Annie Adams Fields, and Jewett, died not long after Cather met them. Distinguished artists Myra Hess, Sigrid Undset, and the Brewsters saw Cather occasionally but lived overseas. The Menuhin children were faithful companions and rejuvenated Cather with their musical brilliance, intelligence, and charm, but she was nearly sixty when they first met.

Surely, Cather's friendship with Ethel Herr Litchfield deserves a place among the most satisfying of all these relationships. Her closeness to Isabelle Hambourg and Edith Lewis enabled her to inhabit Cather's innermost circle. She also was one of the few musicians with whom Cather could discuss music and attend concerts, activities that remained vital for her until her death (Brown 325). Further research may confirm how much Cather absorbed from Litchfield and wove into her fiction and to what extent Litchfield relied on Cather texts for song settings and what Cather thought of these compositions. But evidence already available indicates the two formed an exceptionally durable and collegial friendship, shared similar career paths and pitfalls, enjoyed each other's friends, and provided intellectual stimulation for each other. And, recalling a phrase from Litchfield's 1912 essay, each certainly brought into the other's increasingly lonely life a much-needed "leavening proportion of happiness."

## NOTES

1. Ten years later, the essay was reprinted in *The Musical Forecast* (Pittsburgh), vol. 3, no. 2, October 1922, p. 1.

2. The manuscript of "The Swedish Mother" is undated, but it was written before 5 April 1921, when Litchfield and contralto Rosa K. Hamilton (1891–1993) performed the song, with no mention of Cather's authorship, for the Tuesday Musical Club (Ford and Bybee 34–35; *Tuesday Musical Club Members Book 1921–1922* 31).

3. I refer to the essay's subject as "Jones" when discussing her life before marriage and thereafter as "Litchfield." There is some confusion surrounding Litchfield's preferred name. Litchfield used the middle initial "H." in legal documents, but press notices of her musical performances variously refer to her as "Mrs. Lawrence Litchfield," "Ethel Litchfield," "Ethel Jones Litchfield," "Mrs. Ethel Herr Litchfield," and "Ethel Herr Litchfield." I have adopted the last version for this essay, which is the version used in her 1975 obituary and, with the addition of "Mrs.," for her 1912 essay referred to above.

4. Hine (1867–1954) and Acheson (1871–1954) are the "old friends" Cather mentions in a 1943 letter to Harrison Blaine explaining the connection between High Mowing and *My Ántonia* (*Selected Letters* 619). Byrne and Snyder mistakenly give Acheson's first name as "Edith" (112; "Acheson Obituary").

5. Aman-Jean's portrait of Litchfield was loaned to the eighth annual exhibition of the Carnegie Institute in November 1903 ("Carnegie Art Exhibit").

6. Ethel Carver studied voice, Lawrence Jr., cello, and Margaret, dance ("U. S. Woman"; "Dr. Litchfield's Son"; "Miss Margaret Litchfield").

7. With Selmar Janson, Litchfield recorded for Autograph three rolls of music for four hands by Moszkowski ("The S. Hamilton Company"). Litch-

field's 1924 Duo-Art piano roll of Paderewski's *Cracovienne fantastique* can be heard on YouTube ("Ignacy Jan Paderewski—Cracovienne Fantastique").

8. In her congratulatory letter to Rosina Lhevinne, Litchfield writes that a mutual friend "sat beside us" (letter to Rosina Lhevinne, 16 January 1939).

9. In *Lucy*, Sebastian sings a text by Byron, not the text sung by Bispham (*Lucy Gayheart* 34; Secchi). Cather may have had her own memories of Secchi's song, too, for other singers familiar to her, such as Clara Butt and Ernestine Schumann-Heink, occasionally sang it ("London Ballad Concerts"; "Noted Singer in Fine Recital").

10. Marshall repeated the songs, now collectively titled *Three Impressions*, in a recital at her teacher's studio on 21 February 1924. The accompaniments at this recital were played by Earl Mitchell ("Mrs. Martin's Recital").

11. I am grateful to Elizabeth Burke, Program Specialist at the Cather Project, University of Nebraska–Lincoln, who kindly provided me with photographs of Hambourg's letter and Litchfield's letter to Edith Lewis (see works cited entry).

## WORKS CITED

"Acheson Obituary." *Pittsburgh Post-Gazette*, 14 June 1954, p. 27.

"Among the Musicians." *Sunday Tribune* (Minneapolis), 25 January 1891, p. 11.

Brown, E. K. *Willa Cather: A Critical Biography*. Completed by Leon Edel, U of Nebraska P, 1987.

Byrne, Kathleen D., and Richard C. Snyder. *Chrysalis: Willa Cather in Pittsburgh, 1896–1906*. Historical Society of Western Pennsylvania, 1982.

"Carnegie Art Exhibit." *New York Times*, 6 November 1903, p. 7.

Cather, Willa. *April Twilights and Other Poems*. 1923. Edited by Robert Thacker, Everyman's Library, 2013.

———. *Lucy Gayheart*. 1935. Willa Cather Scholarly Edition, historical essay by David Porter, explanatory notes by Kari A. Ronning and David Porter, textual essay and editing by Frederick M. Link and Kari Ronning, U of Nebraska P, 2015.

———. *The Selected Letters of Willa Cather*. Edited by Andrew Jewell and Janis Stout, Knopf, 2013.

———. *The Song of the Lark*. 1915. Willa Cather Scholarly Edition, historical essay and explanatory notes by Ann Moseley, textual essay and editing by Kari A. Ronning, U of Nebraska P, 2012.

———. *The Troll Garden*. A Variorum Edition, edited by James Woodress, U of Nebraska P, 1983.

————. *Uncle Valentine and Other Stories: Willa Cather's Uncollected Short Fiction 1915–1929*. Edited by Bernice Slote, U of Nebraska P, 1975.

"Concert Calendar." *Chicago Sunday Tribune*, 21 November 1915, pt. 8, p. 3.

"Congregational Church." *Janesville Daily Gazette*, 29 January 1891, p. 4.

"A Distinguished Visitor." *Pittsburgh Gazette*, 24 March 1903, p. 10.

Dressler, Jane. "David Bispham, American Baritone: A Prototype for *Lucy Gayheart*." *Willa Cather Newsletter & Review*, Summer 2014, pp. 7–12.

"Dr. Litchfield Dies in East." *Pittsburgh Post-Gazette*, 16 January 1930, p. 1.

"Dr. Litchfield's Son Appointed to Annapolis." *Pittsburgh Gazette Times*, 11 May 1917, p. 13.

"The Fillion Violin Studios." *The Musical Forecast* (Pittsburgh), June 1926, vol. 10, no. 4, p. 12.

Ford, James E., and Ariel Bybee. "'The Swedish Mother': A Recently Discovered Song Manuscript with Music by Ethel Herr Litchfield and Lyrics by Willa Cather." *Willa Cather Newsletter & Review*, Fall 2008, pp. 33–35.

Hambourg, Isabelle McClung. Letter to Willa Cather, 5 August [1936], Roscoe and Meta Cather Collection (MS 316), Archives & Special Collections, U of Nebraska–Lincoln Libraries.

*Hamburg Passenger Lists, 1850–1934*. Staatsarchiv Hamburg, through Ancestry .com.

"Happenings in Society's Realm." *Pittsburgh Post*, 15 January 1902, p. 4.

Harding, Julia Morgan. "The Club Woman's World." *Pittsburgh Post*, 22 May 1904, pt. 3, p. 3.

————. "In the Realm of Women's Clubs." *Pittsburgh Post*, 6 June 1897, p. 19.

"Ignacy Jan Paderewski—Cracovienne Fantastique" [Performance of piano roll recorded by Ethel Herr Litchfield]. YouTube, uploaded by Marcus Scriptor, 4 August 2011, youtube.com/watch?v=9F4jf5ukOqQ.

"In Society." *Pittsburgh Post*, 3 July 1898, p. 10.

"Jottings About People." *Pittsburgh Gazette Times*, 4 April 1916, p. 16.

Katz, Martin. *The Complete Collaborator: The Pianist as Partner*. Oxford UP, 2009.

Keeble, Glendinning. "Mrs. Litchfield's Trio a Musicianly Work." *Pittsburgh Gazette Times*, 17 March 1914, p. 2.

————. "Music." *Pittsburgh Gazette Times*, 5 April 1914, sec. 8, p. 5.

————. "Music—The Litchfield-Hambourg Trio." *Pittsburgh Gazette Times*, 16 November 1915, p. 9.

Lee, Hermione. *Willa Cather: Double Lives*. Pantheon Books, 1990.

Lewis, Edith. *Willa Cather Living: A Personal Record*. U of Nebraska P, 2000.

"Lhevinne Wins Triumph." *Pittsburgh Press*, 9 April 1907, p. 5.

Litchfield, Ethel Herr. Letter to Edith Lewis, 26 July 1955, Susan J. and James R. Rosowski Cather Collection (MS 228), Archives & Special Collections, U of Nebraska–Lincoln Libraries.

———. Letters to Rosina Lhevinne. Correspondence, Rosina Lhevinne Papers, Music Division, New York Public Library.

———. "Why Should Our Children Study Music?" *The Spectator* (Pittsburgh), 29 November 1912, p. 11.

Litchfield, Lawrence. "A Plea for the Establishment of an American Association for the Prevention of Social Diseases." *Journal of the American Medical Association*, vol. 54, no. 9, 26 February 1910, pp. 692–95, the JAMA Network, DOI:10.1001/jama.1910.92550350001001e.

"Litchfield Obituary." *Washington Post*, 2 June 1975, sec. C, p. 4.

"London Ballad Concerts." *Times* (London), 5 February 1895, p. 14.

Marks, Lucy, and David Porter. *Seeking Life Whole: Willa Cather and the Brewsters*. Fairleigh Dickinson UP, 2009.

"Members Give Program." *Pittsburgh Gazette Times*, 12 March 1913, p. 16.

"Miss Margaret Litchfield Makes Debut as Dancer." *Pittsburgh Gazette Times*, 10 April 1923, p. 10.

"Mrs. Bishop Cheered by 800." *Janesville Daily Gazette*, 31 January 1891, p. 4.

"Mrs. Litchfield's Concerts." *Pittsburgh Gazette Times*, 25 January 1914, sec. 2, p. 4.

"Mrs. Martin's Recital." *Pittsburgh Sunday Post*, 17 February 1924, sec. 6, p. 6.

Münsterberg, Hugo. *American Traits from the Point of View of a German*. Houghton Mifflin, 1901.

"Music." *The Pittsburg Bulletin*, vol. 33, no. 3, 23 May 1896, p. 18, University of Pittsburgh Library System, *Historic Pittsburgh*, www.historicpittsburgh .org/islandora/object/pitt%3A31735068348519/viewer#page/18/mode/2up.

"Music in St. Paul." *Saint Paul Daily Globe*, 25 January 1891, p. 4.

"Music News of the Week." *Pittsburg Press*, 2 May 1915, Women's magazine and society sec., p. 8.

"Music of the Week—Chamber Music Concert." *Pittsburg Press*, 22 November 1914, p. 46.

"Music of the Week—Notable Trio Coming." *Pittsburg Press*, 17 October 1915, Women's magazine and society sec., p. 5.

"The Music World." *Pittsburg Dispatch*, 12 January 1890, p. 5.

Nettels, Elsa. "Youth and Age in the Old and New Worlds: Willa Cather and A. E. Housman." *Cather Studies 4: Willa Cather's Canadian and Old World Connections*, edited by Robert Thacker and Michael A. Peterman, U of Nebraska P, 1999, pp. 284–93.

*New York Passenger Lists, 1820–1957.* Ancestry.com Operations.

"Noted Singer in Fine Recital." *Washington Herald*, 29 March 1919, p. 8.

"Notes of Musical Events." *New York Times*, 14 April 1907, pt. 3, p. 15.

"Obituary News—Rev. David Jones." *Pittsburgh Post*, 29 June 1920, p. 7.

"Pittsburgh Girl Marries Baron van Boetzelaer in Paris." *Pittsburgh Gazette Times*, 29 June 1923, p. 8.

Porter, David. Historical Essay. *Lucy Gayheart*, by Willa Cather, Willa Cather Scholarly Edition, U of Nebraska P, 2015, pp. 251–347.

"Real Estate." *Pittsburgh Commercial Gazette*, 18 April 1899, p. 3.

Secchi, Antonio. "When Two That Love Are Parted" [*Lungi dal caro bene*]. Boosey, 1895. New York Public Library Digital Collections, http://digitalcollections.nypl.org/items/68b1bcce-08b3-33f5-e040-e00a1806754e.

"The S. Hamilton Company." *Pittsburgh Post*, 7 May 1913, sec. 1, p. 4.

"Society." *Pittsburg Press*, 23 August 1896, p. 12.

Suydam, Emma B. "Women's Clubs." *Pittsburgh Sunday Post*, 5 May 1907, sec. 6, p. 7.

"Theatre." *Lincoln Courier*, 20 April 1895, p. 8.

"Trio Will Give First People's Concert." *Indianapolis News*, 13 November 1915, p. 25.

*Tuesday Musical Club Members Book 1920–1921*. Tuesday Musical Club (Pittsburgh), n.p., n.d.

*Tuesday Musical Club Members Book 1921–1922*. Tuesday Musical Club (Pittsburgh), n.p., n.d.

*Tuesday Musical Club Members Book 1939–1940*. Tuesday Musical Club (Pittsburgh), n.p., n.d.

Tudor, M. Kyle. "Lawrence Litchfield Jr. of Alcoa." *The Mines Magazine*, April 1970, vol. 60, no. 4, pp. 12–13, Colorado School of Mines, http://minesmagazine.com/wp-content/uploads/2011/01/Mines_Mag.v60.n4.pdf.

"Twentieth Century Club." *Pittsburgh Sunday Post*, 8 April 1917, sec. 5, p. 3.

Urgo, Joseph R. "Willa Cather's Political Apprenticeship at *McClure's Magazine*." *Willa Cather's New York: New Essays on Cather in the City*, edited by Merrill Maguire Skaggs, Fairleigh Dickinson UP, 2000, 60–74.

*U.S. City Directories, 1822–1995*. Ancestry.com Operations, ancestry.com /interactive/2469/1897182.

*U.S. Consular Registration Certificates, 1907–1918*. National Archives and Records Administration through Ancestry.com.

*U.S. Passport Applications, 1795–1925 [Ethel Herr Litchfield]*. National Archives and Records Administration through Ancestry.com.

*U.S. Passport Applications, 1795–1925 [Margaret Litchfield]*. National Archives
and Records Administration through Ancestry.com.

"U. S. Woman Gets Job of Waiting on Dutch Queen." *Chicago Tribune*, 11
July 1942, p. 5.

"Vera Barstow." *The Canadian Journal of Music*, vol. 4, no. 12, April 1918, p. 165.

Wallace, Robert K. *A Century of Music-Making: The Lives of Josef & Rosina
Lhevinne*. Indiana UP, 1976.

"The Week's Doings among the Women's Clubs." *Pittsburgh Sunday Post*, 22
April 1906, sec. 5, p. 6.

"Woman's City Club." *Pittsburgh Gazette Times*, 31 January 1924, p. 8.

Woodress, James. *Willa Cather: A Literary Life*. U of Nebraska P, 1987.

# 9 Grave and God-Free
## Ethelbert Nevin as a Pivotal Historical Source in "The Professor's Commencement" and *The Professor's House*

KIMBERLY VANDERLAAN

At two points in Willa Cather's writing life, she imagined an academic nearing the end of his career. Emerson Graves in "The Professor's Commencement" (published in *The New England Magazine* in 1902) can be seen as an early blueprint for the more accomplished and pragmatic academic, Godfrey St. Peter, in *The Professor's House* (1925). My argument is multipronged: First, that Cather's friend, the Sewickley-born pianist and composer Ethelbert Nevin, serves as an important historical source for both characters.[1] Second, although both protagonists are teachers, their sensibilities align more imaginatively with the musician, Nevin—a template for all great artists. Third, Ralph Waldo Emerson, the American Transcendentalist, serves as an ideological source for Emerson Graves, and somewhat less directly for Godfrey St. Peter, as Cather uses mid-nineteenth-century educational thought as the basis for her academic characters; for in the final analysis, both fictional men represent the spirit of failed Romanticism.

There are numerous reasons a reader might be tempted to draw parallels between Ethelbert Nevin and Emerson Graves, not the least of which is the timing of the story's publication—just months after the composer's death on February 17, 1901. Additionally, there are myriad temperamental affinities among all three (Nevin, Graves, and St. Peter). Nevin is described by his second biographer, John Tasker Howard, as someone who struggled with an inner demon, at least the last seven or so years of his life. Howard writes euphemistically that Nevin was fighting a "weakness." "[W]hen playing in public proved a strain, he would turn to the enemy he thought was a friend, and as his weakness became an anti-social, solitary habit, it played havoc with his disposition and the natural sweetness of his nature" (221). Solitary drinking is the "enemy" referenced by Howard, though most of Cather's fictional men battle enemies somewhat less tangible.[2] Graves is accused by his sister of being a masochist, who seems to turn on himself and his own potential; she says, "Your real gift is getting all the possible pain out of life" ("Professor's Commencement" 482). St. Peter is similarly divided against himself. Cather writes that he was like two men, one "grafted" (*Professor's House* 267) onto another—that he "now wanted to run away from everything he had intensely cared for" (275). There is clearly an internal conflict at the core of all three, threatening the very fabric of their well-being. Timothy Bintrim argues that neurochemistry was responsible for Nevin's torment—that he was bipolar.[3]

Whatever his personal issues may have been, Nevin's sudden death was a traumatic event in Cather's life, which caused her the kind of despair and disillusionment these fictional protagonists are surely meant to illustrate. Ethelbert Nevin died of a stroke at the age of thirty-eight. In her extended condolence letter, Cather writes to his widow of the "unspeakable" message, using language that clearly shows her distress: "A shadow has come over the sun and nothing seems worth doing" (*Selected Letters* 56).[4] Cather also wrote immediately to the young widow by telegram. Howard recalls: "More than forty telegrams came to Anne the day after that afternoon of February 17. One of them was from Willa Cather" (341). He goes on to cite her telegram: "By my own sorrow, I can understand yours a little. I think there is no more music left on earth" (341).

Cather and Nevin shared a profoundly acute sensibility. Even before Nevin's death there is plenty of evidence that Cather "read" the talent, temperament, and character of her friend plainly. Nevin understood this affinity, writing to his wife in July of 1899, "You have no idea how we miss you ... I am dependent on you. Miss Cather was right—my melodies are you, my harmony is you, and my discords are yours" (qtd. in Howard 322). It is not surprising that Cather the writer would equip her next fictional male artist figure with such sensibilities, nor incorporate similar traits in her more fully realized 1925 artist manqué–academic: "A spasm of emotion contracted" Emerson Graves's vocal chords as he attempted to recite his poem, as "his white hand nervously sought his collar" ("Professor's Commencement" 487). St. Peter also exhibits extreme emotional fluctuations: "Theoretically he knew that life is possible, may be even pleasant, without joy, without passionate griefs. But it had never occurred to him that he might have to live like that" (*Professor's House* 282). One biographer of Nevin recalls that he was "by nature nervous and impetuous, and frequently those who met him casually did not bother to distinguish between artificial and natural exuberance" (Howard 222). Even as a young man of nineteen, the biographer explains, Nevin's "disposition and temperament were given to extremes, the depths of discouragement or the height of enthusiasm" (Howard 38). Nevin's first biographer, Vance Thompson, writes that "both as a composer and as a man ... he was essentially a child. To the last he was an enchanted child" (99). Emerson Graves's sister, Agatha, accuses him of similar traits, saying, "You are a sentimentalist and your vanity is that of a child" ("Professor's Commencement" 482). Godfrey St. Peter's wife accuses him of a similar kind of immaturity—of being self-centered and "intolerant" (*Professor's House* 25), character faults she finds especially offensive when he is such a "poor judge [of his] own behavior" (25).

Further, Cather gives her professors the physicality of impetuous youth as well as the attitude. St. Peter has the "slender hips and springy shoulders of a tireless swimmer" (*Professor's House* 4) and Graves, even on the eve of his retirement, has features that are "as sensitive and mobile as that of a young man" ("Professor's Commencement" 481). Howard describes Nevin as a "sensitive, nervous [youth], a musician with predilections for flowers" (29). Nevin's physical form—based on photographs of him from childhood through adulthood—was slight, slender, graceful, elegant—fastidious. Nevin himself recounted a piano performance from his early twenties, as described by his instructor, "Herr Prof," who marveled, "No wonder he plays so gracefully when every movement of his body is grace" (qtd. in Howard 68). Mr. B. J. Lang, the eminent piano instructor in Boston, whom Nevin sought out in the autumn of 1881, characterized Nevin's playing as "graceful, light and rippling" but critiqued Nevin's lack of "aplomb and firmness" (qtd. in Thompson 24). This assessment of his playing matches all accounts of his character and seems consistent with Nevin's small frame, unobtrusive body language, and delicate hands.

In fact, it was when I took the measure of the diminutive size of the cast of Ethelbert Nevin's right hand on display at the Hillman Library exhibit at the time of the Sixteenth International Seminar that it struck me that this story could very well have been a tribute to Cather's then recently deceased friend. She writes that Graves had "delicate, sensitive hands curving back at the finger ends, with dark purple veins showing prominently on the back. They were exceedingly small, white as a girl's, and well kept as a pianist's" ("Professor's Commencement" 482; see figure 9.1).

Not only do Emerson Graves's hands resemble those of Nevin, represented in the cast, but we can also trace in Cather's terribly charged condolence letter—which she delayed writing for a week or ten days due to the weightiness of the matter—thematic aspects present in both "The Professor's Commencement" and *The Professor's House*.[5] Cather's despair and sorrow border on pathos. She writes to Nevin's widow, "I know that I shall never feel that youthful and genuine enthusiasm for any one's work again, and I feel as though my own youth had died [with him]" (*Selected Letters* 57). A parallel

KIMBERLY VANDERLAAN

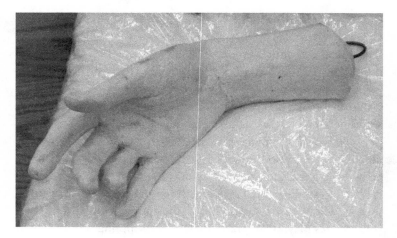

Fig. 9.1. Plaster cast of Ethelbert Nevin's right hand made at Anne Nevin's direction immediately after his death in 1901. Ethelbert Nevin Collection, Center for American Music, University of Pittsburgh Library System.

passage occurs in "The Professor's Commencement," when students recite poems that are inevitably drowned out by the "puffing of the engines in the switchyard" (484). Emerson Graves bemoans the seemingly requisite sacrifice of "the rights of youth" to adult pre-occupations with commerce: "Not even this respite [of the joy of poetry] is left to us; even here the voice of youth is drowned by the voice of the taskmaster that waits for them all impatiently enough" (484). Graves is aware that his long service to his students ("the thirsty young lives [who] had drunk him dry" [486]) forced him to realize that "he had been living from external stimulation from the warm young blood about him" (486). Perhaps even more significant is his eventual recognition that he can no longer vicariously supply those students with the life force required for the mind and for the spirit: "the current of young life had cut away from him" and he is left feeling like "a ruin of some extinct civilization" (486).

In *The Professor's House*, Cather conveys this devastating disillusion-ment via a series of parallels that represents the demise of youth: the

death of Tom Outland, the death of ideas under the assault of com-
mercialism, and the death of Godfrey's early, ideal life. Like Cather
moving from Virginia to Nebraska, Godfrey was forced to uproot
himself from "the lakeside farm" and relocate to "the wheat lands
of central Kansas ... St. Peter nearly died of it" (21). Cather underlines the permanent and destructive nature of the dislocation: "No
later anguish, and he had had his share, went so deep or seemed so
final" (21). The loss of his first ideal, a youthfully cherished location,
is only one of many psychic wounds St. Peter must endure—yet
another way that Cather evolves this 1925 novel beyond its original genesis in the 1902 story. Interestingly, Cather also describes
Tom Outland's hands—though in this later iteration, Tom's hand
becomes both a setting for the precious turquoise and a metonymy
for his whole body; masculine, tanned, and resilient rather than
small and white and effeminate. St. Peter remembers being stirred
by Tom's hand when he came bearing gifts from the Mesa: "the
muscular, many-lined palm, the long, strong fingers with soft ends,
the straight little finger, the flexible, beautifully shaped thumb that
curved back from the rest of the hand as if it were its own master.
What a hand!" (119). The difference between this description of Tom
Outland's hand and that of the hand of Emerson Graves is that
Tom's hand is masculine—his thumb a discreet member as a penis
would be to a male body, whereas Emerson Graves's hand is dainty
and effeminate—posed as holding a rose, a book, or a paper knife.
Still, both appendages, even that of the effeminate, perhaps homo-
erotic Graves, suggest sexuality and eroticism; specifically, a kind of
engorgement and readiness to erupt—the "dark purple veins showing prominently on the back" ("Professor's Commencement" 482).

As demonstrated in the artistic connoisseurship of both Graves
and St. Peter, Cather, too, attributed profound importance to extraordinary art, and to the artists who create it. She writes in the aforementioned letter to Anne Nevin, "A master of any art holds a peculiar
place in the lives of his believers. To them he is the expression of
what seems most rare and precious in life, and when he dies something of themselves goes out with him" (*Selected Letters* 58). James

Woodress adds in *Willa Cather: A Literary Life* that to Cather, Nevin "represented youth, vivacity, golden talent" (132), and reminds us that "she wrote three poems in his memory" (133).[6]

Cather also writes in *The Ladies' Home Journal*: "Temperamentally, Mr. Nevin is much the same blending of the blithe and the *triste* that gives his music its peculiar quality, now exultantly gay, now sunk in melancholy, as whimsical and capricious as April weather" (qtd. in Woodress 132). Emerson's sister, Miss Agatha, points out that her brother is similarly melancholic and inexplicably morose. She chastises him, complaining that his "real gift . . . is extracting needless annoyance from commonplace and trivial things" ("Professor's Commencement" 482). The notion that Emerson Graves (like Nevin) registers the temperamental caprices of his environment (like an Aeolian harp) is consistent with one major motif of Romantic thought; that is, the material world lacks unity and "lies broken and in heaps . . . because man is disunited with himself" (Emerson 65). Cather highlights this kind of correspondence between the physicality of the Romantic hero and his interiority: she describes Graves as having a "bold and prominent nose and chin" and "the high, broad forehead which Nature loves to build about her finely adjusted minds" ("Professor's Commencement" 481), paralleling R. W. Emerson's assertion that "nature is made to conspire with spirit to emancipate us" (Emerson 47). Similarly, Cather describes her 1925 fictional academic as handsome with a "high, polished" forehead "hard as bronze" which was more like a "statue's head than a man's" (*Professor's House* 5), conflating life and art and reminding us of the Romantics' adulation of art, artifice and aesthetic excellence. At first glance, both men (Graves and St. Peter) seem to embody Romantic sublimity.

Susan J. Rosowski may have been the first scholar to note Cather's immersion in Romantic conventions. She writes in *The Voyage Perilous* that Cather's first "premise was the dualism of mind and matter familiar to students of romanticism" (5). Numerous scholars have investigated the duality of Cather's own life as well as that evident in her fiction. Rosowski notes that "Cather wrote of two worlds—the spiritual world and the physical one, an ideal world and an ordinary one" (5). Hermione Lee's biography of Cather is titled with this kind of schism (or fracturing into multiple strands) in mind (*Double Lives* for the U.S. title and *Braided Lives* for the British title). She writes that *The Professor's House* in particular is "about splits and disjunctions" (224).

In both stories, Cather directs us to a reading steeped in the principles of Romanticism through frequent allusions to artists, art works, and literature. Emerson Graves, a "grave" distortion of Ralph Waldo Emerson's transcendent hopefulness, is nonetheless tied to the philosopher by an early reference to "Nature" (capitalized perhaps to remind us of the all-importance and pervasiveness of the natural world). Ralph Waldo's essay celebrates the narrator as "a lover of uncontained and immortal beauty" (Emerson 17) and general aesthetic good taste. Cather humorously writes that Graves's remarkable collection of books "were almost equally apportioned to the accommodation of works on literature and science, suggesting a form of bigamy rarely encountered in society" ("Professor's Commencement" 481). Graves's balanced and remarkable scope of interests reflects R. W. Emerson's call for broad-based knowledge and his admonition to the parochial or restricted scholar. In his essay, "The American Scholar," Emerson charges his audience to be well-versed in all fields, to reject the limitations of the lone statute book or the plow in favor of a more comprehensive education: to strive toward the ideal he calls "Man Thinking" (*Nature* 73). Likewise, Tom Outland is as astute in the academic study of mathematics as he is in the practical work of archaeological digs—and he invents a scientific tool to boot!

Like a true Romantic, Godfrey St. Peter prefers ideas and ideals to material belongings. When his daughter, Rosamond, offers to build him a "little study in the back yard of the new house" (*Professor's House* 59)—a potentially useful hermitage to help him transition from the old to the new house—he responds that he would prefer to "plod on" in the old study. He encourages her to "keep it just an idea—it's better so. Lots of things are" (60). Graves, too, eschews the "scorched and blackened waste" ("Professor's Commencement" 484) of industrial Pittsburgh, and instead, indulges in "his favorite fancy" (483), relishing ideas in books and letters and art work.

Both professors are clearly steeped in nineteenth-century Romantic philosophy, as illuminated by allusions to various Romantic writers. For example, Emerson Graves personally "illustrate[s] the allegory" ("Professor's House" 481) of Nathaniel Hawthorne's "The Great Stone Face," a story that reveals a man's inability to live up to impossibly high expectations. Agatha reminds her brother that he should try to live up to the standards of his humble Pittsburgh milieu, telling him it is time to "do something to justify the faith your friends have always had in you. You owe something to them and to your own name" (482).

The successful Romantic might have achieved a balance between the secular and the sacred: as the original Mr. (Waldo) Emerson explained, success would be to balance the contradictions and the tensions, to almost "fear" one's own gladness, and to revere "the always present," which is simultaneously "inaccessible" (*Nature*). Cather's protagonists are unable to achieve that balance. St. Peter is "very unhappy" (*Professor's House* 135) because the material world has overrun the spiritual, just as Graves finds himself, even at his own celebration of a life devoted to the presumed pursuit of high ideals, facing "utter defeat" ("Professor's Commencement" 488).

Multiple forms of defeat inform this story about a high school teacher retiring after thirty years of scholarship and faithful devotion to what he calls the "old Romance" (484)—Cather writes that "his real work had been to try to secure for youth the rights of youth; the right to be generous, to dream, to enjoy" (484), to help his students inhabit the life of the imagination and the mind. Agatha points out that his first failure is in assuming that these puerile students are able to make use of the tools he has given them: "in that place all your best tools have rusted" (482). She alludes to a second failure: his ignorance or perhaps willed naiveté regarding the true nature of his relationships with his peers. "As for those slovenly persons with offensive manners whom you call your colleagues, do you fancy they appreciate you? They are as envious as green gourds and their mouths pucker when they pay you compliments" (482). Cather's use of the word "fancy" ties Professor Graves to Romantic principles, but his comment to Agatha defending his pupils reveals a kind of naturalistic determinism: "I believe I have, to some at least, in a measure supplied a vital element that their environment failed to give them" (483). If their environment (the city) is in fact a problem for the youths in attaining the broad-based classical education R. W. Emerson conceived in his essay "The American Scholar," and summarized by his phrase "Man Thinking" (73), it is because, in Professor Graves's own words, Pittsburgh controlled at the time "a vast manufacturing region given over to sordid and materialistic ideals" (483).

Echoing the pessimism of Graves's sister, Agatha, about the capacity of his students, colleagues, and family members to make up for the vacuity of his environment, Professor St. Peter critiques a much broader and more ephemeral "place" than Pittsburgh—"The University, his new house, his old house, everything around him seem[s] insupportable, as the boat on which he is imprisoned seems to a sea-sick man" (*Professor's House* 148–49). At this juncture in the novel, his university colleague, Robert Crane (suggesting the extremis of "The Open Boat"), with whom he had heretofore always "fought together in a common cause" (138), has shocked him by threatening to hire a lawyer to gain access to some part of Tom Outland's fortune. Therefore, it is no wonder that the "world [i]s sad" and the town feels "small and tight and airless" (148), nor that he must describe at least *the monetary consequence* of Outland's success as "vulgar" (148).

What I find most telling about this passage in chapter 13 is a significant allusion, from the mid-nineteenth century, to Edgar Allan Poe's "The Pit and the Pendulum," placing Cather's aesthetic attention squarely on the Romantic period. St. Peter remarks, "I feel as if the poor fellow were strapped down on a revolving disk that comes around under the knife just so often" (*Professor's House* 131). Significantly, Poe, an author who seemed fixated on the underbelly of transcendent themes (premature burial, psychological terror, and perverted forms of supernatural phenomena), is tied in Cather's imagination to his Dark Romantic brother, Hawthorne—in his own right obsessed with sin and corruption and multiple levels of failure (on the part of the imagination, the will, and the body). Godfrey St. Peter somewhat perversely insists on working in his old uncomfortable study, cluttered and cold, a figurative head on the body of a dismal, "dead, empty house" (16) the color of "ashes" with a "front porch too narrow for comfort" and a "slanting floor [and] sagging steps" (11). Though there are dozens of repairs to be done ("there were always so many things to fix, and there was not time enough to go round" [12]), in demonstrating St. Peter's stubborn refusal to move to a grander, airier, more modern house, she also insists on his spiritual and psychological stasis. He seems to grasp intuitively that since Tom Outland has died, Romantic inclinations cannot be sustained.

Cather's reference to Nathaniel Hawthorne in "The Professor's Commencement" directly highlights the Romantic period. She uses the phrase "arrested development" (486) to describe Graves's students and implicitly signals his own stasis—a kind of prolonged youth, which he can no longer feed with young blood: "And he himself— what had he done with the youth, the strength, the enthusiasm and splendid equipment he had brought there from Harvard thirty years ago?" (486). So too, the reader senses that Emerson Graves's decision to retire at this particular moment may be driven by an intuition that his powers of Romantic transformation have dwindled, even died. He confesses to his sister: "I feel distraught and weary. You know how I shrink from changes of any sort, and this—why this is the most alarming thing that has ever confronted me." His willingness to cut his life off "at the stalk" as he wonders if it will ever "bud again" conflates hopes for his own future with flower imagery that insists on the ephemeral nature of life. He had just noted that roses never have as lovely a "fragrance as they have in the first sun" ("Professor's Commencement" 482).

St. Peter likewise seems to focus all his remaining energies on cultivating his garden. Both men acknowledge the profound transience of the life of the body and of the mind through their appreciation of flowers. Graves's "garden roses thrust their pink heads close to the screen as though they would not be kept outside" (482), seemingly invading a static space with the vitality of the natural world. In "Uncle Valentine," a story generally understood to be about Nevin, Cather writes about the majesty of "a great white rose, almost as big as a moonflower, its petals beautifully curled" (30). Nevin himself, from an early age, was much enamored by rose songs such as "My Love Is Like the Pure White Rose" and "Rose Bud" (Howard 23). St. Peter's garden is where he "works off his discontent" and where he lives as a "bachelor" when his family goes on vacation to Colorado. Following the Romantic tendency to seek out solitude when weary with the world, and to find the natural world's correspondences with the human spirit, both men need at times to retreat from society, specifically to their garden sanctuaries.

To the point of Cather's intentional (conscious or otherwise) use of Ralph Waldo Emerson's Romantic philosophy—we know that she admired the man of letter's philosophy, prose, and outlook on life. She wrote in the *Lincoln Courier* in 1895 about the "lofty repose and magnificent tranquility" (*World and the Parish* 1: 274) of the philosopher's mind as revealed in his essays. We can glean the key aspects of R. W. Emerson's philosophy in the introduction to his essay *Nature* and also compare it to Willa Cather's own view of nature and art. He writes, "*Nature*, in the common sense, refers to essences unchanged by man; space, the air, the river, the leaf. *Art* is applied to the mixture of his will with the same things, as in a house, a canal, a statue, a picture" (Emerson 13).

There are dozens of important allusions in *The Professor's House* and "The Professor's Commencement" that reveal Cather's longtime (I might suggest lifetime) theme of the failure of the Romantic: individual imagination is not ignited, pessimism wins over optimism, the ecstatic moment is extinguished before it can blossom, and the elevated diction inspired by intersections of the sublime is silenced. Agatha has planned, during Emerson's celebratory retirement dinner, for her brother to correct his failure from decades ago: as a graduating senior, he was not able to recall the lines of Lord Macaulay's narrative poem, "Horatius at the Bridge"—but for a second time, at this dinner, Emerson is unable to recite the lines. It is a complicated moment; one which I think Cather meant to be wrought with ambiguity and tension from potentially warring interpretations. The poem recounts the story of Publius Horatius Cocles, an officer in the army of the ancient Roman Republic, who famously defended the Pons Sublicius from the invading army of Lars Porsena in the late sixth century BC, during the war between Rome and Clusium. Horatius's individual action at a bridge halted the attack and forced Porsena to engage in a protracted siege of Rome rather than sacking it outright. Because a later peace treaty allowed the city to remain intact, Horatius was portrayed in various works of art, starting in the Renaissance, as a valiant hero. Macaulay's poem remained popular in the late nineteenth and early twentieth centuries ("Horatius Cocles").

The Professor's early "humiliation and disgrace, when, in attempting to recite 'Horatius at the Bridge,' he had been unable to recall" the next stanza, constitute a "story that every senior . . . still told the juniors" ("Professor's Commencement" 485), seemingly as a double ritual. His own failures can be seen as reminders that even great men have their moments of struggle; for as Cather writes, even "the least receptive of the Professor's students realized that he had risen to a much higher plane of scholarship than any of his colleagues" (485); but it can also be understood as a call for younger, less-experienced students to embrace the kind of rite of passage that might make them in the end more like their own "bold Horatius" (485). His second "failure" to recite the poem is more than what it appears to be: a simple fault of memory or bout of nerves. His final day at school has been one of intense reflection, processing important memories and recognizing that his decision to stay at the high school beyond the initial planned stint of five years was a response to a different kind of battle: "[T]he desire had come upon him to bring some message of repose and peace to the youth of this work-driven, joyless people, to cry the name of beauty so loud that the roar of the mills could not drown it" (486). This is strong language; Cather seems to suggest that Emerson's noble quest may have been a futile one from the start.

Significantly, she inserts a short passage that ties this early story very closely to the 1925 novel. Each educator has had a brilliant student, a promising protégé, who dies young—wasting awesome ability and potential. Graves recalls, in a retrospective look to his past, appropriately Wordsworthian: "[T]he reward of his first labors had come in the form of his one and only genius; his restless, incorrigible pupil" (486). Similarly reflective, Godfrey notes, "You know, Tom isn't very real to me anymore. Sometimes I think he was just a—a glittering idea" (*Professor's House* 110). Tom Outland, though ostensibly masculine enough, with his "manly and mature voice" (110), is described upon his first meeting with St. Peter as having a body that "seemed shut up in a case" (111). He describes past work "with gravity, as if he had reflected deeply upon irregular behavior" (115), specifically recalling that he had been required to "get a man when he isn't where he ought to be" (115). When Mrs. St. Peter invites him to lunch, he looks "with panic toward the door" and is cajoled by her to "wash his hands" (115) before joining them—all of which implies a kind of deviance. Graves's student with "the gentle eyes and manners of a girl, at once timid and utterly reckless died wretchedly at three-and-twenty in his master's arms" ("Professor's Commencement" 487). He is also a mysterious figure, suggesting effeminacy—or even deviant behavior. Cather has Graves note about himself: "I was not made to shine, for they put a woman's heart in me" (488), suggesting at the very least that his limitations stem from an effeminacy or a sentimentalism at the core of his nature. Interestingly, Cather inverts the stereotypical (or expected) genders of Emerson and his sister; Agatha was "the more alert and masculine character of the two" (482). We recall that Cather's early description of Graves takes the matter further: "He was slight of build and exceedingly frail" (482).

In November of 1900, in *The Ladies' Home Journal*, Cather wrote about Nevin that he "was rather a girlish little boy, always much concerned about his mother's dresses and fond of masquerading in dresses himself" (*World and the Parish* 628). Nevin's first biographer writes frequently of Nevin's "delicate constitution" (Thompson 145) and describes other aspects of his person, such as his "moral strength," being as "rare and fine as a woman's" (145). Thompson also records a friend's recollection of one of Nevin's performances in an intimate parlor scene: "Very slim, in his afternoon coat of black, with a tall white collar, he would come in. There was grey in his boyish hair even then. Laughing a little, in his embarrassed way, he would sit down at the piano" (128). Descriptions of a diminutive, demur artist can be found in biographies, friends' accounts, and even in journalistic accounts of the musician—like those we have read by Cather.

Romantic authors reflecting, in moments of tranquility, upon intense emotional experiences of the past—while simultaneously crafting an artifice of imaginative genius (such as a poem) is a key aspect of the Romantic genre. In both stories, Cather underlines that missing link through her protagonists. Professor Emerson Graves pronounces himself, after losing his emotional self-control at the party his sister organizes for him, "a hopeless dunce" ("Professor's Commencement" 488). Myriad allusions in the early story reinforce the idea that he was "not made to shine" (488) in spite of the admiration of his colleagues who were "full of pride and affection for their scholar and their 'great man'" (487). Cather also grants Professor St. Peter professional respect and public regard for his work. She writes that the "last volumes [of scholarship] brought him a certain international reputation and what were called rewards—among them, the Oxford prize for history, with its five thousand pounds, which had built him the new house" (*Professor's House* 34). Perhaps more significantly, as it may reflect Cather's own sense of having arrived at a mature and unique writerly craft, she allows St. Peter to be an authentic and self-aware artist: "[H]e could feel his hand growing easier with his material, when all the foolish conventions about that kind of writing were falling away and his relation with his work was becoming every day more simple, natural, and happy" (33–34).

Why then, given his multiple forms of professional success, does Cather allow St. Peter to suffer the disillusionment and crisis of identity that he does?—for surely that is her message when she has St. Peter confess, "In a lifetime of teaching, I've encountered just one remarkable mind; but for that, I'd consider my good years largely wasted" (62). Graves also feels exhausted and tossed upon the waste heap, and like St. Peter thinking of Tom Outland, he had known "one and only genius; his restless, incorrigible pupil with the gentle eyes and manner of a girl" ("Professor's Commencement" 486). Both men remind us of the lament of the great Romantic poet, William Wordsworth, on being "out of tune," for his narrator bemoans his culture's material consumption and absence of spiritual substance: "[T]he world is too much with us: late and soon, / Getting and spending, we lay waste our powers: / Little we see in nature that is ours; / We have given our hearts away, a sordid boon!" (559). Likewise, Graves is hurt by what he interprets as the impropriety of his colleagues' reactions to his retirement party, when the merriment lacks seriousness: "Surely this was a time for silence and reflection, if ever such time was" (487). Similarly, Godfrey intuitively understands his dissonance in the world: "He didn't belong there" (*Professor's House* 272). Of course, "there" is the new house, the classroom ("he didn't in the least believe he'd be alive for the fall term" [268]) and his presence on the earth (there came to him a conviction that "he was nearing the end of his life" [267]).

Cather's 1902 version of failed Romanticism has Graves leave his teaching post feeling like an utter failure, unable "to shine" ("Professor's Commencement" 486) and in the 1925 version Cather has Godfrey trying to look back on his life to ascertain "where he ha[d] made his mistake" (*Professor's House* 281). Rosowski points out that Cather's "first principles" involved the "duality of two worlds and two selves" (10)—certainly a theme we see in both these stories about conflicted academics. A secondary theme, "salvation through the imagination" (10), and the efforts to gain such salvation, can be seen in Godfrey's desire to vicariously live his life on the promise of Tom's ardent genius and in Emerson's efforts to gain salvation by granting imaginative space to his students. It is in efforts to attain the third principle, articulated by Rosowski as "exaltation of the artist-priest who can create living art" (10), that both Emerson and Godfrey fall short.

Nevin, however, at least in Cather's mind, could not have fallen short in artistic aptitude, though perhaps she saw his failing in his inability to vanquish what I have heretofore referred to as his "inner demons." Arguably, his most famous song, "Narcissus" (from *Water Scenes*), which reflects his happy boyhood at Vineacre, where there "was music in the river and in the trees, and music in the boy's heart" (Thompson 9), also reflects the symbolic second edge to the double-edged sword of his life. The word "narcissus" is related to "the Greek, *nárke*, or torpor, numbness, a narcotic quality" (Norris 28). It is a significant titular choice, even if inspired by subconscious motivations. Nevin's intense emotional vicissitudes had been noted as early in his life's struggle as 1894, a year in which the musician acknowledged in a letter to Anne, "I tell you, my dearest wife, fame may be a great thing, but it has to be bought at a terrible price; and I'm paying the full" (Thompson 154).[7]

Cather had, by 1925, also gathered and cultivated her emotional and intellectual themes. The convergence of motifs between the two works includes tensions between the sacred and the secular; devotion to family and students above self; interest in private assurance of one's good works, as opposed to public recognition for them; and the wide divide between excellent teaching and original research—all tensions to which teacher-scholars are keenly attuned. Clearly, Cather revisits in this 1925 novel the same tensions between intellectual integrity and material prosperity that pervaded her 1902 story, and which, one might argue, is at the heart of Romantic dualism.

Cather, not coincidentally, equated Nevin's musical genius with the British Romantics in her letter to Anne, writing that when she thinks of Nevin, she thinks "also of the blessed truth of the lines that Shelley wrote to Keats after the world had killed him" (*Selected Letters* 57). Perhaps Cather was thinking when she wrote this of the final lines of Shelley's poem, "Adonais": "The soul of Adonais, like a star. / Beacons from the abode where the Eternal are" (Shelley 636), reminding Anne that Nevin's artistic genius, like that of Keats, had been folded into an eternal realm, never to die. Just as easily, we could use the last lines of the first stanza of Shelley's poem to read the same message: "Forget the Past, his fate and fame shall be / An echo and light unto eternity!" (626). If Nevin was indeed "the embodiment of all the happy privileges of art" (*Selected Letters* 57) for Cather, then when he died, she most certainly would have tried to find a way to express both her sublime satisfaction at having known such a genius and her devastation at having to let him go. Both Emerson Graves and Godfrey St. Peter articulate the same dramatic ambivalence, and Cather, in writing the Romantic vision of Ralph Waldo Emerson into her fictional professors, crafted a fitting tribute to her friend, Ethelbert Nevin.

## NOTES

1. Nevin did not spend much of his adult life at home. He returned to Vineacre only when he had nowhere else to turn and was out of money. Sewickley is an Ohio River town thirteen miles downstream from Pittsburgh, fictionalized as Greenacre in "Uncle Valentine." Edgeworth is a village closest to the Nevin and Slack homes, but the larger community, indeed the entire valley, takes its name from the Big Sewickley Creek. As an alternative prototype for Emerson Graves, in this volume, Mary Ryder posits "the beloved Professor Frederick Merrick" of Pittsburgh's Central High School, stating Merrick's "photograph shows a silver-haired man with kind and expressive eyes, not unlike his literary counterpart whose slight build and silver white hair made him memorable to his students." I agree with Ryder that Merrick may have been the source (or one source among several) for Emerson Graves—as well as for sculptor Harvey Merrick in "The Sculptor's Funeral."

2. The clear exception to this statement is that Valentine Ramsay is portrayed as an alcoholic in "Uncle Valentine."

3. Bintrim posits that by 1901 Cather had become aware of Ethelbert's "liabilities—secretive drinking, borrowing large sums of money from his family or publishers, mysterious illnesses—and, aggravating these problems, what we would call today bipolar disorder" (28).

4. Cather wrote to Anne twice after the death of Ethelbert. Cather's seven-page letter was not known outside Pittsburgh until Timothy Bintrim suggested it be included in a 2013 edition of *Selected Letters*. It had been in the University of Pittsburgh Nevin archive from the 1930s, but was overlooked.

5. Cather did not attend Nevin's funeral, but Isabelle (and probably the Slacks) did, and may have seen the plaster cast. Cather may have visited Anne at Blue Hill, Maine, where Anne asked her to do the biography before Howard was given the task, another occasion she may have seen the cast.

6. Bintrim argues for a fourth ("I Have No House for Love to Shelter Him"), and Robert Thacker, now historical editor of Cather's *Collected Poems*—a volume in the Willa Cather Scholarly Edition—agrees that Nevin was a key source of inspiration for a number of poems: "I Have No Love to Shelter Him," "Song," "The Poor Minstrel," "Winter at Delphi," "Sleep, Minstrel, Sleep," "Arcadian Winter," and "Lament for Marsyas."

7. It seems that Anne admitted his alcoholism in part at least to refute rumors in the papers that her husband was addicted to drugs.

## WORKS CITED

Bintrim, Timothy. "Cather's 'Rosary' and Nevin's Legacy in *April Twilights* (1903)." *Willa Cather Newsletter & Review*, vol. 56, no. 1, Fall–Winter 2012, pp. 28–33.

Byrne, Kathleen D., and Richard C. Snyder. *Chrysalis: Willa Cather in Pittsburgh, 1896–1906*. Historical Society of Western Pennsylvania, 1982.

Cather, Willa. *Collected Poems*. Willa Cather Scholarly Edition, historical essay by Robert Thacker, explanatory notes by Kari A. Ronning and Robert Thacker, textual essay and editing by Kari A. Ronning, forthcoming, U of Nebraska P.

———. "The Novel Démeublé." 1922. *Willa Cather on Writing*, U of Nebraska P, 1988, pp. 35–43.

———. "The Professor's Commencement." 1902. Willa Cather Archive, edited by Andrew Jewell, University of Nebraska–Lincoln.

———. *The Professor's House*. 1925. Willa Cather Scholarly Edition, historical essay by James Woodress, explanatory notes by James Woodress with Kari A. Ronning, textual editing by Frederick M. Link, U of Nebraska P, 2002.

———. *The Selected Letters of Willa Cather*. Edited by Andrew Jewell and Janis Stout, Knopf, 2013.

———. *Uncle Valentine and Other Stories*. Edited by Bernice Slote, U of Nebraska P, 1973.

———. *Willa Cather in Person: Interviews, Speeches, Letters*. Edited by L. Brent Bohlke, U of Nebraska P, 1986.

———. *The World and the Parish: Willa Cather's Articles and Reviews, 1893–1902*. Edited by William M. Curtin, U of Nebraska P, 1970. 2 vols.

Emerson, Ralph Waldo. *Nature: Addresses, and Lectures*. Houghton Mifflin, 1883.

"Horatius Cocles." *Wikipedia, the Free Encyclopedia*. Wikimedia Foundation, 12 February 2018, en.wikipedia.org/w/index.php?title=Horatius_Cocles& oldid=825227910.

Howard, John Tasker. *Ethelbert Nevin: A Biography*. Thomas Y. Crowell, 1935.

Lee, Hermione. *Willa Cather: Double Lives*. Vintage, 1989.

Macaulay, Thomas Babington. "Horatius at the Bridge." 1842. *The World's Best Poetry*, vol. 7, edited by Bliss Carman et al., John D. Morris, 1904, Bartleby .com, 2012, www.bartleby.com/360/7/158.html.

Norris, Mary. "To the Letter: The Pleasures of the Greek Alphabet." *The New Yorker*, 14 January 2019, pp. 24–29.

O'Brien, Sharon. *Willa Cather: The Emerging Voice*. Harvard UP, 1997.

Rosowski, Susan J. *The Voyage Perilous: Willa Cather's Romanticism*. U of Nebraska P, 1986.

Ryder, Mary Ruth. "Growing Pains: The City behind Cather's Pittsburgh Classroom." *Cather Studies 13: Willa Cather's Pittsburgh*, edited by Timothy W. Bintrim, James A. Jaap, and Kimberly Vanderlaan, U of Nebraska P, 2021.

Shelley, Percy Bysshe. "Adonais." 1821. *The Norton Anthology of Poetry*, 3rd ed., Norton, 1983, pp. 626–36.

Thompson, Vance. *The Life of Ethelbert Nevin from His Letters and His Wife's Memories*. Boston Music, 1913. Republished by Forgotten Books, 2012.

Woodress, James. *Willa Cather: A Literary Life*. U of Nebraska P, 1989.

Wordsworth, William. "The World Is Too Much with Us." 1807. *The Norton Anthology of Poetry*, 3rd ed., Norton, 1983, p. 559.

# PART 4

# Later Stories

# 10 "I'm Working, I'm Working"

The Industrious Artist of Pittsburgh in
Willa Cather's *The Century Illustrated
Monthly Magazine* Publications

KELSEY SQUIRE

Willa Cather's move from Nebraska to Pittsburgh in June
1896 represents an important transition in her life from student to
professional. Her early Pittsburgh letters to members of the Gere
family in Lincoln, Nebraska, reflect bursts of excitement and energy
as Cather assumes her working duties at a new periodical, *The Home
Monthly*. In a 29 June 1896 letter to Ellen Gere, Cather explains that
she "will be virtually managing editor," and she delights in having
"a nice desk etc. of my own." Although she's displeased by the magazine's content—"great rot, home and fireside stuff"—Cather assumes
a businesslike attitude, stating, "[T]he financial outlook is good, so I
guess I'll stay by it for a while anyway." Her final signature, "Hurriedly
Willa," conveys the new pace of her professional life in Pittsburgh.
Two weeks later, in a letter to Mariel Gere, Cather's enthusiasm still
shows, but is tempered by signs of isolation and overwork. Cather
writes that the "entire responsibility of the first issue [of *The Home
Monthly*] devolves on me," and that "from days end to days end I see

only the prim old maid who keeps my boarding house and my stenographer." From her initial days at *The Home Monthly*, to her work at the *Pittsburgh Daily Leader*, to her independent articles and stories, Cather's ten years in Pittsburgh exemplify her career pursuits. There, Cather would occupy the role of the "industrious artist," one who works long, grueling hours to achieve mastery in her craft and financial success as well.

Many scholars in the last decade—such as contributors to *Cather Studies 7: Willa Cather as Cultural Icon* (edited by Guy Reynolds, 2007) and David Porter in *On the Divide: The Many Lives of Willa Cather* (2010)—have established Cather's clear and sustained interest in marketing her work, and herself, to the public. This chapter seeks to build on these lines of inquiry by considering how Cather's decade in Pittsburgh shaped her concepts of business and work, and more broadly, how her writing participates in social conversations that surrounded industrialization, labor, productivity, and leisure in the late nineteenth and early twentieth centuries. During this period, I suggest that Cather explored the concept of the "industrious artist," and Pittsburgh provided Cather an excellent backdrop to consider practical questions about the pacing and ideal working conditions of artists, as well as the relationship between this work and measures of success. In order to explore this topic of the "industrious artist," I first turn to three pieces of Cather's journalism from her Pittsburgh period. These pieces—on the Homestead Strike, Stephen Crane, and Ethelbert Nevin—show Cather's exploration of labor and productivity. Next, I examine how *The Century Illustrated Magazine* provided Cather with an avenue to experiment with stories and poetry that catered to popular tastes and trends as a means of increasing her chances at future artistic—and financial—success by experimenting with naturalistic themes.

Cather's career from the 1890s through the 1910s had much in common with other writers we often situate within the school of naturalism. As editor Keith Newlin notes in *The Oxford Handbook of American Literary Naturalism*, "[M]any of the most prominent naturalists—Stephen Crane, Frank Norris, Jack London, Theodore

Dreiser—began their craft as journalists" (105). Like Cather, many of these same writers would find support and success through their work with S. S. McClure. As Amy Ahearn establishes in "Full-Blooded Writing and Journalistic Fictions: Naturalism, the Female Artist, and Willa Cather's *The Song of the Lark*," we have clear evidence of Cather "following the careers of these naturalist writers" and "incorporating their writing styles and their artistic philosophies into her own writings" (144). I propose that pieces from Cather's early journalism career in Pittsburgh highlight her awareness of issues like industrialism, the literary marketplace, and immigration. These issues informed Cather's writing of her short story "The Willing Muse" and other works published in *Century*, which provide us with an opportunity to examine Cather's experimentations with, but ultimate abandonment of, a naturalistic approach to writing. While Cather's *Century* stories exhibit unevenness in artistry, they show her judgment in determining what material was suited to market demands.

Several scholars have traced the impact of Cather's work at *McClure's* on her artistic development.[1] As well, pieces of her Pittsburgh journalism detail her understanding of publishing and contemporary issues that dovetail with magazine fiction of the late nineteenth and early twentieth centuries. In particular, pieces like "The Real Homestead" and "When I Knew Stephen Crane" highlight her understanding of industrialization as well as her awareness of naturalistic writing techniques infusing contemporary journalism and literary prose. Additionally, her essay on Pittsburgh composer Ethelbert Nevin, "The Man Who Wrote 'Narcissus,'" provides insights into a model of the "industrious artist" that Cather might pursue herself.

The notorious and violent strike at Homestead Steel Works in 1892, a Pittsburgh area plant owned by Andrew Carnegie and managed by Henry Clay Frick, brought the tensions between industrial laborers and capitalists into the public awareness through the works of journalists, including Cather. As Carnegie biographer David Nasaw notes, the life and philosophies of Pittsburgh's most famous steel baron contain perplexing contradictions. Carnegie disavowed "hard work" as an indicator of or precursor to success. Nasaw writes that "later in life, when Carnegie was called upon to advise young men on how to succeed in business, he never suggested that unceasing hard work was a prerequisite for acquiring wealth" (82). With each career move in his life, Carnegie would end up earning more money, but working fewer hours; Nasaw relates a story that when Carnegie learned that Pennsylvania businessman A. B. Farquhar arrived at work at 7:00 a.m., he laughed and stated, "[Y]ou must be a lazy man if it takes you ten hours to do a day's work" (184). As Nasaw writes, "[T]here is something charmingly subversive in Carnegie's attempt to disrupt the American success narrative by preaching the virtues of idleness, leisure, and immediate gratification" (203). At his mills, however, "Carnegie's hard-driving policies were legendary. Carnegie, [Henry] Phipps, Captain [William] Jones, [Henry Clay] Frick, and Charlie Schwab pitted department against department, mill against mill, superintendent against superintendent in an ongoing, never-ending race to increase productivity" (Nasaw 400).[2] In writing about Homestead, Cather joins the ranks of Arthur Burgoyne, Hamlin Garland, and Theodore Dreiser who reported on the original strike.[3] Cather's 1901 article for the *Lincoln Courier*, "The Real Homestead," was written amid another round of increasing tensions between labor and management during the U.S. Steel recognition strike of 1901, and provides us with insights into her understanding of industrial labor conditions and her opinions regarding these conditions and underlying social theories. Cather's Homestead article focuses on the incongruity between the capitalists' investments in libraries and performing arts spaces and the workers' inability to use such facilities due to their bosses' hard-driving labor practices. Cather explains to her readers that the mill workers endure exhausting, nonstop, twelve-hour shifts. She quips, "[T]welve-hour shifts are doubtless good economy, but they do not tend to make a literary or music-loving community." "The [Homestead Carnegie] library," she explains, "is full of good things that no one has the leisure to enjoy" (856). If a man "has been working all day in a most exhausting temperature and probably drinking heavily to combat the heat, he wants no music or books or athletics, but all the sleep he can get" before resuming his shift the next day (856). Cather's article points to one of the deep differences in the lives of laborers and their capitalist employers: leisure time.

Artists, of course, are not subjected to the same brutal physical conditions as laborers in steel mills. Cather's "When I Knew Stephen Crane," a highly fictionalized account of meeting Stephen Crane in Lincoln that was published under the pseudonym Henry Nicklemann in a Pittsburgh magazine called *The Library*, dramatizes the hardships of literary labor and the pressures to produce commercialized work. One of the elements most important in Cather's Crane essay is the way in which the demarcations between leisure and labor—so clear in the "Homestead" article—are impossibly blurred for writers. Cather writes, "Though [Crane] was seemingly entirely idle during the few days I knew him, his manner indicated that he was in the throes of work that told terribly on his nerves" (934). The blurring between labor and leisure is also apparent in Cather's physical description of Crane, who appears "slovenly" in his dress and poor in health. When he removed his gloves, Cather "noticed that his hands were singularly fine; long, white, and delicately shaped with thin, nervous fingers" (932–33). Cather is fascinated with Crane's "double literary life; writing in the first place the matter that pleased himself, and doing it very slowly; in the second place, any sort of stuff that would sell" (936). One underlying question in this piece is whether such a "double life" as an artist can be successful, or if the artist must choose to be solely "leisurely" or "industrious" in his or her approach to work.

Similar themes on the "double literary life" appear in Cather's profile of Ethelbert Nevin, "The Man Who Wrote 'Narcissus,'" published in November 1900 in *The Ladies' Home Journal*.[4] Nevin was a prominent composer born near Pittsburgh whom Cather met two years prior. Although Nevin died unexpectedly in 1901 at the age of thirty-eight, Cather found warm friendship and hospitality in the Nevins' household. Her description of Nevin in *The Ladies' Home*

*Journal* emphasizes similar physical traits to her portrait of Stephen Crane. Cather writes that Nevin is a "slight, delicately constructed man, all nerves, with a sort of tenseness in every line of his figure, and the mobile, boyish face of the immortally young." Her description of Nevin's hands—"unmistakably those of a musician, small of palm, with long, supple fingers, and a strong, well-developed thumb"— recalls her description of Crane's hands. In terms of Nevin's composing process, Cather writes that, despite frequent illnesses, he "works almost incessantly, having a dozen or more compositions on hand at once, correcting the proofs of one the same day that he writes the first sketch of another." She also reports that he sleeps very little, and instead, he wanders the house or reads French poetry. "Indeed," Cather notes, "when one considers that in the last ten years he has given nearly six hundred compositions to the world, one wonders that he has found time to sleep at all." In this way, Nevin could be considered Cather's idealized "industrious artist": one who works tirelessly, but one who also produces art that is meaningful and beautiful. This may be tempered, however, by Nevin's financial situation: financial pressure forced Nevin to relocate his family to Vineacre, his family home in Sewickley, Pennsylvania, in 1898.[5] As Cather sought to balance writing for artistic satisfaction and commercial profit, it was natural for her to consider what sorts of pieces would sell well to magazines and periodicals. Although Cather did not hold *The Ladies' Home Journal* in high regard, her portrait of Nevin fit well with the periodical's scope of culture and its readership. Like *The Ladies' Home Journal*, *The Century* aimed at a "cultivated upper middle class" readership (John xi).

## THE CENTURY ILLUSTRATED MONTHLY MAGAZINE AND GENRE-BLENDED NATURALISM

While Cather may not be associated with the classic forms of naturalism that students of American literary history now recognize in the works of Frank Norris and Theodore Dreiser, the magazine scene of the early twentieth century catered to a wide array of readers.

Periodicals like *The Century Illustrated Monthly Magazine* sought to capitalize on new literary trends, but in a way that would not alienate their readership or violate the artistic expectations of editors. As Cather attempted to live the life of the "industrious artist," she turned to *The Century* several times for the publication of both short stories and poetry. I propose that viewing Cather's pieces in *The Century* itself provides a different context, one that situates the stories within Cather's connections to Pittsburgh and broader social conversations involving labor, leisure, and productivity in the early twentieth century.

*The Century* may seem an odd place to take up an examination of how Cather's work abuts the school of naturalism; after all, *Century* editor Richard Watson Gilder famously rejected Stephen Crane's *Maggie: A Girl of the Streets* in 1892 or 1893 for serialization on moral grounds. Yet *The Century* did play an important role in exposing readers to works by individuals like Jack London, Edith Wharton, Hamlin Garland, and Jacob Riis. *The Century*'s serialization of Jack London's *The Sea-Wolf* in 1904 provides an excellent example, perhaps, of the path that Cather sought. Charles Johanningsmeier explains, "The case of Jack London, who complained mightily about being a beset proletarian worker while simultaneously becoming America's first millionaire author, is a curiously contradictory one" (365). *The Century* played an important role in shaping that success. Carol S. Loranger notes, "At the end of 1903, *The Century* paid $4,000 for serial rights to London's next novel [*The Sea-Wolf*], when the second half was still in outline form. When Macmillan released the novel in 1904, the publisher was able to pre-sell 40,000 copies" (377). London's expanded version of "To Build a Fire" would also appear in *The Century* in 1908. Andrew Carnegie, too, saw *The Century* as a potential avenue for increasing his own status and spreading his philosophies. Gilder, while editor at *The Century*, developed a close friendship with Andrew Carnegie; the two men held annual literary dinners at Carnegie's New York residence, and *The Century* company released Carnegie's *Gospel of Wealth* essay collection in book form (see Nasaw 617, 631).

While *The Century* certainly wasn't publishing the edgy pieces that would appear in periodicals such as *McClure's*, authors like Jack

London and Edith Wharton explicitly engaged with social Darwinist ideas in stories that appeared in *The Century* just prior to Cather's first publication with the magazine, "The Willing Muse," in 1907.[6] In London's *The Sea-Wolf*, narrator Humphry van Weyden, "a literary critic and a man of leisure," is forced into serving as cabin boy to Captain "Wolf" Larsen, a position Humphry finds demeaning and physically painful (*Century* February 1904, 585). Although Humphry describes Wolf as "primitive" and objects to his Herbert Spencerian approach to life—the captain insists that just as two particles of yeast cannot "wrong each other by striving to devour each other," so "man cannot wrong another man. He can only wrong himself" (1904, 695, 696)—Humphry emerges at the end of the story stronger and more responsible as a result of his physical ordeal as captive. Ultimately, London's story as published in *The Century* blends classic elements of romance (adventure, unbelievable coincidences, and romantic tension between two characters) with his "survival of the fittest" message. In the end, readers see Humphry transformed from a literary man of leisure into a thriving, able-bodied, and competent specimen.

Edith Wharton's short story "Afterward" (*Century*, January 1910) also engages directly with Darwinist philosophies, but through mixing with a different genre: the ghost story. In this riveting but somewhat predictable supernatural tale, midwestern engineer Ned Boyne and his wife, Mary, retire to a life of leisure in Southwest England after he strikes it rich in the Blue Star Mine. After her husband disappears, however, Mary learns that Ned's business deal was completed shrewdly to his own advantage; in speaking of Bob Elwell, a man disadvantaged by the deal, Ned's associate Mr. Parvis says that "Elwell wasn't smart enough, that's all.... It's the kind of thing that happens every day in business. I guess it's what the scientists call the survival of the fittest" (336). In the end, Bob Elwell has his revenge. The trajectory of Ned Boyne's career from engineer to man of wealth evokes the life of a Carnegie or Rockefeller; as the mystery unfolds and Ned's corruption is exposed, readers are ultimately satisfied when his past deeds come back—literally—to haunt him.

Making any generalizations about the tone and direction of *The Century* during Cather's years of publication there (1907–19) is challenging; during that same period, the magazine had five different editors, each of whom attempted to address the magazine's loss of subscribers in the face of competition from "an influx of new, less expensive, and livelier competitors" like *The Ladies' Home Journal* and *McClure's* (John 233).[7] What is notable about these pieces by London and Wharton is that both incorporate direct references to Spencerian "survival of the fittest" philosophies while blending other genres of writing, including romance or ghost stories.

While Cather's publications with *The Century* aren't as explicit as these examples by London and Wharton in their evocation of social Darwinism or "survival of the fittest" philosophies, Cather does use her *Century* pieces to explore the economic forces and social conditions that limit the choices of her characters and shape their outlook on life. Cather's short story "The Willing Muse" was published in *The Century* magazine in August 1907, one year after Cather moved to New York from Pittsburgh. Although sustained critical discussion is slight, this story does pop up frequently as an exemplar of Cather's awkward Jamesian attempts at fiction and is often situated in relationship to the stories she published in *The Troll Garden* and her first novel, *Alexander's Bridge*. In *Willa Cather's Imagination*, David Stouck summarizes the story thus: "In this story an impractical and unworldly novelist [Kenneth Gray] marries a woman [Bertha Torrance] who is also a writer, but her ambition far exceeds his and he is eventually reduced to being her secretary and publicity agent. In the end he saves himself by leaving her and disappearing altogether" (183). The Jamesian elements include Kenneth's occupation as a writer, the narrative voice (which is conveyed through one of Kenneth's friends), and the story's opening, which examines the upcoming marriage of Kenneth and Bertha. While there is significant merit and value in these Jamesian readings, a study of the story's echoes of Pittsburgh reveals Cather's keen interest in exploring the dynamics of the life of the industrious artist through Kenneth's and Bertha's careers.

Cather paints a bleak portrait of industry through brief but strategic descriptions concerning Kenneth's longtime residence, the fictional Olympia, Ohio. Once a bucolic village, home to a college and many literary people, Kenneth explains that Olympia has been "ruined completely" due to invading industrialization, and that "the place is black with smoke and thick with noise from sunrise to sunset." Seen in the light of Cather's Pittsburgh journalism, this portrait of Olympia first invokes Vineacre, Ethelbert Nevin's home on the Ohio River, and the encroaching industrialization recalls Cather's portrait of how steel mills transformed Homestead. Early discussions of "The Willing Muse" by Edward and Lillian Bloom (*Willa Cather's Gift of Sympathy*, published in 1962) and David Stouck (*Willa Cather's Imagination*, published in 1975) find links between the destruction of Olympia and Kenneth's romantic—but ultimately unsuccessful—approach to his literary career.

Cather's descriptions of Kenneth's nervousness and slow pace of composition echo her descriptions of Stephen Crane and Ethelbert Nevin. In "When I Knew Stephen Crane" Cather focuses her attention on Crane's hands, which "were singularly fine; long, white, and delicately shaped with thin, nervous fingers" (933), and in *The Ladies' Home Journal* article, Nevin's fingers appear "long [and] supple." Of Nevin, Cather writes that his hands "are never still when he is talking." In "The Willing Muse," Cather also focuses on Kenneth's hands; while holding an anxious conversation with the narrator, Kenneth is described as "rapidly twirling a paper-cutter between his long fingers." While these descriptions of Kenneth link him to Cather's portraits of "industrious artists," Kenneth's lack of productivity stands in stark relief. Prior to his marriage, Kenneth produced his first book, "Charles de Montpensier." The book appears to his friends to be "overworked": Kenneth "spent years in developing" it over "several laborious summers in France and Italy." The final product, however, was "reduced to a shadowy atmosphere." His second work, by contrast—"an exquisite prose idyll" titled "The Wood of Ronsard"—brought his admirers relief. After his marriage, however, Kenneth's work grinds to a halt. His friends chide him that he should learn to be more "industrious" from his wife, Bertha Torrance. His reply, "I'm working, I'm working," captures the stress of the industrious artist Cather highlighted in her essays on Crane and Nevin—but for Kenneth, this comes without product.

Kenneth's wife, the popular writer Bertha, likewise, plays a complex role in the story. Bertha is a prolific writer whose work achieves commercial and popular success. As demands for her work grow, Kenneth accepts more and more of the business responsibilities to lighten her load. He responds not only to her piles of correspondence, but also reads and replies to manuscripts sent to Bertha for feedback by aspiring writers.[8] Stouck describes Bertha as "vampire-like" because she becomes more radiant and energetic as Kenneth takes on the additional business duties. However, Kenneth's friends seem more disturbed by his inability to produce work than by Bertha's success. Kenneth and his friends do not disparage Bertha for the literary material that she produces—historical romances, which fall into the "cheap" category that Kenneth seeks desperately to avoid. Instead, Bertha is admired and respected for her productivity. As Janis Stout points out, there may be gendered factors at work here: "In 'The Willing Muse,' the one story that undermines gender expectations, with a wife whose writing flourishes after her marriage while her husband's declines from even his earlier halting pace, this situation is regarded as deplorable, as if the wife *should* take the traditional role of muse." Stout also presents an intriguing alternative hypothesis: that Bertha is typing up material by Kenneth, and publishing it under her own name, because he is "too proud to be sullied by hasty work" (Stout 98). In either case, Bertha is hardly a sinister succubus who exploits her husband. While Bertha has adapted herself better to the labor conditions under which writing must occur, she doesn't seem to have the unlimited leisure time that was enjoyed by the industrial capitalists like Andrew Carnegie and J. P. Morgan. At the end of the day, Bertha is still a laborer, one judged solely by her literary output.

In her Homestead article, Cather critiqued the "survival of the fittest" philosophies put forth by Herbert Spencer and embraced by the industrial capitalists. She acknowledges that "an ideal democracy, that is, a complete and consistent democracy, would completely disapprove all of Herbert Spencer's system of philosophy" (858). In the end of "The Willing Muse" Kenneth's disappearance from the world—his permanent strike—seems to be an attempt to remove himself from this "survival of the fittest" literary marketplace. This ending suggests that while individuals may not be able to shape the market forces surrounding them, individuals can decide to "opt out" and leave that system entirely. The story ends, however, without our knowing if his removal from society and market forces allows him to write or increases his happiness.

## ADDITIONAL *CENTURY* PUBLICATIONS

While Kenneth attempts to escape the literary marketplace, Cather's publication of "The Willing Muse" represents an opposing approach as she "opts in" to producing periodical pieces of varying quality in order to enhance her financial success and authorial status. While "The Willing Muse" offers Cather's most detailed portrait of the "industrious artist," she continues to explore themes of work and art within her subsequent *Century* pieces. These pieces, to a varying extent, echo themes of naturalism as characters attempt to navigate desperate situations in which they have little control. In "The Joy of Nelly Deane" (*Century*, October 1911) and "Scandal" (August 1919), Cather presents stories of female musicians. In the former, the title character Nelly Deane has prodigious musical talent, but the fallout from a jilted lover leaves her stuck in a small Nebraska town in a less-than-ideal marriage. In "Scandal," Cather returns to the character of Kitty Ayreshire, who also appeared in her Pittsburgh story "A Gold Slipper" (*Harper's Monthly Magazine*, January 1917). In "Scandal," Siegmund Stein, a Jewish "department store millionaire," attempts to fool the public by hiring a girl (Ruby Mohr) to impersonate the legendary singer Connie Ayrshire. Connie's reaction to the gossipy story of Stein emphasizes a naturalistic surrender, as Connie states that both she and Ruby are "the victims of circumstance" who must adapt to the whims of the wealthy and powerful. In "The Bookkeeper's Wife" (*Century*, May 1916) and "Ardessa" (*Century*, May 1918) Cather explores the dynamics of the modern workplace through the Remsen Paper Company and *The Outcry* office (a muckraking periodical that resembles *McClure's*). In both stories, the characters struggle to move up or maintain their current positions, to dire consequences. In "The Bookkeeper's Wife," Percy Bixby's lack of an appropriate salary to support his wife leads him to steal money from the company. Ultimately, he loses his job and marriage in the fallout when his accounting crimes are revealed. In "Ardessa," Ardessa Devine holds a comfortable, powerful job as the main secretary to *The Outcry* chief, O'Mally. Ardessa loses her job after outsourcing elements of her work to the aspiring, hardworking Becky Tietelba. And finally, in her poem "Street in Packingtown" (*Century*, May 1915), Cather paints a desperate portrait of urban immigrant life. The poem centers on the narrator's descriptions of a child—labeled "a Polack's brat"—torturing a feral cat in an alley. The most pressing element is the boy's demeanor: his torture of the animal is described as "joyless," and he persists despite the cat's aggressiveness (the boy's arms are covered in scratches) and the presence of the narrator.[9]

It is clear that both Cather and periodical publishers were not entirely satisfied with many of these pieces. Of the *Century* stories, only "Scandal" was republished in Cather's short-story collection, *Youth and the Bright Medusa* (1920).[10] As Lisa Marcus notes, drawing on James Woodress's *Willa Cather: A Literary Life*, "Scandal" was written in 1916, but "took years for her agent to place. When it finally appeared in *The Century* in 1919, it had been rejected fifteen times" (78). Clearly, many editors did not feel that "Scandal" met the interests of their readers nor the scope of their publications. Both "Scandal" and "Ardessa" contain uncomfortable stereotypes of Jewish characters.[11] And the portrait of immigrants in "Street in Packingtown" is startling given Cather's sympathetic portraits of immigrants in *O Pioneers!*, *The Song of the Lark*, and *My Ántonia*. Although Cather would continue to experiment with poetry sporadically and republish an expanded version of *April Twilights* in 1923, "Street in Packingtown" was not selected for republication.

These stories, particularly "The Willing Muse," reveal Cather's negotiation process as she attempted to navigate the "double literary life" that she met in Pittsburgh, writing for pleasure and artistic satisfaction on the one hand, and for commercial success on the other. In *Willa Cather: A Memoir*, Elizabeth Shepley Sergeant reflects back on the summer of 1914, writing, "It used to surprise me that with all her talk of Pittsburgh and for all her connections with *McClure's*, Willa never once mentioned to me those Pittsburgh steel mills which, during the age of reform, came in for so much social criticism" (126). While Cather, even at this stage of her career, made explicit statements against the sort of realistic fiction that seemed to contain a didactic or social message, Cather's life in Pittsburgh was influential in shaping her awareness of industry and labor. Like Kenneth's refrain "I'm working, I'm working," Cather's letters from Pittsburgh back to family and friends in Nebraska contained messages of pride about her increasing professionalization, but also exhaustion at the pace of her work and her duties. Her early journalism—pieces like "The Real Homestead" and "When I Knew Stephen Crane"—can be useful in documenting Cather's exposure to and opinions on issues of labor, and, while she did not take up the path of a muckraking journalist or brutal naturalist writer, stories like "The Willing Muse" highlight her ability to incorporate reflections on industry and industriousness into her fiction in an allusive way. Although Cather's *Century* stories may not be her best, her completion of these stories showcases her engagement with the tastes of the market, her development as a writer, and ultimately, her ability to use "good economy."

## NOTES

1. See, for example, "Willa Cather's Political Apprenticeship at *McClure's Magazine*" by Joseph R. Urgo in *Willa Cather's New York: New Essays on Cather in the City*; "The Standard Oil Treatment: Willa Cather, 'The Life of Mary Baker G. Eddy,' and Early Twentieth Century Collaborative Authorship" by Ashley Squires; "'It's Through Myself That I Knew and Felt Her': S. S. McClure's 'My Autobiography' and the Development of Willa Cather's Autobiographical Realism" by Robert Thacker; Ellen Gruber Garvey's

"Important, Responsible Work: Willa Cather's Office Stories and Her Necessary Editorial Career"; and Donal Harris's *On Company Time: American Modernism in the Big Magazines.*

2. All of the men included here were notable figures in the Pennsylvania steel industry during the late nineteenth and early twentieth centuries. Henry Phipps was a partner at the Carnegie Steel Company. Captain William Jones took his title from his service in the Civil War; he worked in many capacities for Carnegie's Edgar Thompson Steel Works in both supervising roles and as the inventor of numerous mechanical devices for the plant (see Nasaw 147–48). Henry Clay Frick began his career in coke manufacturing; in the 1880s, Frick and Carnegie formed formal relationships between their coke and steel businesses—a partnership that helped to keep Carnegie's production costs low. Nasaw describes Charlie Schwab as Carnegie's protégé (374); he served as the general superintendent at Edgar Thompson and Homestead in the 1880s before rising to the position of president of the Carnegie Steel Corporation.

3. Arthur Burgoyne, a Pittsburgh journalist, published *The Homestead Strike of 1892*, in 1893. Cather and Burgoyne worked together at the *Pittsburgh Leader* in 1897–98, and may have discussed political issues of the day. Hamlin Garland, according to Nasaw, "snuck into the works through a hole in the fence" with an illustrator (461); Garland published "Homestead and Its Perilous Trades—Impressions of a Visit" in *McClure's* in 1884 (June, vol. 3, no. 1). Theodore Dreiser worked for the *Pittsburgh Dispatch* in the early 1890s and wrote numerous articles critical of Carnegie and his business practices (see Nasaw 373–74).

4. Prior to "The Man Who Wrote 'Narcissus,'" Cather placed "Ethelbert Nevin: Return of Narcissus" in the *Lincoln Courier*, February 5, 1898. Much of the information in *The Ladies' Home Journal* piece was published in the *Courier* previously, on July 15, 1899. For more, see Curtin, pages 532–38 and 627–37.

5. See the note for "Ethelbert Nevin" in Cather's letter to Mariel Gere (#0055).

6. In *The Best Years of "The Century,"* Arthur John details the differences between the two publications. He writes: "[M]ore striking than any difference in subject matter was the livelier tone of *McClure's*, achieved in part by a liberal use of photographs, but perhaps even more by a journalistic approach to nearly all subjects. Whether an article was about a famous musician, a foreign statesman, or an American writer, *McClure's* usually dwelt on the personality of the subject. *The Century* tried to match this emphasis on occasion, but essentially the personal note was out of keeping with Gilder's stress on dignity and ideal standards" (236).

7. See especially "Postscript" in Arthur John's *The Best Years of "The Century,"* pp. 270–71. During Cather's years of publication with the magazine, these editors included the following:

Richard Watson Gilder: 1881–1909 (died 1909)
Robert Underwood Johnson: 1909–13
Robert S. Yard: 1913–14
Douglas Z. Doty: 1915–18
Thomas H. Smith: 1919

8. The relationship between Kenneth and Bertha seems to reverse the relationship that Cather outlines between Nevin and his wife, Anne, in "The Man Who Wrote 'Narcissus.'" Cather opined, "[I]t is almost impossible to write of Mr. Nevin without writing of his wife, so closely are they associated in everything. She is practically his business manager, is thoroughly posted in all her husband's work, and is his most constant if not his most impartial critic." The dynamics between Kenneth and Bertha also evoke the relationship between another Nevin prototype, Valentine Ramsey, and his ex-wife, Janet Oglethorpe, in "Uncle Valentine."

9. The tenor of this poem recalls another of Cather's Henry Nicklemann pieces, "Pittsburgh's Mulberry Street." Writing as Nicklemann, Cather provides detailed descriptions of immigrant lives and living conditions, much in the manner of Jacob Riis in *How the Other Half Lives* (1890).

10. Mark J. Madigan provides a complete publishing history for "Scandal" in his historical notes for the Cather Scholarly Edition of *Youth and the Bright Medusa*.

11. For more analysis of Cather's representation of Jewish characters, see Lisa Marcus's "Willa Cather and the Geography of Jewishness" and Donald Pizer's *American Naturalism and the Jews: Garland, Norris, Dreiser, Wharton, and Cather*.

## WORKS CITED

Ahearn, Amy. "Full-Blooded Writing and Journalistic Fictions: Naturalism, the Female Artist and Willa Cather's *The Song of the Lark.*" *American Literary Realism*, vol. 33, no. 2, 2001, pp. 143–56.
Bloom, Edward A., and Lillian D. Bloom. *Willa Cather's Gift of Sympathy*. Southern Illinois UP, 1962.

Cather, Willa. #0025: Willa Cather to Ellen Gere [29 June 1898]. *The Complete Letters of Willa Cather*, edited by the Willa Cather Archive Team, the Willa Cather Archive, 2018, www.cather.unl.edu/letters/let0025.

———. #0026: Willa Cather to Mariel E. Clapham Gere, 13 July [1896]. *The Complete Letters of Willa Cather*, edited by the Willa Cather Archive Team, the Willa Cather Archive, 2018, www.cather.unl.edu/letters/let0026.

———. #0055: Willa Cather to Mariel Gere [Dec. 1898]. *The Complete Letters of Willa Cather*, edited by the Willa Cather Archive Team, the Willa Cather Archive, 2018, www.cather.unl.edu/letters/let0055.

———. "Ardessa." The Willa Cather Archive, www.cather.unl.edu/ss048.html.

———. "The Bookkeeper's Wife." The Willa Cather Archive, www.cather.unl.edu/ss047.html.

———. "The Joy of Nelly Deane." The Willa Cather Archive, www.cather.unl.edu/ss014.html.

———. "The Man Who Wrote 'Narcissus.'" The Willa Cather Archive, www.cather.unl.edu/nf059.html.

———. "Pittsburgh's Mulberry Street." *The World and the Parish: Willa Cather's Articles and Reviews, 1893–1902*, edited by William M. Curtin, U of Nebraska P, 1970, pp. 2: 869–74.

———. "The Real Homestead." *The World and the Parish: Willa Cather's Articles and Reviews, 1893–1902*, edited by William M. Curtin, U of Nebraska P, 1970, pp. 2: 854–59.

———. "Scandal." The Willa Cather Archive, www.cather.unl.edu/ss055.html.

———. "Street in Packingtown." *The Century Illustrated Monthly Magazine*, vol. 90, no. 1, May 1915, p. 23.

———. "When I Knew Stephen Crane." *Willa Cather: Stories, Poems, and Other Writings*, Library of America, Viking Press, 1992, pp. 932–38.

———. "The Willing Muse." The Willa Cather Archive, www.cather.unl.edu/ss016.html.

Curtin, William M., editor. *The World and the Parish: Willa Cather's Articles and Reviews, 1893–1902*. U of Nebraska P, 1970. 2 vols.

Garvey, Ellen Gruber. "'Important, Responsible Work': Willa Cather's Office Stories and Her Necessary Editorial Career." *Studies in American Fiction*, vol. 36, no. 2, 2008, pp. 177–96, Project MUSE, DOI:10.1353/saf.2008.0020.

Harris, Donal. *On Company Time: American Modernism in the Big Magazines*. Columbia UP, 2016.

Johanningsmeier, Charles. "Naturalist Authors and the American Literary Marketplace." *The Oxford Handbook of American Literary Naturalism*, Oxford UP, 2011, pp. 357–72.

John, Arthur. *The Best Years of the "Century": Richard Watson Gilder, "Scribner's Monthly," and the "Century Magazine," 1870–1909*. U of Illinois P, 1981.

London, Jack. "The Sea-Wolf." *The Century Illustrated Monthly Magazine*, vol. 67, no. 4, February 1904, pp. 585–97.

———. "The Sea-Wolf." *The Century Illustrated Monthly Magazine*, vol. 67, no. 5, March 1904, pp. 693–708.

Loranger, Carol S. "Consolation, Affirmation, and Convention: The Popular Reception of American Naturalist Texts." *The Oxford Handbook of American Literary Naturalism*, edited by Keith Newlin, Oxford UP, 2011, pp. 373–88.

Madigan, Mark J. Historical Essay. *Youth and the Bright Medusa*. Explanatory notes by Mark Madigan, textual essay and editing by Frederick M. Link, Charles W. Mignon, Judith Boss, and Kari A. Ronning, U of Nebraska P, 2009, pp. 313–75.

Marcus, Lisa. "Willa Cather and the Geography of Jewishness." *The Cambridge Companion to Willa Cather*, edited by Marilee Lindemann, Cambridge UP, 2005, pp. 66–85.

Nasaw, David. *Andrew Carnegie*. Penguin Press, 2007.

Newlin, Keith. "Introduction: The Naturalistic Imagination and the Aesthetics of Excess." *The Oxford Handbook of American Literary Naturalism*, edited by Keith Newlin, Oxford UP, 2011, pp. 3–17.

Pizer, Donald. *American Naturalism and the Jews: Garland, Norris, Dreiser, Wharton, and Cather*. U of Illinois P, 2008.

Porter, David H. *On the Divide: The Many Lives of Willa Cather*. U of Nebraska P, 2008.

Reynolds, Guy, editor. *Cather Studies 7: Willa Cather as Cultural Icon*. U of Nebraska P, 2007.

Sergeant, Elizabeth Shepley. *Willa Cather: A Memoir*. U of Nebraska P, 1963.

Squires, Ashley. "The Standard Oil Treatment: Willa Cather, 'The Life of Mary Baker G. Eddy,' and Early Twentieth Century Collaborative Authorship." *Studies in the Novel*, vol. 45, no. 3, 2013, pp. 328–48.

Stouck, David. *Willa Cather's Imagination*. U of Nebraska P, 1975.

Stout, Janis P. *Willa Cather: The Writer and Her World*. UP of Virginia, 2000.

Thacker, Robert. "'It's Through Myself That I Knew and Felt Her': S. S. McClure's *My Autobiography* and the Development of Willa Cather's Autobiographical Realism." *American Literary Realism*, vol. 33, no. 2, 2001, pp. 123–42.

Urgo, Joseph R. "Willa Cather's Political Apprenticeship at *McClure's Magazine*." *Willa Cather's New York: New Essays on Cather in the City*, edited by Merrill Maguire Skaggs, Fairleigh Dickinson UP, 2000, pp. 60–74.

Wharton, Edith. "Afterward." *The Century Illustrated Monthly Magazine*, vol. 79, no. 3, January 1910, pp. 321–39.

## 11 Venetian Window

### Pittsburgh Glass and Modernist Community in "Double Birthday"

JOSEPH C. MURPHY

"Double Birthday" (1929) is Willa Cather's glass story. Its centerpiece is "a large stained-glass window representing a scene on the Grand Canal in Venice" ("Double Birthday" 48), installed in the spectacular late-nineteenth-century Allegheny City, present-day North Side, home of the Engelhardts, a once affluent family of Pittsburgh glass manufacturers who have since fallen into ruin and obscurity. Their last survivors by the late 1920s are one son (of the original five) and an uncle, aged fifty-five and eighty, respectively, both named Albert, both bachelors, sharing the same birthday and, at this point, the same upper floor of a house they split with a glassworker's family on Pittsburgh's South Side, the Engelhardts' last surviving property. Once neglected by critics, "Double Birthday" has in recent years attracted notice for its dialectical representation of space and time. I have studied how Cather "integrates four sections of Pittsburgh—South Side, Squirrel Hill, Allegheny, and downtown—conventionally separated by forces of class and history" (Murphy, "Dialectics" 255–56). Joshua Doležal identifies "a remarkable synergism of past and future," "a coupling of worlds in time" that is Cather's answer to political progressivism (414, 425). In their biographical study, Timothy Bintrim and Kari Ronning ground the story's spatiotemporal coordinates in the tragic but industrious life of Cather's Allegheny friend and mentor George Gerwig. Most recently, David Porter discusses "Double Birthday" as a "pivot" text between the largely comic energies of *The Song of the Lark* (1915) and the tragic mood of *Lucy Gayheart* (1935). Here I will reconsider the story's dialectical structure through its most distinctive architectural feature: its central Venetian window, which serves as an entryway to Cather's depiction of modernist consciousness and community.

In their Allegheny City heyday, the Engelhardts of "Double Birthday" were known by their stained-glass window. The progress of the story's tragic heroine, the budding vocal artist Marguerite Thiesinger, from Pittsburgh to a burgeoning career in New York under Uncle Albert's sponsorship, originates from her instinctive desire "to see that beautiful window from the inside" (49). But the reader is not privy to Marguerite's inside view of the window. That view remains a hidden source of illumination—one of the story's many lacunae—an index to an entire world obliterated, emotionally if not physically, by the Great War, the fault line dividing the narrative's present and past. To reconstruct an insider's knowledge of this window, I am seeking here to understand its aesthetic form, its Venetian subject, and ultimately its emotional register for the Engelhardts and the surrounding community at a time when Pittsburgh was the leading glass-manufacturing city in the United States.[1] I am also trying to account for the Venetian window's elusive presence—why the experience of it, so familiar to the characters, is largely withheld from the reader. As such, I will read deeply and broadly into a relatively succinct architectural detail, albeit one exhibiting a characteristically Catherian expansiveness that permeates the narrative and opens into history. My study will involve the battle of styles in late nineteenth-century American stained glass—especially the phenomenon of opalescent glass—and the contemporaneous iconology of Venice, as well as the modernist technique Cather pursues in this mature, uncollected story of the late 1920s. Throughout, I will consider the Venetian window as a work of art that constructs a particular relationship with its audience (both within and outside the narrative) through its social and historical significance, its visual dynamics, and its Venetian imagery.

## THE INNER SANCTUM

In "Double Birthday," the Venetian window is a teasing sign of both openness and exclusivity. It is the public face of the Engelhardts, a prominent German family in a neighborhood then known as Deutschtown, facing west toward Allegheny market: "Everyone knew the Engelhardt house, built of many-colored bricks, with gables and turrets, and on the west a large stained-glass window representing a scene on the Grand Canal in Venice, the Church of Santa Maria della Salute in the background, in the foreground a gondola with a slender gondolier" (48). As public image, the stained glass duly represents August Engelhardt as a glass magnate in the nation's glassmaking capital, while at the same time distinguishing, through fine artisanal work, his family's domestic retreat as a separate sphere from their "flourishing glass factory up the river" (42). The window is the most distinctive feature of a house—"big, many-gabled, so-German" (45)—that pegs the family as affluent but also singular and ethnic, with "that queer German streak in them" (42). In its touristic associations, the window seems to foretell the Engelhardt sons' drift from their father's business toward "fantastic individual enterprises" (42). Images of the Allegheny household dwell on its external, theatrical signs of leisure, calling to mind "people in a book or a play": "flowers and bird cages and striped awnings, boys lying about in tennis clothes, making mint juleps before lunch, having coffee under the sycamore trees after dinner" (57); "flowering shrubs and greenhouses . . . so well known in Allegheny" (53).

While the Engelhardts play out their lives as a kind of theater under the sign of the Venetian window, the window, in its impermeability, also establishes the limits of their public intercourse. More than a medium for light, the window is a façade. Cather's matter-of-fact description emphasizes its scenic elements—canal, church, gondola, gondolier—rather than its translucence as stained glass. The eyes of the public fasten on the window, yearning for the personal touch, openly visible, that will glimpse the underlying domestic intimacy of "a public-spirited citizen and a generous employer of labor" (43). When that intimacy is not forthcoming, the people imagine it for themselves: "People said August and Mrs. Engelhardt should be solidly seated in the prow [of the gondola] to make the picture complete," a public daydream that persists even after August Engelhardt's death (48). The empty space in the gondola creates for the reader a sense of aesthetic incompleteness, a phantom presence generating an atmosphere of suspense and possibility.

The Venetian window's impermeability and incompletion heighten the drama of gaining access. Everyone knows the house with the Venetian window, but only inductees like Marguerite Thiesinger and Margaret ("Marjorie") Hammersley, linked by their given names, are chosen to enter its inner sanctum. For Marguerite, her voice is her passport. Uncle Albert has the opportunity to distinguish her "one Voice" among a larger chorus because "the chapel windows were open" as he passes Allegheny High School on his customary morning walk. Following that voice to its source in the chapel, he encounters Marguerite singing, solo now, Carl Bohm's "Still Wie die Nacht," and invites her to have lunch and sing in the Engelhardt home. Marguerite's reply—"Oh, yes! ... [S]he'd always wanted to see that beautiful window from the inside"—sketches the terms of a covenant still under negotiation: Uncle Albert, having apprehended her voice through the open chapel windows, will cultivate that voice behind the Venetian window, the private sanctum of the Engelhardt home replacing the public sanctuary of the school chapel. In exchange, Marguerite gains access to a German clan who outclass her own "very ordinary" German people, and to the inner view of the Venetian window, which becomes invested with her voice's potential (48–49). By contrast, as a social peer, young Marjorie Hammersley's access to the Engelhardt house requires no display of artistic talent, only a desire to escape the mating rituals of "the young men in her set," who "grabbed [a girl] rather brutally," and to enjoy a family who appreciates her "aesthetically" (57). For both Marguerite and Marjorie, however, the Venetian window marks an exclusive passageway into an aesthetic realm that suspends the city's materialistic ambitions. As Uncle Albert counsels Marguerite, "There is something vulgar about ambition. Now we will play for higher stakes; for ambition read aspiration!" (51).

From the story's 1920s present, the memory of the Allegheny house with its signature window becomes a metonym for the irrecoverable world "before-the-war" (60). So it is for the adult Marjorie Hammersley (now the widow Mrs. Parmenter) who recalls the house as a "wonderful" place of "music" and a thing to "cherish" (61). Back in the day, it impressed Marguerite as "magnificent" (49). The Alberts, in their household ways and wares, have re-created something of the Allegheny house's luster in their "workingman's house" on the South Side (45), which Marjorie calls "the only spot I know in the world that is before-the-war. . . . You've got a period shut up in here," she tells them, "the last ten years of one century, and the first ten of another" (60–61). Nephew and uncle, in dignified poverty, tend the embers of an all-but-vanished age. However, the reader never experiences what would be the visual apotheosis of this one-time magnificence: the stained-glass image of Venice on the west side of the Allegheny house as Marguerite long desired it, *privately viewed from within*, backlit by the afternoon sun. This spectacle, so carefully intimated, never appears in the story. The principal characters share luminous experiences of the window to which the reader has no access.

OPALESCENCE

It would seem arbitrary to make an issue of what Cather *doesn't* describe, were the alternative not so plausible. Cather understood the phantasmagoric potential of glass. When Black Hawk is frozen over in *My Ántonia* (1918), narrator Jim Burden feels the unconscious pull exerted by the Methodist Church window: "I can remember how glad I was when there happened to be a light in the church, and the painted glass window shone out at us as we came along the frozen street.... Without knowing why, we used to linger on the sidewalk outside the church ... shivering and talking until our feet were like lumps of ice. The crude reds and greens and blues of that colored glass held us there" (168–69). In *One of Ours* (1922), Claude Wheeler spends an hour in Rouen's church of St. Ouen contemplating "[t]he purple and crimson and peacock-green" light of the rose window that "[h]e felt distinctly ... went through him" (452). Or consider, in *Shadows on the Rock* (1931), the light show performed for Cécile by Count Frontenac's "crystal bowl full of glowing fruits of coloured glass: purple figs, yellow-green grapes with gold vine-leaves, apricots, nectarines, and a dark citron stuck up endwise among the grapes. The fruits were hollow, and the light played in them, throwing coloured reflections into the mirror and upon the wall above" (71). Clearly Cather was not blind to the power of glass as a subject for word painting.

The preeminent example of the era, in a work she admired, is Henry Adams's meditation on the twelfth-century glass of Chartres Cathedral in *Mont-Saint-Michel and Chartres* (1904).[2] "[N]o opaque color laid on with a brush, can compare with translucent glass," writes Adams, transfixed by "the limpidity of the blues; the depth of the red; the intensity of the green; the complicated harmonies; the sparkle and splendor of the light" (124, 132). On her own visit to Rouen in 1902, Cather marveled at "the burning blue and crimson of two rose windows" in the cathedral "almost as beautiful as those of Notre Dame" (*World and the Parish* 2: 923). For Cather, the luminosity of stained glass served as a handy metaphor. She once thanked her publishers, the Knopfs, for an especially fine case of Rothschild wine from the South of France, which she praised in terms of glass and light: "It is a superb wine, and shall be reserved for special occasions when I feel a little hard and want to have a glow put into things, a kind of stained glass treatment of pallid daylight" (*Selected Letters* 331).

Fig. 11.1. Opalescent window, 820 Cedar Avenue, Pittsburgh, Pennsylvania. Probably Rudy Brothers Studio, 1894 or after. Photograph by Joseph C. Murphy.

Why, then, the inertness of Cather's Venetian window, her neglect of its translucence and her decision not to capitalize on its spectacular potential as glass? I'll pursue these questions on two levels, first in regard to the type of stained glass Cather had in mind, and second in regard to her modernist goals in "Double Birthday." In other words, what would the Venetian window have looked like, and why does Cather's representation of it matter for an interpretation of her modernism?

Historical models for the Venetian window are elusive but not beyond reach. The search begins with the prototype of the Engelhardt house at 906 (formerly 66) Cedar Avenue on Pittsburgh's North Side, formerly the residence of Cather's Lincoln friend George Gerwig—a historical context already richly detailed by Peter M. Sullivan as well as Bintrim and Ronning. This gabled and turreted house, probably dating from the 1870s, contains no window depicting a Venetian scene, though it does feature a handsome iris-motif window on the second floor west façade. Neighboring houses at 902 and 820 Cedar contain turn-of-the-century stained glass, facing Suismon Avenue, depicting scenes that, though not specifically Venetian, do feature boat-and-water motifs with vaguely Italianate scenery: peninsulas, poplars, turrets, a loggia with Romanesque arches. In the 820 Cedar window, a solo boatman, his image doubled in the water, is a stout forerunner of Cather's "slender gondolier" (figure II.I). These two scenic windows, which Cather would certainly have noticed while visiting the Gerwig house and commuting to her job at nearby Allegheny High School (Bintrim and Ronning 83), may be the closest we come to locating prototypes for her fictional Venetian window. Both these windows are examples of the opalescent style popularized by John La Farge and his rival Louis Comfort Tiffany beginning in the 1880s, characterized by glass "in multicoloured, marbleized sheets, often with an iridescent sheen" (Raguin 224).[3] Throughout the United States, opalescent windows became the upper-middle-class fashion for homes as well as religious and educational buildings. American glass studios adopted opalescent glass as their primary medium, defining the period between 1880 and 1920 as the "opalescent era" and making "American Glass" synonymous with opalescent glass (Raguin 224, 230; Tannler, "Classical Perspective"). Veteran Pittsburgh glass restorer John Kelly identifies the Cedar Avenue scenic windows as, without question, the work of the Rudy Brothers, who operated one of the major opalescent glass workshops in Pittsburgh at the century's turn.[4] The brothers Frank, J. Horace, Jesse, and Isaiah Rudy opened their first shop in Pittsburgh's East Liberty section in 1894. An early patron was industrialist H. J. Heinz, who commissioned stained-glass windows for his Point Breeze neighborhood residence and his factory ("Guide"). A list of the Rudy company's clientele "reads like a litany of the new managerial and middle class: broker, pay master, physician, lawyer, superintendent, dentist, doctor, and so on" (Madarasz 101–2).

As a status symbol, opalescent glass would have been the obvious choice for an industrialist like August Engelhardt; moreover, its nature is consistent with Cather's muted rendering of her Venetian window. Modernizing the antique "pot metal" technique—in which glass pieces colored by metal oxides were stitched together by prominent leadwork (Gossman et al. 40)—opalescent windows subordinated the leadwork to a pictorial design showcasing milky streaks and whorls of color. Opal or milk glass, which had long been used in tableware, is formed by incorporating a compound of "peroxide of tin or stannic acid, antimonic acid, chloride of silver, phosphate of lime, or bone ashes" into the glass (La Farge 1). La Farge's innovation was his use of opal glass for windows by combining it with ordinary colored glass in long sheets, stacking several plates on top of one another, and fastening them with lead (Raguin 231–32).

The opalescent style exhibits three hallmark properties. One is iridescence, that is, a slow-burning shimmer achieved by distributing light throughout the sheet rather than allowing it to pass through. Less translucent than medieval stained glass, and in some cases almost opaque, opalescent glass achieves its unique "movement and life when light illuminates it from behind" (Isenberg and Isenberg 4), giving piquancy to Marguerite Thiesinger's desire to see the Venetian window "from the inside." A second feature of opalescent glass is its subtle gradation of color, layered like paint but actually inherent in the glass itself. As such, opalescent glass diverges from the tradition of painted glass, dating from the Renaissance, in which paint was applied to the surface of clear glass (Gossman et al. 41–43). The third hallmark, extending from the second, is its formal imi-

Fig. 11.2. John La Farge, *Fortune on Her Wheel*, 1902, Frick Building, Pittsburgh, Pennsylvania. Photograph by Albert Vitiello.

tation of perspectival painting. As La Farge explained in his 1879 patent application, opalescent glass enabled him, "by checking or graduating" the passage of light, "to gain effects as to depth, softness, and modulation of color" and achieve a higher degree of "realistic representation" (1). Cather's description of the Venetian window calls attention to this illusionistic strategy—it is a window "representing a scene," she writes—and deploys perspectival signposts to depict a cityscape formally at odds with the two-dimensionality of glass: "the Church of Santa Maria della Salute in the background, in the foreground a gondola." Cather's presentation of the Venetian window as painterly rather than translucent, then, captures an essential feature of opalescent glass.

Cather had many opportunities to experience opalescent windows throughout her career. In addition to the Allegheny neighborhood windows, she must have known La Farge's monumental opalescent window *Fortune on Her Wheel,* installed in 1902 in the lobby of the Frick Building across from the Pittsburgh courthouse where Albert and Judge Hammersley meet in the opening scene of "Double Birthday" (figure 11.2). It depicts Fortune as a dramatic figure of turbulence, riding her wheel on choppy waters. Certainly, Cather admired the work of La Farge, who outfitted Manhattan's Church of the Ascension, her "favourite church in New York" (Lewis 151), with four opalescent windows as well as the grand mural *The Ascension of Our Lord* (1887) above the altar. In an intriguing detail in a letter to her niece Margaret during a stay at Williams College, Massachusetts, in 1942, Cather describes herself "studying the stained glass in the chapel" (*Selected Letters* 612). The masterpiece of Williams's Thompson Memorial Chapel is, in fact, an opalescent window by La Farge— his exquisite, layered rendering of *Abraham and an Angel* from 1882, dedicated to the memory of President James A. Garfield—suggesting the continuing allure of opalescent windows for Cather in later years.

The memorial function of stained glass was on Cather's mind during mid-1928 when she was working on "Double Birthday," as she was then considering options for a window in memory of her father in Red Cloud's Grace Episcopal Church.[5] In this endeavor she was assisted by her Red Cloud friend Carrie Miner Sherwood, whom she wrote from New York on 13 June 1928: "I find stained glass a difficult thing to go shopping for, and I have decided to let Father's window go over until next fall, when I hope I will have more energy." By the following January she could write Carrie with more assurance, "I like the design you sent for Father's window very much," and, referring to another window Carrie was overseeing for the church, remarked: "I realize what a lot of work it takes to put anything of that kind through" (21 January 1929).

Fig. 11.3. *The Good Shepherd*, Emil Frei Company, St. Louis and Munich, dedicated 5 December 1937. Cather memorial window, Grace Episcopal Church, Red Cloud, Nebraska. Photograph by Joseph C. Murphy.

Cather's sense of the difficulty of selecting a church window must have derived in part from her awareness of the array of contending styles available. The windows she ultimately chose to honor each of her parents are examples of the Munich style, manufactured by Emil Frei Company of St. Louis and Munich (figure 11.3).[6] Like the opalescent style, the Munich style, established in the early nineteenth century under the sponsorship of Ludwig I of Bavaria, represented a compromise between traditional medieval glass and post-Renaissance painted glass (Gossman et al. 44), but it clung much more closely to the latter tradition. While "made of traditional hand-blown antique glass," Munich glass windows relied almost entirely on applied paint for an "idealized naturalism and spatial realism" that spread across the pane with less pronounced leading than medieval glass (Tannler, "Leo Thomas"). Painted glass maximizes the window's pictorialism but minimizes its translucency, as far less light penetrates the enamel paint. Both the Munich and the opalescent styles were rejected by neo-Gothic boosters like Henry Adams, who believed that illusionistic perspective had no place in stained glass. "The twelfth-century glassworker would sooner have worn a landscape on his back than have costumed his church with it," Adams protested. "He wanted to keep the colored window flat, like a rug hung on the wall" (126).

In any case, Cather opted to memorialize her parents in a style Adams trivialized as "opaque color laid on with a brush," rather than in the neo-Gothic or opalescent styles (the latter being somewhat out of vogue by the 1920s [Raguin 235]). Her taste was evidently more eclectic than Adams's. Finding aesthetic value in all these traditions, Cather was aware of a broad continuum between the translucent glass of the Middle Ages, at one extreme, and the "painted glass window" of *My Ántonia*'s Methodist Church, with its "crude reds and greens and blues," on the other. Opalescent and Munich glass both fell along this continuum, but it was opalescent glass that more completely fused the medieval and Renaissance traditions, captivating the viewer with both its pictorialism and its intrinsic qualities as glass. It is this complex appeal of opalescence—the favored style for upper-middle-class homes before World War I—that an informed historical reading restores to the Engelhardts' Venetian window.

## GLASSWORK

The subdued quality of Cather's Venetian window corresponds not only to the opalescent style but also, I will suggest, to the aesthetic and narrative sensibility she cultivates in "Double Birthday." This sensibility is perhaps best summarized in Albert Engelhardt's meditations (communicated through free indirect discourse) as he commutes home for his uncle's birthday dinner and brushes aside any consideration of his own birthday: "If one stopped to think of that, there was a shiver waiting round the corner" (57). Crossing the Smithfield Street Bridge, surveying the flow of the Monongahela River beneath him and the heights of Mount Washington above, he truncates his thinking: "Better not reflect too much" (57). The line could serve as the motto for a story that implies reflection or mirroring in its title, "Double Birthday," but here discourages reflection as a mental habit, even as it features a stained-glass window in which the reflective, refractive, and translucent properties of glass are restrained. Albert's self-conscious chastening of reflection upholds Cather's own modernist method, as described in "The Novel Démeublé" (1922), of creating "the emotional aura of the fact or the thing or the deed" "without . . . specifically nam[ing]" it (41–42).

Significantly, the story's guarded attitude toward reflection—reflection in mind, reflection in glass—puts it at odds with the aesthetic tradition on which young Albert was weaned: the 1890s Decadent works of Aubrey Beardsley, Ernest Dowson, Oscar Wilde, even "a complete file of the *Yellow Book*," which still line the shelves of his library but look, "though so recent, . . . already immensely far away and diminished" (45–46). For the Decadents, who savored moods of loss and aftermath, the complex and diminishing play of light on reflective surfaces was irresistible. In *Decadence and the Invention of Modernism*, Vincent Sherry details the "familiarly decadent emphasis on reflected and secondary light" in a tradition extending from Henry

Fig. 11.4. *The Holy Family*, Emil Frei Company, St. Louis and Munich, dedicated 5 December 1937. Cather memorial window, Grace Episcopal Church, Red Cloud, Nebraska. Photograph by Joseph C. Murphy.

James to T. S. Eliot (273). Ellis Hanson, in *Decadence and Catholicism*, discusses stained glass as a Decadent figure for the aestheticized twilight of Christian belief, flickering and fading (10). Cather's story at turns indulges and resists such aestheticized regret as it serves up scenes from the twilight of an American family. Uncle Albert prolongs a state of mourning for his "lost Lenore," Marguerite (47, 62), her career cut short by a terminal illness, and even rekindles his faded Catholicism with occasional visits to "an old German graveyard and a monastery" (53). But the narrative foregrounds his more sanguine routines with Albert and with the Rudder family downstairs.

Cather's alternative to the scattered light of the Decadents is iridescence, the peculiar property of opalescent glass, which holds light within itself by distributing it across the pane—making it appear "as if lighted by the sun" even on "a cloudy or dark day" (La Farge 2). The hidden iridescence of Cather's Venetian window permeates and sustains the human relationships that develop around it. I have already suggested a bond between Marguerite Thiesinger and the Venetian window. Marguerite is the window's secret sharer because she is herself a medium of light: "glowing with health," "like a big peony just burst into bloom and full of sunshine—sunshine in her auburn hair, in her rather small hazel eyes," "greenish yellow, with a glint of gold in them" (49, 50). Marguerite's light is not scattered but focused in Uncle Albert. Even when, bitterly disappointed by her elopement, he burns her photographs—as if her light were contained in those effigies—she returns to him brighter than before. Nearing death, Marguerite resembles the stained glass that once captivated her, with "still a stain of color in her cheeks" (52). In her New York hospital room Uncle Albert mutters *"Pourquoi, pourquoi?"* at the window but receives no answer from "that brutal square of glass" (52), that is, an industrial window lacking any of the Venetian window's iridescence. (As noted above, the story's other variation on the term "brutal" describes the crass mating rituals of Marjorie's social set, in contrast to the gentle refinement of the Engelhardt boys.) The answer comes only when Uncle Albert himself takes on the quality of opalescent glass, allowing Marguerite's death-struggle to permeate his body, like light. "She never knew a death-struggle—she went to sleep," he recalls. "That struggle took place in my body. Her dissolution occurred within me." Through this struggle "something within [Uncle Albert] seemed to rise and travel" with the "puffy white clouds like the cherub-heads in Raphael's pictures" (53). His absorption of Marguerite's death recasts, in iridescent terms, an exemplum of the Virgin Birth popular among medieval commentators, that Christ passed into the world through Mary as light passes through a window: "[A]s light pierces glass without breaking it, so, too, God pierced Mary without breaking her" (Harris 303).[7] But if Marguerite's "dissolution" within Uncle Albert does not break him, it certainly haunts him, like light suspended within an opalescent window. Her long twilight modulates inside him in his half-conscious moments before sleep, while listening to his nephew's piano music: "[T]he look of wisdom and professional authority faded, and many changes went over his face, . . . moods of scorn and contempt, of rakish vanity, sentimental melancholy . . . and something remote and lonely" (46).

In sum, the opalescent style I am identifying in "Double Birthday"—in its signature window and an associated modernist sensibility—is distinct from the styles associated with both the medieval Gothic cathedral and its secular revival by the Decadent Movement. If the translucent stained glass of the Gothic cathedral elevated its medieval viewers toward the divine, the opalescent glass of the Venetian window only hints at transcendence. And if the Decadents savored secondary and reflected light, the opalescent style entails the preservation of light, analogous to the steady and protracted commitments that bind the urban community of Cather's story. The narrative itself exhibits this same quality of iridescence, its illuminations restrained and muted.

## PITTSBURGH'S VENICE

I must turn now from the window's medium to its message, and briefly inquire: Why Venice? The window's Venetian subject is by no means accidental; rather, it crystalizes a cluster of associations that resonate with the story's plot, temporality, social vision, and position in Cather's career.

Originally, for August Engelhardt the window would have advertised his cultural sophistication, enshrining an iconic view from the Grand Tour in the heart of bourgeois Deutschtown. European themes, notes Pittsburgh glassman John Kelly, "were heavily favored by the new American clientele who were able to afford a 'commission' for a landing window."[8] Given Venice's historical renown as a glassmaking center—Pittsburgh's Old World predecessor— the Venetian theme suited old August's industrial as well as cultural aspirations and extended directly from its medium. For the aspiring singer Marguerite, it is Venice's rich historical association with vocal music that must underlie her attraction to the window. Nineteenth-century Pittsburgh as a whole had Venetian aspirations: its glassworks; its bridge-strewn, water-locked landscape; even H. H. Richardson's romantic Bridge of Sighs linking the Allegheny County Courthouse (figure 11.5, the "gray stone Court House" where "Double Birthday" opens [41]) to its adjoining jail, refers to a Venetian original. For the next generation of Engelhardts the window would have accrued, with their dissipated status, associations of perpetual decline long attached to the sinking city of the Adriatic—a mood that suits Albert's postwar reflection, crossing the Monongahela River, that "kingdoms and empires had fallen" (57). More personally, the window's representation of Santa Maria della Salute ("Saint Mary of Health"), a Baroque church completed in 1681 to memorialize plague victims, captures in a single image both Marguerite's "glowing . . . health" and her premature death.[9]

While living in Pittsburgh, Cather developed her own dualistic impressions of Venice prior to her first visit there in 1908. She discovered an upbeat Venice in Pittsburgh composer Ethelbert Nevin's popular piano suite *A Day in Venice*, which she heard him perform in 1899 at his rural Vineacre estate outside Pittsburgh, after his return from a year on the Grand Canal. The program notes included in Cather's essay "An Evening at Vineacre" depict an amusement ride

Fig. 11.5. Henry Hobson Richardson, *Bridge of Sighs*, Allegheny County Courthouse and Jail, Pittsburgh, 1888. Detroit Publishing Company photograph collection, Library of Congress Prints and Photographs Division, LC-DIG-DET-4A10829.

through a bracing and rejuvenating cityscape: "The gondoliers are off for the day, out upon the historic waterways, gliding down the Grand Canal, under the arched stone bridges, through deep, still streets where the stone walls on either side are mossed with age, and the shadows make the water green and the air is cool—and out again into the broad sunlit lagoons" (*World and the Parish* 2: 631–32). Cather describes in similar terms a Venetian scene by Spanish painter Martin Rico y Ortega that she viewed at Pittsburgh's Carnegie Museum of Art: "very blue skies, a silvery canal, white and red houses, bridges and gay gondolas, and in the foreground the dear Lombard poplars, the gayest and saddest of trees, rustling green and silver in the sunlight" (*World and the Parish* 2: 762–63). In her 1905 Pittsburgh story "Paul's Case," it is before such a "blue Rico" that her art-struck protagonist Paul "lost himself" at the Carnegie (218).[10]

The "middle class," Cather observes, prefer such idealized Venetian scenes to "those of greater painters ... who have darkened the canals of the city with the shadows of her past" (*World and the Parish* 2: 845). She encountered this darker, brooding Venice in the pages of Gabriele D'Annunzio's roman à clef *The Flame of Life* (1900), which she reviewed for the *Lincoln Courier* in 1901, observing: "[T]he city with its dark and stirring past, the present decrepitude and decay, are used to cleverly emphasize the picture of the aged and ailing actress," a character based on D'Annunzio's estranged lover Eleonora Duse (*World and the Parish* 2: 861). Perusing "Double Birthday," one notes, beyond the window itself, an accumulation of conventional Venetian touches, both light and dark: Marguerite's soprano voice sounding in the street, Elsa Rudder and her fiancé, Carl, dressed for masquerade, the city's suspect air, "not good for the throat" (48), and above all, the fate of the suffering artist. By 1929, the motif of the suffering or dying artist in Venice, exemplified in the career of Wagner and dramatized in the fiction of D'Annunzio, Vernon Lee, and Thomas Mann, had hardened into a modernist archetype.[11] In "Paul's Case" Cather specifies "the blue of Adriatic water" among the final thoughts of Paul who, jumping into an oncoming train, catches an afterimage of the "blue Rico" he had admired at Pittsburgh's Carnegie (252).

In Cather's Venetian window, these multivalent tropes of Venice coalesce around the intriguing figure of the "slender gondolier." We have seen that this gondolier engages the viewer's imagination, inviting Deutschtown to envision Mr. and Mrs. Engelhardt "solidly seated in the prow to make the picture complete." In relation to Marguerite's death, the gondolier takes on the darker guise of Charon, the ferryman of Hades. For Albert, schooled in Decadent culture, the gondolier would have suggested more risqué associations. In the code of the English Decadents, for whom Venice was a bewitching destination (featured several times in Albert's complete set of *The Yellow Book*), a "slender gondolier" carried a potentially erotic charge, by association with late-nineteenth-century male tourists seeking casual relations with the Venetian working class (Brady

207–17).[12] More broadly, it signaled the opportunity for the tourist
to experience "a certain wholeness" through "intense forms of life
in the here and now" (Booth 172)—an intensity of pleasure that
Cather herself associates with gondoliers in her notes on Nevin's *A
Day in Venice*: "The gondolier laughs—at nothing—at everything, at
life and youth, laughs because the sky is blue and the sun is warm,
laughs for joy at the gladness and beauty of another day—a day in
Venice" (*World and the Parish* 2: 631). As such, the lone gondolier adds
a dash of frisson to the interclass communion among Engelhardts,
Rudders, and Hammersleys on Pittsburgh's South Side, but one
wouldn't want to push this analogy too far. The gondolier is not so
much a figure to be interpreted, as a template for the stream of historical associations that play across the window's surface. Despite
its apparent inertia, the Venetian window is a vital register of the
desires that have continually reanimated it, like the various moods
that flicker across Uncle Albert's face before sleep or the features
of young Albert exhibiting "a kind of quick-silver mobility" (41). It
is finally a medium not for light but for the history through which
the story's characters have persevered. One could say of the window,
in its kaleidoscopic associations, what Cather says of Albert: that it
"had lived to the full all the revolutions in art and music that [its]
period covered" (55).

Among the revolutions the window registers are those of Cather's
own career: the plot and Venetian motif of "Double Birthday" quite
explicitly recast, in a tragic mode, the materials of her 1915 novel *The
Song of the Lark*.[13] The rise of Wagnerian diva Thea Kronborg, stew-
arded by her mentor Dr. Archie, culminates in the closing conceit
of the nightly tides refreshing the Venetian lagoons, even as the
"tidings" of youthful careers refresh the citizens of Moonstone, Colorado (*Song of the Lark* 539). "Double Birthday" reprises the device
of a medical doctor shepherding a vibrant young singer's career;
however, Cather sacrifices Marguerite to a fate Thea is spared, while
darkening the allusion to Venice. Here the picture of Venice, and
the figure of storytelling, shifts from the irrepressible motion of
tides through a "network of shining water-ways," to the purposeful

progress of a slender man through the Grand Canal, represented in glass. As such, storytelling devolves from a Wagnerian force of nature to something more fragile, though perhaps as powerful as Thea's success in stoking a community's "memories" and "dreams" (*Song of the Lark* 539).

In a particularly insightful account of Cather's project, Richard Millington distinguishes between her "two modernisms": an "authenticity" modernism, typified by *The Professor's House* and classics by Fitzgerald and Hemingway, seeking "aestheticized" authenticities in an environment of "inauthentic values and degraded emotions infected by the economic" (3); and an "anthropological" or "readerly" modernism, evident in novels like *My Ántonia* and *Shadows on the Rock*, centered upon "acts of heightened or illuminated witnessing" within a particular cultural locale (11). According to Millington, Cather's anthropological modernism, by abandoning the traditional developmental plot of the Victorian novel (which "authenticity" narratives like *The Professor's House* also follow), "frees its readers, no less than its characters, from a customary repertoire of response, ... from the depth-seeking, ending-hungry, explanation-driven trajectories of Victorian culture" (15). In "Double Birthday," Cather charts a transition between these modernisms of authenticity and anthropology by depicting an unorthodox community of Pittsburghers forged in the afterglow of exhausted experiments and frustrated careers. On the one hand, both Alberts derive a "feeling of distinction" (48) from their nonconformist, artistic lives, and a sheen of authenticity from their aestheticized experiences of loss: Uncle Albert's Gothic Romanticism (his "lost Lenore") and Albert's faded Decadence. On the other hand, these personal authenticities—lacking the aesthetic intensity of high modernism—quietly resolve into a domestic partnership sustained by an assortment of Pittsburgh friends. From the outset of "Double Birthday," Cather signals that her anthropological interests will not follow a traditional developmental plot. "Even in American cities, which seem so much alike," the story begins, "where people seem all to be living the same lives, striving for the same things, thinking the same thoughts, there are still individuals a little out of tune with the times—there are still survivals of a past more loosely woven, there are disconcerting beginnings of a future yet unforeseen" (41). Quirky throwbacks like the Alberts, aloof from the city's ambitions, are heralds of a future beyond view. Their double birthday awaits another birth.

Likewise, the meaning of Cather's Venetian window never comes fully into focus: there is no definitive way "to make the picture complete"; the seat in the prow of the gondola is open to any passenger, any reader. The Venetian window offers a paradigm for the values held suspended here and elsewhere in Cather's modernism: between authenticity and witnessing; naming and not naming; decline and renewal. In an echo likely to be missed, Cather's story balances these tensions when Uncle Albert's closing utterance *"Even in our ashes"* (63)—quoting Thomas Gray's elegiac line, "E'en in our ashes live their wonted fires" (line 92)—recasts the opening sentence "Even in American cities . . ." The narrative moves between cities and ashes, embracing the polarities of glass itself, which erects the modern city from the base matter of molten sand and ash. The Venetian window, vestige of "a past more loosely woven," is the hidden eye of the story's revolutions: the fin-de-siècle artwork revitalizing centuries of glassmaking tradition, glimpsing through its opalescent medium and its Venetian subject "the disconcerting beginnings of a future yet unforeseen."

## NOTES

Research on this essay was funded by a grant from the Ministry of Science and Technology, Taiwan (MOST 104-2410-H-030-041-MY2).

1. Starting with two glasshouses in 1797, Pittsburgh became the center of the American glass industry by the Civil War. By 1880, fifty-one factories produced almost 30 percent of the nation's glass, and by 1920 Western Pennsylvania's glass output, combined with West Virginia's and Ohio's, comprised 80 percent of U.S. production (Madarasz 2–6). As a journalist and editor in Pittsburgh at the turn of the century, Cather took an active interest in the workings of the city's industries, including its glass production—once even

attending a picnic of the Glassblowers' Union with the labor editor of the *Pittsburgh Leader* (Byrne and Snyder 44).

2. *Mont-Saint-Michel and Chartres* (reissued by Houghton Mifflin in 1913) is very likely the Adams book for which Cather thanks Ferris Greenslet in a letter on 12 January 1914 (*Calendar* #0273). In one of her final letters (12 April 1947), Cather told her biographer E. K. Brown: "I wish I could have had a comfortable boardinghouse near Chartres when Henry Adams used to prowl about the cathedral" (*Selected Letters* 672).

3. Eight months after La Farge's patent was granted on 24 February 1880, Tiffany applied for his own patent, which was granted on 8 February 1881. As Sloan summarizes the case, "La Farge's patent was for the use of the material, while Tiffany's was for its assembly" (part 2). La Farge and Tiffany carried on a protracted battle over their respective claims, first in the courts and later in the media. Tiffany's marketing savvy prevailed, eventually making his name synonymous with opalescent glass; however, by 1883 many studios were using the medium (Sloan).

4. John Kelly of Kelly Art Glass, Pittsburgh, after examining photographs of these windows, wrote that he was "certain" they are the Rudy Brothers' work: "I have been restoring glass from that studio for 35 years and can spot the Rudy style and method of execution from a distance. Each older commissioning studio can be identified [through] a number of visible traits." (14 July 2017).

5. By late 1928, "Double Birthday" had been accepted by *The Forum* for the February 1929 issue (*Selected Letters* 413), but apparently Cather had written an early draft, not ready to show, by 15 February 1928 (*Calendar* #1838).

6. Emil Frei (1869–1942) was among the masters of the Munich style. Born in Bavaria, he immigrated to New York and eventually settled in St. Louis, where he founded Emil Frei Art Glass in 1898 and won the grand prize at the 1904 Louisiana Purchase Exposition. His company continues to operate today under the direction of the fifth generation of the Frei family ("History").

7. In his essay "The Blessed Virgin and the Sunbeam through Glass," Breeze traces this topos to fifth- or sixth-century North Africa (23).

8. Kelly, "Re: Rudy windows," 28 June 2017.

9. Cather reports a morning visit to Santa Maria della Salute "to see another Titian and a beautiful Tintoretto," in a postcard to Isabelle McClung dated 14 July [1908] (*Selected Letters* 115).

10. Jaap identifies this painting as *San Trovaso, Venice*, the only Rico then owned by the Carnegie (Jaap et al. 19).

11. Barker traces the legacy of Wagner's death in Venice through numerous works of European literature. In "A Wicked Voice" (1890), Vernon Lee, whose Italian writings Cather called "capricious and self-conscious" (*Selected Letters* 112), depicts Venice as "a miasma of long-dead melodies" (Lee 208) that stifle her Wagnerian composer Magnus, a character nicely contextualized in Caballero's study. D'Annunzio's *The Flame of Life* concludes with a fictionalized rendition of Wagner's funeral procession in Venice (399–403). The first American translations of Mann's *Death in Venice* (1912), by Kenneth Burke (1924) and Helen Tracy Lowe-Porter (1928), were issued by Cather's publisher Knopf (Boes 429–30).

12. Venice appears as a significant setting in four stories in the thirteen volumes of *The Yellow Book*, published between 1894 and 1897: Kenneth Grahame's "Long Odds" (vol. 6), Vernon Lee's "Prince Alberic and the Snake Lady" (vol. 10), Lena Milman's "Marcel: An Hotel-Child" (vol. 12), and Dora Greenwell McChesney's "At Old Italian Casements" (vol. 13). Venice also figures in Henry James's essay on George Sand, "He and She: Recent Documents" (vol. 12).

13. Porter has identified interconnections between *Song of the Lark* and *Lucy Gayheart* running through "Double Birthday." I build on Porter's work here by noting the 1929 story's recasting of *Song*'s Venetian imagery.

## WORKS CITED

Adams, Henry. *Mont-Saint-Michel and Chartres*. 1904. Penguin, 1986.

Barker, John W. *Wagner and Venice Fictionalized: Variations on a Theme*. U of Rochester P, 2012.

Bintrim, Timothy, and Kari Ronning. "George Gerwig's Double Tragedy and Cather's 'Double Birthday.'" *Willa Cather Newsletter & Review*, vol. 53, no. 3, Spring 2010, pp. 77–84.

Boes, Tobias. "Aschenbach Crosses the Waters: Reading *Death in Venice* in America." *Modernism/Modernity*, vol. 21, no. 2, April 2014, pp. 429–45, Project MUSE, DOI: 10.1353/mod.2014.0039.

Booth, Howard J. "John Addington Symonds, Venice and the Gaze." *English Studies*, vol. 94, no. 2, 2013, pp. 171–87, Taylor and Francis Online, DOI: 10.1080/0013838X.2013.764084.

Brady, Sean. "John Addington Symonds, Horatio Brown and Venice: Friendship, Gondoliers and Homosexuality." *Italian Sexualities Uncovered, 1789–1914*, edited by Valeria P. Babini, Chiara Beccalossi, and Lucy Riall, Palgrave, 2015, pp. 207–27.

Breeze, Andrew. "The Blessed Virgin and the Sunbeam through Glass." *Celtica*, vol. 23, 1999, pp. 19–29.

Byrne, Kathleen D., and Richard Snyder. *Chrysalis: Willa Cather in Pittsburgh, 1896–1906*. Historical Society of Pennsylvania, 1980.

Caballero, Carlo. "'A Wicked Voice': On Vernon Lee, Wagner, and the Effects of Music." *Victorian Studies*, vol. 35, no. 4, 1992, pp. 385–408, JSTOR, www.jstor.org/stable/3828463.

Cather, Willa. *A Calendar of the Letters of Willa Cather: An Expanded Digital Edition*. Edited by Andrew Jewell and Janis P. Stout, Willa Cather Archive, edited by Andrew Jewell, U of Nebraska–Lincoln, www.cather.unl.edu /index.calendar.html.

———. "Double Birthday." 1929. *Uncle Valentine and Other Stories: Willa Cather's Uncollected Short Fiction, 1915–1929*, edited by Bernice Slote, U of Nebraska P, 1973, pp. 41–63.

———. Letters to Carrie Miner Sherwood. 13 June 1928, 21 January 1929, Willa Cather Foundation, Red Cloud, Nebraska.

———. *My Ántonia*. 1918. With illustrations by W. T. Benda, edited by Charles Mignon with Kari A. Ronning, historical essay by James Woodress, contributions by Kari Ronning, Kathleen Danker, and Emily Levine, U of Nebraska P, 1995.

———. "The Novel Démeublé." 1922. *Willa Cather on Writing: Critical Studies on Writing as an Art*, foreword by Stephen Tennant, U of Nebraska P, 1988, pp. 35–43.

———. *One of Ours*. 1922. Willa Cather Scholarly Edition, historical essay and explanatory notes by Richard C. Harris, textual essay and editing by Frederick M. Link with Kari A. Ronning, U of Nebraska P, 2006.

———. "Paul's Case: A Study in Temperament." *The Troll Garden*. McClure, Phillips, 1905, pp. 213-53. Willa Cather Archive, edited by Andrew Jewell, U of Nebraska–Lincoln, cather.unl.edu/writings/books/0006.

———. *The Selected Letters of Willa Cather*. Edited by Andrew Jewell and Janis Stout, Knopf, 2013.

———. *Shadows on the Rock*. 1931. Willa Cather Scholarly Edition, historical essay by John J. Murphy and David Stouck, explanatory notes by John Murphy and David Stouck, textual editing by Frederick M. Link, U of Nebraska P, 2005.

———. *The Song of the Lark*. 1915. Willa Cather Scholarly Edition, historical essay and explanatory notes by Ann Moseley, textual essay and editing by Kari A. Ronning, U of Nebraska P, 2012.

———. *The World and the Parish: Willa Cather's Articles and Reviews, 1893–1902*. Edited by William M. Curtin, U of Nebraska P, 1970. 2 vols.

D'Annunzio, Gabriele. *The Flame of Life*. Translated by Kassandra Vivaria, L. C. Page, 1900, Internet Archive, archive.org/details /flameoflifenovel00danniala/page/n7.

Doležal, Joshua. "The Fire in the Ash: Dissent and Progressivism in Cather's 'Double Birthday.'" *Cather Studies 8: Willa Cather; A Writer's Worlds*, edited by John J. Murphy, Françoise Palleau-Papin, and Robert Thacker, U of Nebraska P, 2010, pp. 412–27.

Gossman, Lionel, et al. *A Stained Glass Masterpiece in Victorian Glasgow: Stephen Adam's Celebration of Industrial Labor*. Lionel Gossman, Work on the Web, commons.princeton.edu/lgossman/wp-content/uploads/sites /64/2018/04/Adam.pdf.

Gray, Thomas. "Elegy Written in a Country Churchyard." *Norton Anthology of English Literature*, edited by M. H. Abrams et al., 4th ed., vol. 1, Norton, 1979, pp. 2444–47.

"Guide to the Records of the Rudy Brothers Company, 1894–1979." *Historic Pittsburgh*, U of Pittsburgh Library System, historicpittsburgh.org /islandora/object/pitt%3AUS-QQS-MSS278.

Hanson, Ellis. *Decadence and Catholicism*. Harvard UP, 1998.

Harris, Anne F. "Glazing and Glossing: Stained Glass as Literary Interpretation." *Journal of Glass Studies*, vol. 56, 2014, pp. 303–16.

"History." Emil Frei, Stained Glass Artisans Since 1898, www.emilfrei.com /history/.

Isenberg, Anita, and Seymour Isenberg. *How to Work in Stained Glass*. Chilton Book Company, 1972.

Jaap, James A., et al. "Cather Camp." *Willa Cather Newsletter & Review*, vol. 56, no. 3, Fall 2013, pp. 19–23.

Kelly, John (Kelly Art Glass, Pittsburgh). "Re: Rudy windows." Email to the author, 28 June 2017, 14 July 2017.

La Farge, John. Colored-Glass Window. US224831A, United States Patent Office, 24 February 1880, application filed 10 November 1879, Google Patents, www.patents.google.com/patent/US224831A/en.

Lee, Vernon. "A Wicked Voice." *Hauntings: Fantastic Stories*, Heinemann, 1890, pp. 193–237. Victorian Women Writers Project, Indiana University, purl .dlib.indiana.edu/iudl/vwwp/VAB7073.

Lewis, Edith. *Willa Cather Living: A Personal Record*. 1953. Introduction by John J. Murphy, U of Nebraska P, 2000.

Madarasz, Anne. *Glass: Shattering Notions*. Historical Society of Western Pennsylvania, 1998.

Millington, Richard. "Willa Cather's Two Modernisms." 2013. English Language and Literature: Faculty Publications 2, Smith ScholarWorks, Smith College, scholarworks.smith.edu/eng_facpubs/2/.

Murphy, Joseph C. "The Dialectics of Seeing in Cather's Pittsburgh: 'Double Birthday' and Urban Allegory." *Cather Studies 7: Willa Cather as Cultural Icon*, edited by Guy Reynolds, U of Nebraska P, 2007, pp. 253–68.

Porter, David. "From *The Song of the Lark* to *Lucy Gayheart*, and *Die Walküre* to *Die Winterreise*." *Cather Studies 11: Willa Cather at the Modernist Crux*, edited by Ann Moseley, John J. Murphy, and Robert Thacker, U of Nebraska P, 2017, pp. 149–69.

Raguin, Virginia Chieffo. *The History of Stained Glass: The Art of Light Medieval to Contemporary*. Contribution by Mary Clerkin Higgins, Thames and Hudson, 2003.

Sherry, Vincent. *Decadence and the Invention of Modernism*. Cambridge UP, 2015.

Sloan, Julie L. "The Rivalry between Louis Comfort Tiffany and John La Farge." Julie L. Sloan, LLC, Consultants in Stained Glass, www.jlsloan.com /louis-comfort-tiffany-and-john-la-farge.

Sullivan, Peter M. "The Gerwig House: Willa Cather's Friends on Pittsburgh's North Side." *Western Pennsylvania History*, vol. 86, no. 2, Summer 2003, pp. 21–28.

Tannler, Albert M. "Classical Perspective, Industrial Art, and American Gothic." *Architectural Glass in Pittsburgh*, Pittsburgh History and Landmarks Foundation, phlf.org/education-department/architectural -history/architectural-glass-artists-and-sites-in-metropolitan-pittsburgh /classical-perspective-industrial-art-and-american-gothic/.

———. "Leo Thomas (1876–1950) for George Boos (1859–1937), Munich, Germany." *Architectural Glass in Pittsburgh*, Pittsburgh History and Landmarks Foundation, phlf.org/2008/03/21/leo-thomas-1876-1950-for -george-boos-1859-1937-munich-germany/.

*The Yellow Book: An Illustrated Quarterly*. 13 vols., 1894–1897, Heidelberg Historic Literature—Digitized, Heidelberg U Library, digi.ub.uni -heidelberg.de/diglit/yellow_book.

## 12 Cather's Pittsburgh and the Alchemy of Social Class

ANGELA CONRAD

In Willa Cather's stories of Pittsburgh, we expect to find a discourse of social class that explains the characters' climbs up and down the hills and the social register. What we might not expect to find is alchemy—that ancient practice of transmutation of one substance into another, both for financial gain and for spiritual symbolism. Indeed, in Cather's time, the city seemed full of such transformations—iron and coal into steel; sand, soda, and lime into glass; Scottish immigrants into capitalist kings. The history of alchemy is marked by magnificent hope, scurrilous fraud, and fantastic failures. It is also full of symbolism, spirituality, and sludge. It is difficult to gauge how much Cather knew about alchemy, but its concepts appeared in the works of many authors she admired and in the works of her contemporaries.[1] The highs and lows of Pittsburgh's topography and the fortunes of characters in Cather's Pittsburgh stories mirror the up-and-down motion of substances in alchemical practice and the refinement process common to both industry and culture. Two Pittsburgh stories written more than twenty years apart, "Paul's Case" (1905) and "Double Birthday" (1929) demonstrate how

Cather used alchemical symbolism over time to contrast genuine transformation through cultural purgation with the false transformations created solely through increasing wealth.

There have been many critical studies of "Paul's Case" but fewer of "Double Birthday," and though none of them focus on the subject of alchemy, some place their emphasis on dialectics and divisions between opposites. Several critics have seen "Paul's Case" as a case study of Paul's condition, essentially at odds with his station in life (See Wasserman 121). Paul may be understood as "a glutton in Bohemia because he is famished for spiritual, aesthetic, and emotional food in Presbyteria" as Sharon O'Brien argues (283), or a social outcast because of either his perceived homosexuality or a personality disorder (Rubin 127; Saari 389). Timothy Bintrim has explored Paul as adhering to Baudelaire's category of dandy and being welcomed or reviled for this "disguise" (23). Whatever the approach, critics see Paul as an outsider, a misfit preferring the arts to the mundane reality of commercial and industrial work. I will show that this same polar division of the world into the refined and the base underlies the metaphysics of alchemy in the story.

Studies of "Double Birthday," the late story so infused with Pittsburgh, focus mainly on Cather's attitude toward the city and her friendship with the Seibels, whose house and activities are reflected in the residence of the namesakes, the two Albert Engelhardts (Byrne and Snyder 21–22; Woodress 119). Cather herself was enthusiastic about the story and wrote to her sister Elsie that she hoped her sketch of Dr. Tyndale (uncle of her college friend Fritz Westermann) as the older Albert Engelhardt would not annoy the doctor (*Selected Letters* 412–13). Critics find many instances of division and doubling as the main characters move between social classes and from attitudes of extreme commercial devotion to utter Bohemian culture-worship. Joseph C. Murphy states that the story "portrays the artist-intellectual trying to domesticate the city by bringing its spatial and historical coordinates into dialogue" (253). Joshua Doležal, however, looks for clues to Cather's attitude toward the future and her progressivism. He claims that Cather "was in some senses progressive but that she looked ahead by looking back" (412). It is this mix of looking back while projecting into the future that makes Cather's use of the ancient lore of alchemy suited to her era—one in which alchemy was experiencing a modernist resurgence.

Though alchemy had, by the early twentieth century, been discredited as a pseudo-science, its combination of magic, science, and charlatanism pervaded Western thought. Alchemy appeared in many works of art, literature, and philosophy at the time of Cather's sojourn in Pittsburgh and well beyond. Because Cather never wrote specifically about alchemy, it is important to prove that she must have been aware of its reputation as well as its spiritual application in her own time. Most of the early works of literature that featured the character of the alchemist and his practices treated it as the province of con artists. Dante Alighieri relegated alchemists to the eighth circle of hell in Canto 29 of *The Inferno*. The Canon's Yeoman of Chaucer's *The Canterbury Tales* exposes alchemy's misdeeds, causing the canon to abandon plans to con the pilgrims. Shakespeare's *The Tempest* shows Prospero using some of the techniques of alchemy, and the Bard's Sonnet 33 renders the dawn tinting all with gold by performing "alchemy." Ben Jonson's *The Alchemist* (1610), according to a recent study, "ridicules alchemists and especially the gullibility of those who are willing to sacrifice everything for the promise of quick riches, while taking aim at the hypocrisy of contemporary society" (Ziolkowski 50).

Cather knew well the legend of Faust that arose in the Middle Ages and was first published in 1587. Early versions represented Faust as an alchemist, frustrated with his inability to achieve alchemical transformations, turning to a devil character who promises him greater knowledge in exchange for his soul ("The Legend of Faust"). Images of Faust in art and literature connect him with fire and distillation equipment. Modern dramatizations of the story did not please Cather universally. She objected to the emphasis on the "garden scene," which she calls "one of the stupidest and most monotonous of all love scenes. There is absolutely no action, no obstacle to overcome, nothing to call out great emotion, no great temptation"

(*Kingdom of Art* 279). She absolutely rejected any attempt to lighten the plot, to turn the story's tragic magnificence into anything comedic. Indeed, she preferred Goethe's poem to any English translation or dramatization (280).

Cather also knew the operatic version of Faust's tale by Gounod that was loosely based on Goethe's poem. Goethe's Faust, unlike earlier manifestations of the character, was not explicitly an alchemist, but Goethe himself had direct experience with alchemy, and "the figure of the alchemist plays a major role in two key passages" of the tale, notes Ziolkowski (90). Faust's dark magic, provided by a covenant with Mephistopheles that gives Faust an elixir of youth and enables him to live transformed, is often conflated with alchemy.

Many French writers of the nineteenth century, for whom Cather had a confessed enthusiasm, made use of the figure of the alchemist and put in motion a new emphasis on the philosophical and spiritual aspects of the practice. In Victor Hugo's *The Hunchback of Notre Dame* (1831), Claude Frollo places all his faith in alchemy; Alexandre Dumas (*père*) wrote a five-act verse drama, *L'Alchimiste* in 1839; and Honoré de Balzac's *The Quest of the Absolute* (1834) presents a practitioner obsessed; all include alchemist figures in a spiritual configuration (Ziolkowski 105, 106, 109). Some of these authors were favorites of the reading gatherings between Cather and the Seibels whose house doubled as the Engelhardts' in "Double Birthday" (Seibel 11–21). Even Gustave Flaubert, one of Cather's idols, tried his hand at the figure of the alchemist early in his career with the short story "Dream of Hell" (1835).

In the United States, too, the figure of the obsessed alchemist was evident in nineteenth-century literature. Nathaniel Hawthorne referenced the elixir of life in his short story "Dr. Heidegger's Experiment," and images of the forge are used for self-transformation in "Ethan Brand." Most explicitly, Hawthorne showed the alchemist figure in "The Birth-Mark," in which scientist Aylmer experiments on his wife to remove her birthmark. The story specifically mentions "alchemy" and Aylmer's reading of Paracelsus. When the wife/victim reads the journals of her husband's experiments, she learns that they were all failures. Hawthorne even provides readers a glimpse of the alchemical equipment that was thought typical of the practice:

> The first thing that struck her eye was the furnace, that hot and feverish worker, with the intense glow of its fire, which by the quantities of soot clustered above it seemed to have been burning for ages. There was a distilling apparatus in full operation. Around the room were retorts, tubes, cylinders, crucibles, and other apparatus of chemical research. An electrical machine stood ready for immediate use. The atmosphere felt oppressively close, and was tainted with gaseous odors which had been tormented forth by the processes of science. (100)

Hawthorne's story uses the archetypes of the madness of the alchemist and the grotesque, idiot-savant lab assistant. With all these depictions of alchemists and alchemy Cather found in her reading, she would likely have been aware of the key elements of the practice: transformation of base to pure through distillation, obsessed practitioners, and failed experiments.

Cather did not need to have a deep historical knowledge of alchemical history and signification in order to manipulate these well-known symbols. First in importance is the refinement process by which alchemists planned to bring about transformations of base materials. Even casual readers knew that alchemists attempted to transform lead into gold. Indeed, the earliest alchemists believed that all material substances were composed of four elements (earth, air, fire, and water) in different proportions. That natural philosophy suggested that one material could be changed into another by adjusting its proportions of the various elements (Atwood 26). Gold and silver had monetary value, to be sure, and some alchemists were primarily after the financial gain that would come from turning lead into gold. This conviction opened the gullible and greedy believers to the risks and ridicule of being taken in by con artists, as happens in Ben Jonson's comedy. The purer practitioner of alchemy was motivated by knowledge and for the spiritual edification of refining base materials into fine ones (Atwood 27). The dual nature of alchemy—one aspect metallurgical and one spiritual—permits it a rich base of symbolism.

Most alchemical processes required heat and vessels (a flask or tube or other device) to bring about the combination of materials and the distillation of those combinations. One symbol, the Star of David, also held special significance in that it shows the interlocking importance of up (the triangle pointed upward) and down (the opposite triangle). The base materials would be purified up through heat and evaporation and then sink down as they cooled. Once purified, the distillate would need to be remixed with base materials and subjected to the process again for further purification. The alchemist Henning Brand, in 1669, isolated the first chemical element, phosphorus, by performing similar processes on human urine. By leaving urine to evaporate and decay, then refining it through a series of distillations to produce a glowing, beautiful substance, Brand seemed to confirm that a lot of smelly sludge could be transformed into something ethereal (Morris 70–71).

In the process of refinement, base materials were thought to go through a series of color shifts: first blackening (nigredo), then whitening (albedo), and finally reddening (rubedo). The blackening represents the phase known as "putrefaction," in which the mystical marriage occurs between opposite elements, sulfur and mercury (also known as quicksilver). Sulfur, the masculine (active) element, was associated with heat or fire, while mercury, the feminine (passive) element, flowed like water. The union of the two would fecundate the mixture and bring about a new creation. This new life was known as "genesis in the retort" (Roob 146). The psychological significance of this type of change fascinated Carl Jung, who wrote extensively on the symbolism of alchemy. When his conclusions were published posthumously in 1970, they compared this transformation to the psychological process of individuation (170).[2]

The artist, analogously, seemed able to transform base materials into refined ones with the stroke of a brush or pen. Though he came to his conclusions rather later in the century, Marcel Duchamp—hero of the Armory Show—became fascinated with alchemy and produced a number of works that he believed demonstrated the artist's alchemy. In fact, the poem that inspired Duchamp's famous *Nude Descending a Staircase* was "Encore à cet astre" by Jules Laforgue.[3] According to John F. Moffit, this poem

> is full of blatantly alchemical motifs. . . . The climax of [the] poem metaphorically represents a false procedure, one that has led to the loss of the elusive Philosopher's Gold. As a consequence, the resulting alchemical material becomes a mockery of its original intention: darkened, spotted, blemished, eaten up, and corrupted due to a lack of spiritual integration. (50–51)

In this poem and others, the alchemist must have pure motives in order to effect the full transformation. A forced, or fake transformation—not to culture, but to the trappings of wealth that often accompany it—drew Cather's interest in "Paul's Case."

Paul's frustrated attempts to transform himself into an elite member of society drive him to impersonate the gold standard of the wealthy elites. Edward Pitcher has compared Paul's "self-destructive acts" to "Faust's electing to sell his soul for the gratification of his desires" (543). According to Pitcher, Paul's theft of Denny & Carson's deposit is the moment he sells his soul, like Faust, for the temporary advantages in this world (543). Moreover, the heat and cold of Paul's pursuit, his elevation and descent, correspond to evaporation and condensation, and his color scheme, moving from black, to white, to red, all identify him with the failed alchemist.

Paul's last arc of suicide at the end of the story demonstrates that his attempts at self-transformation are a failure. Like Faust, Paul rejects the Great Work of slow learning, the actual change that comes from hard work and education, to take a shortcut to gaining his desires. Paul's teachers report his many "misdemeanours," chief of which is the "contempt which they all knew he felt for them" (199, 200). He seems not to regret the loss of their esteem, for it is "the Soldiers' Chorus from *Faust*" that Paul is whistling as he "ran down the hill" from the Pittsburgh High School (203). Paul's downward motion parallels Faust's putrefaction in the deal with Mephistopheles.

Paul nourishes his dreams in a land of fantasy, the theater, where he helps actor Charley Edwards get into costume and complete the artificial transformation that the theater requires. He rehearses his own apotheosis, imagining himself magically going "after [the German soprano up the steps into the Schenley Hotel,] a tropical world of shiny, glistening surfaces and basking ease" (207). But an hour later he is shivering in the basement of his father's house "down one of the side streets" from Fifth Avenue and "sinking back forever into the ugliness and commonness" of Cordelia Street (208, 209). The motion of going up to the theater and the Schenley should signify Paul's alchemical purgation through fire, and his sinking back to Cordelia Street should represent his remixing with base materials to begin anew the purification process. But they do not. Though he is "delicately fired" by the performances he witnesses, he repudiates "the natural" world, which is the basis of the alchemical transmutation. He needs instead a "certain element of artificiality" in order to see beauty—he prefers the fake transformation (216)—perhaps a signal that his whole transient pursuit is wrong-headed.

His escape to New York, then, is based on fraud and theft, though he regards his solution as "wonderfully simple" and feels freed from the "meshes of the lies he had told" as well as the fear they occasioned (222). His ascent to the ultimate upper-class luxury hotel—the Waldorf—relies on a false transformation, that can only result in apparent, not real, refinement. The ingredients and colors of alchemy are there for his transformation. The sulfur and heat lie in his desire for luxury; he goes out looking for entertainment "hot for pleasure," and he burns "like a faggot in a tempest" (225). The cold of the swirling snow and champagne, "that cold, precious, bubbling stuff that creamed and foamed in his glass," like laboratory glassware, should cool and condense his finer temperament (226). But the flaws in his design involve both his motivation and his goal. Éliphas Lévi, French popularizer of the artist-as-alchemist theory in the late nineteenth century, insisted that "the alchemically symbolizing Artist . . . is poor. His poverty arises because he has voluntarily renounced material wealth, pursuing instead the immaterial goals of his inspired imagination" (Moffit 42). The alchemist should not be motivated by a lust for wealth, but rather a quest for purification and real refinement. Paul, surrounded in luxury unearned, instead "wondered that there were honest men in the world at all." He concludes that luxury is the goal, that "this was what all the world was fighting for" (226).

His failure of self-refinement is punctuated by a suicide and by the mockery of the color transformation characteristic of alchemical theory. The blackening phase that should represent putrefaction and fertility, for Paul corresponds to the reality of Cordelia Street, which, after he realizes his fraud is exposed, falls on him "like a weight of black water" (231–32). This is the juncture at which he adopts his false faith, "that money was everything" (232). The whitening of alchemy should represent the purification through fire and the joining of opposites in a mystical marriage. In Paul's story, it is merely the snow—the numbing element in which he eventually buries the ruins of his red carnation, before he leaps in front of a train. The red carnation, which should then be the proof of the success of the transformation, is subsumed in the sterile white of the snow. In the moments after he jumps into the path of the oncoming train "the folly of haste occurred to him with merciless clearness, the vastness of what he had left undone" (234). In the one moment before his death, Paul realizes that his rush toward the appearance of transformation left him with the Great Work of his life "undone," like many an alchemist before him.

"Double Birthday," written more than twenty years later, is also filled with characters trekking up and down Pittsburgh's fabled hills, some tempted by the outward shows of success, and the Alberts, at least, refining themselves in cultural terms. It seems Cather linked Pittsburgh, whose forges produced mythical quantities of steel and glass by merely chemical means, with these attempts at alchemical transformations; a return to Pittsburgh means a return to the laboratory and the arising to and falling from social, financial, and cultural success. The tale focuses on two main figures. The elder Albert Engelhardt, or "Uncle Doctor," as he is known, escapes his obsessive drive to transform a woman, while the younger namesake, Albert Engelhardt, falls from the heights of Allegheny City and a family glass fortune of his youth, to a genteel poverty; however, his transformation seems at least partially successful in the end. Though Judge Hammersley looks on the spending of the Engelhardt fortune as a great waste of resources, the purity of both Alberts by the estimation of the judge's daughter Margaret Parmenter must prove that their lives, by Cather's measure, were well spent.

Doctor Albert is connected with alchemy in both his name (perhaps a reference to Albertus Magnus, great alchemist of the thirteenth century), as well as through his clear identification with Doctor Faustus, who made a pact with Mephistopheles to court a much younger, innocent woman named Margaret (or Gretchen)— Marguerite Thiesinger, in Cather's story. Doctor Albert's attempts to turn his "cabbage rose" into a great soprano are limited by the girl's weak imagination and by the constraints of nature. After years of treating the throats of traveling singers whose voices were damaged by the "Pittsburgh air" that was "not good for the throat," Doctor Albert met his base material in Marguerite (48). He falls in love with her voice before even seeing her, and after only a short period of observation, he decides to "finance her" and "stake everything upon this voice" (50). His willingness to risk financial ruin to foster an artist proves his pure motives, yet he hopes to master a young woman and purify her, instead of himself—a move which proves damaging.

At first, the doctor realizes that Marguerite has "no ambition" and is "not very intelligent" but urges her to have "application and ambition" (49, 51). She is his base material that he wishes to transform through culture to a refined product. Her humility, like that of Goethe's Marguerite, nearly frustrates the designs of the older doctor when she elopes with an insurance agent, but just as jewels persuade Faust's Gretchen, eventually Marguerite develops a desire to be famous, to be trained by a New York teacher as Doctor Albert had offered (51). Unlike Paul's superficial transformation, Marguerite's is to be one of substance and true artistic mastery. Doctor Albert, the throat specialist, swallows his pride and counsels her: "Take note, Gretchen, that I change the prescription. There is something vulgar about ambition. Now we will play for higher stakes; for ambition read aspiration!"

(51). But the alchemical process is strewn with unexpected disasters. After two years in New York, the great changes she shows are ones of illness and dissolution; cancer cuts short her life, and she regrets that she wasted time "running off with Phil" and not completing the work in the world of the arts (52). Her incomplete transformation is what haunts Uncle Albert's twilight years and makes him toast the young woman as his "Lost Lenore" (47). Uncle Albert attempts to refine another person, and in doing so becomes more like Faust or Hawthorne's Aylmer than the successful artist-alchemist. Though the elder Albert's motives seem pure, his result is consistent with the fact that alchemy often fails due to faulty materials.

Only young Albert Engelhardt—whose features have "a quicksilver mobility" (suggesting mercury, one of the elemental ingredients of alchemy)—seems able to make the full transformation into the refined object Cather admires. He starts his journey on a height—as Judge Hammersley remembers with scorn, the Engelhardt brothers "began with a flourishing glass factory up the river, a comfortable fortune, a fine old house on the park in Allegheny, a good standing in the community; and it was all gone, melted away" (42). In the alchemical iconography, a fortune "melted away" is as conspicuous as it is for a family of glassmakers, in which melting is the first step in creating something new, beautiful and strong. Indeed, in the crucible of youth and cultural growth, Albert moves from a well-to-do industrialist's child to a true lover of the arts. He moves up culturally—"always running over to New York," the judge remembers, and eventually makes his way to one of the pinnacles of cultural life—Rome (42). When the judge suggests to his daughter that Albert had "better have been in Homestead," Margaret recoils, pointing out that "Albert would never have been much use in Homestead, and he was very useful to Mrs. Sterrett in Rome" (44).[4] To the judge, the usefulness of a man is measured by the fortune he makes in upper management. Among the "heavyweights" of the wealthy families congregating in Rome, too serious and successful by Mrs. Parmenter's measure, "There must be some butterflies." She reminds her father that Albert "had a gorgeous time" and "learned to speak

Italian very well" (44). The staid and gruff judge finds this kind of cultural elevation a waste of time, especially in a city as devoted to material wealth as Pittsburgh then was.

After meeting the judge at the courthouse, Albert cools and descends socially to his home on the South Side.[5] While the judge "was settling down," isolated in his large home, "empty for himself and his books," Albert sits up "in a garnet velvet smoking-jacket" at his "upright piano, playing Schumann's *Kreisleriana* for his old uncle" (45). The red jacket signifies the successful search for the philosopher's gold, or culture, which he preserves in his home, among the humble dwellings of his modest neighborhood. Cather makes clear the contrast between the splendor of Albert's castle-like Allegheny home and the humble stature of his current home: "They lived, certainly, in a queer part of the city, on one of the dingy streets that run uphill off noisy Carson street, in a little two-story brick house, a workingman's house, that Albert's father had taken over long ago in satisfaction of a bad debt" (45). It is a multifamily dwelling that Albert and his uncle share with "an old German glass engraver" who worked for his father. But into this modest home, Albert has crammed a wealth of culture from his lifetime: a "Degas drawing in black and red—three ballet girls at the bar," fine rugs and his "collection of books . . . large and very personal." He keeps "a complete file of The Yellow Book," a British periodical featuring the works of Aesthetic writers. Indeed, he also treasures works of various artists of the period: "drawings of Aubrey Beardsley—decadent, had they been called? A slender, padded volume—the complete works of a great, new poet, Ernest Dowson" who coined the phrase "they are not long, the days of wine and roses," and works by Oscar Wilde (45–46; Dowson 1)—known for his ardent pursuit of art for art's sake. Albert recognizes what Paul could not, that the values of refinement are not sartorial and luxurious, but inherently evanescent.

His recognition of this fact is what allows young Albert to make the walks around Pittsburgh, to navigate the ups and downs of financial success, as well as the *"solve et coagula"* of the purification process, without regret or rancor. Albert might feel physical discomfort by having to walk uphill in the snow to the judge's home to retrieve two bottles of wine for Uncle Albert's birthday, but the judge's embarrassment makes no impact on him. As he looks on the homes of Squirrel Hill, he "did not feel sorry for himself" (54) because he knows his cultural and spiritual refinement outweigh the advantages of the wealthy:

> He thought he had had the best of it; he had gone a-Maying while it was May. This solid comfort, this iron-bound security, didn't appeal to him much. These massive houses, after all, held nothing but the heavy domestic routine; all the frictions and jealousies and discontents of family life. Albert felt light and free, going up the hill in his thin overcoat. He believed he had had a more interesting life than most of his friends who owned real estate. . . . [H]e had lived to the full all the revolutions in art and music that his period covered. He wouldn't at this moment exchange his life and his memories . . . for any one of these massive houses. . . . If Mephistopheles were to emerge from the rhododendrons and stand behind his shoulder with such an offer, he wouldn't hesitate. Money? Oh, yes, he would like to have some, but not what went with it. (55)

Albert's successful alchemical transformation enables him to reject the offer of ease and young women that Mephistopheles placed in front of Faust, and instead proceed with his life of genteel poverty, free of envy. As critic Titus Burkhardt explains, "That is the spiritual threshold which the alchemist has to cross. The ethical threshold . . . is the temptation to pursue the alchemical art only on account of gold. Alchemists constantly insist that the greatest obstacle to their work is covetousness" (31–32). As young Albert walks home to celebrate his old uncle's birthday, he crosses that threshold in the form of the Smithfield Street Bridge and looks on "the sheer cliffs of Mount Washington, high above the river," not with greed, or the desire to mine its rich coal deposits for industrial gold, but with imagination and pleasure, as he did when he was a boy, and thought of the place as "some far-away, cloud-set city in Asia; the forbidden city" (57).

The celebration of the double birthday is ultimately satisfactory because it is full of "good wine, good music and beautiful women," that Doctor Albert says are "all there is worth turning over the hand for" (62). Another beautiful and appreciative Margaret (Mrs. Parmenter) has come to them with lush praise and red roses of alchemical success. Both Alberts have foregone financial success in lieu of true cultural refinement and have reaped their reward.

Paul exits his story having been taken in by the fraud of wealth, its false refinement, regretting not using his ardor to create a purer, more refined life. Conversely, the two Alberts of "Double Birthday" work throughout their lives to attempt transformations of hardship into true cultural refinement—to gamble everything material on the hope of change. Finally, it is their ability to give up material prosperity that allows both Alberts the chance to become adepts, to learn the mystery of alchemical success. This knowledge is shared by the two men in a moment of reflection, after their guest has gone home, when Uncle Albert makes reference to Thomas Gray's "Elegy in a Country Church-Yard," a poem that reflects on the need of the dead to have their work and life remembered. He cites the last line of the most alchemical of the poem's passages:

> On some fond breast the parting soul relies,
>     Some pious drops the closing eye requires;
> Ev'n from the tomb the voice of Nature cries,
>     Ev'n in our ashes live their wonted fires. (ll. 89–92)

The spiritual element of nature that burns to ashes yet lives on is the ideal for alchemical imagery. It signifies purification to the point of becoming the elixir of life, or the philosopher's stone. The artwork of the living will ensure the eternal life of those who have gone. For Willa Cather, as for many of her artist contemporaries, it is only through the spiritual elevation and purification brought about by the artist-alchemist, that human beings can hope to avoid the false idol of material wealth, and instead live a life of true transformation.

## NOTES

1. In his account of Cather's involvement in amateur theatricals in Red Cloud, James Woodress notes that she "appeared as the old alchemist in the Merchants' Carnival," an appearance sponsored by her then employer, Cook's Drugstore (58). Even as a teenager, she was exploring the role of the alchemist.

2. Jung began his writings on alchemy in 1942 with his "Paracelsus als geistige Erscheinung" *Paracelsica: Zwei Vorlesungen über den Arzt und Philosophen Theophrastus* (Zurich: Rascher, 1942). There is no evidence that Cather ever met Jung, but her good friend Elizabeth Shepley Sergeant studied with him in the mid-1930s, according to the Elizabeth Shepley Sergeant papers, Special Collections Department, Bryn Mawr College Library.

3. Cather seems not to have known Duchamp personally, though her traditionalism was compared to the modernism of Duchamp in a review by Katherine Ann Porter in 1952, as is examined by Janis Stout (153).

4. The timing of young Albert's visit to Rome (circa 1904) did not correspond to the 1892 Homestead Strike, nor would the Battle of Homestead have been of recent memory to readers of "Double Birthday" in 1929, but the gritty, reputation of the mill town remained. The judge and his daughter disagree about how a man can make himself useful, given his family inheritance and the spirit of the times. Young Albert's sacrifice to higher culture goes to the alchemical goal of transforming the rough materials with which one begins.

5. There is some question as to the relative elevation of the courthouse in those years in relation to the South Side Flats neighborhood. The elevation of the courthouse was altered so the South Side may have been in fact a few meters higher. Nonetheless, Cather and her readers would have certainly recognized the lower socioeconomic status of the Flats and seen it as "lower."

## WORKS CITED

Atwood, M. A. *Hermetic Philosophy and Alchemy*. Julian Press, 1960.

Bennett, Mildred. "Willa Cather in Pittsburgh." *Prairie Schooner*, vol. 1, Spring 1959, pp. 64–76.

Bintrim, Timothy W. "Exit Smiling: The Case for Paul's Dandyism." *Willa Cather and Aestheticism: From Romanticism to Modernism*, edited by Sarah Cheney Watson and Ann Moseley, Fairleigh Dickinson UP, 2012, pp. 17–28.

Burckhardt, Titus. *Alchemy: Science of the Cosmos, Science of the Soul*. Translated by William Stoddart, Fons Vitae, 1997.

Byrne, Kathleen D., and Richard C. Snyder. *Chrysalis: Willa Cather in Pittsburgh, 1896–1906*. Historical Society of Western Pennsylvania, 1980.

Cather, Willa. "Double Birthday." *Uncle Valentine and Other Stories*, edited by Bernice Slote, U of Nebraska P, 1973, pp. 40–63.

———. *The Kingdom of Art: Willa Cather's First Principles and Critical Statements 1893–1896*. Edited by Bernice Slote, U of Nebraska P, 1966.

———. "Paul's Case." *Youth and the Bright Medusa*. 1920. Willa Cather Scholarly Edition, historical essay and explanatory notes by Mark J. Madigan, textual essay and editing by Frederick M. Link, Charles W. Mignon, Judith Boss, and Kari A. Ronning, U of Nebraska P, 2009, pp. 199–234.

———. *The Selected Letters of Willa Cather*. Edited by Andrew Jewell and Janis Stout, Knopf, 2013.

Doležal, Joshua. "The Fire in the Ash: Dissent and Progressivism in Cather's 'Double Birthday.'" *Cather Studies 8: Willa Cather; A Writer's Worlds*, edited by John J. Murphy, Françoise Palleau-Papin, and Robert Thacker, U of Nebraska P, 2010, pp. 412–27.

Dowson, Ernest. "Vitae Summa Brevis Spem Nos Vetat Incohare Longam." www.poetscollective.org/publicdomain/vitae-summa-brevis/.

Goethe, Wolfgang Johann von. *Faust Parts I and II*. Poetry in Translation, translated by A. S. Kilne, www.poetryintranslation.com/pitbr/German/Fausthome.php.

Gray, Thomas. *Elegy Written in a Country Church-Yard*. Thomas Gray Archive, edited by Alexander Huber, www.thomasgray.org/cgi-bin/display.cgi?text=elcc.

Hawthorne, Nathaniel. *The Portable Hawthorne*. Edited by William C. Spengemann, Penguin Books, 2005.

Jung, Carl. *The Collected Works of C.G Jung*, vol. 12, translated by R. F. C. Hull, Princeton UP, 1967.

"The Legend of Faust." http://www.faust.com.

Moffit, John F. *The Case of Marcel Duchamp: Alchemist of the Avant-Garde*. State U of New York P, 2003.

Morris, Richard. *The Last Sorcerers: The Path from Alchemy to the Periodic Table*. Joseph Henry Press, 2003.

Murphy, Joseph C. "The Dialectics of Seeing in Cather's Pittsburgh: 'Double Birthday' and Urban Allegory." *Cather Studies 7: Willa Cather as Cultural Icon*, edited by Guy Reynolds, U of Nebraska P, 2007.

O'Brien, Sharon. *Willa Cather: The Emerging Voice*. Oxford UP, 1987.

Pitcher, Edward W. "Willa Cather's 'Paul's Case' and the Faustian Temperament." *Studies in Short Fiction*, vol. 28, no. 4, Fall 1991, pp. 543–52.

Roob, Alexander. *Alchemy & Mysticism*. Taschen 2005.

Rubin, Larry. "The Homosexual Motif in Willa Cather's 'Paul's Case.'" *Studies in Short Fiction*, vol. 12, no. 2, March 1975, pp. 127–31.

Saari, Rob. "'Paul's Case': A Narcissistic Personality Disorder." *Studies in Short Fiction*, vol. 34, no. 3, Summer 1997, pp. 389–95.

Seibel, George. "Willa Cather from Nebraska." *The New Colophon*, vol. 2, no. 7, September 1949, pp. 195–208, reprinted in *Willa Cather Remembered*, compiled by L. Brent Bohlke and Sharon Hoover, edited by Sharon Hoover, U of Nebraska P, 2002, pp. 11–21.

Wassermann, Loretta. "Is Cather's Paul a Case?" *Modern Fiction Studies*, vol. 36, no. 1, 1990, pp. 120–29.

Woodress, James. *Willa Cather: A Literary Life*. U of Nebraska P, 1987.

Ziolkowski, Theodore. *The Alchemist in Literature: From Dante to the Present*. Oxford UP, 2015.

# Epilogue
## Why Willa Cather? A Retrospective

In June 2014 scholars gathered in Rome for a three-day symposium to celebrate Willa Cather and boost her reputation in Europe, where compared to other American modernists she remains relatively unknown. What dawned on me at the end of the three days was that none of the papers, including my own, asked or attempted to answer why we would want to promote the reading of Cather. Is it for her art? Her humanity? For the life principles manifest in her fiction? As an academic promoting the reading of Cather for over fifty years and exploring the complexity behind the pleasure, I want to suggest answers to the question unasked and unanswered in Rome. My effort is anecdotal at times, for it amounts to what Cather means to me.

### DESCRIPTION

Willa Cather is known for landscape description, a vehicle for something like Emily Dickinson's circumference without that vehicle impeding the process. This proficiency was her initial appeal, although Cather was not my first American landscape enthusiasm. That was Hawthorne, who communicated circumference via New England mountains and countryside, especially in tales like "The Great Stone Face" and "Ethan Brand," rivaling the best of the Hudson River school of painters. But in Hawthorne, allegory and excessive language often impede picture. Comparing parallel landscape passages from *The Marble Faun* and *Death Comes for the Archbishop*, for example, reveals differences that credit Cather with (in her words) "finding what conventions of form and what detail one can do without and yet preserve the spirit of the whole" (*On Writing* 102).

In the Hawthorne novel, the American sculptor Kenyon is about to accompany the Count of Monte Beni on a tour of central Italy. Description is filtered through the visitor, who feels "magnified" by the

wide . . . Umbrian valley that suddenly opened before him, set in its grand frame-work of nearer and more distant hills. It seemed as if all Italy lay under his eyes, in that one picture. For there was the broad, sunny smile of God, which we fancy to spread over that favoured land more abundantly than on other regions, and, beneath it, glowed a most rich and varied fertility. The trim vineyards were there, and the fig-trees, and the mulberries, and the smokey-hued tracts of the olive-orchards; there, too, were fields of every kind of grain. . . . White villas, gray convents, church-spires, villages, towns, each with its battlemented walls and towered gateway, were scattered upon this spacious map; a river gleamed across it; and lakes opened their blue eyes in its face, reflecting Heaven. (*Novels* 1065)

In the *Archbishop*, Jean Latour, accompanied by his Native guide, travels through the desert country east of Ácoma pueblo. As in the Hawthorne passage, the country is filtered through the visitor, a Frenchman, who responds to its vastness:

In all his travels the Bishop had seen no country like this. From the flat red sea of sand rose great rock mesas, generally Gothic in outline, resembling vast cathedrals. They were not crowded together in disorder but placed in wide spaces, long vistas between. This plain might once have been an enormous city, all the smaller quarters destroyed by time, only the public buildings left,—piles of architecture that were like mountains. The sandy soil of the plain had a light sprinkling of junipers, and was splotched with masses of blooming rabbit brush,—that olive-coloured plant that grows in high waves like a tossing sea, at this season covered with a thatch of bloom, yellow as gorse, or orange like marigolds. (99)

In order to satisfy Cather's "higher processes of art" (which as a modernist she reduced to "simplification"), to "disregard" and "subordinate ... to a higher and truer effect" (*On Writing* 40), I would delete as implied Hawthorne's "grand frame-work" and "one picture" and substitute the "smile of God," introducing his catalogue of vineyards, fig-trees, and foliage with something like: "Beneath an expansive sun-filled sky glowed a rich and varied country." In his next sentence, "towered gateway" seems implied, as does "spacious," and the "blue eyes" reflection might be replaced with "lakes mirrored the heavens." Moralizing needs to be subtle in modernist description, and language subordinated to picture. Cather achieves similar effects with fewer words, her landscape made vivid through metaphors that create picture with contrasting images of "sea," "Gothic ... cathedrals," and "enormous city." Her use of color in describing the blooming vegetation suggests the influence of Impressionism, an improvement over the blur of Hawthorne's "smokey-hued tracts."

These passages represent both authors communicating landscapes encountered later in life, not familiar home country, which explains the filtering through visitors. More significantly, both landscapes focus on the sky and storms and reveal a predisposition toward transcendence. As Kenyon watches a thunderstorm moving across the valley,

the sky was heavy with tumbling vapours. . . . [T]he spectator could not tell rocky height from impalpable cloud. Far into this misty cloud-region, however,—within the domain of Chaos, as it were—hill-tops were seen brightening in the sunshine; they looked like fragments of the world, broken adrift and based on nothingness, or like portions of sphere destined to exist, but not yet finally compacted. The sculptor . . . fancied that the scene represented the process of the Creator, when He held the new, imperfect Earth in His hand, and modelled it. (1072)

Latour is fascinated by the same elements—storm clouds, sunlight, and Genesis aspects—but Cather has shuffled them and inserted specificity:

This mesa plain had an appearance of great antiquity, and of incompleteness; as if, with all the materials for world-making assembled, the Creator had desisted, gone away and left everything on the point of being brought together, on the eve of being arranged into mountain, plain, plateau. . . . The great tables of granite set down in an empty plain were inconceivable without their attendant clouds, which were a part of them, as the smoke is part of the censer, or the foam of the wave. . . . [R]ain began to fall as if it were spilled from a cloud-burst. . . . Looking out over the great plain spotted with mesas and glittering with rain sheets, the Bishop saw the distant mountains bright with sunlight. Again he thought that the first Creation morning might have looked like this when the dry land was drawn up out of the deep, and all was confusion. (99–100, 104)

Aside from these culturally rich landscapes, both writers were adept at mythologizing country familiar to them since childhood. Hawthorne bequeathed to his readers New England forests haunted by *The Scarlet Letter*'s Hester, Arthur, and Pearl, and the complex fates of characters in dozens of tales. I will never forget my first trip, in 1972, to Cather's Nebraska, to Webster County and Red Cloud. Traveling south from Hastings at dusk in a Pinto station wagon with my wife and four kids, the landscape was magic, at once Homeric sea and unmade country unfolding under an almost full moon. I can only second Cather's self-estimate to an interviewer that "descriptive work" is "the thing I do best" (Mahoney 39).

## ACHIEVEMENT

The saga of *Death Comes for the Archbishop* begins and ends with an invitation to journey, a diligence horn echoing in the Auvergne mountains calling two young priests to Paris to prepare for missionary work in the American Midwest and Southwest, eventually to head new dioceses in New Mexico and Colorado. Theirs is arguably the most historically spectacular of Cather success stories but only one among many, for a major appeal of this fiction is its call to achievement to those disadvantaged by geography or society, or both.

Earlier works also prioritize middle America—in class as well as location. For a second-generation American like myself, the first in a blue-collar family to attend college, Jim Burden's experiences in *My Ántonia* at a provincial university of serious young men "who hung on through the four years" on "only a summer's wages" (250) were as familiar in 1950s Brooklyn, New York, as in 1890s Lincoln, Nebraska. My being in New York City offset his privileged social status, although our discoveries were similar. My best teacher made literature so alive and significant that I changed my major from history to English and supplemented it with theatre, concerts, opera, ballet. Like Jim, I could appreciate the "people of my own infinitesimal past" (254), my parents and especially my Irish grandmother, who began to recite Tennyson's "Song of the Brook" one evening as I read it aloud to her. She had memorized it in school in Donegal during the years Jim Burden was reading Virgil with his teacher Gaston Cleric. Her American daughters had little literary schooling, which helped me understand the cultural deprivation of children of poor immigrants.

For half of my academic life I taught first-generation college students from the depressed mill cities in Massachusetts strung along the Merrimack River, sharing and introducing literature and the related fine arts and hoping my students' lives would be enriched like mine had been. Perhaps we've been too hard on Jim Burden, emphasizing his failures, sexual squeamishness, disengagement, and self-deception rather than his successful engagement with the arts in bequeathing to us the greater success story of an immigrant girl overcoming rejection and shame to become, as Cather intended her to be, "a rich mine of life, like the founders of early races" (342).

More dramatic than either story is Thea Kronborg's rise from Moonstone, Colorado, to the world stage of opera in *The Song of the Lark*. Hers is one of ongoing struggle to identify her talent, cope with poverty and disappointment, and familiarize herself with the cultural tradition she needs for artistic success. Thea's discovery of her place in this ascent occurs in an Arizona canyon and is strategically positioned subsequent to her breaking out of the restrictions of her upbringing, what artists and perhaps all the truly educated must experience—what Cather describes in her Katherine Mansfield essay as "escaping, running away, trying to break the net which circumstances and . . . affections have woven about [one]" (*On Writing* 109). In Thea's case there is a vast distance between the world she enters and the world she leaves behind. The break occurs on a train bound for Chicago after a less than successful visit home: "As the train pulled out she looked back at her mother and father and [brother] Thor. They . . . did not know, they did not understand. Something pulled in her—and broke" (273). Separation and isolation are the price of success, although not necessarily unqualified. Canadian novelist Gabrielle Roy envisions such a break as a summons, maybe a love call, to teachers and artists, "to withhold [oneself] . . . along the road, and then to catch up with the others, to rejoin them and cry joyously, 'Here I am, and here is what I've found for you along the way!'" (209).

Claude Wheeler's story in *One of Ours* resembles Thea's in provincial upbringing, escape to a larger world, and brush with heroic theater, but is one in which Cather plaits success with the tragic. As such, it recalls Alexandra Bergson in *O Pioneers!* and anticipates Godfrey St. Peter and Tom Outland in *The Professor's House*, as well as *Lucy Gayheart*. In Claude's case, war disturbingly replaces art as the venue of success. On leave from the front line in France, he listens to his companion David Gerhardt play Saint-Saens's third violin concerto with Claire Fleury and is torn between admiration and bitter envy at never having "been taught to do anything at all," at being "tongue-tied, foot-tied, hand-tied" during his years on his family's Nebraska farm. But the sound of artillery fire from the front restores his self-confidence and belief that the war will make the future different, rescue the world from the "strait-jacket" of "business proposition," and be his "adventure," his "Destiny" (551–54). Getting "his men in hand" when "they were going soft under his eyes" at the approach of German bombers, successfully holding back the enemy, and discovering while mortally wounded that "he commanded wonderful men" (596–97) fulfills Lieutenant Wheeler's destiny. His mother's reflection that "he must have found his life," that "[h]e died believing his own country better than it is, and France better than any country can ever be," defines his success. If these values seem illusory, they are also visionary; Mrs. Wheeler concludes, "[T]hose were beautiful beliefs to die with" (604).

Visionary components of success are also apparent in subsequent Cather novels. Apparitions encapsulate the height of success for both Professor St. Peter and Tom Outland. The Professor's occurs off the south coast of Spain, below the towering peaks of the Sierra Nevada, "high beyond the flight of fancy"; as he "lay looking up at them … the design of his [prize-winning history] book unfolded in the air above him. … He had accepted it as inevitable, … and it had seen him through" (105). Tom's "high tide" also occurs from a supine position but at the bottom of a Blue Mesa canyon: "high above me the canyon walls … dyed flame-colour … and the Cliff City lay in a gold haze against its dark cavern. … This was the first time I ever saw [the mesa] as a whole. It all came together. … For me the mesa was … a religious emotion" (249–50). Tom delivers this narration after his university graduation, after making his way from amateur archaeologist and student of Virgil to physicist. Both visionary experiences are recalled rather than occurring in the present and are tarnished by tragic circumstances: Tom's heartless rejection of his best friend, his own death in the Great War, and the disastrous legal and monetary consequences of his invention; the Professor's loss of Tom, family discord, despair, and flirtation with death.

Outland's departure for the war in France, his leaving behind marriage and life in the Midwest, echoes Claude's. Father Duchene, Tom's mentor, offers an interpretation of the mesa's ancient inhabitants easily applicable to the ideals Claude believed he was saving. The tribe, Duchene speculates, was "a superior people," who "developed the arts of peace," had "a distinct feeling for design," and "purif[ied] life by religious ceremonies and observances.... They were probably wiped out, utterly exterminated, by some roving Indian tribe without culture or domestic virtues" (217–19). The description reads like a palimpsest, echoing the earlier text of Claude's war of the worlds between his brother's buying and selling and his own high ideals, of life "reinforced by something that endured, ... a background that held together" (*One of Ours* 535).

St. Peter's relinquishing "something very precious" late in his story duplicates what Thea broke with: "He didn't . . . feel any obligations toward his family. . . . He doubted whether his family would ever realize that he was not the same man." He would seek refuge in a larger family, in "the bloomless side of life he had always run away from," one embodied in the devout family seamstress, Augusta, "with whom one was outward bound" (280–82). The Professor's is, perhaps, the darkest of Catherian success stories, one of "letting go with the heart" (Sergeant 215), as Cather indicated to Robert Frost, borrowing the phrase from his poem "Wild Grapes."

Shadows are evident in each of these successful journeys and in those that follow: Myra Henshawe's in *My Mortal Enemy*, Sapphira Colbert's in *Sapphira and the Slave Girl*, and in "Old Mrs. Harris" and "Before Breakfast." Success is qualified by modernist complexities and realism, and redefined to include the visionary, individual integrity, and even illusion.

## EDUCATION

It is 13 October 2015, and I have just returned from an exhibition of Dutch painting in the age of Rembrandt and Vermeer at Boston's Museum of Fine Arts. As a Cather scholar I was anxious to get to the opening, for it was to such an exhibition and to the sonata form that Cather credited the experimental structure of *The*

*Professor's House*. Bernice Slote gave a lecture at Merrimack College in 1972 titled "The Secret Web," explaining that a "web of connections and relationships ... illuminate and ... define [Willa Cather] as a person and as an artist," that her art "is apparent simplicity, actual complexity," and that the web "always moved outward from this time and place" (2, 9, 8). Those of us fortunate enough to have worked on the Willa Cather Scholarly Edition will emphatically agree. Exploring a Cather text for what exists in, above, or beneath it amounts to a liberal education, and while the extent of the web, if not always secret, is fathomless, following where it leads into locales, histories, literary texts, and the fine arts profoundly expands our worlds. Cather texts of "complexity ... determined by simplification" (Slote 19) have directed much of my study, interests, travel over the years—in fact, defined much of my life.

The web connects to the American writers Cather admired and/ or was influenced by. During the 1960s and early '70s, when paperback editions of the novels were unavailable and most American literature professors ignored Cather or offered "Paul's Case" as a sample, many of us struggled to make her novels integral to the canon. Certainly, Ántonia Shimerda could be discussed with Huck Finn as an American type, and Jim Burden with Huck as the narrator of a comparable and apparently episodic narrative. We could argue that including Cather actually discloses the canon. Burden's account at the beginning of *My Ántonia* of leaning against a warm yellow pumpkin and being dissolved into the universal, "whether it is sun and air, or goodness and knowledge" (18), echoes the transparent eyeball passage at the beginning of Emerson's *Nature* and later a child's love of nature: "I expand and live in the warm day like corn and melons" (*Essays* 38). Jim approaches his new world with new eyes, as Emerson encourages, building his own world and his own heaven. Emerson's disciple Walt Whitman, whom Myra Henshawe in *My Mortal Enemy* slyly labels a "dirty old man" (66), inspired Cather's cosmic vision in *O Pioneers!*, which takes its title from one of his poems. The mating of earth and air, the yield of the earth to the plow, Alexandra Bergson's yearning for the spirit breathing across the land owe to "Song of Myself," as does the novel's final sentiment that hearts like hers will be received by the earth to live again in wheat and corn. Alexandra's insights on death after her brother's murder affirm those of the persona in "The Sleepers."

Cather has Cardinal Allande drolly refer to Fenimore Cooper in the prologue to the *Archbishop*, perhaps her hint that there are clear parallels between Cooper's Leatherstocking and Littlepage novels and her own Nebraska ones, from the ocean metaphor describing shaggy grass in *The Prairie* and *My Ántonia* to the environmental impact and social decline of settlement recorded in *The Prairie* and Littlepage series and from *O Pioneers!* to *A Lost Lady*. Natty Bumppo's escape *to* the prairie from western New York due to plunder serves as an ironic foil for Niel Herbert's flight *from* the prairie as petty businessmen "destroy and cut up [the vast territory] into profitable bits" (*Lost Lady* 102). One of the American books Cather singles out for praise in her preface on Sarah Orne Jewett is *The Scarlet Letter*, which she refers to earlier in "The Novel Démeublé" as an example of creating without naming. Its influence is felt in the sympathy nature accords to the lovers in *O Pioneers!*, and I detect Hawthorne in both *My Ántonia* and the *Archbishop*: Jim Burden seems a clone of the narrator of *The Blithedale Romance*, Miles Coverdale, and the execution of Fray Baltazar a dead ringer for the murder of Miriam's model in *The Marble Faun*.

Elizabeth Sergeant recalls that at their first meeting Cather recognized her as a fellow Jamesian and somewhat brusquely questioned why Sergeant "joined the reforming pamphleteers" (35). Henry James was a lifelong model of sorts for Cather's fiction and occasional essays on fiction, which she, too, related to the fine arts. Her early and awkward Jamesian imitations, such as "Eleanor's House" and "The Willing Muse," and several, like "Flavia and Her Artists," on writers and artists, prepared her for perhaps her best story on art and performance, "Coming, Aphrodite!" Even after Cather admitted in a 1905 letter to Viola Roseboro' a certain impatience with James's later fiction, a mature Cather, as Sharon O'Brien explains, "assimilated James' influence . . . and could accommodate his technique

for her own purposes" (310). Cather's maturity involved her introduction to the Southwest, an altered view of her home country, and
the influence of Sarah Orne Jewett, whose work exemplified How-
ellsian theories of realism, and also American Naturalists Stephen
Crane and Frank Norris, the first for style and perhaps the drowning
scene in *Alexander's Bridge*, the second for violence in early prairie
stories, for Wick Cutter in *My Ántonia*, and the suicide of Ántonia's
father. Cather was able to recast the Jamesian consciousness to new
locales and situations. This is especially evident in male characters
in her later novels: Latour in the *Archbishop*, Auclair in *Shadows on
the Rock*, Henry Colbert in *Sapphira and the Slave Girl*. All three are
informed by literature, the arts, philosophy, religion, and capable of
metaphoric thinking. Latour, for example, filters the New Mexico
landscape through Genesis and compares mountains and clouds to
censer and smoke, wave and foam. An intimacy with the American
canon is a requirement for following Cather's "Secret Web."

The British canon is the most familiar and shortest step from the
American in tracing Cather connections. Shakespeare, the Romantic poets (Wordsworth and Keats primarily), and the Victorians significantly informed Cather's vision and provided artistic models.
However, as several scholars have demonstrated, French and Russian
writers are at least as important. Flaubert's *Madame Bovary* should
be required reading for us and perhaps Alphonse Daudet's *Letters
from My Mill* for its arrangement of sketches as well as the flavor
of Provence, which permeates Cather settings from *O Pioneers!* to
the Avignon fragment "Hard Punishments." As for the Russians,
Tolstoy's *Confession* informs the final book of *The Professor's House*,
and fables like "What Men Live By," "The Three Hermits," and "Master
and Man," which a youthful Cather would have dismissed as "wea-
risome" because written "for a moral purpose" (*Kingdom of Art* 378),
resonate in the "miraculous" vignettes a mature Cather wove into
her "Catholic novels." Similarly, a minor work of Turgenev, "Bezhin
Meadow," from *A Sportsman's Notebook*, suggested the structure of
"The Enchanted Bluff" (and also the picnic scene in *My Ántonia*).
Five boys sit around a fire near a river and tell stories. The contrast

between Old and New World mentalities is of significance: the Russian boys are obsessed with superstitions, death, and doomsday; the Americans see the legendary past as an opportunity for adventure, although one never realized. In both, a river, birds, fish, stars, moon, sunset, sunrise give cosmic life to the setting, and each ends with the revelation of the future death of one of the boys. A Latinist well-versed in the classics, Cather knew Virgil, Homer, the tragic dramatists, and also Dante. *The Aeneid* is referred to repeatedly throughout the Cather canon, and *The Georgics* is arguably the major literary source for *My Ántonia*. Dante's world is that of the *Archbishop*, *Shadows*, and "Hard Punishments," and the stories embroidered in the *Commedia* inform, like Tolstoy's fables, both novels.

Willa Cather was a prodigious educational traveler. Her readers and scholars have followed her from the grasslands of Webster County, Nebraska, and Cather family sites in Red Cloud; to Lincoln, where she studied; to the northern Virginia mountains, where she was born; to Pittsburgh, where she taught school; to New York, where she worked and lived most of her life; to New Hampshire, where she wrote and is buried; and to Grand Manan Island, where she owned real estate and summered. But beyond her home places, which provided settings, Cather the tourist expanded the scope of her fiction from Chicago to Avignon. Through a wealth of details, like a Southwest tower seen through falling snow, a copper flash on the dome of St. Peter's, the yellow of a New Mexico cliff evoking the Palace of the Popes, exotic places become immediate. They invite study, entice visits and adventures well beyond the web—for me a hike up the Puy de Dome, the view of Rome from Parco Savello, of Percé Rock from a boat, a decade of choir in Archbishop Lamy's (Latour's) cathedral.

The Boston Museum of Fine Art's exhibition of Dutch paintings reminded me that serious exploration of Cather's writings takes us beyond the strictly literary and into the fine arts. Her critical essays reveal that fiction is a fine art, and she collapses the distinctions among them. The fragment "Light on Adobe Walls" groups Beethoven, Shakespeare, and Leonardo as equal players in "the game of make-believe" (*On Writing* 125). The "Casta Diva" aria from Bellini's

*Norma* reveals Myra Henshawe's situation and character in *My Mortal Enemy*; the Hudson River luminist painters inspire the sunsets in *My Ántonia* and "Tom Outland's Story"; hearing Dvořák's Symphony in E Minor, "From the New World," becomes a formative occasion for Thea Kronborg; the Central Park afternoon scene in "The Diamond Mine" is Cather's take on her Impressionist painter contemporaries. Correspondences with the fine arts have proven a field day for scholars: Schubert's *Die Winterreise* and *Lucy Gayheart*, Puvis de Chavannes murals and the *Archbishop*, Wagner's *Parsifal* and *One of Ours*, *La Dame à la licorne* tapestries and *Shadows*. And we should explore the symphonic structure of Cather narratives, her scenic arrangements, and use of chiaroscuro in them. Edith Lewis describes the diet of opera she and Cather enjoyed in their early days in New York: "We lived very economically.... Our practice of economy was, however, accompanied by extravagance.... [W]e went often to the opera, sitting high up, in the cheap seats" (74). The influence of theater, especially opera, is detectable in the love and death scene in "The White Mulberry Tree" in *O Pioneers!* and in the farewell scene in *My Ántonia*'s "The Pioneer Woman's Story," a duet, really, staged beneath the moon at sunset. Cather challenges us to make the fine arts as much a part of our lives as reading. They were for her and are detectable in the particular cadence and quality of her voice.

## TRANSCENDENCE

As an artist Cather cherished and delighted in the physical world, and her fascination with our appetites is evident in a variety of characters, from Thea Kronborg to Grandma Harris, Bartley Alexander to Jean Marie Latour, and in situations as diverse as Marie and Emil's lovemaking beneath the white mulberry tree and Cécile Auclair pulling Jacques on her sled up Holy Family Hill to enjoy a Quebec sunset. Always, however, something somewhere beyond is predictably present if unnamed, what Flannery O'Connor explains as the mystery "left over" that "cannot be accounted for" when the fiction writer is done with nature and manners (*Mystery* 153). Count

Frontenac's contemplation of death in *Shadows* is my favorite Cather passage on this mystery, that he believed "his spirit would go before God to be judged. . . . because he had been taught it in childhood, and because he knew there was something in himself and in other men that this world did not explain. Even the Indians had to make a story to account for something in their lives that did not come out of their appetites" (284).

Among Cather scholars, my work, although hopefully balanced by aesthetic and historical concerns, is usually associated with the issue of Cather and religion. I first read Cather and then taught her in belief contexts, at Catholic and Mormon schools, which, as O'Connor argues, might be more liberating than restricting—as introductions to "a larger universe" (*Mystery* 175). Critics as disparate as E. K. Brown, who identifies *The Professor's House* as "a religious novel" (246), grouping it with the three novels subsequent to it, and Joan Acocella, who recognizes Christianity as "central to [Cather's] work" but "as an instance [and] not the summation of Cather's idealism" (84, 86), seem to justify approaching Cather, at least partially and unsentimentally, from the perspective of religion. Acocella's observation is insightful in distinguishing religious attitudes beyond Judeo-Christianity and sectarianism. I go back to *The Marble Faun* for a metaphor encapsulating these distinctions. During their ramble through Umbria, the sculptor Kenyon and the Count visit many churches, and the American is fascinated by the brilliance of the stained glass, by the depicted "religious truth and sacred story" made radiant by the bright Italian sunshine. "[V]iewed from the warm interior of Belief . . . Christian Faith," Kenyon claims, "is a grand Cathedral, with divinely pictured windows." But, he continues, "standing without, you see no glory, nor can imagine any" (*Novels* 1107). Later when his Puritan girlfriend softens toward Catholicism, Kenyon condemns its truths and stories as "a brilliant illusion" and situates himself outside, declaring, "[b]ut, give me—to live and die in—the pure, white light of Heaven!" (1156–57). Erase the defensiveness and condemnation and this duality clarifies the stance toward religion in much of Cather's fiction.

Frontenac situates himself both within and outside the cathedral. He accepts the "religious truth and sacred story" of his church, recognizing these as creations, versions of the inexplicable. Belief becomes both a matter of interpretation and of culture and art. In *Shadows on the Rock*, the range of faith within the same belief system is extraordinary, from the innocent acceptance of Cécile and Jacques to the rational qualifications of Euclide Auclair and Frontenac, from the administrative orderliness of Bishop Laval to the conservative hysteria of recluse Jeanne Le Ber and martyr Noël Chabanel, and to Father Hector Saint-Cyr's benign interpretation of that Jesuit's life as Christlike self-sacrifice. Through the nuns of Quebec, Cather envisions the church as a "world of the mind," a "lovingly arranged and ordered universe" in which one could feel "at home" (115). The physical counterpart is Jean Marie Latour's Midi Romanesque cathedral, built to represent Catholicism at its aesthetic best in a new country. Like *Shadows*, the *Archbishop* contains a diverse range of belief: the literalness of Father Vaillant, Sada's servility, Latour's developing ecumenism regarding religious traditions outside Christianity. Both novels might be considered illustrations of Professor St. Peter's argument that "art and religion . . . are the same thing, in the end," cultural constructs "giv[ing] man the only happiness he has ever had" (*Professor's House* 69).

Whatever her own religious beliefs, Willa Cather was fascinated by and took comfort in the culture of belief and made it a major component of her fiction and life. She was confirmed in the Episcopal church in Red Cloud, Nebraska, and in New York attended the Episcopal Church of the Ascension, although, as Flannery O'Connor claimed, "scratch an Episcopalian and you're liable to find most anything" (*Collected* 1057). The art in this Fifth Avenue church was its attraction. Cather "loved the beautiful altar, with John La Farge's great fresco [*The Ascension of Our Lord*] above; and for years went regularly to the vesper services, where the organist . . . conducted one of the best-trained choirs in New York," writes Edith Lewis (151–52). In one of her last letters, Cather wished she "could have had a comfortable boardinghouse near Chartres when Henry Adams used to prowl about the cathedral" (*Letters* 672). She, too, was inspired by pictured windows.

However, the transcendent aspect of Cather's fiction is my main concern here, the ongoing offering of grace and vision to her characters when acceptance is tantamount to human transcendence, what theologian Karl Rahner describes as "God's self-communication to man as a free being" capable of "an absolute 'yes' or 'no' to God" (118). Instances of such offers regularly occur beyond the pages of Cather texts. In *O Pioneers!*, the mystery left over from Alexandra Bergson's "resolution" to go to her brother's killer, Frank Shabata, in jail, is an example, a decision "formed" during the several days she lies bedridden (252). Similar reserve is evident in the *Archbishop*, where we are removed from Latour's painful decision to release Vaillant to the Colorado mission in spite of deep personal need. The "Bishop . . . was shut in his study all morning" (256), subsequently presenting Vaillant with a challenge he responds to enthusiastically. In *Sapphira and the Slave Girl*, the death of her granddaughter Betty becomes Sapphira's opportunity to overcome her long alienation from her daughter, Rachel, after slave-girl Nancy's escape. Again, Cather distances us from the mystery: "[T]he Mistress was thinking, turning things over in her mind. . . . [W]hen she had quite made up her mind, she put her hand on her husband's drooping shoulder" (262), and asks him to invite their daughter home.

All three are positive examples, but there are negative ones as well. Harry Gordon's refusal of Lucy Gayheart's request for a ride, the result of which is a life haunted by guilt: "Lucy had suffered for a few hours. . . . But with him it was there to stay. . . . [a] dark place in his mind" (*Lucy Gayheart* 232–33). Tom Outland's rejection of Roddy Blake is perhaps the most dramatic in Cather, and is a struggle less distanced. "There was an ache in my arms to reach out and detain him," Tom confesses, "but there was something also that made me absolutely powerless to do so." Following this negative prompting is a clear positive one to rise above anger, disappointment, and a hurt ego as Roddy pauses to echo the Golden Rule: "And I'm glad it's you that's doing this to me, Tom; not me that's doing it to you"

(*Professor's House* 247). The result for Tom is a dark place in his mind: "But the older I grow, the more I understand what it was I did that night on the mesa. Anyone who requites faith and friendship as I did, will have to pay for it" (252).

Arguably, the most protracted of transcendent opportunities, one filled with negatives but positive in outcome, occurs in *My Mortal Enemy*, involving Myra Henshawe in the final stage of her life. Narrator Nellie takes her to a headland above the Pacific, where a twisted cedar and intense sunlight complement the spare realism of the text. "From a distance I could see her leaning against her tree and looking off to sea, as if she were waiting for something.... The afternoon light ... grew stronger and yellower, ... beating from the west on her cliff as if thrown by a burning-glass"—an obvious symbol of grace. Myra's smile becomes "soft," her face "lovely." The transformation is viewed from the outside, its mystery distanced. "Light and silence," she claims, "heal all one's wounds ... but one, and that is healed by dark and silence" (60–61). Her need for healing, sense of guilt, and hope for forgiveness intensify the sun setting into the sea, like the cedar, a traditional Crucifixion image.

I've saved two major examples from English literature relevant to that "something" in human nature "that this world did not explain," the King James Bible and John Bunyan. The King James, the more important, served Cather not only as a source of direct quotes and indirect reference through the arts, but for archetypes enhancing her material and language arranged in seamless and evocative poetic clusters. Characters as diverse as Claude Wheeler and Grandma Harris reveal themselves negatively and positively through scriptural reference. Claude is so terrified by bodily decay during his college years that he pins assurance of privileged escape on Psalm 16:10: "[N]either wilt thou suffer thine Holy One to see corruption," betraying a crippling narcissism (*One of Ours* 75). Mrs. Harris, in contrast, accepts a servile role in her daughter's house, is thankful for each night's rest on her thin mattress, taking comfort in Psalm 23: "To be off her feet, to lie flat, to say over the psalm beginning: '*The Lord is my shepherd*,' was comfort enough" (*Obscure Destinies* 80). Perhaps Cather's greatest achievement in mining the King James is the evolution of a poetic style drawn from scriptural clusters. In the *Archbishop*, for example, chapter two of the seventh book opens with Jean Latour racked by doubts about his missionary work in New Mexico and in need of the support of his vicar serving far off in Arizona. Latour is "unable to sleep, . . . failure clutching at his heart." His prayers seem "empty words," his bed becomes "a bed of thorns," his soul "a barren field," and his work "a house built upon the sands" (221). The restless night and thorns in the flesh are humbling experiences in, respectively, Job 7:4 and 2 Corinthians 12:7; the barren field and house built on sand are parable images referring to unsuccessful missionary endeavor in, respectively, Matthew 13:4–7, 20–22, and 7:26–27.

Bunyan's *The Pilgrim's Progress* and *Holy War* are referred to directly and used archetypally in Cather texts. As Grandma Harris on her deathbed begins to listen to her young grandson read her a story, her mind drifts into a passage from Bunyan's allegory, where Christian's wife, Christiana, her family, and her friend Mercy "come to the arbour on the Hill of Difficulty: *'Then said Mercy, how sweet is rest to them that labour'*" (*Obscure Destinies* 150–52). Allegorical landscapes and nomenclature link *Pilgrim's Progress* and the *Archbishop*. The *Holy War*, an allegory Bunyan wrote between the first and second parts of the more famous *Pilgrim's Progress*, is introduced in *Sapphira and the Slave Girl* during Henry Colbert's struggle over his attraction to the slave Nancy, whose sexuality he mitigates by associating her with Bunyan's Mercy.

"Saul Bellow once said that all great modern novelists were really attempting a definition of human nature in order to justify the continuation of their craft," writes James Wood (74). This certainly seems applicable to Cather, who clothed human activity and aspiration, success and failure in the mystery left over that cannot be accounted for.

### DISAPPROVAL

I use this single term for consistency in the final part of this retrospective and to respect Cather's claim in a 1941 letter that she was not a social critic, never tried to write "any propaganda—any rules . . .

or theories about the betterment of human society," especially "when disguised as fiction" (*Letters* 597). However, through characters and situations and clear complaints in essays, she reveals disapproval, bitter at times, of the course of American society. This is evident in her earliest work, in stories like "The Sculptor's Funeral," and, prior to her recourse into history, casts shadows on all her more or less contemporary novels from *O Pioneers!* to *The Professor's House*. Her 1923 essay in *The Nation*, "Nebraska: The End of the First Cycle," should be required reading for aficionados of her Nebraska novels and a featured text for some future Cather Spring Conference in Red Cloud. Her denunciations of the "Americanization" (237) of the state that was her residence from 1883 to 1896 and provided the setting for much of her fiction emphasizes discrimination against foreign immigrants, suppression of foreign languages, the decline of cookery and craft, and, most importantly, the "eclipse" of the humanities by the study of "mercantile processes" at her alma mater, the University of Nebraska (238).

Cultural decline seems to be inversely proportional to the prosperity and modernization following the state's recovery from depression in the 1890s. New houses lit by electricity and equipped with bathrooms, well-kept towns, happy-looking and well-nourished schoolchildren with opportunities for university study are eclipsed by "the ugly crest of materialism.... Too much prosperity, too many moving-picture shows, too much gaudy fiction have colored the taste and manners of so many of these Nebraskans of the future. There, as elsewhere, one finds the frenzy to be showy ... a coming generation which tries to cheat its aesthetic sense by buying things instead of making anything" (238). The phrase "There, as elsewhere" is strategic, for what is being castigated in 1923 is these United States, the cultural standard to which Nebraska has succumbed. By 1923, after *One of Ours* and two years prior to *The Professor's House*, her argument with Nebraska had expanded to the whole country and, perhaps, beyond. The question we have to ask concerns the current relevancy of Cather's disapproval, which assumes several literary forms, most successfully satire, although more frequently and less successfully character-belittling diatribe, jeremiad, confession, and lecture.

*O Pioneers!*, composed when she was still enthused about her "home pasture," contains one of her sharpest satiric episodes. The newly prosperous Bergson clan assembles for dinner in Alexandra's dining room, which the local furniture dealer "had conscientiously done his best to make ... like his display window" (92). The talk is in English because her brother Oscar's wife, "from the malaria district of Missouri, was ashamed of marrying a foreigner, and his boys did not understand a word of Swedish" (94). Oscar is jealous because Alexandra is buying a piano for brother Lou's daughter. Lou fears gossip about his sister keeping the Bible-reading Norwegian hermit Ivar on her farm because, as Ivar puts it, "the way here is for all to do alike" (88). The surprise arrival of the Bergsons' old neighbor, Carl Linstrum from New York, prompts Lou's wife, Annie, to primp herself and boast of her daughter's piano skills and wood-burning art, her husband's success, and their plans to move into town "as soon as her girls are old enough to go out into company" (104). Lou swaggers to the New Yorker about William Jennings Bryan and how the "West is going to make itself heard" (104). As Annie appears for departure "in a hat that looked like the model of a battleship" (105), the brothers draw Alexandra aside to warn her that Carl might be after her money. With much left unnamed, Cather introduces the portrait of pioneer patriarch John Bergson hanging in Alexandra's sitting room, noting its "sad eyes that looked forward into the distance, as if they already beheld the New World" (98). In all these scenes, consumer culture is satirized and materialism is questioned.

In *My Ántonia*, and especially in *A Lost Lady*, Cather seems to have lost patience with the society if not the terrain of her "home pasture," and the result, diatribe and jeremiad, is less successful. Jim Burden's denouncement of the town of Black Hawk is an example of the former. Put off by the townspeople's dismissal of foreigners as "ignorant people who couldn't speak English," by their fear of immigrant girls from the country as a menace to the social order, and by the "respect for respectability" (*My Ántonia* 194–95) of Black Hawk youth like himself who enjoy frolicking with these hired girls before marrying conventional ones, Burden walks the streets of the town at night "scowling" at the flimsy houses sheltering lives "made up of evasions and negations" (212). Yet Cather tempers his criticism, identifying him through a "grown-up" neighbor as a "romantic" given to exaggeration (145, 222). Similar subjectivity accompanies Niel Herbert's musing on the demise of the pioneer West; Niel is rigid, described as "stiff" (60), and cruelly dismissive of Marian Forrester for not satisfying his heroic expectations. Although compromised, Cather's criticism is extended through Niel from the local indictment of a town to "all the vast territory of the Old West" and capped with a dire prophecy of the future: "[S]ettled by ... great-hearted adventurers[,] ... the vast territory they had won was to be at the mercy of ["shrewd young men"] ... who. ... would drink up the mirage, dispel the morning freshness, root out the great brooding spirit of freedom" (102). This is the environment Claude Wheeler inherits in *One of Ours*.

Claude's story and that of Godfrey St. Peter in *The Professor's House*, if explored for social disapproval, represent a transition on Cather's part and require a change of key. Both are confessional literature of sorts: Claude's a bildungsroman and St. Peter's a disclosure of artistic, political, and religious struggle. Unlike Jim's and Niel's adolescent memoirs highlighting female symbols of setting, Claude's and St. Peter's stories are extremely intimate, self-focused—and deadly. Restricted by a social environment valuing mechanical toys over education and passing to shrewd young men trained to petty economies, Claude courts distinction in going to war in France for humanistic ideals that will save the world. Social disapproval here has broadened from province to nation: Claude "had begun to believe" that Americans "were always buying and selling, building and pulling down ... [,] were a people of shallow emotions" (535). "[P]erhaps he would never go home at all ... would buy a little farm and stay here for the rest of his life" (534).

In *The Professor's House*, bickering over money and status in his family (more corrupting than anything in *O Pioneers!*), in his university, and in general society made "[t]he world ... sad to St. Peter ... small and tight and airless. ... [E]verything around him ... seemed insupportable. ... [T]he little world ... might become like that; a boat on which one could travel no longer" (148–49). Disapproval here is summarized in the lecture St. Peter gives early on, universalizing Cather's Nebraska essay. All of Western history is the context: the biblical era, the Middle Ages, the Renaissance. The Professor's subject is the development of science at the expense of much else—science here read as psychiatry dismissive of sin, physics "revolutionizing aviation" (42) but debasing a family, technology in the service of profitmaking and physical comfort at the expense of moral impoverishment. However we define "science" in this novel, "the other side of the medal" (to borrow a phrase from the Nebraska essay) is stamped with "[a]rt and religion (they are the same thing, in the end)" (69). "The classics, the humanities, are having their dark hour," Cather lamented in her essay (238) two years prior to the publication of St. Peter's story, which frames the extension of decline to America's capital city in "Tom Outland's Story," a materialistic narrative set ironically in a landscape much touted for its liberating style.

There is a dichotomy in the Catherian sensibility. A jarring addendum to the Professor's lecture is Cather's comment in her 11 August 1945 letter to Sidney Florance that "the atomic bomb has sent a shudder of horror (and fear) through all the world" (*Selected Letters* 652), yet the previous year, in "Before Breakfast," she has her aging protagonist, Henry Grenfell, watch a young woman take an early morning plunge in "the death-chill" waters of the North Atlantic and, despite his chagrin and decrepitude, recover his optimism, "chuckling to himself: 'Anyhow, when that first amphibious frog-toad found his water hole dried up behind him, and jumped out to hop along till he could find another,—well, he started on a long hop'" (*Collected* 406–7). Saul Bellow's comment again seems appropriate: "[A]ll great modern novelists were really attempting ... to justify the continuation of their craft." Mildred Bennett quotes Robert Frost's observation that "with Carl Sandburg, it was 'the people yes.' With Willa Cather, it was 'the people, no'" (149). Cather's disapproval turned toward the "Stupid Faces" that confront Thea Kronborg, turned toward conventional society, its fads, misplaced values, rumors and faulty education. She gave her assent to those who rose above such limitations, those who, in spite of them, quietly or dramatically achieved.

## WORKS CITED

Acocella, Joan. *Willa Cather and the Politics of Criticism*. U of Nebraska P, 2000.

Bennett, Mildred R. *The World of Willa Cather*. 1951. Bison Edition, U of Nebraska P, 1961.

Brown, E. K. *Willa Cather: A Critical Biography*. Knopf, 1953.

Cather, Willa. *Collected Stories*. Vintage, Random House, 1992.

———. *Death Comes for the Archbishop*. 1927. Willa Cather Scholarly Edition, historical essay and explanatory notes by John J. Murphy, textual editing by Charles W. Mignon with Frederick M. Link and Kari A. Ronning, U of Nebraska P, 1999.

———. Letter to Viola Roseboro' (October 1905). Witter Bynner Collection, Houghton Library, Harvard U, Cambridge.

———. *A Lost Lady*. 1923. Willa Cather Scholarly Edition, historical essay by Susan J. Rosowski with Kari A. Ronning, explanatory notes by Ronning, textual editing by Charles W. Mignon and Frederick M. Link with Ronning, U of Nebraska P, 1997.

———. *Lucy Gayheart*. 1935. Willa Cather Scholarly Edition, historical essay by David Porter, explanatory notes by Kari A. Ronning and Porter, textual essay and editing by Frederick M. Link and Ronning, U of Nebraska P, 2015.

———. *The Kingdom of Art: Willa Cather's First Principles and Critical Statements, 1893–1896*. Edited by Bernice Slote, U of Nebraska P, 1966.

———. *My Ántonia*. 1918. Willa Cather Scholarly Edition, with illustrations by W. T. Benda, edited by Charles Mignon with Kari A. Ronning, historical essay by James Woodress, with contributions by Ronning, Kathleen Danker, and Emily Levine, U of Nebraska P, 1994.

———. "Nebraska: The End of the First Cycle." *Nation*, 5 September 1923, 236–38.

———. *Obscure Destinies*. 1932. Willa Cather Scholarly Edition, historical essay and explanatory notes by Kari A. Ronning, textual essay by Frederick M. Link with Mark Kamrath and Kari Ronning, U of Nebraska P, 1998.

———. *One of Ours*. 1922. Willa Cather Scholarly Edition, historical essay and explanatory notes by Richard C. Harris, textual essay and editing by Frederick M. Link with Kari A. Ronning, U of Nebraska P, 2006.

———. *On Writing: Critical Studies on Writing as an Art*. Knopf, 1949.

———. *O Pioneers!* 1913. Willa Cather Scholarly Edition, edited by Susan J. Rosowski and Charles W. Mignon with Kathleen Danker, historical essay and explanatory notes by David Stouck, U of Nebraska P, 1993.

————. *The Professor's House.* 1925. Willa Cather Scholarly Edition, historical essay by James Woodress, explanatory notes by Woodress with Kari A. Ronning, textual editing by Frederick M. Link, U of Nebraska P, 2002.

————. *Sapphira and the Slave Girl.* 1940. Willa Cather Scholarly Edition, historical essay and explanatory notes by Ann Romines, textual essay and editing by Charles W. Mignon, Kari A. Ronning, and Frederick M. Link, U of Nebraska P, 2009.

————. *The Selected Letters of Willa Cather.* Edited by Andrew Jewell and Janis Stout, Knopf, 2013.

————. *Shadows on the Rock.* 1931. Willa Cather Scholarly Edition, historical essay and explanatory notes by John J. Murphy and David Stouck, textual editing by Frederick M. Link, U of Nebraska P, 2005.

————. *The Song of the Lark.* 1915. Willa Cather Scholarly Edition, historical essay and explanatory notes by Ann Moseley, textual essay and editing by Kari A. Ronning, U of Nebraska P, 2012.

Emerson, Ralph Waldo. *Essays and Lectures.* Edited by Joel Porte, Library of America, 1983.

Hawthorne, Nathaniel. *Novels.* Edited by Millicent Bell, Library of America, 1983.

Lewis, Edith. *Willa Cather Living: A Personal Record.* 1953. Bison Edition, edited by John J. Murphy, U of Nebraska P, 2000.

Mahoney, Eva. "How Willa Cather Found Herself." 1921. *Willa Cather in Person: Interviews, Speeches, and Letters,* edited by L. Brent Bohlke, U of Nebraska P, 1986, pp. 33–39.

O'Brien, Sharon. *Willa Cather: The Emerging Voice.* Oxford UP, 1987.

O'Connor, Flannery. *Collected Works.* Edited by Sally Fitzgerald. Library of America, 1988.

————. *Mystery and Manners: Occasional Prose.* Edited by Sally and Robert Fitzgerald, Farrar, Straus and Giroux, 1969.

Rahner, Karl. *Foundations of Christian Faith: An Introduction to the Idea of Christianity.* Translated by William V. Dych, Crossroad, 1989.

Roy, Gabrielle. *Street of Riches.* Translated by Harry Binsse, Harcourt, Brace, 1957.

Sergeant, Elizabeth Shepley. *Willa Cather: A Memoir.* 1953. Bison Edition, U of Nebraska P, 1963.

Slote, Bernice. "The Secret Web." *Five Essays on Willa Cather: The Merrimack Symposium,* edited by John J. Murphy, Merrimack College, 1974, pp. 1–19.

Wood, James. "The Art of Witness." *The New Yorker,* 28 September 2015, pp. 68–75.

TIMOTHY BINTRIM is professor of English at Saint Francis University in Loretto, Pennsylvania. His fascination with Cather's Pittsburgh began with a weekend observance celebrating the centennial of her arrival in the city hosted by Duquesne University in June 1996 and peaked with the Sixteenth International Seminar, also hosted by Duquesne, in June 2017. Much of his work has explored her writing for *The Home Monthly*, *The National Stockman and Farmer*, the *Evening Leader*, and the short-lived Pittsburgh magazine *The Library*.

ANGELA CONRAD, a longtime scholar and friend of the Willa Cather community, taught for thirteen years at Bloomfield College in Bloomfield, New Jersey. Among other accomplishments, Angela wrote a book about Emily Dickinson, *The Wayward Nun of Amherst*, was a critical organizer of the Willa Cather International Seminar in New York City in 1998, and she was also a member of the New Jersey Council for the Arts for close to four years. She has published many articles in *The Willa Cather Newsletter & Review* as well as Cather Studies. After an eight-year battle with cancer, Angela passed away on 27 March 2019, leaving behind her devoted husband, Roberto Osti, son, Massimo, and daughter, Emilia.

JOHN H. FLANNIGAN is a retired professor of English at Prairie State College, Chicago Heights, Illinois, where he taught American, African American, and British literatures and composition and was president of the Faculty Federation from 2004 to 2013. His essays on Cather, music, and opera have appeared in Cather Studies, *Modern Fiction Studies*, *Studies in Short Fiction*, and the *Willa Cather Pioneer Memorial Newsletter*.

MICHAEL GORMAN is a professor at Hiroshima City University in Japan. His teaching and research interests include rural American civilization as well as multicultural, environmental, and transnational literatures. Recent publications include "Willa Cather, Cultural Imperialism, and the 'The Coming Man'" (2018) and "Climates of Violence, Spirits of Resistance: Chang-rae Lee's *On Such a Full Sea* and Louise Erdrich's *Future Home of the Living God*" (2019).

CHARMION GUSTKE is an assistant professor of English and the director of the First-Year Seminar Program at Belmont University in Nashville, where she teaches courses in writing, literature, and cultural theory. Her Cather research examines the material and gendered trajectories in Cather's life and in her writing. Other scholarly interests include transatlantic literary studies and the work of Henry David Thoreau, on which she has published articles. She is committed to community engagement and employs her service-learning classes to connect students to nonprofit organizations in her continued support of sustainable food practices, social advocacy, and the liberal arts.

JAMES A. JAAP is currently a teaching professor of English and the assistant chief academic officer at the Greater Allegheny campus of the Pennsylvania State University. Recently published pieces include an article on Cather and Southwest painter Ernest Blumenschein in *Cather Studies 11* and a discussion of the art and industrial connections in "Paul's Case" in *Cather Studies 12*. In addition to co-directing the 2017 Cather International Seminar in Pittsburgh, he currently serves on the Willa Cather Foundation Board of Governors. He lives in the Friendship neighborhood of Pittsburgh with his wife and two children, not far from where Cather stayed while living in the city.

JOHN J. MURPHY, professor emeritus, Brigham Young University, and a thirty-year veteran of the Cather Foundation Board of Governors, published his first essay on Cather in 1963 and has since contributed scores of essays to leading literary journals and to books. He is the author of *My Ántonia: The Road Home*; editor and coeditor, respectively, of the Cather Scholarly Edition volumes of *Death Comes for the Archbishop* and *Shadows on the Rock*; the editor of Penguin's Big Read *My Ántonia*; and coeditor of *Cather Studies 8* and *Cather Studies 11*. In 1981 he directed the first International Cather Seminar and co-directed the 2007 Seminar in France and the 2013 Seminar in Arizona; he has taught Cather in China, Taiwan, and Europe, and conducted graduate seminars on Cather at the universities of Rome and of Leon and Santiago in Spain. He lives with his wife, Sally, in Newton, Massachusetts.

JOSEPH C. MURPHY is associate professor in the English Department at Fu Jen Catholic University. His essays have appeared in Cather Studies, *Forum for Modern Language Studies*, *American Literary Scholarship*, and other journals and collections. His current research situates Cather in relation to modern cultures of spectacle and performance.

DARYL W. PALMER is professor of English at Regis University in Denver, Colorado. His most recent book is *Becoming Willa Cather: Creation and Career* (2019). His articles on Willa Cather and the American West have appeared in journals such as *American Literary Realism*, *Great Plains Quarterly*, *Kansas History*, *Theory & Event*, and *The Willa Cather Review*.

DIANE PRENATT is professor of English emerita at Marian University and faculty mentor in the Scholarly Concentration in Medical Humanities at Indiana University School of Medicine. Her research interests include the representation of domestic arts and ethnic identity in narrative, especially in the fiction of Willa Cather. She has published several essays in Cather Studies and the *Willa Cather Newsletter & Review*. She is writing a life of the writer and social activist Elizabeth Shepley Sergeant.

TODD RICHARDSON is an associate professor in the University of Nebraska at Omaha's Goodrich Scholarship Program. He is the editor of *Louise Pound: A Folklore and Literature Miscellany* and coauthor of *Implied Nowhere: Absence and Folklore Studies*.

*Contributors*

ANN ROMINES is professor emerita of English at the George Washington University and a longtime member of the Board of Governors of the Willa Cather Foundation. She is author or editor of several books about Willa Cather, including the Nebraska Scholarly Edition of *Sapphira and the Slave Girl*, and of numerous essays about American women's writing and cultures. She is an editor of *Willa Cather Review*.

MARY RUTH RYDER is a distinguished professor emerita of English of South Dakota State University where she taught and directed Graduate Studies in English. A longtime member of the Willa Cather Foundation, she has published widely on Cather, including in *Cather Studies 6*, *Teaching the Works of Willa Cather*, *The Literature of the Great War Reconsidered: Beyond Modern Memory*, *American Woman Nature Writers*, and *Willa Cather's Southern Connections: New Essays on Cather and the South*. Her book *Willa Cather and Classical Myth: The Search for a New Parnassus* (1990) was recognized by the journal *Classical and Modern Literature* with its prize for outstanding scholarship. She has also published in *The Willa Cather Review* and in *Teaching Cather*, among other journals. She continues to do research on American realism and naturalism and on Midwest farm fiction by women in the golden age of agriculture.

KELSEY SQUIRE is associate professor of English at Ohio Dominican University, where she teaches courses in writing and American literature. She has published previously in *Great Plains Quarterly*, *The Willa Cather Review*, *Cather Studies 9*, *Willa Cather and Modern Cultures*, and *Reception*. Her book *Willa Cather: The Critical Conversation* was published in June 2020 by Boydell and Brewer as part of their Literary Criticism in Perspective series.

KIMBERLY VANDERLAAN earned her PhD in 2006 from the University of Delaware in the area of late nineteenth-century and early twentieth-century American literature and is now an associate professor of English at California University of Pennsylvania, where she teaches upper-level American literature courses, critical theory, and composition. She has published extensively on an array of authors in such journals and series as *American Literary Realism*, *Western American Literature*, *The Explicator*, *Journal of American Studies*, *The Journal of American Culture*, Cather Studies, *The Willa Cather Review*, and others.

# INDEX

CPSIA information can be obtained
at www.ICGtesting.com
Printed in the USA
LVHW092318120721
692535LV00003B/67